Presented to

The Official Guide to
American Historic
Bed & Breakfast
Inns and Guesthouses

The Official Guide to
American Historic
Bed & Breakfast
Inns and Guesthouses

Deborah Edwards Sakach
Timothy J. Sakach

Association of American Historic Inns and Guesthouses
Dana Point, California

Published by:

The Association of American Historic Inns and Guesthouses

P. O. Box 336

Dana Point, California 92629

Front cover: The Williams House, The Dalles, Oregon. Photo by Timothy Sakach.

Back cover photo: Mainstay Inn, Cape May, New Jersey. Photo provided by the innkeeper.

ISBN: 0-9615481-3-4

Library of Congress Catalog Card Number: 87-71501

Printed in the United States of America

Contents

Acknowledgments

ur appreciation and thanks go to each of the innkeepers who provided the historical information, brochures, drawings, copies of newspaper articles, photographs, and local folklore about their inns. Most of all we are grateful for their constant enthusiasm and support for the project all along the way.

We give special credit to our art department, Claire Read, Melissa Latham-Stevens, and Craig Thornsley, whose skill and dedication helped produce some of the finest pen and ink inn drawings we have seen.

To our son Tim, for his advice and encouragement, and to our son David, for his enthusiastic proofreading and research, we express our deep appreciation. We also thank Douglas Edwards, our diligent cataloger and researcher, for the exceedingly long hours he gave to the project, and Sue Duggan and Tammy Cantu for their help in researching the many inns. Our son Stephen, daughter Suzanne, and friend Matt Swanson deserve a special thank you for managing the many mailings required. We appreciate Joyce Smith's extracurricular assistance for several months. And we also thank Debby Bodo and Cheryl Heidner whose help gave us the time we needed to see the project through to its completion.

A heartfelt thanks to Catherine Bowers, our editor, for her many insightful suggestions and skill, and to Herb Primosch, whose patience, advice, and assistance will long be appreciated.

We are grateful to Richard Everett of Colorcraft Press for the high quality workmanship he provided and for his fast response to our many requests for help.

Most of all I wish to thank Angela Edwards, coal-miner's daughter, university graduate, post graduate scholar, everyone's favorite schoolteacher, and my mother. When I was seven years old and recovering from polio with braces on, she taught me to ride a bike and provided me with *Little Engine That Could* stories throughout my child and adulthood.

Tim & Deborah Sakach

How to use this book

After many years of experience, making reservations for thousands of prospective inn-goers and using the available guides, it seemed that the most logical structure for a guide be alphabetical -- by state, by city, and by the inn's name. Our experience with regionally organized references at times proved very frustrating, particularly when we knew in advance the name of the city but not the arbitrary region. Considering the fact that most of us already know the fifty states and the regions they define, what better structure could there be?

We also found that by using a road map in conjunction with this guide, it is very easy to locate the city using the map's index and coordinates. Nearby cities can also be checked very quickly.

Some of the inns desired to also be included under the listing for a nearby city or town. This is helpful to travelers who may not be familiar with the proximity of a lesser known town to a major city. This cross reference should be checked if you are considering a stay at the major city.

Codes

The listings use codes where possible to help condense the information. We have kept the use of codes to a minimum and have used them only to refer to those things with which we are all very familiar.

Credit Cards:

Visa ....(no change)
MC ....Master Charge
AE ....American Express
CB ....Carte Blanche
DC ....Diner's Club

Beds:

K ....King size bed
Q ....Queen-size bed
D ....Double size bed
T ....Twin beds
W ....Waterbed
C ....Crib available.

Meals:

Continental breakfast: coffee, juice, toast, or pastry.

Continental-plus breakfast: A continental breakfast plus a variety of breads, cheeses, fruit.

Deluxe continental: more elaborate version of the continental plus. Eggs Flambeau?

Full breakfast: Coffee, juice, breads and an egg or meat entree.

B&B: Breakfast (full or continental) included in the price of the room.

AP: American Plan. All three meals are included in the price of the room. Check to see if quoted for two people or per person.

MAP: Modified American Plan. Breakfast and dinner are included in the price of the room.

EP: European Plan. No meals are included.

Introduction

il Bennet had often postponed the trip, even though he had a strong desire to get away from the pressures of Boston. The White Mountains, according to the handbill, offered a time to relax, to enjoy some peace and quiet, and to gaze out on some of the most beautiful scenery this side of the Mississippi. The worst part of the trip, the part that Wil hated, was getting there.

He had traveled long distances by stage before, and he was not looking forward to it again.

However, the time had come to depart. He had packed his bag in anticipation of the difficult journey to northern New Hampshire. He carried the usual changes of clothes, some bread and tea, extra blankets in case the evenings turned cold, some writing paper, and other supplies.

The trip was expected to last several days. The weather of the early fall was as unpredictable as ever.

The horses stirred nervously. Other passengers waited as their bags were loaded into the basket on the back of the stage. Wil noticed that the driver had just cut a plug of tobacco and popped it into his mouth. Wil shuddered as he imagined getting splattered with tobacco juice.

The stage always looked small to Wil. Today, it was even smaller. Six passengers were inside the cab, three more on top, the driver and his assistant up front. Hardly room to stretch or turn.

Passengers and luggage on board, the driver turned and waved to the station attendants. He cracked his whip over the lead horse's head, and the stage jerked into motion.

Cobblestones were fine for keeping down the dust and for preventing ruts from forming in the road, but Wil cursed them while in a stage. As they picked up speed the vibration became unbearable. Wil gripped the window ledge and looked at the other passengers. A young woman tried to maintain her dignified appearance in spite of the noise and the shaking.

The increase in dust coming through the open windows was evidence that the noisy cobblestones were coming to an end. Wil pulled a bandana from his coat pocket and tied it around his face. He pulled it up almost to his eyes hoping to eliminate any dust from entering his nose and mouth. It was too hot and humid, and the breeze from the windows was welcomed by all passengers in spite of the dust.

Soon beads of perspiration began to roll down Wil's forehead and mix with the dust. He wished it would rain.

The ladies sat in the center seats. The gentlemen were situated beside the windows because they had to help the driver. Wil could see the hills ahead and knew that the straight and dusty road was going to be replaced by twisting, sloping paths. Passengers began tucking away their belongings. The three men on the top were checking the baggage basket on the back to make sure everything was secure. The horses slowed as they climbed a small hill. On the downhill side the driver pressed his foot on the brake lever to keep the stage from over-running the horses.

"Gentlemen, to your left!" the driver shouted as the stage entered a turn to the left.

The men on the top moved quickly to the left side of the stage. Two men on the inside pushed their bodies through the windows and hung on to the sides. The stage leaned precariously to the right. Wil looked out his window and could see down into the gulley on the right side.

The men climbed back inside and rested as the stage rumbled on.

"Gentlemen, to your right!" barked the driver.

It was Wil's turn to hang out the window. As he did the stage hit a rut and Wil's back slammed against the bottom of the window opening. The pain shot up his backbone. This is going to be a long trip he thought.

Several dusty, twisting and jostling hours later the stage pulled to a stop. As the dust settled Wil could see the lights.

It was a most welcomed sight.

In the twilight, through the trees with smoke coming from the cooking chimney was the INN.

He jumped from the stage, shaking the dust from his clothes and beating his hat against his leg.

The innkeeper stood in the doorway wiping his hands with a kitchen towel. The smell of the burning wood mingled with the smell of the evening meal. Hot water boiled in huge pots in the large cooking fireplace. The thought of a hot bath brought a smile to Wil's face. Nothing he thought was more welcome today than this inn. In spite of the difficulties of the stage travel the inn somehow made it all worthwhile.

Tonight he was going to eat, relax, enjoy the fire, talk some with the other guests, and sleep. Tomorrow? That's another day.

Those days are long gone. Today, we just pack a bag, jump into our air-conditioned, plushly upholstered automobile, with its highly engineered suspension system, cruise control, quadraphonic sound system, radar detector, adjustable posture-controlled seating, cellular telephone and cigar lighter. A couple of hours and a hundred or so miles later we arrive at our destination.

And there it is, a most welcomed sight.

In the twilight, through the trees with smoke coming from the cooking chimney is the INN.

The innkeeper stands in the doorway wiping his hands with a kitchen towel. The smell of the burning wood mingles with the smell of the evening meal. The thought of a hot bath brings a smile to our face. Nothing is more welcome today than this inn. In spite of the difficulties or ease of the travel, the inn somehow makes it all worthwhile.

Tonight we are going to eat, relax, enjoy the fire, talk some with the other guests, and sleep. Tomorrow? That's another day.

Americans have rediscovered the joy of traveling from inn to inn. Fortunately, innkeepers are responding by making it easier than ever for travelers to find country inns and bed and breakfasts. New innkeepers are restoring historic properties and opening them to the traveling public. The growth is phenomenal. Every corner of the country now offers historic bed and breakfasts, inns and guesthouses.

You can't easily take a stagecoach across America these days, but you can still experience adventure just around the next bend by staying in a bed and breakfast. Whether it's an old sea captain's mansion in Nantucket, a country inn in Vermont, a pre-Civil War plantation in Mississippi, an adobe inn in New Mexico, a gold miner's inn in the West, or an old stone house in Pennsylvania you will double your travel value. You'll learn folk lore, relive the history of the area, enjoy regional specialties for breakfast, and meet real people.

Best of all you'll take home twice as many memories. How could anyone ever forget staying at the Captain Lord Mansion in Kennebunkport, Maine, a sea captain's house tucked behind a white picket fence with a four-story spiral staircase, fireplaces in the guest rooms and views from the cupola where wives and townsfolk of years ago would look for inbound ships.

A businessman from Seattle summed it up when he said, "I've been in ten different hotels in ten days and can't remember a thing about the other nine or even where they were, but I'll remember Harrison House (Guthrie, Oklahoma) forever."

Most of the inns included in **The Official Guide to American Historic Bed & Breakfast Inns and Guesthouses** are of true vintage character having been built in the 1700s and 1800s. The majority of us, raised in post-World War II houses, rarely get to spend time in an older house. So for this guide we have only included B&Bs, inns, and guesthouses built prior to 1940.

What is Bed & Breakfast?

Though there are regional preferences in defining a B&B all of the following come under the umbrella term: bed and breakfast. In general "bed and breakfast" is a travel term which means that one price includes both the lodging and breakfast.

Bed and Breakfast Inn: Used interchangeably with country and city inn in some regions of the country. In general, it implys a professional lodging establishment that has met local ordinances, licensing and signage requirements. It is often owner-occupied, with from three to thirty sleeping rooms. Breakfast is included in the price. Emphasis is placed upon ambience, congeniality and often on breakfast specialties.

Country Inn: In the Country Inn, the restaurant, rather than the lodging, is usually the focal point, and is open to the public as well as the overnight guests. Country inns often provide the finest gourmet dining in the area. They are professional lodging and dining establishment having met local ordinances and licensing requirements.

Guesthouse or Tourist Home: A lodging accommodation that may have signs, is usually less expensive than inns, and sometimes available for long-term stays. Most often found in older homes, tourist homes and guesthouses are survivors from an earlier era and have found a new identity with the interest in bed and breakfast. Although meals may not be included in the price of a night's stay, many are beginning to offer this service as a result of the bed and breakfast movement.

Homestays: These are private homes which may have one or more guest rooms available for travelers. There are no signs outside, and travelers can generally find them only through a reservation service organization. Breakfast is included in the price. Some folks insist this is the only true form of bed and breakfast.

Other uses: Because of the tremendous amount of publicity bed and breakfast has achieved large hotel chains have taken note and are offering breakfast. The Countryside Inn chain and the Country Inn chain have one-hundred-room "bed and breakfast" hotels. This commercial use of the term may add to the confusion of the traveler who seeks a true "inn" experience. Although these establishments may increase public awareness of the bed and breakfast concept, travelers now have to choose carefully to insure the travel experience they expect.

Children.

Many inns restrict accommodating young children because of the abundance of fine crystal, antique furnishings or perhaps because of an open staircase.

Minimum stay requirements.

When traveling in peak seasons, expect two-night minimums.

Advance Reservations Required.

For weekend travel to resort areas during peak seasons many inns will fill up six to twelve or more weeks ahead.

What to do if all the inns you call are full:

- Ask the inn for a recommendation, perhaps a new inn or one a little off the beaten path.
- Call a reservation service that covers the area or a national reservation service that can make a recommendation. See page 259.
- Call the local Chamber of Commerce in the town you hope to visit and ask if a new inn may have recently opened.
- Call the state tourism bureau. See page 265.

Rates.

The rates in this guidebook have been expressed in ranges. The ranges reflect the high and low prices given to us by the innkeepers at the time of publication. However, the lowest prices are usually only available during the off-season. Therefore you should always check the rates with the inns when making your reservations. Information in this book is current at press time but is subject to change so please check. Always verify important features with the innkeeper.

Note: When the word "Rates" is preceded by two asterisks (**Rates:), reservations can be made through your travel agent or through Reservation Service Organizations serving that area.

Reservation Form

See the reservation form in the back of the book to help make phone and mail reservations.

Inn Evaluation Form

Because of the scope of this reference it was impossible for the authors to personally "inspect" each of the inns listed. Rather we encourage you to do your own "inspection". Please feel free to make copies of and use the **Inn Evaluation Form** in the back and to return copies to the publisher so that we can catalog and rate the inns based on consumer evaluations.

As the inn-going public becomes more aware of the quality of travel possible in bed and breakfasts, it is our hope that innkeepers at those few inns that might be considered by some to be below a standard will be encouraged to improve and maintain their properties at the highest standards possible. Most innkeepers, knowing the needs and desires of travelers, are continually and conscientiously striving to provide the utmost in quality travel accommodations.

Alabama

Mentone

Mentone Inn
Highway 117
Mentone AL 35984
(205) 634-4836

Circa 1927. Mentone is a refreshing stop for those looking for the cool breezes and natural air-conditioning of the mountains. Here antique treasures mingle with the modern-day conveniences and a sun deck and spa complete the experience. Sequoyah Caverns, Little River Canyon, DeSoto Falls and Desoto Park are just moments away, as well as the inn's own hiking trails. There is also a cabin on the grounds.

Location: On Lookout Mountain in the northeast section of Alabama.
**Rates: $35-$70. Season: May 1 to October 31.
Innkeeper(s): Amelia & Bob Brooks.
12 Rooms. 12 Private Baths. Hot Tub. Conference Room. Guest phone available. Children 10 & up. TV available. Beds: QT. Meals: Full breakfast.

Mobile

Vincent-Doan Home
1664 Springhill Ave
Mobile AL 36604
(205) 433-7121

Circa 1827. This home is the only building of French Creole architecture in Mobile. It is one of the old 'summer houses' from days gone by.

Location: In Dauphin Way Historic District.
Rates: $40-$50. Season: All year.
Innkeeper(s): Betty Doan.
3 Rooms. 3 Private Baths. Children. Credit Cards: Visa, MC. Meals: Full breakfast.

Opelika

Under the Oaks
707 Geneva St
Opelika AL 36801
(205) 745-2449

Circa 1825. This Greek Revival homestead features two-story columns rising from the entrance way, under graceful oak trees. There are six guest rooms decorated and furnished with antiques or white wicker. A continental-plus breakfast is served.

Rates: $50-$60.
Innkeeper(s): Debbie & Mike Whitley, Danny Tankersley.

Scottsboro

Brunton House
PO Box 1006, 112 College Ave
Scottsboro AL 35768
(205) 259-1298

Circa 1921. This late Victorian home is painted Williamsburg Blue with oyster and federal red trim. It has ten-foot-high ceilings and is on a park-like lot with an acre of lawn and dogwood trees. The office of the inn was the original cotton gin office. All the rooms are tastefully decorated. The Brunton House is one of the first bed and breakfast inns in Alabama. Down the street from the inn at Courthouse Square, an old-time drugstore operates its original soda fountain.

Location: One mile from Rt 72.
**Rates: $29-$42.
Innkeeper(s): Norman & Jerry Brunton.
6 Rooms. 1 Private Baths. Children 2 & up. Handicap access provided. Smoking OK. Meals: Full breakfast.

Alaska

Anchorage

Alaska Private Lodgings
PO Box 110135 South Station
Anchorage AK 99511
(907) 345-2222

Susan Hansen operates this bed and breakfast reservation service. She lists several historic properties including an original log house built by a pioneer.

Location: Represents hosts in several Alaska cities.
Rates: $30-$55.

Gustavus

Gustavus Inn
PO Box 31
Gustavus AK 99826
(907) 697-3311

Circa 1928. This inn provides guests three full meals included in the room rate. It is located near the Salmon River and Glacier Bay National Park. There is a library and a wine and root cellar. Bicycles, fishing poles, flight-seeing and boat trips are available.

Rates: $80. Season: May 1 to September 30.
Innkeeper(s): David & Joann Lesh.
10 Rooms. Meals: Full breakfast.

Homer

Driftwood Inn
135-T W Bunnell Ave
Homer AK 99603
(907) 235-8019

Circa 1920. Clean, comfortable and unpretentious, the Driftwood Inn is in a historic building on the shores of Kachemak Bay. The inn caters to families and sportsmen. All-you-can-eat breakfasts are a special feature of the inn.

Location: On the beach and overlooking the mountains, glaciers and Kachemak Bay.
Rates: $35-$70.
Innkeeper(s): Jeff & Gail Murphy.

Skagway

Golden North Hotel
PO Box 431
Skagway AK 99840
(907) 983-2294

Circa 1898. The Golden North is the oldest hotel in Alaska. It provides a restaurant and bar, a sitting room and gift shop. The inn is furnished in antiques.

Rates: $60-$75.
34 Rooms. 30 Private Baths. Children. Smoking OK.

Arizona

Cochise

Cochise Hotel
PO Box 27
Cochise AZ 85606
(602) 384-3156
  Circa 1882. Authentic 1800s furnishings typical of the Arizona lifestyle back at the turn of the century are used in the inn.

Rates: $15-$24.
Innkeeper(s): Lillie Harrington.
5 Rooms. 5 Private Baths. Meals: B&B.

Flagstaff

Dierker House Bed & Breakfast
423 West Cherry
Flagstaff AZ 86001
(602) 774-3249
  Circa 1914. A charming old Victorian house with spacious antique-filled rooms, the Dierker House offers privacy and European comforts. Down comforters and a fireplace warms the cold winter nights after an excursion to the Grand Canyon or nearby Indian areas. In the summer, guests enjoy the garden room. Your hosts can provide information on area skiing and Colorado River rafting.

Location: Ninety miles south of the Grand Canyon.
Rates: $25-$35
Innkeeper(s): Dorothea Dierker.

Rainbow Ranch
2860 North Fremont
Flagstaff AZ 86001
(602) 774-3724
  Circa 1886. An old farmhouse on seven acres, Rainbow Ranch is furnished with antiques. Eggs are gathered in the morning for your breakfast and homemade breads and jams are served as well. Just next door is the Museum of Northern Arizona.

Rates: $40. Season: All.
Innkeeper(s): Miriam Pederson.
3 Rooms. Children. Meals: Full breakfast.

Sasabe

Rancho de la Osa
PO Box 1
Sasabe AZ 85633
(602) 823-4257
  Circa 1890. This home was constructed in a quadrangle style and furnished in a 1930s decor with a Mexican motif. The inn is adjacent to the Papago Indian Reservation. Horseback riding and local dances are enjoyed by guests as well as a dip in the inn's pool and spa.

Location: One mile from the Mexican border.
Rates: $300-$390 per person weekly.
Innkeeper(s): Fran & Bill Davis.
20 Rooms. 20 Private Baths. Credit Cards: Visa, MC, AE. Meals: All meals are included.

Tempe

Mi Casa-Su Casa Bed & Breakfast
PO Box 950
Tempe AZ 85281
(602) 990-0682
  This reservation service represents homes throughout the state and Ruth Young, coordinator, knows Arizona like her own backyard. Many of her listings are historic homes and depict the full southwest experience. A directory may be ordered for three dollars that provides a wide selection of private homestays.

Location: Covers all of Arizona. Rates: Call.

Arkansas

Brinkley

The Great Southern Hotel
127 West Cedar
Brinkley AR 72021
(501) 734-4955

Circa 1915. Built on the site of a hotel which burned to the ground, the Great Southern Hotel is a Victorian building with frontage on the Rock Island tracks and adjacent to the Union Passenger Depot. With the decline of the railroad the hotel fell into disrepair but was recently restored. An elegant and serene atmosphere now prevails and includes two large balconies and a wraparound veranda.

Location: One mile off I-30, midway between Memphis & Little Rock.
**Rates: $36-$40. Season: All year.
Innkeeper(s): Stanley & Dorcas Prince. TV in room. Meals: Continental breakfast brought to the room.

Eureka Springs

Crescent Cottage Inn
211 Spring St
Eureka Springs AR 72632
(501) 253-6022

Circa 1881. The first governor of Arkansas, Powell Clayton, built Crescent Cottage after the Reconstruction. This Victorian Gothic-style house lends flavor and atmosphere to the furnishing and the guest rooms. A large veranda overlooks the East Mountains. The inn is just a short walk past memorable views, landscaped springs and long-standing dogwoods, oaks and maples on the way to the historic downtown area of town.

Location: In the historic residential area of town.
Rates: $55-$65. Season: All year.
Innkeeper(s): Ron & Brenda Bell.

4 Rooms. 2 Private Baths. 2 Shared Baths. Guest phone available. TV available. Credit Cards: Visa, MC. Beds: D. Meals: Full breakfast.

"Of all the B&B places we've stayed, yours was the best, not only your house but you two made it wonderful."

"The food was fantastic. Thanks."

Dairy Hollow House & Cottage at Dairy Hollow
Rt 4, PO Box 1
Eureka Springs AR 72632
(501) 253-7444

Circa 1888. A restored Ozark farmhouse, Eureka Springs' first bed and breakfast inn offers a warm, beguiling home-base for exploring this quirky, charming mountain town. Visitors can enjoy Victorian architecture, fine arts, crafts, antiques, festivals, nearby

lakes and rivers. The inn offers outstanding "Noveau 'zarks" cuisine, by reservation only, and is the home of the award-winning *Dairy Hollow House Cookbook*.

Location: Just off Dairy Hollow Rd, the cottage is at the junction of Spring & Dairy Hollow Rd.
Rates: $69-$149. Season: All year.
Innkeeper(s): Ned Shank & Crescent Dragonwagon.
5 Rooms. 5 Private Baths. Hot Tub. Conference Room. Guest phone available. Children By arrangement. Credit Cards: All.

Beds: QDT. Meals: Full breakfast. "Noveau 'Zarks" dinner by reservation only.

"The height of unpretentious luxury."

"One of the loveliest experiences we've ever had. It's rare to have something come up to the expectations of my imagination as this has."

"Wonderfully romantic hideaway. Outstanding food, great rooms and conversation."

"Grand!! Spectacular dining."

Singleton House Bed & Breakfast
11 Singleton
Eureka Springs AR 72632
(501) 253-9111

Circa 1895. Singleton is an old-fashioned Victorian with interesting collections and furnishings. A pretty garden with a pond, flowers, arches, and stone paths is often the site for breakfast.

Location: In the historic district.
**Rates: $45-$65.
Innkeeper(s): Barbara Gavron.

Sweet Seasons Guest Cottages
26 Spring Street
Eureka Springs AR 72632
(501) 253-7603

Circa 1890. Sweet Seasons is a collection of authentic Victorian cottages built at the turn of the century. Each has been lovingly restored and renovated to preserve a charming atmosphere of wood floors, decorative molding, gingerbread trimmings, and doors. Embellishments include stencils on walls, floors and cupboards. Period and reproduction light

fixtures, wallpapers and antique furnishings give character to the cottages. Both ceiling fans and air

conditioning are provided as well as four-poster beds and porch swings.

Location: In the historic district of downtown Eureka Springs.
**Rates: $55-$89. Season: All year.
Innkeeper(s): Marcia Yearsley.
8 Rooms. 8 Private Baths. Children. Pets OK. TV in room. Smoking OK. Credit Cards: Visa, MC, AE. Beds: KQ. Meals: Each cottage has a fully furnished kitchen.

The Heartstone Inn
35 King's Highway
Eureka Springs AR 72632
(501) 253-8916

Circa 1903. Described as "a pink and white confection", this restored 1903 home with wraparound veranda is located in the historic district. Each room fea-

tures antique furnishings and decor, and the picket fence surrounding the inviting garden is lined with pink roses.

Location: Northwest Arkansas, in the historic district of Eureka Springs.
Rates: $47-$65. Season: All year.
Innkeeper(s): Iris & Bill Simantel.
10 Rooms. 10 Private Baths. Guest phone available. Children. TV in room. Smoking OK. Credit Cards: Visa, MC. Beds: QC. Meals: Full breakfast.

"Extraordinary! Best breakfasts anywhere!"

"The highlight of our vacation..."

"Our fourth stay and it gets better each time..."

"Beyond our expectations...just like coming home. Thanks for the memories."

Everton

Corn Cob Inn
Rt 1, PO Box 183
Everton AR 72633
(501) 429-6545

Circa 1910. This two-story native stone building was first a general store for local zinc miners. It then became a corncob pipe factory where thousands of pipes were made each week. In 1937, it was converted to a home because of its splendid location on the banks of Clear Creek. Surrounded by the peaceful Ozark countryside, the creek's private beach beckons to those who wish to fish, swim or float.

**Rates: $30-$35. Season: All year.
Innkeeper(s): Anna & Dave Borg.
3 Rooms. 1 Shared Baths. Children. Beds: Q. Meals: B&B.

Fayetteville

Mt Kessler Inn
Mt Kessler Road
Fayetteville AR 72701
(501) 442-6743

Circa 1930. The inn is made from rocks gathered from the landscape and there is an enormous stone fireplace in both dining and living rooms. An appeal-

ing tennis court is nestled in the pine trees. Croquet, volleyball, horseshoes, badminton and hiking are other popular activities. Two miles of cleared trails for hiking in the beautiful Ozark woods afford visitors many spots from which to enjoy magnificent views.

Location: Four miles from downtown on the top of the hill at the end of the road.

Rates: $200-$400 whole inn. Season: April 1 to December 1.
Innkeeper(s): Betty Harrison.
6 Rooms. 1 Private Baths. 2 Shared Baths. Conference Room. Guest phone available. Children. Smoking OK. Beds: D. Meals: Continental breakfast.

Hot Springs

Williams House Inn
420 Quapaw St
Hot Springs AR 71901
(501) 624-4275

Circa 1890. Williams House is a brownstone and brick Victorian nestled among towering trees. The inn

is dedicated to personal, romantic and comfortable lodgings for travelers and visitors to the Hot Springs National Park. The carriage house, hitching posts, and mounting blocks are still on the property and the inn is listed in the National Register of Historic Places.

Location: Fifty miles southwest of Little Rock, five blocks off Hwy 7.
Rates: $50-$70. Season: All year.
Innkeeper(s): Mary & Gary Riley.
6 Rooms. 4 Private Baths. 2 Shared Baths. Guest phone available. Children 10 & up. TV available. Credit Cards: Visa, MC. Beds: QDT. Meals: Full breakfast.

Little Rock

The Great Southern Hotel
See: Brinkley, AR.

California

Albion

Fensalden Bed & Breakfast
PO Box 99
Albion CA 95410
(707) 937-4042
   Circa 1860. Originally a stagecoach way station house, Fensalden looks out over the Pacific Ocean as

it has for more than one hundred years. The Tavern Room has witnessed many a rowdy scene and bullet holes are evident in the original redwood ceilings. The inn's twenty acres provide a wonderful place to enjoy walks, bicycling, whale-watching, and viewing deer.

Location: Seven miles south of Mendocino, on Hwy 1.
**Rates: $75-$125. Season: All year.
Innkeeper(s): Scott & Frances Brazil.
7 Rooms. 7 Private Baths. Conference Room. Guest phone available. Children 11 & up. Handicap access provided. Credit Cards: Visa, MC. Beds: KQ. Meals: Continental-plus breakfast.
   "What a beautiful ocean view."
   "Our bike ride was superb, and we enjoyed lounging on the porch, watching the sun set over the ocean. What a way to end a wonderful weekend."
   "Our three days here have been balm to my soul."
   "The hors d'oeuvres and breakfasts are yummy."

Anaheim

Anaheim Country Inn
856 South Walnut St
Anaheim CA 92802
(714) 778-0150
   Circa 1910. Just a mile from Disneyland, the Anaheim Country Inn is an elegant farmhouse surrounded by nearly an acre of lawns, gardens and avocado trees. The house was built by Mayor John Cook of Anaheim. Beautifully detailed woodwork graces the entry and staircase while beveled and leaded windows cast rainbows in the parlor and dining room. Just outside the honeymoon suite sits a gazebo and spa. Balconies and a circular porch accent one of the few old homes left in the area.

**Rates: $32-$75. Season: All year.
Innkeeper(s): Lois Ramont & Marilyn Watson
8 Rooms. 4 Private Baths. 2 Shared Baths. Guest phone available. Children 12 & up. TV available. Credit Cards: Visa, MC, AE, Discover. Beds: QT. Meals: Full breakfast.
   "I wanted to thank you for the lovely, restful, quiet time, which we spent at your inn. My husband is still telling anyone who'll listen how good the breakfasts were."
   "Many thanks for your warm hospitality and extremely good food. You helped make Lisa's wedding a very memorable occasion."

Aptos

Mangels House
570 Aptos Creek Rd, PO Box 302
Aptos CA 95001
(408) 688-7982
   Circa 1886. Claus Mangels built this country house when he started the California sugar beet industry with the famous Spreckels family. The inn is reminis-

cent of a southern mansion with its encircling veranda, lawns and orchards. It is bounded by the Forest of Nisene Marks with 10,000 acres of redwoods, creeks and trails, and just three-quarters of a mile away is

Monterey Bay. Today the inn is a happy blend of periods creating a comfortable yet sophisticated atmosphere.

Location: Central Coast.
**Rates: $78-$96. Season: All year but Christmas.
Innkeeper(s): Jacqueline Fisher.
5 Rooms. 2 Private Baths. 3 Shared Baths. Conference Room. Guest phone available. Children 12 & up. Credit Cards: Visa, MC. Beds: KQT. Meals: Full breakfast.

"Compliments on the lovely atmosphere we enjoyed as guests in your wonderful house. We look forward to sharing our discovery with friends and returning with them."

Arcata

Lady Ann
902 14th St
Arcata CA 95521
(707) 822-2797
Circa 1888. This Queen Anne Victorian overlooks Humboldt Bay and the town of Arcata. It is within walking distance of shops and the Humboldt State University. The round three-story corner tower and redwood in-terior make this a showcase home. It is known as the Stone House because it was built by Wesley Stone.

Rates: $40-$60.
Innkeeper(s): Sam Pennisi.

Arroyo Grande

Guest House
120 Hart Ln
Arroyo Grande CA 93420
(805) 481-9304
Circa 1850. This New England Colonial is set among old-fashioned gardens just seventeen miles south of San Luis Obispo. The inn was built by a New England

sea captain and the flavor of that period is kept alive with many family heirlooms and a colorful garden terrace. Local wineries, beaches, antique shops and Hearst Castle are nearby.

Location: In the old village.
Rates: $40-$50. Season: All year.
Innkeeper(s): Mark V. Migger.
3 Rooms. 2 Shared Baths. Guest phone available. Smoking OK. Beds: QD. Meals: A hearty breakfast.

"Home away from home, warm and wonderful."
"Charming, great hosts."
"This home is a treasure, beautiful."
"The charm of the home is only exceeded by that of the hosts."

Auburn

Powers Mansion Inn
164 Cleveland Ave
Auburn CA 95603
(916) 885-1166

Circa 1886. This Victorian mansion was built by Mr. Power from the gold-mining millions he excavated from Auburn's richest mine. The house was always

filled with children and according to a neighbor, there was always something happening over there, games and parties or going together to Clarke's Hole on the American River for swimming. Many prominent folk, such as engineer Herbert Hoover, visited in the Powers Mansion. Throughout the second floor halls of this elegantly restored mansion are notes and memorabilia that tell the history of the inn. The luxury and extravagance of the inn is typified by the heart-shaped tub and fireplace at the foot of a lacy bed in the honeymoon suite.

Location: In the heart of downtown Auburn.
**Rates: $65-$150. Season: All year.
Innkeeper(s): Don & Sandy Martin.
15 Rooms. 15 Private Baths. Conference Room. Guest phone in room. Children. TV available. Handicap access provided. Credit Cards: Visa, MC, AE. Beds: Q. Meals: Full breakfast.

"A perfect place to come for a romantic getaway."
"Breakfast wasn't only delicious, but unbelievable!"
"Seems like a different place and time. Thank you for providing such a lovely place to be in love in."

Avalon

Zane Grey Pueblo Hotel
PO Box 216
Avalon CA 90704
(213) 510-0966

Circa 1926. The famous western novelist, Zane Grey, built this pueblo as his home. Resting on a bluff only three blocks from Avalon's charming main street, it has fantastic views of the bay, town and hills. The original living room houses a grand piano and fireplace.

Location: Catalina Island.
**Rates: $65-$100. Season: All year.
Innkeeper(s): Bob, Robin, John.
18 Rooms. Swimming Pool. Conference Room. Guest phone available. Children. TV available. Smoking OK. Credit Cards: Visa, MC, AE. Beds: Q. Meals: Continental breakfast.

Bakersfield

Helen Kay Inn
2105 19th St
Bakersfield CA 93301
(805) 325-5451

Circa 1901.

Location: Corner of 19th and "D", in downtown Westchester section.
**Rates: $55-$85.
Innkeeper(s): Sheila Dormier & Colleen McGauley.

Ben Lomond

Fairview Manor
245 Fairview Ave
Ben Lomond CA 95005
(408) 336-3355

Circa 1920. Fairview Manor is a redwood house on a woodsy two-and-a-half acres in the Santa Cruz Mountains. Even though very private and secluded it is just a short walk to town. There are five guest rooms and a huge fireplace of stone.

Location: On San Lorenzo River in Santa Cruz County.
**Rates: $89-$99.
Innkeeper(s): Frank Feely & Nancy Glasson.

Big Bear City

Gold Mountain Manor
1117 Anita, PO Box 2027
Big Bear City CA 92314
(714) 585-6997

Circa 1926. A spectacular 1920s log mansion, Gold Mountain Manor was once a hideaway for the rich and famous. At one time it was even a bordello! Eight magnificent fireplaces provide a roaring fire in each room in fall and winter and a hand-hewn, sugar-pine staircase graces the dining room. The Lucky Baldwin

Room features a hearth made from stones of gold gathered in the famous Lucky Baldwin mine nearby.

In the Clark Gable room is the actual fireplace Clark Gable and Carole Lombard enjoyed on their honeymoon.

Location: Two hours northeast of Los Angeles and Orange County, 7,000 feet high in San Bernardino Mountains.
**Rates: $70-$135. Season: All year.
Innkeeper(s): Lynn Montgomery & Richard Kriegler.
7 Rooms. 6 Private Baths. 1 Shared Baths. Conference Room. Guest phone available. Children 12 & up. TV available. Beds: Q. Meals: Full breakfast.

"In the words of Robert Taylor to Deborah Kerr in Quo Vadis, 'Nothing that I see that is not perfection!'"

"We especially enjoyed the visit from the spirits of Clark Gable and Carole Lombard, though their passionate cries kept us up most of the night!"

"A majestic experience! In this magnificent house, history comes alive!"

Big Bear Lake

Knickerbocker Mansion
869 S Knickerbocker Rd
Big Bear Lake CA 92315
(714) 866-8221
  Circa 1917. This unusual vertical log mansion welcomes families and couples to a mountain experience in a beautiful inn.

**Rates: $75-$150.
Innkeeper(s): Phyllis Knight & Eden Wynn.

Calistoga

Scarlett's Country Inn
3918 Silverado Trail North
Calistoga CA 94515
(707) 942-6669
  Circa 1900. This restored farmhouse occupies property that was a Wappo Indian campground in the days when the Indians migrated from the mountains in winter to hunt deer on the coast. They gathered obsidian to make arrowheads from nearby Glass Mountain. Guests can enjoy tranquility, green lawns and refreshing vistas in this peaceful woodland setting at the edge of country vineyards. Fruit trees abound and guests are free to sample their wares. Breakfast is often taken beneath the apple trees or poolside.

Location: Napa Valley Wine Country.
**Rates: $75-$95. Season: All year.
Innkeeper(s): Scarlett & Derek Dwyer.
3 Rooms. 3 Private Baths. Swimming Pool. Conference Room. Guest phone in room. Children. TV available. Smoking OK. Credit Cards: Visa, MC. Beds: QC. Meals: Continental-plus breakfast.

"Wonderful, peaceful, serene."
"The friendly and gracious hosts made our vacation."
"Scarlett's extra touches and that beautiful breakfast were a complete surprise. We'll be back."
"The beds were the best we've had."

Carmel

Cypress Inn
7th & Lincoln Sts, PO Box Y
Carmel CA 93921
(408) 624-3871
  Circa 1929. The Cypress Inn is a small Mediterranean-style hotel in the heart of Carmel. Period details include oak floors, imported Italian tiles, and

beamed cathedral ceilings, all carefully restored. There is a large living room with fireplace, an in-

timate library overlooking a private garden courtyard, and ocean views.

Location: One block south of Ocean Ave in center of the village.
**Rates: $80-$150. Season: All year.
Innkeeper(s): David Wolf.
33 Rooms. 33 Private Baths. Guest phone in room. TV in room. Smoking OK. Credit Cards: Visa, MC, AE. Beds: KQT. Meals: Continental breakfast.

"Thank you for your hospitality...your hotel is delightful and beautiful to look at, warm and comfortable, but what made our stay special was your staff. Cheers to Jeanne, Elisabeth Paz and all the rest."

Happy Landing Inn
Monte Verde between 5th and 6th ST, PO Box 2619
Carmel CA 93921
(408) 624-7917
  Circa 1925. Built as a family retreat, this early Comstock design inn has evolved into one of Carmel's most romantic places to stay. The Hansel-and-Gretel

look is accentuated with a central garden and gazebo, pond and flagstone paths. There are cathedral ceilings and the rooms are filled with antiques.

Location: One & one half blocks to the main street of Carmel, 4 blocks to the beach.
Rates: $75-$120. Season: All year.
Innkeeper(s): Bob Anderson & Dick Stewart.
7 Rooms. 7 Private Baths. Guest phone available. Children 12 & up. TV in room. Handicap access provided. Credit Cards: Visa, MC. Beds: KQ. Meals: Continental breakfast.

San Antonio House
San Antonio between Ocean & 7th
Carmel CA 93921
(408) 624-4334
  Circa 1900.

Location: One and a half blocks from Carmel Beach and five blocks from the village.
Rates: $95-$115.
Innkeeper(s): Jewell Brown.

Chico

Bullard House
256 E 1st Ave
Chico CA 95926
(916) 342-5912
  Circa 1902. Bullard House is a completely restored country Victorian. It has been honored with the Golden Rose Award from the Greater Chico Chamber of Commerce and was picked as the "Decorator's

Dream House". Centrally located near the college, hospitals and historic Bidwell Mansion, it also provides visitors easy access to hunting, fishing and boating.

Rates: $50-$60. Season: All year.
4 Rooms. 2 Shared Baths. Guest phone available. TV available. Meals: Continental breakfast.

Cloverdale

Vintage Towers Inn
302 N Main St
Cloverdale CA 95425
(707) 894-4535

Circa 1900. There are three guest rooms in the towers of this gracious Victorian. The towers were built in three shapes, one a square, one a round and the other tower an octagon. Bicycles are provided for guests to ride through the nearby vineyards.

Location: Six blocks from the Russian River.
Rates: $45-$80. Season: All year.
8 Rooms. 6 Private Baths. 2 Shared Baths. Conference Room. Guest phone available. Children. Beds: Q. Meals: Full breakfast.

Coloma

American River Inn
See: Georgetown, CA.

Davenport

New Davenport Bed & Breakfast
#31 Davenport Ave
Davenport CA 95017
(408) 425-1818

Circa 1902. Captain John Davenport came here to harvest the gray whales that pass close to the shore

during migration. The oldest remaining original building began as a public bath, became a bar, restaurant and dance hall before being converted to a private home. It has been completely renovated and houses four of the inn's rooms.

Location: Halfway between Carmel and San Francisco on the coast.

**Rates: $55-$105. Season: All year.
Innkeeper(s): Bruce and Marcia McDougal.
12 Rooms. 12 Private Baths. Guest phone in room. Children. Handicap access provided. Credit Cards: Visa, MC, AE. Beds: KQ. Meals: Continental-plus breakfast.

"We have been in California for over twenty-five years and never knew there was a place called Davenport! I cannot express the wonderful thrill at the first glimpse of our room with its lovely country appeal and garden right out our window."

"So peaceful and quaint, you tend to forget there is a jungle out there."

Del Mar

Rock Haus Bed & Breakfast
410 15th St
Del Mar CA 92014
(619) 481-3764

Circa 1910. The Rock Haus is a Craftsman-style, California bungalow on a half-acre hillside with panoramic ocean views. It once served as a church. Common areas include a large living room with fireplace and glass-enclosed veranda, while antique-filled rooms and down comforters complete the luxury touch. Nearby is the famous Del Mar Racetrack.

Location: Twenty minutes north of San Diego, 1/2 block east of Coast Hwy in the seaside village of Del Mar.
**Rates: $70-$135. Season: All year.
Innkeeper(s): Verlee J. Warfield.
10 Rooms. 4 Private Baths. 6 Shared Baths. Guest phone available. Credit Cards: Visa, MC, Discover. Beds: KQT. Meals: Continental-plus breakfast.

Dulzura

Brookside Farm
1373 Marron Valley Rd
Dulzura CA 92017
(619) 468-3043

Circa 1928. From the farmhouse, ancient oaks shade terraces that lead to a murmuring brook. Behind a large stone barn nearby there is a grape arbor and

beneath it, a spa. Each room in the inn has a personality all its own, furnished with vintage pieces and handmade quilts. There are two romantic cottages on the property as well. The adventurous hiker will enjoy an exploration of mines dating from the gold rush of 1908. Cooking classes are given by the innkeepers, former award-winning restaurant owners.

Location: Thirty-five minutes southeast of San Diego.
**Rates: $45-$65. Season: All year.
Innkeeper(s): Edd & Judy Guishard.
9 Rooms. 3 Shared Baths. Conference Room. Guest phone available. Smoking OK. Beds: QD. Meals: Full breakfast and dinner by prior arrangement.

Elk

Harbor House
5600 South Hwy One
Elk CA 95432
(707) 877-9997
　Circa 1916. Built by a lumber company for its visiting executives from the East, the inn is constructed en-

tirely of redwood. A vaulted, carved ceiling and redwood paneling were all sealed by hot beeswax that was hand-rubbed by the builders. An Edwardian decor adds elegance to the guest rooms. Views of the ocean and the arches carved in the massive rocks that jut from the sea may be seen from the blufftop cottages. Benches are nestled along a path edged with wild flowers that winds down the bluff to the sea.

Rates: $110-$165 MAP. Season: All year.
Innkeeper(s): Dean & Helen Turner.
9 Rooms. 9 Private Baths. Guest phone available. Meals: Full breakfast and dinner included.

Eureka

Carter House
1033 Third St
Eureka CA 95501
(707) 445-1390
　Circa 1982. Owner Mark Carter found a pattern book in an antique shop and built the Carter House according to the plans of an 1890 San Francisco Vic-

torian. The plans were made by the same architect (Joseph Newsom) who created the Carson House across the street. Both airy and light, the house has three open parlors with bay windows and marble fireplaces. Guests are free to visit the kitchen in quest of coffee and views of the bay.

Location: Corner of Third & L Streets in Old Town.
Rates: $45-$150. Season: All year.
Innkeeper(s): Mark & Christi Carter.
7 Rooms. 4 Private Baths. 1 Shared Baths. Conference Room. Guest phone available. Children 10 & up. TV available. Handicap access provided. Credit Cards: Visa, MC, AE. Beds: QD. Meals: B&B.
　"We've traveled extensively throughout the U.S. and stayed in the finest hotels--You've got them all beat!! The accommodations, the food, the atmosphere and the friendly hosts are the very best of the best."
　"We'll be back--even sooner definitely since we've found the perfect place to stay!"
　"The most memorable night I can remember."
　"We loved every minute of our stay in this special home."

Gingerbread Mansion
See: Ferndale, CA.

Fairfield

Frietas House Inn
744 Jackson St
Fairfield CA 94533
(707) 425-1366
  Circa 1925.

Location: Northeast of San Francisco Hwy 1-80, 45 minutes.
**Rates: $80-$100.
Innkeeper(s): Jackie Benson.

Ferndale

Gingerbread Mansion
400 Berding St
Ferndale CA 95536
(707) 786-4000
  Circa 1899. Built for Dr. H.J. Ring, the Gingerbread Mansion is now the most photographed of Northern

California inns. Near Eureka, it is in the fairy-tale Victorian village of Ferndale (a state Historical Landmark). Outside the inn are formal English gardens. Gingerbread Mansion is a unique combination of Queen Anne and Eastlake styles with elaborate gingerbread trim. Inside are spacious and elegant rooms including a suite with "his" and "her" bathtubs. There are four parlors. Bicycles are available for riding through town and the surrounding countryside.

Location: Near Eureka, five miles off Hwy 101.
**Rates: $55-$95. Season: All year.
Innkeeper(s): Wendy Hatfield & Ken Torbert.
8 Rooms. 5 Private Baths. 2 Shared Baths. Conference Room. Guest phone available. Children 10 & up. Credit Cards: Visa, MC. Beds: QT. Meals: Continental-plus breakfast.
  "Easily the most beautiful and the classiest B&B on the coast."
  "Absolutely the most charming, friendly and delightful place we have ever stayed at. See you again.!"
  "That was one of the nicest, quietest, hidden vacations I have ever had!" Paul (Pete) McCloskey, Jr., Former Congressman.
  "You are a most wonderful and unique couple and extend the most gracious, warm and heartfelt hospitality anyone could imagine. We have lived in the afterglow of our weekend with you all week and our thoughts turn to you frequently." Charles Percy

Fort Bragg

Country Inn
632 North Main St
Fort Bragg CA 95437
(707) 964-3737
  Circa 1890. This two-story town house with bay windows was once the office and residence of the owner

of the Union Lumber Company, Charles Russell Johnson. Johnson was also Fort Bragg's first mayor and founder of the California Western Railroad. The house is built of native redwood and features rooms with slanted and peaked ceilings. Camellia trees, flower boxes and a white picket fence accent the landscaping, while just two blocks away a railroad carries visitors on excursions through the redwoods.

**Rates: $58-$68. Season: All year.
Innkeeper(s): Don & Helen Miller.
8 Rooms. 8 Private Baths. Guest phone available. Handicap access provided. Credit Cards: Visa, MC, AE. Beds: KQ. Meals: Continental-plus breakfast.
  "Each room is so charming, how do you choose one?"
  "We wouldn't stay anywhere else."
  "Like visiting my favorite aunt and uncle."

Glass Beach Bed and Breakfast
726 N Main
Fort Bragg CA 95437
(707) 964-6774

Circa 1900. Born and raised in Fort Bragg, the inn-keeper can remember the 'skid cabins' behind the inn that were used by original land owners for logging

camps. Renovated in 1980, the inn received an award from the city for maintaining its architectural integrity. Several unique and charming rooms include the Attic Room with a swinging bed.

Rates: $49-$83. Season: All year.
Innkeeper(s): Robert & Beverly Sallinen.
9 Rooms. 9 Private Baths. Hot Tub. Guest phone available. TV available. Credit Cards: Visa, MC. Beds: Q. Meals: Hearty full breakfast.

"So much character and so friendly every time we stay here. We wouldn't think of staying anywhere else."

"Yo ho yo, a pirates life for us. We loved the nautical touch."

Grey Whale Inn
615 N Main St
Fort Bragg CA 95437
(707) 964-0640

Circa 1915. Built in the classic style of old growth redwood, this stately historic building served as the Redwood Coast Hospital until 1971. A skillfully executed renovation has created airy and spacious rooms and a warm and wonderful inn.

Location: In historic North Fort Bragg, two blocks from center of town.
**Rates: $55-$85. Season: All year.
Innkeeper(s): Colette Bailey.
14 Rooms. 12 Private Baths. 2 Shared Baths. Guest phone available. Children 12 & up. TV available. Credit Cards: Visa, MC, AE. Beds: KQT. Meals: Full breakfast.

"The Grey Whale Inn is as perfect a bed and breakfast as one could hope to find." Georgia Hesse, **San Francisco Examiner.**

"Just spent the loveliest week in our traveling history...the inn surpassed any Hyatt Regency in service and attitude. The accommodations were superb...I could go on and on."

Pudding Creek Inn
700 North Main St
Fort Bragg CA 95437
(707) 964-9529

Circa 1889. Originally constructed by a Russian count, the inn's two picturesque Victorian buildings are adjoined by a lush enclosed garden court featuring begonias, fuchsias and ferns. Rumor has it that

there could be jewels buried on the grounds because the count is said to have fled his homeland with riches that were not his own. The guest rooms are cozy and casual country style.

Location: Corner of Bush and North Main St.
**Rates: $45-$75. Season: February through December.
Innkeeper(s): Marilyn & Gene Gundersen
10 Rooms. 10 Private Baths. Guest phone available. Children 10 & up. Credit Cards: Visa, MC. Beds: KQDT. Meals: Continental-plus breakfast.

"Our second time here...such a special treat." Beverly Garland (actress), Hollywood.

"Lovely, like a trip down memory lane."
"Best stop on our trip!"
"Our second time...just as enchanting as the first."

Georgetown

American River Inn
Orleans St, PO Box 43
Georgetown CA 95634
(916) 333-4499

Circa 1853. Just a few miles away from where gold was discovered in Coloma, stands Georgetown and the American River Inn, a completely restored 1853 miners' boarding house. Mining cars dating to the original Woodside Mine Camp are visible. The lode

still runs under the inn, but no one knows exactly where. One of the more famous nuggets from the mine weighed in at 126 ounces! An antique shop on the property doubles as an intriguing guest room. The American River provides white water rafting trips.

**Rates: $59-$69. Season: All year.
Innkeeper(s): Neal & Carol.
20 Rooms. 5 Private Baths. 15 Shared Baths. Hot Tub. Swimming Pool. Conference Room. Guest phone available. Children 8 & up. TV available. Handicap access provided. Smoking OK. Credit Cards: Visa, MC. Beds: KQ. Meals: Full breakfast.

"Our third visit to your inn, our home away from home, We love it, we fell in love here in all its beauty and will be back for our 4th visit in April, another honeymoon for six days."

Grass Valley

Domike's Inn
220 Colfax Ave
Grass Valley CA 95945
(916) 273-9010

Circa 1894. Domike's is an impressive white Victorian with green trim accentuating the abundant

gingerbread. Huge trees and a white picket fence with climbing roses surround the inn. Canopy beds and down comforters are among the pleasures enjoyed here.

Location: Grass Valley is on the Western slope of the Sierra Nevada, in the Gold Country.
**Rates: $50-$75.
Innkeeper(s): Joyce & Don Domike.

Gualala

Old Milano Hotel
38300 Highway One
Gualala CA 95445
(707) 884-3256

Circa 1905. The Old Milano Hotel is located 100 miles north of San Francisco on the dramatic Mendocino Coast. Its romantic location, extensive restoration, and history have earned it a place in the National Registry of Historic Places. The Caboose is a railroader's fantasy tucked among the cedars for privacy. Most rooms have ocean views and if not guests can linger longer on the cliffside where the jacuzzi tub is situated.

Rates: $75-$130. Season: All year.
Innkeeper(s): Leslie L. Linscheid.
9 Rooms. 3 Private Baths. 2 Shared Baths. Jacuzzi Tubs. Guest phone available. Credit Cards: Visa, MC, AE. Beds: QD. Meals: Gourmet breakfast.

Half Moon Bay

San Benito House
356 Main St
Half Moon Bay CA 94019
(415) 726-3425

Circa 1905. The restored San Benito House has been reopened its upper floor as a country inn in the tradition of the auberges of Europe, and the wayside hostelry of New England. An ornate stairway, Victorian and country decor, brass beds, and historical photographs add to the Old World atmosphere. A sun deck, croquet lawn and flower gardens provide rest and relaxation.

**Rates: $49-$108.
Innkeeper(s): Carol Mickelsen.
12 Rooms. 9 Private Baths. 3 Shared Baths. Sauna. Conference Room. Guest phone available. Children 5 & up. Smoking OK. Credit Cards: Visa, MC, DC. Beds: QDT. Meals: Full breakfast and innovative California cuisine in the small restaurant.

"A refreshing unpretentious place to eat, drink and rest."

Healdsburg

Camellia Inn
211 North St
Healdsburg CA 95448
(707) 433-8182

Circa 1869. The Camellia is an elegant Italianate Victorian townhouse. There are twin marble parlor fireplaces and an ornate mahogany dining-room fireplace. Antiques fill the guest rooms and the award-winning grounds are accentuated with a pool. At one time the Camellia was the town's hospital.

Location: Heart of Sonoma Wine Country.
**Rates: $45-$75. Season: All year.
Innkeeper(s): Ray & Del Lewana.
7 Rooms. 5 Private Baths. 1 Shared Baths. Swimming Pool. Guest phone available. Children 10 & up. Handicap access provided. Credit Cards: Visa, MC. Beds: QT. Meals: Full breakfast.

Grape Leaf Inn
539 Johnson St
Healdsburg CA 95448
(707) 433-8140

Circa 1900. This magnificently restored Queen Anne home was built in what was considered the "Nob Hill" of Healdsburg and was typical of a turn-of-the-century middle-class dream house. It is situated near the Russian River and the town center. Seventeen skylights provide an abundance of sunlight, fresh air, and stained glass. Antiques and whirlpool tubs add to the ambience.

Rates: $60-$95. Season: All year.
Innkeeper(s): Kathy Cookson.
7 Rooms. 7 Private Baths. Hot Tub. Guest phone available. Children 10 & up. Handicap access provided. Credit Cards: Visa, MC. Beds: QT. Meals: Full country breakfast.

Haydon House
321 Haydon St
Healdsburg CA 95448
(707) 433-5228

Circa 1912. This unique home shows the influence of several architectural styles. It has the curving porch and general shape of a Queen Anne Victorian, the expansive areas of siding and unadorned columns of the Bungalow style, and the exposed roof rafters of the Craftsman style.

Location: Western Sonoma County, heart of the wine country.
**Rates: $50-$90. Season: All year.
Innkeeper(s): Richard & Joanne Claus.
8 Rooms. 4 Private Baths. 4 Shared Baths. Conference Room. Guest phone available. Children 12 & up. TV available. Credit Cards: Visa, MC. Beds: QT. Meals: Full breakfast.

"Staying at the Haydon House has been wonderful - adjectives like class, warmth, beauty, thoughtfulness with the right amount of privacy, attention to details relating to comfort, all come to mind...Thank you for the care and elegance."

"A warm friendly welcome to a delightful and comfortable home and a delectable breakfast. We feel so fortunate to have been your guests at the Haydon House."

Healdsburg Inn on the Plaza
116 Matheson St, PO Box 1196
Healdsburg CA 95448
(707) 433-6991

Circa 1900. A former Wells Fargo building, the inn is a renovated brick gingerbread overlooking the plaza in historic downtown Healdsburg. Ornate bay windows, embossed wood paneling and broad, paneled stairs present a welcome entrance. There are fireplaces and the halls are filled with sunlight from vaulted glass skylights. A roof garden-solarium is the setting for breakfast. A large covered porch extends along the entire rear of the building. Shops on the premises sell gifts, toys, quilts and fabric. A bakery and art gallery can be found there as well.

Location: On the historic square.
Rates: $45-$115. Season: All year.
Innkeeper(s): Genny Jenkins.
9 Rooms. 9 Private Baths. Conference Room. Guest phone available. Children 10 & up. TV available. Handicap access provided.
Credit Cards: Visa, MC, AE. Beds: Q. Meals: Full breakfast.

L'Auberge du Sans-Souci
25 West Grant
Healdsburg CA 95448
(707) 431-1110

Circa 1900. This stately redwood Victorian home is nestled under spruce, cedar and redwood trees. One of the gardens was planted by the original owner, Mr. John Miller. (Miller & Sons Food Company flourished when Sonoma County was famous for its prunes and pears.) Your hostess Madame Ginette pampers you with down comforters and full breakfasts.

Location: Sonoma County Wine Country.
Rates: $60-$70. Season: All year.
Innkeeper(s): Madame Ginette.
5 Rooms. 3 Private Baths. 2 Shared Baths. Conference Room. Guest phone available. Children 13 & up. TV available. Credit Cards: Visa, MC. Beds: Q. Meals: Full French breakfast.

Raford House
10630 Wohler Rd
Healdsburg CA 95448
(707) 887-9573

Circa 1880. This turn-of-the-century Victorian sits above the vineyards of Sonoma County, near many wineries. Known for a long time as the Wohler Ranch, the home was built for Raford Peterson. Originally, there were over 400 acres of hops surrounding the home and the foundations of the hop kilns can still be seen. A large front porch overlooks

vineyards and orchards with grassy patios and rose gardens nearby. Favorite activities are swimming and canoeing on the Russian River, wine tasting at local wineries, and biking along the country roads.

Location: North of San Francisco, from Hwy 101 3 miles north of Santa Rosa.
Rates: $54-$80. Season: All year.
Innkeeper(s): Alan & Beth.
7 Rooms. 5 Private Baths. 2 Shared Baths. Guest phone available.
Credit Cards: Visa, AE. Beds: QT. Meals: Continental breakfast.

Homewood

Rockwood Lodge
5295 West Lake Blvd, PO Box 544
Homewood CA 95718
(916) 525-4663

Circa 1930. On the west shore of Lake Tahoe, the Rockwood Lodge is situated among towering pines just down from the Kaiser Estate where *The Godfather, Part II* was filmed. It was built by a wealthy valley dairyman as a summer home. There is a small his-

toric marina across from the inn. The inn has a huge stone fireplace in the parlor, hand-hewn beams and pine paneling restored to their natural aged golden color. The generous use of indigenous rock in the walls and fireplace blends into the natural surroundings. European and American antiques are accented with fabrics by Laura Ashley, and together with the large beds, puffy down comforters and pillows give a luxurious country feel to the inn. Ask for the room with the seven-foot Roman tub.

Location: Lake Tahoe.
Rates: $100-$150.
Innkeeper(s): Louis Reinkens, Constance Stevens.
4 Rooms. 3 Private Baths. Beds: QD. Meals: B&B.

"The way a mountain chalet ought to be." K. C., Ski Magazine.

Inverness

Ten Inverness Way
10 Inverness Way
Inverness CA 94937
(415) 669-1648

Circa 1904. A stone fireplace, good books, and access to a great hiking area are some of the many specialties of this cozy inn. According to local folk lore a ghost used to call Ten Inverness Way his home. Since the innkeepers had each room of the house blessed several years ago he seems to have disappeared for good. Now, the inn is known for providing a refreshing renewal experience.

Rates: $43-$55. Season: All year.
Innkeeper(s): Mary Davies, Ruth Kalter & Stephen Kimball.
5 Rooms. Meals: Full breakfast.

Ione

The Heirloom
214 Shakeley Lane, PO Box 322
Ione CA 95640
(209) 274-4468

Circa 1863. A two-story Colonial house with columns and balconies, the antebellum Heirloom, has

a spacious private English garden. Inside, there is a square grand piano once owned by Lola Montez, and many other heirloom antiques. The building was dedicated by the Native Sons of the Golden West as a historic site.

Location: California Gold Country.
Rates: $50-$75. Season: All year.
Innkeeper(s): Melisande Hubbs & Patricia Cross.
6 Rooms. 4 Private Baths. 2 Shared Baths. Guest phone available. Children 10 & up. Smoking OK. Beds: KQ. Meals: Full breakfast.
"As usual our stay was fantastic."

"Thank you for making our stay with you so joyful."
"We appreciated your elegant breakfast in bed."
"Thank for the restful atmosphere you've created."

Jamestown

National Hotel
Main St, P.O. Box 502
Jamestown CA 95327
(209) 984-3446

Circa 1859. One of the oldest continuously operating hotels in California, the National has many stories to tell. The saloon contains the original nineteenth-century redwood bar over which thousands of dollars in gold dust were spent. *Bon Appetite* magazine lauded the hotel as one of the most interesting places to visit

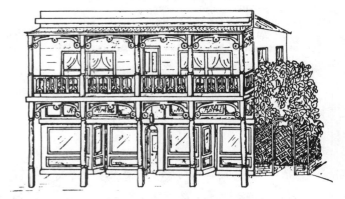

in the Gold Country. And indeed, the restaurant has the reputation of being one of the finest in the Mother Lode.

Location: Center of town.
**Rates: $35-$55. Season: All year.
Innkeeper(s): Stephen Willey.
11 Rooms. 5 Private Baths. 6 Shared Baths. Conference Room. Guest phone available. Children 8 & up. TV available. Smoking OK. Credit Cards: Visa, MC. Beds: QT. Meals: Continental-plus breakfast.
"Delightful!"
"Excellent, wonderful place!"
"Extremely pleased."
"Super."

Julian

Julian Gold Rush Hotel
2032 Main St, PO Box 856
Julian CA 92036
(619) 765-0201

Circa 1897. The dream of a former slave and his wife lives today as the sole surviving hotel in Southern California's "Mother Lode of Gold Mining." This Victorian charmer is listed in the National Register of Historic Places and is designated State of California Point of Historic Interest #SDI-09. Guests enjoy the feeling of a visit to grandma's and get a kick out of reading one hundred years of guest registration in the old hotel book.

Location: Center of the historic gold mining town.
**Rates: $50-$105. Season: All year.
Innkeeper(s): Steve & Gig Ballinger.
17 Rooms. 4 Private Baths. 13 Shared Baths. Conference Room. Guest phone available. Children By prior arrangement. Smoking OK. Beds: DT. Meals: Full breakfast.

"Any thoughts you have about the 20th Century will leave you when you walk into the lobby of this grand hotel."

Knights Ferry

Knights Ferry Hotel
17713 Main St
Knights Ferry CA 95361
(209) 881-3271

Circa 1854. Knights Ferry is the oldest hotel to survive the raging fires and floods which plagued this little gold mining town nestled along the Stanislaus River. The nearby covered bridge is the longest and

oldest west of the Mississippi, 330 feet long. Army Captain Ulysses S. Grant is said to have stayed here.

Location: Two hours east of San Francisco, one and one half hours from Yosemite.
**Rates: $25-$75. Season: All year.
Innkeeper(s): Richard Olson & Chris Coleman Ehmig.
6 Rooms. 2 Shared Baths. Guest phone available. TV available. Handicap access provided. Beds: QTC. Meals: B&B.

Kyburz

Strawberry Lodge
Kyburz CA 95720
(916) 659-7200

Circa 1858. Brass beds and hand-painted furniture provide a cozy setting in this historic lodge nestled in the Sierra Nevada mountains, high above Lake Tahoe. Ski resorts are just ten minutes away. In other seasons there is swimming, tennis, rock climbing and cycling. German brown trout and rainbow trout may be fished out of the south fork. Golden eagles nest on the high cliffs of nearby Lover's Leap. The inn was named after its builder, Ira Fuller Berry, who was so tight-fisted he passed off straw for hay to teamsters driving their wagons up to the lodge. When they arrived, they would yell, "Got any more of that straw, Berry?" A welcome sight to miners of the gold and silver fields, Strawberry Lodge has maintained a warm and serene atmosphere through the years.

Location: On Highway 50, 90 minutes east of Sacramento, 25 minutes from Tahoe.
**Rates: $33-$65. Season: All year.
31 Rooms. 26 Private Baths. 5 Shared Baths. Swimming Pool. Conference Room. Guest phone available. Children. Pets OK. TV available. Smoking OK. Credit Cards: Visa, MC, AE. Beds: KQT. Meals: EP.

La Jolla

The Bed & Breakfast Inn at La Jolla
7753 Draper Ave
La Jolla CA 92037
(619) 456-2066

Circa 1913. Irving Gill, the "father of tilt slab construction", is the architect for whom this inn is historically designated.

Location: One block from the Ocean.
**Rates: $65-$175. Season: All year.
Innkeeper(s): Betty Albee.
16 Rooms. 15 Private Baths. 1 Shared Baths. Guest phone available. Pets OK. TV available. Credit Cards: Visa, MC. Beds: QT. Meals: Continental-plus breakfast.

Laguna Beach

Carriage House
1322 Catalina St
Laguna Beach CA 92651
(714) 494-8945

Circa 1920. The inn is one of Laguna Beach's designated historical landmarks. A New Orleans style inn with a Cape clapboard exterior, the inn is a warm and

welcome sight. It was owned by Louis B. Mayer. Later it housed an art gallery, a bakery, and then was made into apartments, with large rooms, parlors and kitchens. The courtyard contains a fountain and flowers, shaded by a large carrotwood tree with hanging moss.

Location: Two blocks off Coast Highway on residential street.
**Rates: $75-$110. Season: All year.
Innkeeper(s): Dee & Vernon Taylor.
6 Rooms. 6 Private Baths. Guest phone available. Children. TV available. Smoking OK. Beds: KQDT. Meals: Continental-plus breakfast.

"Close to the beach, shop and restaurants, art galleries and town, yet so quiet. A true home away from home with all the extra touches added in."

"Great having my own parlor and lots of space after a day at the beach."

Casa Laguna Inn
2510 South Coast Hwy
Laguna Beach CA 92651
(714) 494-2996

Circa 1930. Recently restored to its original charm as a romantic combination of California Mission and Spanish Revival architecture, the inn's Mission House

and cottages were built in the early 1930's as guest facilities for the Villa Rockledge of Frank Miller, owner of the picturesque Riverside Inn. The Casitas, consisting of nineteen courtyard rooms, balcony rooms and suites, were added in the 1940's to serve visitors to the growing artist colony of Laguna Beach. The inn's hillside setting of secluded gardens, winding paths and flower-splashed patios invite guests to linger and enjoy the ocean view. Guests often enjoy watching the sunset over the Pacific Ocean from the Bell Tower high above the inn or from the deck surrounding the swimming pool.

Location: Across the street from the ocean on an ocean view hillside setting.
**Rates: $85-$170. Season: All year.
Innkeeper(s): Jerry & Luanne Siegel.
20 Rooms. 20 Private Baths. Swimming Pool. Guest phone available. Children. TV in room. Smoking OK. Credit Cards: Visa, MC, AE, DC. Beds: KQTC. Meals: Continental-plus breakfast, afternoon hors d'oeuvres.

"You really went out of your way to make sure everything was perfect for our vacation and we can't thank you enough."

"We had such a wonderful time at your delightful inn that we have regretted leaving every day we have been home."

"Such a beautiful place! Thanks for making it that way for us."

"Thank you it was superb! Charming in every way and everyone so gracious."

Eiler's Inn
741 South Coast Highway
Laguna Beach CA 92651
(714) 494-3004

Circa 1940. This New Orleans style inn is centered around a lush courtyard with fountain. The inn was named after Eiler Larsen, the famous town "greeter" of Laguna Beach. Located on the ocean-side of the Pacific Coast Highway, the inn is just a stone's throw from some of the most gorgeous beaches in Southern California.

Location: In the heart of the village.
Rates: $95-$150.
Innkeeper(s): Jonna Iverson.
12 Rooms. 12 Private Baths. Guest phone available. TV available. Smoking OK. Beds: KQT. Meals: B&B.

"Who could find a paradise more relaxing than an old-fashioned bed and breakfast with Mozart and Vivaldi, a charming fountain, wonderful fresh-baked bread, ocean air and Henk's conversational wit!"

"Eiler's Inn allows us to stop our hectic lives, the atmosphere allows us to relax and reflect. We come at least every year. It's our place to fall back in love with ourselves, each other and with life."

Little River

The Victorian Farmhouse
7001 N Highway One, PO Box 357
Little River CA 95456
(707) 937-0697

Circa 1877. Built as a private residence, this Victorian farmhouse is located on two-and-a-half acres in Little River, two miles south of the historic village of Mendocino. The inn offers a relaxed country setting with deer, quail, apple orchard and a running creek. Guests can enjoy breakfast in their room next to the fireplace and ocean views.

Rates: $67-$75.
Innkeeper(s): George & Carole Molnar.
6 Rooms. 6 Private Baths. Guest phone available. Children 10 & up. Handicap access provided. Credit Cards: Visa, MC, AE, DC. Beds: KQ. Meals: B&B.

Long Beach

Crane's Nest
316 Cedar Ave
Long Beach CA 90802
(213) 435-4084

Circa 1904. This California bungalow was built by the famous architects, Charles and Henry Greene, who built the renowned Gamble house in Pasadena. It is located in the newly renovated center of downtown Long Beach. Nearby are a shopping mall, restaurants, the Long Beach Convention Center, Queen Mary, Spruce Goose, Catalina cruises, the World Trade Center and Seaport Village.

Location: Heart of old historic downtown Long Beach.
**Rates: $45-$55. Season: All year.
Innkeeper(s): Ione Washburn.
2 Rooms. 1 Shared Baths. Guest phone available. TV available. Beds: QT. Meals: Continental breakfast.

Seal Beach Inn & Gardens
See: Seal Beach, CA.

Los Angeles

Bed & Breakfast of Los Angeles (Reservation Service)
32127 Harborview Lane
Los Angeles CA 91361
(818) 889-7325 or 889-8870

Peg and Angie have operated this Southern California reservation service for the past several years providing both homestay-type bed and breakfast accommodations as well as inn-stays. All the properties they serve have been inspected for the assurance of a pleasant and comfortable stay. A directory will be mailed for a $2.00 fee and a self-addressed, stamped envelope. Write to the address above.

Location: Over one hundred host homes throughout Greater Los Angeles.
Rates: $25-$100.

Casa Laguna Inn
See: Laguna Beach, CA.

Eastlake Victorian Inn
1442 Kellam Ave
Los Angeles CA 90026
(213) 250-1620

Circa 1887. Faithfully restored, decorated and furnished, the 1887 Eastlake Victorian Inn is located in Los Angeles' first historic preservations zone. Private tours of two Victorian, National Register homes is available as are old-fashioned hot-air ballooning, gondola cruises and other nearby attractions.

Location: Near downtown, museums and music center.

**Rates: $45-$125. Season: All year.
Innkeeper(s): Murray Burns & Planaria Price.
7 Rooms. 2 Private Baths. 5 Shared Baths. Conference Room. Guest phone available. Children 10 and above. TV available. Smoking not permitted. Credit Cards: Visa, MC, AE. Beds: Q. Meals: B&B.

"The Eastlake Inn took excellent care of us...so very helpful with restaurant recommendations and road directions."

"Perfect breakfasts."

"Meticulously restored." Travel & Leisure Magazine.

Salisbury House

2273 West 20th St
Los Angeles CA 90018
(213) 737-7817

Circa 1909. Salisbury House is located in Arlington Heights, part of the old West Adams area of Los Angeles. The inn features original stained and leaded

glass windows, wood-beamed ceilings, and an abundance of wood paneling. Salisbury House has been used as a location for movies and commercials. Many know Salisbury House for its famous gourmet breakfasts and old-fashioned graciousness.

**Rates: $55-$70. Season: All year.
Innkeeper(s): Kathleen & Bill

5 Rooms. 3 Private Baths. 2 Shared Baths. Guest phone available. Children 10 & up. TV available. Credit Cards: Visa, MC, AE. Beds: KQT. Meals: Full breakfast.

"This is without question, the finest bed and breakfast we've ever seen. Not only is the house exquisite but the hospitality is unmatched! Oh yes, what a breakfast!"

Terrace Manor

1353 Alvarado Terrace
Los Angeles CA 90006
(213) 381-1478

Circa 1902. This gracious three-story Tudor home is a National Register Landmark home. Your host

Sandy, is a practicing magician with **The Magic Castle**, a private magic club often frequented by well-known Hollywood personalities. Guests at the inn are also invited to be guests at the Castle. Terrace Manor is tastefully decorated and has many incredible stained glass windows, installed by the original builder who owned of a turn-of-a-century stained glass factory.

Location: Downtown Los Angeles.
**Rates: $55-$85. Season: All year.
Innkeeper(s): Sandy & Shirley Spillman.
5 Rooms. 5 Private Baths. Conference Room. Guest phone available. Children 12 & up. TV available. Credit Cards: Visa, MC, AE. Beds: KQ. Meals: Full breakfast.

"Lovely! Sandy does magic in the parlor; Shirley in the kitchen!"

"Here we are again! What a great way to visit L. A. !"

"Thanks your loving hospitality and for calming my life!"

Mendocino

Country Inn
See: Fort Bragg, CA.

Fensalden Bed & Breakfast
See: Albion, CA.

Harbor House
See: Elk, CA.

Howard Creek Ranch
40501 North Hwy, PO Box 121 Westport
Mendocino CA 95488
(707) 964-6725

  Circa 1871. First settled as a land grant of thousands of acres, Howard Creek Ranch is a twenty-acre farm on the Pacific Ocean with sweeping views of the ocean, sandy beaches and rolling mountains. A 75-

foot bridge spans a creek that flows past barns and outbuildings to the beach 200 yards away. The farmhouse is surrounded by green lawns, an award-winning flower garden, and grazing cows and horses. This rustic rural location is highlighted with antiques and collectibles.

Location: Mendocino Coast on the ocean.
Rates: $48-$75. Season: All year.
Innkeeper(s): Charles & Sally Grigg
7 Rooms. 3 Private Baths. 4 Shared Baths. Jacuzzi Tubs. Hot Tub. Sauna. Swimming Pool. Guest phone available. Children By prior arrangement. Beds: KQD. Meals: Hearty ranch breakfast.

  "Of the dozen or so inns on the West Coast we have visited, this is easily the most enchanting one."
  "This place is magical."

Joshua Grindle Inn
44800 Little Lake Rd, PO Box 647
Mendocino CA 95460
(707) 937-4143

  Circa 1879. Joshua Grindle, a Maine raftsman, moved to Mendocino and opened the first bank in town. He built his home on two acres of land. Light

and airy guest rooms are filled with New England antiques and collections of cast-iron shooting gallery pieces, candle molds, samplers, antique bicycles, church pews and chests. Two rooms are situated in The Tower and have commanding views of the coastline and Mendocino.

Location: On the Pacific Ocean, 150 miles north of San Francisco.
Rates: $65-$85. Season: All year.
Innkeeper(s): Bill & Gwen Jacobson
10 Rooms. 10 Private Baths. Guest phone available. Children 8 & up. Handicap access provided. Credit Cards: Visa, MC, DC. Beds: QT. Meals: New England-style breakfast.

  "We are basking in the memories of our stay. We loved every moment. You have created a beautiful warm place appointed in impeccable taste. We truly felt like privileged guests in a good friend's home."

MacCallum House Inn
45020 Albion St
Mendocino CA 95460
(707) 937-0289

  Circa 1882. Built by William H. Kelley for his newlywed daughter Daisy MacCallum, MacCallum House Inn is one of the most splendid examples of New England architecture in the Victorian village of Mendocino. Besides the main house, accommodations include the barn, carriage house, greenhouse, garden gazebo and water tower rooms.

Location: California North Coast.
**Rates: $45-$125. Season: All year.
Innkeeper(s): Melanie & Joe Reding.
20 Rooms. 7 Private Baths. 13 Shared Baths. Guest phone available. Children. Handicap access provided. Smoking OK. Credit Cards: Visa, MC, AE. Beds: KQTC. Meals: B&B and restaurant at the inn.

Mendocino Village Inn
44860 Main St, PO Box 626
Mendocino CA 95460
(707) 937-0246

Circa 1882. Originally the home of physician, Dr. William McCornack, the inn is comfortably located across the street from the ocean and just a stroll from

businesses in town. It has been beautifully restored and is now one of the architectural gems of Mendocino. A variety of rooms offer both Victorian and country-style decor, and seven of the rooms have their own fireplaces with firewood laid neatly each night. Just beyond the white picket fence are all the pleasures of the stunning North Coast.

Rates: $49-$95. Season: All year.
Innkeeper(s): Sue & Tom Allen.
12 Rooms. 10 Private Baths. 2 Shared Baths. Guest phone available. Children 10 & up. Credit Cards: Visa, MC. Beds: Q. Meals: Full breakfast.

"Thanks for making our visit very special! We enjoyed the ambience you provided - Vivaldi, Diamond Lil, homemade breakfast and of course, Mendocino charm!"

Monterey

Roserox Country Inn By-The-Sea
See: Pacific Grove, CA.

Murphys

Murphy's Hotel
457 Main St
Murphys CA 95247

(209) 728-3444

Circa 1856. Built as a stopover for visitors to the Calaveras Big Trees, a grove of giant sequoias, the hotel's many guests include such notables as President Grant, Mark Twain, and Horatio Alger Jr. Just a mile away are the Mercer Caverns.

Location: In historic gold rush town of Murphys.
**Rates: $45-$55.
Innkeeper(s): Robert Walker.

Napa

Coombs Residence "Inn on the Park"
720 Seminary St
Napa CA 94559
(707) 257-0789

Circa 1852. This two-story Victorian was built as the home of Frank Coombs, son of Nathan Coombs who

laid out the city of Napa and was the Ambassador to Japan during President Harrison's term. The inn is decorated with European and American antiques. Across the street is the historical Fuller Park.

Location: Wine Country, one hour from San Francisco.
**Rates: $65-$95. Season: All year.
Innkeeper(s): Rena Ruby
4 Rooms. 1 Private Baths. 3 Shared Baths. Guest phone available. Children 16 & up. TV available. Credit Cards: Visa, MC. Beds: KQDT. Meals: B&B.

"We feel like we are back in Europe! Your hospitality is unmatched! Simple elegance with warm friendly atmosphere. Our favorite B & B, a house with its own personality."

Gallery Osgood Bed & Breakfast Inn
2230 First St
Napa CA 94559
(707) 224-0100
Circa 1898. The artist-owners invite you to share and delight in their perfectly preserved Queen Anne

home, complete with period furnishings, stained glass and fine art. You'll enjoy an extraordinary wine country experience with your hosts' enthusiasm for Napa Valley, their home and showplace flower garden, and their knowledge of fine cuisine and art.

Location: In town.
**Rates: $77. Season: All year.
Innkeeper(s): Joan Osgood Moehrke & Howard Moehrke.
3 Rooms. 0 1 Shared Baths. Children 12 & up. Smoking OK. Credit Cards: Visa, MC, AE. Beds: QD. Meals: Full breakfast.

"We feel at home, except the food is better...the wineries paled by comparison...a warm, friendly visit, our honeymoon all over again, incredible attention to detail, five star...Ahhhhh!"

Grape Leaf Inn
See: Healdsburg, CA.

Napa Inn
1137 Warren St
Napa CA 94559
(707) 257-1444
Circa 1885. This Victorian mansion is nestled in the heart of the wine country in a quiet neighborhood.

Some of the rooms have their own kitchens enabling guests to pack a picnic lunch and start off for an afternoon of wine touring.

Rates: $50-$80. Season: All year.
Innkeeper(s): Dean & Helen Turner.
4 Rooms. 2 Private Baths. Children. Smoking OK. Meals: Continental-plus breakfast.

Scarlett's Country Inn
See: Calistoga, CA.

Nevada City

Piety Hill Inn
523 Sacramento St
Nevada City CA 95959
(916) 265-2245
Circa 1933. Located in the gold rush town of Nevada City, Piety Hill Inn is a 1930s auto court transformed into seven charming, uniquely decorated cottages. Some of the walls are hand stenciled. Others have wall hangings and Victorian and early American antiques. All the rooms overlook a grassy, tree-shaded courtyard with picnic tables and barbecues.

Location: Sierra Nevada foothills, one hour from Sacramento, two and a half hours from San Francisco.
**Rates: $50-$80. Season: All year.

Innkeeper(s): Trieve & Barbara Tanner.
7 Rooms. 7 Private Baths. Hot Tub. Guest phone available. Children. TV in room. Handicap access provided. Credit Cards: Visa, MC. Beds: K. Meals: Continental-plus breakfast.

Newport Beach

Doryman's Inn
2102 West Ocean Front
Newport Beach CA 92663
(714) 675-7300

Circa 1880. The Doryman's is an oceanfront inn with romantic Victorian rooms. French and American antiques enhance luxury appointments, Italian marble sunken bathtubs, gilt-edged, beveled mirrors, and etched French glass fixtures. Ferns and skylights are everywhere. Candlelit dinners are catered by one of Newport's finest gourmet seafood restaurants.

**Rates: $135-$275. Season: All year.
Innkeeper(s): Michael Palitz. 10 Rooms. 10 Private Baths. Hot Tub. Guest phone available. Children 12 & up. TV available. Smoking OK. Credit Cards: Visa, MC, AE, DC, CB. Beds: KQ. Meals: Continental-plus breakfast.
"Terrific service." Neil & Marsha Diamond.
"Had a wonderful stay." Jerry Lewis, comedian.

Pacific Grove

Green Gables Inn
104 5th St
Pacific Grove CA 93950
(408) 375-2095

Circa 1890. The Green Gables is a beautiful Victorian house anytime of day but it is a spectacular sight in the evening, jutting out over the bay with windows from every gable awash with light.

Rates: $95-$135. Season: All year.
10 Rooms. 6 Private Baths. Meals: Continental breakfast.

House of Seven Gables
555 Ocean View
Pacific Grove CA 93950
(408) 372-4341

Circa 1886. Along the oceanfront of the Monterey Peninsula, the Seven Gables has an unobstructed view of the Monterey Bay. The inn is owned by the Flatley family who had operated a guest house since 1958 just a few blocks from this one. Those rooms with ocean views also provide their guests with sights of sea otters, harbor seals and whales as well as the crashing surf.

Rates: $85-$125. Season: All year.
12 Rooms. 12 Private Baths. Meals: B&B.

Old St Angela Inn
321 Central Ave
Pacific Grove CA 93950
(408) 372-3246

Circa 1890. A restored former convent, the inn is a Cape style and includes a glass solarium where breakfast is served. Under the gazebo in the back garden is a jacuzzi and the ocean is a block away.

Rates: $85-$125.
Innkeeper(s): Donna & Carmen.
8 Rooms. 5 Private Baths. Credit Cards: Visa, MC. Beds: QT. Meals: Champagne breakfast.

Roserox Country Inn By-The-Sea
557 Ocean View Boulevard
Pacific Grove CA 93950
(408) 373-7673

Circa 1904. Roserox was designed and built by Dr. Julia Platt, the first woman mayor of Pacific Grove, a

Doctor of Zoology, and a world-renowned scientist. Today, the home is a warm, intimate four-story inn, enhanced by original patterned oak floors and ten-foot-high redwood beamed ceilings.

Location: Oceanfront, Monterey Peninsula.
**Rates: $85-$185. Season: All year.
Innkeeper(s): Dawn V. Browncroft.
8 Rooms. 4 Private Baths. 4 Shared Baths. Conference Room. Guest phone available. Children 13 & up. Beds: QT. Meals: Continental-plus breakfast.
"Unbelievable ocean views, enchanting rooms, a total and complete getaway, like being on our Honeymoon again."
"I could never return to Monterey without staying at Roserox."
"Totally charming and cozy...super breakfast, fun wine and cheese hour; but what really impressed us the most was Dawn and Deborah, the innkeepers. Those two cared so much!...they give it their all."

"The best thing that ever happened to our marriage."

Palo Alto

The Victorian on Lytton
555 Lytton Ave
Palo Alto CA 94301
(415) 322-8555

Circa 1890. This Queen Anne home was built for Hannah Clapp and her partner, Elizabeth Babcock. Miss Clapp was a descendant of Massachusetts Bay colonist, Roger Clapp. In 1859, threatened by tuberculosis, she sought health in the West and crossed the

plains on horseback wearing bloomers so she could ride astride with a pistol at her belt to ward off any who thought her costume invited frivolity. Later she opened a preparatory school and pursued other educational leadership roles. This elegant inn was fully restored in 1986. All rooms include a sitting area and canopy or four-poster beds.

Rates: Call. Season: All year.
Innkeeper(s): Susan Max Hall.
9 Rooms. 9 Private Baths. Guest phone available. Beds: KQ. Meals: Continental breakfast.

"Thank you for a lovely home away from home. You have created a serene and welcoming atmosphere. The appointments have been chosen with care and your warm hospitality compliments this fine house."

Placerville

Chichester House Bed & Breakfast
800 Spring St
Placerville CA 95667

(916) 626-1882

Circa 1892. D. W. Chichester, a partner in the local sawmill, built this gracious home for his wife. It is said

to be the first home in Placerville with built-in plumbing. Guests enjoy the pump organ in the parlor, fireplaces, the library and conservatory. The guest rooms are decorated with family treasures and antiques.

Location: On historic Highway 49, one and a half block from downtown.
Rates: $60-$65. Season: All year.
Innkeeper(s): Nan & Woody Carson.
3 Rooms. 4 Private Baths. 1 Shared Baths. Conference Room. Guest phone available. Beds: D. Meals: B&B.

"The most relaxing and enjoyable trip I've ever taken."

"You really helped to make Placerville a little bit more like home. A particular thank you for last night, starting with the relaxing sherry, then migrating into the dining room for my favorite dessert, followed by a presentation of trophy pinecones and a tour of a rare art gallery."

Historic Combellack-Blair House
3059 Cedar Ravine
Placerville CA 95667
(916) 622-3764

Circa 1895. The Combellack-Blair house is in the National Register of Historical Places, nominated after eleven years of restoration projects. When it was built in 1895, this Queen Anne house was proclaimed, an "elaborate, artistic and a handsome addition to the community." This statement is still an accurate description of the house with its white picket fence, sloping green lawn, and an ornate gable with turned spools in a sunburst design. The charming tower

room is accessed by a free-standing, stairway. Beautifully decorated to accent the outstanding stained glass and rich woods, the inn is a great place to stay while in the gold country.

Location: One-and-a-half blocks from downtown Placerville.
Rates: $55. Season: All year except Christmas and Thanksgiving.
Innkeeper(s): Cec & Jim Mazzuchi.
2 Rooms. 2 Shared Baths. Beds: D. Meals: New England country breakfast or miner's breakfast.

Quincy

The Feather Bed
542 Jackson St, PO Box 3200
Quincy CA 95971
(916) 283-0102
Circa 1893. At the turn of the century, this charming Queen Anne was renovated when electricity and a Greaco-Roman facade were added.

Location: High Sierra region, 75 miles northwest of Reno, NV.
**Rates: $50-$65.
Innkeeper(s): Chuck & Dianna Goubert.

Rancho Cucamonga

Christmas House Bed & Breakfast Inn
9240 Archibald Ave
Rancho Cucamonga CA 91730
(714) 980-6450
Circa 1904. This Queen Anne Victorian has been newly renovated in period elegance emphasizing its intricate wood carvings and red and green stained glass windows. It was once surrounded by eighty acres of citrus groves and grape vineyards. The wide, sweeping veranda is a favorite place for lounging while look-

ing out over the lawns and palm trees. The elegant ambience and quiet attract the business traveler, the romance seeker, and the vacationer.

Location: Thirty seven miles east of downtown Los Angeles, three miles from Ontario International Airport.
**Rates: $50-$95. Season: All year.
Innkeeper(s): Jay & Janice Ilsley.
4 Rooms. 2 Shared Baths. Conference Room. Guest phone available. TV available. Beds: D. Meals: Continental on weekdays, full breakfast weekends.

"Coming to Christmas House is like stepping through a magic door into an enchanted land."
"Our stay put me in a nostalgic romantic mood."
"It really was an emotional experience!"

Red Bluff

Faulkner House
1029 Jefferson St
Red Bluff CA 96080
(916) 529-0520
Circa 1890. Built by jeweler Herman H. Wiendieck this Queen Anne Victorian was bought by Dr. and Mrs. James L. Faulkner in 1933. The house has original stained glass windows, ornate molding, and eight-foot pocket doors separating the front and back parlors.

**Rates: $43-$60. Season: All year.
Innkeeper(s): Harvey & Mary Klingler.
4 Rooms. 1 Private Baths. 3 Shared Baths. Guest phone available. Smoking On the porch. Beds: Q. Meals: Continental breakfast.

Sacramento

Briggs House B&B
2209 Capitol Ave
Sacramento CA 95816
(916) 441-3214

Circa 1901. Surrounded by stately trees, this elegantly restored Cube Colonial is filled with European and American antiques creating a setting of peaceful

splendor. The spacious rooms have rich wood paneling, inlaid hardwood floors, and oriental rugs. Hospitality here is practiced to such an extent that guests are welcome to raid the refrigerator where wine, sparkling water and cider are kept.

Location: Mid-town, seven blocks from the Capitol.
**Rates: $55-$95. Season: All year.
Innkeeper(s): Sue Garmston, Barbara Stoltz, Kathy Yeaks, Paula Rawles & Leslie Hopper.
7 Rooms. 5 Private Baths. 2 Shared Baths. Hot Tub. Sauna. Conference Room. Guest phone in room. Children. Credit Cards: Visa, MC, AE. Beds: KQT. Meals: Full breakfast.

"I have experienced a real change in what is accomplished at business meetings held at inns as opposed to hotel rooms. People become friendlier, more relaxed and more productive. The sense of caring...nurtures the harried traveler."

"...a wonderful change from the impersonal hotels we've slept in. It's the start of an entirely new way of planning future trips!"

"We were treated with overflowing abundances of thoughtfulness, from the storage of our bikes, to brandy when we came in from the cold, to having our fire started for us."

"We have enjoyed country inns around the world, and this ranks as one of the top small inns."

Powers Mansion Inn
See: Auburn, CA.

San Diego

Britt House
406 Maple St
San Diego CA 42103
(619) 234-2926

Circa 1887. This one-hundred-year-old Queen Anne Victorian boasts two-story stained glass windows,

carved oak fretwork, and wainscoting. Formal English gardens surround the inn which stands on a large lot.

Location: City, parkside.
**Rates: $80-$100. Season: All year.
Innkeeper(s): Dawn Martin.
10 Rooms. 1 Private Baths. 4 Shared Baths. Guest phone in room. Children. TV available. Credit Cards: Visa, MC, AE. Beds: Q. Meals: B&B and afternoon tea.

"The 'Gold Standard' for California B&B's."

Brookside Farm
See: Dulzura, CA.

Casa Laguna Inn
See: Laguna Beach, CA.

Heritage Park Bed & Breakfast
2470 Heritage Park Row
San Diego CA 92110
(619) 295-7088

Circa 1889. Proudly situated on a seven-acre Victorian park in the heart of Old Town, the inn is one of seven classic period structures that are preserved in the park. It was built for Hartfield and Myrtle

Christian and was featured in *The Golden Era* magazine where it was called an "outstandingly beautiful home of Southern California." It has a variety of chimneys, shingles, a two-story corner tower, and an encircling veranda.

Location: In the heart of historic Old Town.
**Rates: $75-$115.
Innkeeper(s): Lori Chandler.

Rock Haus Bed & Breakfast
See: Del Mar, CA.

Surf Manor & Cottages
PO Box 7695
San Diego CA 92107
(619) 225-9765

Circa 1930. Four of the few remaining original beach cottages in the popular area of South Mission

Beach, Surf Manor provides quiet accommodations with a living room, bedroom, kitchen and bath in each cottage. Guests enter through the picket fence, and onto a small front porch. An English garden surrounds each cottage, adding to the ambience. Only steps away are both the Pacific Ocean beach and the bay.

Location: South Mission Beach.
Rates: $60-$120. Season: All year.
Innkeeper(s): Jerri Grady.
4 Rooms. 4 Private Baths. Children. TV available. Smoking OK.
Beds: D. Meals: B&B.

The Bed & Breakfast Inn at La Jolla
See: La Jolla, CA.

San Francisco

Art Center Wamsley Bed & Breakfast
1902 Filbert St
San Francisco CA 94123
(415) 567-1526

Circa 1857. The Art Center B&B was built during the Louisiana movement to San Francisco during the gold rush. The late Mario Musehi, editor of a daily

Italian newspaper said the building was next to what was called Washer Woman's Cove. It was the only permanent structure on the path between the Presidio and Yerba Buena village. The freshwater lagoon here at the foot of Laguna Street served as the village laundry. There are four guest apartments here, convenient to much of San Francisco.

Location: Two blocks south of Lombard (Rt 101) on Laguna.
**Rates: $65-$115. Season: All year.
Innkeeper(s): George & Helvi Wamsley.
4 Rooms. 4 Private Baths. Guest phone available. TV in room.
Credit Cards: Visa, MC, AE, DC, CB. Beds: QT. Meals: Kitchen with B&B.

Aurora Manor
1328 Sixteenth Ave
San Francisco CA 94122
(415) 564-2480

Circa 1930. Dutch, German, French and Norwegian are spoken in this international guesthouse. Your hostess is from Holland and has been an RN for many

many years. Dutch clean, this home has a special kitchen guests may use for fixing a light lunch. Tea and coffee are always available. A living room with fireplace is often used as guests relax.

Location: Near Golden Gate Park.
**Rates: $42. Season: All year.
Innkeeper(s): Saskia Thiadens.
5 Rooms. 2 Shared Baths. Guest phone available. TV available. Credit Cards: Visa, MC. Beds: QDT. Meals: Full breakfast.

"Thank you for the excellent hospitality; the breakfasts were superb; the directions for tours convinced us again that B&B lodging is superior, and the warmth of your personality helped make this stay in San Francisco unforgettable and justify this run-on sentence."

Casa Madrona Hotel
See: Sausalito, CA.

Chestelson House
See: St. Helena, CA.

Coombs Residence "Inn on the Park"
See: Napa, CA.

Hermitage House
2224 Sacramento St
San Francisco CA 94115
(415) 921-5515
  Circa 1901.

Location: Pacific Heights
**Rates: $80-$120.
Innkeeper(s): Marian Binkley & Jane Selzer.

Moffatt House
431 Hugo St
San Francisco CA 94122
(415) 661-6210
  Circa 1910. A simple two-story Edwardian home, The Moffatt House has a vivid stained glass window which contrasts with the light, neutral-toned interior. Color moods enhance each artfully eclectic guest room. Some guests linger to enjoy garden views while others jump on a MUNI bus for a quick ride to downtown. The inn is just a block to the major attractions in Golden Gate Park.

Location: San Francisco, 1 block from Golden Gate Park.
**Rates: $34-$49. Season: All year.
Innkeeper(s): Ruth Moffatt.
4 Rooms. 4 Shared Baths. Guest phone available. Children. TV in room. Smoking OK. Credit Cards: Visa, MC. Beds: QTC. Meals: Continental-plus breakfast.

Spencer House
1080 Haight St
San Francisco CA 94117
(415) 626-9205
  Circa 1890. This grand mansion, which sits on three city lots, is one of San Francisco's finest examples of Queen Ann Victorian architecture. Ornate parquet floors, original wallpapers, gas lights, and antique linens are featured. The elegantly paneled dining room, where breakfast is served with crystal and silver, is a room you may never forget. The opulence of Spencer House is even more enjoyable because of your hosts unpretentious good taste.

Location: Ten minutes from the wharf.
**Rates: $85-$130. Season: All year.
Innkeeper(s): Barbara & Jack Chambers.
6 Rooms. 3 Private Baths. Conference Room. Guest phone available. TV available. Beds: KQD. Meals: Full breakfast.

The Inn San Francisco
943 S Van Ness Ave
San Francisco CA 94110
(415) 641-0188
  Circa 1872. Built on Mansion Row, this Italianate Victorian was the home of John English and his fami-

ly. He was a city commissioner known as "The Potato King" because of his vast holdings in potato commodities. Champion race horses were raised on the grounds. Now, restored to an elegant Victorian, guests enjoy ornate woodwork and marble fireplaces.

**Rates: $56-$160. Season: All year.
Innkeeper(s): Joel Daily & Deborah Stedman.
15 Rooms. 12 Private Baths. 3 Shared Baths. Guest phone in room. Children 12 & up. TV in room. Smoking OK. Credit Cards: Visa, MC, AE. Beds: Q. Meals: Buffet continental breakfast.

"We were thrilled with the many small touches and extras provided. We felt at home and safe in a country very foreign to us." B.W., Australia.

"We loved our room and hot tub. Your thoughtfulness made our stay even better and our 31st anniversary will be remembered for years to come."

The Mansion Hotel
2220 Sacramento St
San Francisco CA 94115
(415) 929-9444
Circa 1887. Set high on a floral knoll, in Pacific Heights, San Francisco's most prestigious neighborhood, this Registered Historic Landmark, is a Queen

Anne Victorian on a grand scale. Guests enjoy the multimillion-dollar art collection, treasured Victorian memorabilia, and the Bufano Sculpture gardens. The invisible fingers of the resident ghost play classical requests in the haunted parlor every night. Magnificent dining is provided in the stained glass room.

Location: Pacific Heights area of San Francisco.
**Rates: $79-$200 Season: All year.
Innkeeper(s): Bob Pritikin.
19 Rooms. 19 Private Baths. Conference Room. Guest phone in room. Children. TV available. Smoking OK. Credit Cards: Visa, MC, AE, DC. Beds: QT. Meals: Full gourmet breakfast. Restaurant.

"Upstairs, Downstairs is still a way of life at the Mansion Hotel." Wall Street Journal.

"Lovely...marvelous hospitality." Barbra Streisand
"You jump back a century, slow down a bit, and breathe an atmosphere of forgotten elegance." Christian Science Monitor.

The Monte Cristo
600 Presidio Ave
San Francisco CA 94115
(415) 931-1875
Circa 1875. Each guest room is elegantly furnished with authentic period pieces. The inn is two blocks from the restored Victorian shops on Sacramento St.

**Rates: $50-$95.
Innkeeper(s): Frances Allan.

San Jose

Madison Street Inn
See: Santa Clara, CA.

San Rafael

Panama Hotel
4 Bayview St
San Rafael CA 94901
(415) 457-3993
Circa 1910.

Location: Fifteen miles north of San Francisco on 101.
Rates: $35-$85.
Innkeeper(s): Dan Miller & Paul Morrison.

Santa Ana

The Craftsman
2900 N Flower St
Santa Ana CA 92706
(714) 543-1168 or 558-1067
Circa 1910. A two-story Craftsman historical home, the inn was built by the Smiley family, well-known orchard growers in the Santa Ana area. The house is one of the few stately Craftsman homes still in the area. One of the original orange groves remains across the street. American and Danish antiques furnish the interiors.

Location: Orange County, Disneyland area.
**Rates: $40-$50.
Innkeeper(s): Philip and Iren Chinn.

Santa Barbara

Bella Maggiore Inn
See: Ventura, CA.

Cheshire Cat Inn
36 W Valerio
Santa Barbara CA 93101
(805) 569-1610

Circa 1892. The Eberle family built two graceful homes side by side, one a Queen Anne the other a Colonial Revival. The Eberles were blacksmiths, lawyers, and teachers. In 1896 one of them entertained President McKinley on his visit to Santa Barbara. Special features of the inn are its pagoda-like porch and both a square bay and a curved angular bay. Laura Ashley wallpapers and fabrics now enhance the elegance of the inn. The fireplace and balcony are favorite guest spots sometimes rivaling the garden gazebo with its spa and the large lawns and rose gardens.

Location: Downtown.
**Rates: $99-$149, $79-$129. Season: All year.
Innkeeper(s): George Mari & Carol Ryder.
10 Rooms. 10 Private Baths. Conference Room. Guest phone in room. Children 14 & up. TV available. Beds: KQT. Meals: Continental-plus breakfast.

"Staffing is absolutely marvelous, food delicious, decor beautiful."

"Elegant and warm environment. Would highly recommend."

"Fantastic accommodations, personal touch evident."

Old Yacht Club Inn
431 Corona Del Mar
Santa Barbara CA 93101
(805) 962-1277

Circa 1912. This 1912 California Craftsman house was the home of the Santa Barbara Yacht Club during the roaring twenties. It was opened as Santa Barbara's first B&B and is the only inn at the beach. It has become renown for it's gourmet food and superb hospitality.

Location: East Beach.
**Rates: $60-$115. Season: All year.
Innkeeper(s): Nancy Donaldson, Sandy Hunt & Lu Caruso.
9 Rooms. 5 Private Baths. 2 Shared Baths. Conference Room. Guest phone available. Children 12 & up. TV available. Credit Cards: Visa, MC, AE. Beds: KQ. Meals: Full gourmet breakfast.

"I also like the Old Yacht Club Inn because it is run by a driven genius named Nancy Donaldson...One bite of one of her omelets and you'll know you've met the Renoir of food." Eve Babitz, Los Angeles Magazine.

Olive House
1604 Olive St
Santa Barbara CA 93101
(805) 962-4902

Circa 1904.

**Rates: $65-$90.
Innkeeper(s): Nancy Flint & Jeannine Hunt.
"As you enter the Olive House, it is as if you are stepping into Grandma's house with its redwood-paneled parlor, high ceilings, and full breakfasts."

Red Rose Inn
1416 Castillo St
Santa Barbara CA 93101
(805) 966-1470

Circa 1886. This Victorian is pictured in the Santa Barbara Historical Society's publication, **Survivors**, as one of the city's outstanding examples of Victorian architecture. The inn has been fully restored and offers polished hardwood floors, stained glass windows, antique furnishings throughout, and an elegant walnut fireplace in the parlor. There is also a rose garden and a large avocado tree that shades the patio. The rooms in the inn were named for the great-grandmothers of the innkeeper. Ella's room features a bed that is believed to have been owned by Abraham Lincoln.

Location: Four blocks from downtown, fourteen blocks from Pacific Ocean.

Rates: $55-$100. Season: All year.
Innkeeper(s): Rick & Neile Ifland.
4 Rooms. 2 Private Baths. 1 Shared Baths. Guest phone available.
Children 13 & up. Credit Cards: Visa, MC. Beds: Q. Meals: Continental-plus breakfast.

"One of the most exquisite B&B's in Southern California."

"The Red Rose Inn is our favorite place!"

The Parsonage
1600 Olive St
Santa Barbara CA 93101
(805) 962-9336

Circa 1892. Built for the Trinity Episcopal Church, the Parsonage is one of Santa Barbara's most notable Queen Anne Victorians. It is nestled between downtown Santa Barbara and the foothills, in a quiet residential, upper eastside neighborhood. The inn is within walking distance of the mission, shopping, theater, and dining.

**Rates: $65-$120.
Innkeeper(s): Hilde Michemore.

Upham Hotel
1404 De La Vina St
Santa Barbara CA 93101
(805) 962-0058

Circa 1871. The Upham is a historic Victorian hotel with period furnishings including antique armoires and four-poster beds. Fireplaces warm the garden cottages where occasionally a hammock can be seen

swaying between the trees. Just two blocks away is the main street of Santa Barbara where guests will find gourmet restaurants, theaters, and fine shops.

**Rates: $75-$200. Season: All year.
Innkeeper(s): Andrea Gallant, General Manager.
39 Rooms. 39 Private Baths. Conference Room. Guest phone in room. Children. TV in room. Smoking OK. Credit Cards: Visa, MC, AE, Discover. Beds: KQC. Meals: Continental breakfast. Restaurant.

Santa Clara

Madison Street Inn
1390 Madison St
Santa Clara CA 95050
(408) 249-5541

Circa 1890. This Queen Anne Victorian still has the original doors and locks. "No Peddlers or Agents" is

engraved in the cement of the original carriageway. But guests always receive a warm and gracious welcome. High-ceilinged rooms are furnished in antiques, Oriental rugs, and Victorian wallpapers.

Location: Santa Rosa.
**Rates: $55-$75.
Innkeeper(s): Ralph & Theresa Wigginton.

5 Rooms. 3 Private Baths. 2 Shared Baths. Hot Tub. Sauna. Swimming Pool. Guest phone in room. Children 5 & up. TV available. Credit Cards: Visa, MC, AE. Beds: QT. Meals: B&B.

"Everything a B & B should be."

"Just like staying with old friends or coming home."

"Good food, good company; good fun."

Santa Cruz

Babbling Brook Bed & Breakfast Inn
1025 Laurel St
Santa Cruz CA 95060
(408) 427-2437

Circa 1909. A cascading waterfall and meandering creek grace the acre of gardens and redwoods that surround this secluded inn. It was built on the foundations of an 1870 tannery and a 1790 grist mill. Country French decor, cozy fireplaces and deep soaking whirlpool tubs are luxurious features of the inn.

Location: Two blocks from Highway One. Within walking distance to the beach, shopping and tennis.
**Rates: $75-125. Season: All year.
Innkeeper(s): Tom & Helen King.
12 Rooms. 12 Private Baths. Children 13 & up. TV in room. Handicap access provided. Smoking OK. Credit Cards: Visa, MC, AE, Discover. Beds: KQT. Meals: B&B.

Chateau Victorian
118 First St
Santa Cruz CA 95060
(408) 458-9458

Circa 1890. Chateau Victorian was built by a prosperous young sea captain from the east coast who made Santa Cruz his home port. On one of his journeys he met and fell in love with a beautiful native girl from the Solomon Islands. He sent his ship on without him after instructing the crew to tell the story that he had died at sea. Many years later, nearing death, he tried to return home to Santa Cruz and his family but died aboard ship returning to California. This beautiful Victorian has been renovated into an elegant inn.

Location: One block from the beach near the boardwalk and the wharf.
Rates: $80-$110. Season: All year.
Innkeeper(s): Franz & Alice-June Benjamin.
7 Rooms. 7 Private Baths. Guest phone available. Credit Cards: Visa, MC, AE. Beds: Q. Meals: Continental-plus breakfast.

"You went out of your way to make our stay pleasant and memorable. Thank you."

"We thoroughly enjoyed the Chateau Victorian, and the company was an added plus."

"...the perfect place for a romantic, hassle-free weekend on the Pacific coast. Attentive without being intrusive."

Cliff Crest
407 Cliff St
Santa Cruz CA 95060
(408) 427-2609

Circa 1887. Warmth, friendliness and comfort characterize this elegantly restored Queen Anne Victorian. An octagonal solarium, tall stained glass windows, and a belvedere overlook Monterey Bay and the Santa Cruz mountains. The mood is airy and romantic. The spacious gardens were designed by John McLaren, landscape architect for Golden Gate Park. Antiques and fresh flowers fill the rooms, once home to William Jeter, Lieutenant Governor of California.

Location: Crest of Beach Hill, just 1 1/2 blocks from the beach and boardwalk.
**Rates: $75-$115. Season: All year.
5 Rooms. 5 Private Baths. Guest phone available. Credit Cards: Visa, MC, AE. Beds: KQ. Meals: Full hearty breakfast.

New Davenport Bed & Breakfast
See: Davenport, CA.

Sausalito

Casa Madrona Hotel
801 Bridgeway
Sausalito CA 94965
(415) 332-0502

Circa 1885. The Victorian mansion is a registered Sausalito Historical Landmark. The old Casa on the hilltop is the oldest building in town. It started as a lumber baron's mansion in 1885. As time went on additional buildings were added to the property giving it a distinctly European look. Following the traditional inn style dating back to who knows when, each room has its own unique name and charm. "Lord Ashley's Lookout", "Kathmandu", "Mariner Room", "Fireside Room" and "Gramma's Room" are only a few of the many rooms available, and the appointments are as varied as the names. Each room had been given over to a professional bay area decorator, and "they have plied their arts to a fare-thee-well." The Casa Madronna faces San Francisco Bay, and guests frequently enjoy the barking seals, the evening fog and the beautiful sunrises.

Location: Downtown Sausalito.
Rates: $60-$195. Season: All year.
Innkeeper(s): John W. Mays.
35 Rooms. 33 Private Baths. 2 Shared Baths. Hot Tub. Conference Room. Guest phone in room. Children. TV in room. Handicap access provided. Smoking OK. Checks not accepted. Credit Cards: Visa, MC, AE, DC, CB. Meals: B&B & restaurant.

"Wonderful stay at the Casa Madrona. Had to pinch myself several times to be sure it was real! Is this heaven? With this view it sure feels like it."
"A throwback to the good ole days."
"Incredibly terrific."

Seal Beach

Seal Beach Inn & Gardens
212 5th St
Seal Beach CA 90740
(213) 493-2416

Circa 1924. From this exquisitely restored inn it is a very easy walk to Seal Beach's historical points of interest. In the old days, the Hollywood crowd would arrive by Red Car to gamble and drink rum. Lindberg and his buddies would fly in from the East coast. (His former haunt, The Glide 'Er Inn, remains as an aviation-theme eatery. The Red Car still stands on Electric Street. All the rooms are appointed with fine antiques and historical pieces, and a tin ceiling graces

the library. Outside gardens blaze with colors. Napoleonic *jardinieres* are filled with flowers. There is

a 300-year-old fountain from France and museum quality art in the garden. A grand antique Parisian fence surrounds the property.

Location: Quaint seaside village just 300 yards from the ocean in a quiet residential neighborhood.
**Rates: $78-$145. Season: All year.
Innkeeper(s): Marjorie Bettenhausen.
23 Rooms. Swimming Pool. Conference Room. Children. TV in room. Credit Cards: Visa, MC, AE, CB. Beds: KQTC. Meals: B&B.
  "The closest thing to Europe since I left there."
  "It just sings as song as you walk by."
  "Anybody shall have poetical feelings in this place."
(Gentleman from Tokyo).

Sonoma

Overview Farm
15650 Arnold Dr
Sonoma CA 95476
(707) 938-8574

Circa 1880. Historic Landmark #140, this Victorian farmhouse was once a part of the famed Spreckels estate. It has been revitalized to capture the gracious living styles of turn-of-the-century Sonoma. Large guest rooms with ten-foot ceilings house a fine collec-

tion of early American treasures. Manicured gardens, espaliered fruit trees, and captivating views complement the beauty of the interior.

Location: Wine country.
**Rates: $85. Season: All year.
Innkeeper(s): Judy & Robert Weiss.
3 Rooms. 3 Private Baths. Guest phone available. Beds: QD. Meals: Full breakfast.

  "We thank you very much for our wonderful stay in your house. It was extremely romantic and the best part was that we met you." Goldie Hawn & Kurt Russell.

Sonora

Barretta Gardens Inn
700 S Barretta St
Sonora CA 95370
(209) 532-6039
  Circa 1904.

Location: Off Hwy 108.
**Rates: $55-$60.
Innkeeper(s): Don & Vivian Easler.

The Ryan House Bed & Breakfast
153 S Shepherd St
Sonora CA 95370
(209) 533-3445
  Circa 1855. This homestead-style house is set well back from the street, in a quiet residential area. Green lawns and gardens with thirty-five different roses blooming all summer, surround the house. Each room is individually decorated in handsome antiques.

The inn cat often peeks around the corner to see if you are enjoying your stay.

Location: Two blocks from the heart of historic Sonora.
**Rates: $39-$65. Season: All year.
Innkeeper(s): Maureen Kelley & Ken Brunges.

4 Rooms. 2 Private Baths. 2 Shared Baths. Guest phone available. Children. Credit Cards: Visa, MC, AE, DC. Beds: QD. Meals: Full breakfast.

  "Staying at the Ryan House was everything our friends said it would be: warm, comfortable and great breakfasts!

  "You made us feel like long-lost friends the moment we arrived."

St. Helena

Chestelson House
1417 Kearny St
St. Helena CA 94574
(707) 963-2238
  Circa 1904. This Queen Anne Victorian has a wraparound veranda and French country furnishings. The rooms are named after Robert Louis Stevenson's

Child's Garden of Verses. The Silverado Museum is only a few blocks away.

Location: Napa Valley -- Wine country.
**Rates: $75-$95. Season: All year.
Innkeeper(s): Jackie Sweet.
3 Rooms. 3 Private Baths. Children 12 & above. Smoking on porch Beds: Q. Meals: B&B.

  "...comfortable & charming accommodations reflect a special ambience of tradition...exceptional breakfast is an outstanding highlight... friendly & generous hospitality makes the stay memorable...welcoming countryside invites us to return!

Scarlett's Country Inn
See: Calistoga, CA.

White Ranch
707 White Lane
St. Helena CA 94574
(707) 963-4635

Circa 1865. This nineteenth century yellow farmhouse was built by Asa White, a Methodist minister, who brought his family across the prairie in a covered wagon. Situated among vineyards, it provides an intimate lodging experience for one couple. Qualifying in both B&B categories, it is listed as an inn but is still a family house. A separate entrance leads to the guest room in its own wing, private porch, and fireplace. There are horses in the pasture, turkeys in the barn, old walnut trees out front and vineyards all around.

Rates: $70. Season: All year.
1 Rooms. 1 Private Baths. Guest phone available. TV in room. Beds: Q. Meals: Continental-plus breakfast.

Sutter Creek

Nancy & Bob's 9 Eureka Street Inn
9 Eureka St
Sutter Creek CA 95685
(209) 267-0342

Circa 1916. A California bungalow, the inn mirrors the graciousness and charm of a bygone era, complete with beautiful rich woods, antiques, stained glass windows, and guest rooms decorated in the mode of the past.

Location: Highway 49 in the Gold Country.
Rates: $65-$75. Season: February to December.
Innkeeper(s): Nancy & Bob Brahmst.
5 Rooms. 5 Private Baths. Conference Room. Guest phone available. Credit Cards: Visa, MC. Beds: QT. Meals: Full breakfast.

Tahoe City

Mayfield House
256 Grove St
Tahoe City CA 95730
(916) 583-1001

Circa 1930. One of the finest examples of old Tahoe architecture, the Mayfield House is named after its builder, Lake Tahoe's pioneer contractor.

Location: Downtown Tahoe City, Hwy 28.
Rates: $65-$95.
Innkeeper(s): Jawie Kaye.

Templeton

Country House Inn
91 Main St, PO Box 179
Templeton CA 93465
(805) 434-1598

Circa 1886.

Location: Twenty miles north of San Luis Obispo on Hwy 101.
**Rates: $60-$75.
Innkeeper(s): Dianne Garth.

Ventura

Bella Maggiore Inn
67 S California St
Ventura CA 93001
(805) 652-0277

Circa 1925.

Location: Two blocks from the beach. Close to restaurants and shops.
**Rates: $60-$90.
Innkeeper(s): Ms. Lisa Koenig.

La Mer
411 Poli St
Ventura CA 93001
(805) 643-3600

Circa 1890. La Mer is a three-story Cape Cod Victorian. The second floor has high ceilings and large windows that overlook the heart of historic San Buenaventura and the spectacular California coastline. Each room is decorated to capture the feeling of a specific European country. French, German, Austrian, Norwegian and English-style accommodations are available. The inn is just a few blocks from the beach and within walking or biking distance of Ventura's many shops and restaurants. Gisela, the hostess, is a native of Siegerland, Germany.

Location: Second house north of city hall.
**Rates: $65-$105. Season: All year.
Innkeeper(s): Gisela & Michael Baida.
5 Rooms. 5 Private Baths. Guest phone available. TV available. Credit Cards: Visa, MC. Beds: Q. Meals: Full Bavarian breakfasts.

"Where to begin? The exquisite surroundings, the scrumptious meals, the warm feeling from your generous hospitality?!? What an unforgettable weekend all had in your heavenly home. Counting the moments 'til we'll be back."

Yuba City

Harkey House Bed & Breakfast
212 C St
Yuba City CA 95991
(916) 674-1942

Circa 1864. Sheriff of Sutter County, William Harkey built this Victorian house as a family residence. Painted cream, blue, and burgundy, the house contains an art gallery, library, back-to-back marble fireplaces, and three guest rooms. Guests enjoy the grounds and gardens that surround a pool, spa, and a basketball court.

Location: Two hours from San Francisco and Tahoe, 40 miles from Sacramento.
**Rates: $50-$70.
Innkeeper(s): Bob & Lee Jones.

Colorado

Aspen

Sardy House
128 East Main St
Aspen CO 81611
(303) 920-2525
   Circa 1892. Sardy House was built by J. William Atkinson, often called "three-fingered Jack". He was one of the owners of the "Little Annie" mine and Aspen's

first freight company. He served as sheriff of Aspen for fourteen years. The inn is one of the finest examples of Queen Anne Victorian architecture in Aspen with its thick brick walls, sandstone detailing, and wood ornamental trim. One of the Colorado Blue Spruce on the grounds is over ninety feet high and is the tallest in Aspen. Deluxe guest rooms are in both the main house and the Carriage House. Guests enjoy the unexpected and the ultimate in pampered luxury.

****Rates: $160-$360. Season: November to April 19 and June 12 to October.
Innkeeper(s): Jayne Poss.
21 Rooms. 21 Private Baths. Hot Tub. Sauna. Swimming Pool. Conference Room. Guest phone in room. Children. TV in room.

Credit Cards: Visa, MC, AE, DC. Beds: KQT. Meals: Full breakfast. Restaurant.
   "Many, many thanks for our marvelous stay at the Sardy House. As you know it was my first trip to Aspen and everything far exceeded expectations, particularly your beautiful establishment. Sardy House is wonderful and unique. The level of service is superb, all of which I am looking forward to returning to."

Boulder

Bed & Breakfast Colorado, Ltd
PO Box 6061
Boulder CO 80306
(303) 442-6664
   From grand Victorian Queen Anne inns to small honeymoon-type cottages with fireplaces and jacuzzi tubs, all accommodations have been carefully inspected by Lois La Croux, owner of this reservation service. There is a wide selection from which to pick the accommodation just right for you.

Location: Historic homes and inns throughout Colorado.
Rates: $25-$100.

Carbondale

Crystal River Inn
Hell Roaring Ranch, 12954 Hwy 133.
Carbondale CO 81657
(303) 963-3902
   Circa 1895. This Victorian home is on 150 acres of privately owned land. A pond nearby is often used for skating in the winter. Two fireplaces warm the inn and to keep guests even warmer slippers are provided.

Location: Five miles north of Redstone on Crystal River.
****Rates: $48-$60.
Innkeeper(s): Robyn King.

Colorado Springs

Bed & Breakfast Colorado, Ltd
See: Boulder, CO.

Bed & Breakfast Rocky Mountains
PO Box 804
Colorado Springs CO 80901
(303) 630-3433

This reservation service is owned by Kate Peterson, one of the dynamic leaders of the bed and breakfast movement. Kate has organized over 100 host homes and inns in these four states. Favorite B&Bs are near the Buffalo Bill Museum and in ski areas such as Aspen, Vail, Copper Mountain, Breckenridge, Winter Park and Steamboat. The many scenic forests and state parks offer opportunities for hiking, gold panning, white water-rafting, ballooning, snowmobiling, horseback riding, sleigh rides, fishing and of course skiing. When you call for reservations state that you prefer a *historic* inn or home because Kate has many other listings.

Location: B&Bs in Colorado, Montana, Wyoming and New Mexico.
Rates: $17-$95.

Billy's Cottage
See: Manitou Springs, CO.

Hearthstone Inn
506 N Cascade Ave
Colorado Springs CO 80903
(303) 473-4413

Circa 1885. This elegant Queen Anne inn is actually two lovely houses joined by an unusual walkway that

is an old carriage house. The inn has been restored into a period showplace with six working fireplaces, carved oak staircases and magnificent antiques throughout. A green, lush lawn suitable for croquet surrounds the house. Flower beds match the Victorian colors of the exterior of the inn.

Location: On a tree-lined boulevard of central Colorado Springs, two minutes from I-25.
**Rates: $50-$90. Season: All year.
Innkeeper(s): Dorothy Williams - Ruth Williams (no relation).
25 Rooms. 23 Private Baths. 1 Shared Baths. Guest phone available. Children. Smoking OK. Credit Cards: Visa, MC, AE. Beds: KQDTC. Meals: Hearty country breakfast.

"So welcoming! Like going to Grandmother's!"

"We try to get away and come to the Hearthstone at least twice a year because people really care about you!"

Crested Butte

Purple Mountain Lodge
PO Box 897, 714 Gothic Avenue
Crested Butte CO 81224
(303) 349-5888

Circa 1927. Purple Mountain is a small lodge in a historic town full of interesting shops and nearby cross-country ski trails and downhill skiing spots.

**Rates: $22-$55
Innkeeper(s): Walter & Sherron Green.

Cripple Creek

Imperial Hotel
123 N Third St
Cripple Creek CO 80813
(303) 689-2922, 689-2713

Circa 1896. The only original Cripple Creek hotel still standing, the inn is filled with antiques and has a collection of Gay 90's memorabilia. The inn is known for its excellent cuisine and its cabaret-style melodrama that is performed twice daily.

Location: Center of town.
**Rates: $30-$40.
Innkeeper(s): Stephen & Bonnie Mackin.

Denver

Bed & Breakfast Colorado, Ltd
See: Boulder, CO.

Queen Anne Inn
2147 Tremont Place
Denver CO 80205
(303) 296-6666

Circa 1879. The Queen Anne is a beautifully restored three-story home situated among other meticulously-restored homes and gardens in the nationally registered Clements Historic District. It is Denver's oldest, continuously occupied residential neighborhood. The inn was designed by Colorado's most famous architect. It has private baths and air conditioning in addition to its many elegant furnishings. Music, art, and a grand old oak stairway add to the Victorian experience. For a special treat select the *Fountain Room* with its five windows and views of Benedict Fountain and Park, or soak in the sunken tub with its golden fixtures, or fall asleep in the big canopied bed. There is an antique Queen Anne style writing desk and a comfy sofa arrangement. One room is in the peak of the turret. Another has the cupola and one is tucked under the branches of an ancient maple tree.

Location: Four blocks from the center of town.
**Rates: $55-$85. Season: All year.
Innkeeper(s): Ann & Chuck Hillestad.
10 Rooms. 10 Private Baths. Guest phone in room. Children 15 & up. Credit Cards: Visa, MC. Beds: QDT. Meals: Continental breakfast.

The Dove Inn
See: Golden, CO.

Victoria Oaks Inn
1575 Race St
Denver CO 80218
(303) 355-1818
  Circa 1894. Victoria Oaks was originally built as a boarding house. The floor plan, dramatic hanging oak

staircase, and four wood-and-tile working fireplaces make for an interesting and enjoyable visit. All rooms are furnished in restored antiques, soft pastel colors,

and custom bedspreads. The inn is close to many of Denver's historic attractions. Bicycles can be rented from the inn.

Location: Close to downtown.
Rates: $39-$79. Season: All year.
Innkeeper(s): John Kelly & Kim Stephens. 9 Rooms. 1 Private Baths. 3 Shared Baths. Conference Room. TV available. Smoking OK. Credit Cards: All. Beds: QT. Meals: Continental-plus breakfast.

Durango

Bed & Breakfast Colorado, Ltd
See: Boulder, CO.

Empire

The Peck House
PO Box 423
Empire CO 80438
(303) 569-9870
  Circa 1860. Built as a residence for James Peck, the house is the oldest hotel still in operation in

Colorado. Its future as a hotel was assured as investors for Peck's gold mines flooded in from the East. Much of the original furniture brought by ox cart remains. Some rooms such as *Mountain View* provide magnificent views of the eastern slope of the Rockies. The *Mint Lode,* the *Hideaway* and the *Governor's Quarters* are old fashioned and comfortable with such items as walnut headboards and a red antique fainting couch.

**Rates: $35-$80. Season: All year.
Innkeeper(s): Gary & Sally St. Clair.

11 Rooms. 9 Private Baths. 2 Shared Baths. Conference Room. Guest phone available. Children. Smoking OK. Credit Cards: All. Beds: DT. Meals: Restaurant. EP.

Ft Collins

Elizabeth Street Guesthouse
202 E Elizabeth
Ft Collins CO 80524
(303) 493-2337
 Circa 1905. A restored American four-square brick inn, Elizabeth Street Guest House has all the gracious amenities of an earlier day of skilled craftsmanship and a slower pace. Leaded windows and polished oak woodwork are highlighted with plants and antiques. The inn is in the nationally designated Laurel School Historic District.

Location: Center of Ft Collins, one block east of Colorado State University.
**Rates: $30-$42.
Innkeeper(s): John & Sheryl Clark.

Golden

The Dove Inn
711 14th St
Golden CO 80401
(303) 278-2209
 Circa 1889. The Dove Inn is a charming Victorian that features an airy bay window overlooking giant

blue spruce and the foothills of the Rockies. Breakfast is served before the 100-year-old fireplace or outdoors on the porch or on the deck with its old-fashioned lawn furniture. In the same neighborhood

are the beautiful old homes that housed the leaders of the former territorial capital of Colorado. (The innkeepers prefer no unmarried couples.)

**Rates: $29-$49 Season: All year.
Innkeeper(s): Ken & Jean Sims.
5 Rooms. 5 Private Baths. Guest phone in room. Children. TV in room. Smoking In two rooms. Credit Cards: All. Beds: QDC. Meals: Full breakfast.
"Our first experience at a bed and breakfast was delightful, thanks to your hospitality at the Dove Inn."
"Thanks for making our honeymoon stay a special one."
"An unforgettable experience."

La Veta

1899 Bed & Breakfast Inn
314 S Main
La Veta CO 81055
(303) 742-3576
 Circa 1899. Stone walls that are eighteen-inches thick add to the substantial feel of this inn. A wood burning stove makes it warm and cozy inside in the winter, while the large front porch and the porch swing are perfect spots for a summer evening. Bicycles can be borrowed or you can browse through the inn's gift shop.

Location: Next to the museum and library, Rt 12 in Southern Colorado.
Rates: $22.50-$32.
Innkeeper(s): Marilyn Hall.

Manitou Springs

Billy's Cottage
117 Deer Path
Manitou Springs CO 80829
(303) 685-1828
 Circa 1909. A beautifully restored Victorian cottage, this inn features family heirloom furniture and original wood floors. There is a pot belly stove and an antique marble sink yet the vintage setting is perfectly blended with modern function. A private patio leads to the hosts' hot tub that is available for guests private use. The cottage is perfect for the honeymoon couple or family with children. It has a kitchen, sunny breakfast room and dining area with spectacular mountain view. Before the turn of the century the ultimate tourist attraction in the area was to view the sunrise from the top of Pikes Peak. Burros jolted many a saddle-sore traveler the twenty-six miles from the village

up and down the mountain. Travel weary folks were treated to a dip in the famous mineral springs.

Location: Nestled at the foot of Pikes Peak, four miles from Colorado Springs.
**Rates: $55-$85. Season: All year.
1 Rooms. 1 Private Baths. Jacuzzi Tubs. Guest phone in room. Children. Pets OK. TV in room. Handicap access provided. Smoking OK. Credit Cards: Visa, MC. Beds: Q.

BILLY'S COTTAGE   BUILT·1909 ; RESTORED·1986
117 DEERPATH
MANITOU SPRINGS, COLORADO

"The charm of historic Manitou plus the wonderful mountain setting perfectly sets off Billy's Cottage as an absolutely delightful getaway. We just hate to leave."

Silver Plume

Brewery Inn
246 Main St, PO Box 473
Silver Plume CO 80476
(303) 571-1151 or 569-2277
Circa 1890. The Brewery Inn is a restored Victorian home with fireplaces, antiques, wallpapers and down

comforters. Located within the National Historic District, a walk through the town will recapture the feel-

ings of an 1880s silver mining town. Nearby is the Silver Plume museum and the Georgetown Loop Narrow Gauge Train Ride.

Location: I-70 exit 226, fifty miles west of Denver.
Rates: $40-$60 Season: All year.
Innkeeper(s): Mary P. Joss & Jeanette Rizzardi.
4 Rooms. 1 Private Baths. 1 Shared Baths. Conference Room. Guest phone available. Children. Smoking OK. Credit Cards: Visa, MC. Beds: QT. Meals: B&B. Restaurant.

"Charming, cozy, comfortable! It makes one ponder the real need for the 'necessities' of life, (TV, telephone). It was wonderful to go back and be free of everyday stresses."

Silverton

Grand Imperial Hotel
1219 Green St
Silverton CO 81433
(303) 387-5527 or 387-5333
Circa 1882. The Grand Imperial was built by a wealthy perfume merchant from London who owned part of the Martha Rose smelter in town. A saloon within the hotel, the Hub, became the social center of the entire town and is said to have been the birthplace of

the song, "There's a Hot Time in the Old Town Tonight." The hotel was a glittering hostess to Bat Masterson, Wyatt Earp, Lillian Russell, and Diamond Jim Brady. The hotel was known as the "home of the silver kings."

Location: Main street in town.
**Rates: $35-$100. Season: March to November.
Innkeeper(s): Ken Marlin & Mary Helen Marlin.
40 Rooms. 40 Private Baths. Conference Room. Guest phone available. Children. TV in room. Credit Cards: Visa, MC. Beds: QDTC. Meals: AP. Restaurant on premises.

Connecticut

Bolton

Jared Cone House
25 Hebron Rd
Bolton CT 06040
(203) 643-8538

Circa 1775. Situated in hilly woodland and farmland this authentically furnished historic inn has a large Palladian window above the front door, a massive stone fireplace in the kitchen and seven other fireplaces. The original owner was an early Bolton farmer who built the house in two phases. Classical music is played in the parlor in the evening. In the morning guests awake to lovely views of the scenic countryside.

Location: Ten minutes east of Hartford.
Rates: $55.
Children. Smoking OK. Credit Cards: Visa, MC. Beds: Q. Meals: B&B.

Chester

Riverwind
See: Deep River, CT.

Deep River

Riverwind
209 Main St
Deep River CT 06417
(203) 526-2014

Circa 1850. Renovated almost single-handedly by the innkeeper herself, this inn features a wraparound gingerbread porch filled with gleaming white wicker furniture. Most of the inn is decorated with antiques from the innkeeper's Virginia home. There are fireplaces everywhere including a twelve-foot cooking fireplace in the keeping room.

Location: Center of town.
Rates: $70-$125.
Innkeeper(s): Barbara Barlow.
8 Rooms. 8 Private Baths. TV available. Smoking OK. Beds: D. Meals: Southern Virginia breakfast.

"If we felt any more welcome we'd have our Time subscription sent here."

"After 30 years we have finally found what are looking for - a charming innkeeper and a most relaxing inn."

"We've stayed in many inns and B&B's in Ireland, England, New England and California...this is one of the best."

"As innkeepers in Newport, Rhode Island, we rate your inn a 10."

East Haddam

Riverwind
See: Deep River, CT.

Essex

Riverwind
See: Deep River, CT.

Glastonbury

Butternut Farm
1654 Main St
Glastonbury CT 06033
(203) 633-7197

Circa 1720. A colonial-style house situated on two acres of woodlands, the farm is home to prize-winning goats, pigeons and chickens all housed in the old barn behind the house. Authentic eighteenth-century Connecticut antiques, such as a cherry highboy and a cherry pencil-post canopy bed, are used throughout the inn and enhance the natural beauty of the pumpkin-pine floors and brick fireplaces.

Location: South of Glastonbury Center, 1 1/2 miles, 15 minutes from Hartford.
Rates: $50-$65.
Innkeeper(s): Don Reid.
4 Rooms. Guest phone available. Children. TV available. Meals: Continental breakfast.

Greenwich

Homestead Inn
420 Field Point Rd
Greenwich CT 06830
(203) 869-7500

Circa 1799. A judge and gentleman farmer, Augustus Mead built the Homestead as a typical farmhouse. Later it was remodeled to a fanciful Carpenter Gothic Victorian style. A full veranda is filled with wicker furnishings and offers views of rolling lawns and shady trees. The inn was renovated by noted designers John and Virginia Saladino and with its fine collection of antiques, classic French restaurant, and intimate library with fireplace, it is often the site of romantic weddings.

Rates: $80-$150. Season: All year.
Innkeeper(s): Nancy Smith & Lessie Davison.
23 Rooms. 23 Private Baths. Guest phone available. Children. TV available. Smoking OK. Credit Cards: All. Meals: B&B.

Groton Long Point

Shore Inne
54 East Shore Rd
Groton Long Point CT 06340
(203) 536-1180

Circa 1915. Waterfront on Long Island Sound, the Shore Inne is a colonial-style house that features water views from many of the inn's common rooms and six of the guest rooms.

Location: Three-and-a-half miles from Mystic.
Rates: $35-$48.
Innkeeper(s): Helen Ellison.
7 Rooms. 3 Private Baths. Guest phone available. Children. TV available. Smoking OK. Credit Cards: Visa, MC. Meals: B&B.

Litchfield

Tollgate Hill Inn
Route 202 and Tollgate Rd
Litchfield CT 06759
(203) 567-4545

Circa 1745. Formerly known as the Captain Bull Tavern, the inn underwent extensive renovations in 1983. Listed in the National Register, features include Indian shutters, wide pine-paneled walls, a Dutch door fireplace, and an upstairs ballroom. Next door is a historic schoolhouse which houses four of the inn's guestrooms.

Rates: $75-$85. Season: All year.
Innkeeper(s): Frederick Zivic.
10 Rooms. 10 Private Baths. Children. Pets OK. Smoking OK. Meals: Continental breakfast.

Mystic

Harbour Inne and Cottage
Edgemont St
Mystic CT 06355
(203) 572-9253
Circa 1898.

Location: On Mystic River two blocks from the railroad station.
**Rates: $35-$165. Season: All year.
Innkeeper(s): Charles Lecouras, Jr. 6 Rooms. 6 Private Baths. Guest phone available. Children. Pets OK. TV available. Smoking OK. Beds: D. Meals: B&B.

New Preston

Inn on Lake Waramaug
North Shore Rd
New Preston CT 06777
(203) 868-0563

Circa 1760. The inn is a colonial home on 130 acres with a swimming pool and private beach.

Rates: $60-89 per person double occupancy.
Innkeeper(s): Richard Bonynge Combs & family.

Norfolk

Manor House
Maple Ave
Norfolk CT 06058
(203) 542-5690

Circa 1898. Built in 1898 by Charles Spofford, designer of the underground system in London and son of Ainsworth Rand Spofford, Librarian of Congress

under Abraham Lincoln. The inn has exquisite cherry paneling, a grand staircase, Moorish arches and Tiffany windows. Guests often enjoy hot mulled cider after a sleigh ride, hay ride, or horse-and-carriage drive along the country lanes nearby.

Location: Northwestern Connecticut.
**Rates: $55-$150.
Innkeeper(s): Hank & Diane Tremblay.
8 Rooms. 4 Private Baths. 2 Shared Baths. Conference Room. Guest phone available. Children 12 & up. TV available. Smoking OK. Credit Cards: Visa, MC, AE. Beds: KQT. Meals: Full breakfast.

"Queen Victoria, eat your heart out."
"A castle and a home - exquisite."
"Wonderful trip to the romantic world of days gone by."
"Blueberry pancakes and waffles are tops - truly paradise."

Norwalk

Silvermine Tavern
Silvermine & Perry Avenues
Norwalk CT 06850
(203) 847-4778

Circa 1786. The Silvermine consists of the Old Mill, the Country Store, the Coach House and the Tavern itself. Primitive paintings and furnishings as well as family heirlooms have been used to decorate the inn. The guest rooms and dining rooms overlook the Old Mill, the waterfall and the swans gliding across the millpond.

Rates: $36-$61. Season: All year.
Innkeeper(s): Frank Whitman, Jr.
10 Rooms. 10 Private Baths. Children. Smoking OK. Credit Cards: All. Meals: B&B.

Old Lyme

Old Lyme Inn
85 Lyme St
Old Lyme CT 06371
(203) 454-2600

Circa 1850. This elegantly restored mansion features original wall paintings in the front hall that portray historic Old Lyme buildings and the scenic countryside. At one time the 300-acre farm housed a riding academy where it is said that Jacqueline Kennedy Onassis took lessons. Elegance is reflected

throughout the inn with marble fireplaces, antique mirrors and Victorian and Empire furnishings.

**Rates: $75-$115. Season: Closed Mondays and Christmas week.
Innkeeper(s): Diana Field Atwood.
13 Rooms. 13 Private Baths. Conference Room. Guest phone available. Children. Pets OK. TV available. Handicap access provided. Smoking OK. Credit Cards: All. Beds: QT. Meals: Continental breakfast. Gourmet restaurant.

"Gracious and romantic rooms with exquisite dining...our favorite inn!"
"Fantastic to find something old and nice in modern United States." Swedish visitor.

"Best pillows we ever laid our heads on plus a great queen-size bed!"

Old Mystic

Red Brook Inn and Haley Tavern
10 Wells Rd
Old Mystic CT 06372
(203) 572-0349

Circa 1760. This New England colonial has a traditional center chimney and sits high on a bluff surrounded by stone walls and woodlands. Two fireplaces with beehive ovens are in the inn. One of these is in the keeping room. Here hot breakfasts are served each morning. Additional rooms are housed in the Haley Tavern, nearby.

Rates: $75-$125.
Innkeeper(s): Ruthe Keyes & Verne Sasek.
9 Rooms. 7 Private Baths. Guest phone available. Children 9 & up. TV available. Credit Cards: Visa, MC. Meals: B&B.

Waterbury

The Parsonage
18 Hewlett St
Waterbury CT 06710
(203) 574-2855

Circa 1900. Located on a maple-tree lined street, this former church rectory is a fifteen-room, central-hallway Victorian. A sweeping front porch has large stately columns.

Location: Five minutes from I-84 & Rt 8.
**Rates: $45-$60.
Innkeeper(s): Lonetta Baysinger.

Woodstock

Inn at Woodstock Hill
Plaine Hill Rd
Woodstock CT 06267
(203) 928-7587

Circa 1816. Now a Georgian Federal gentleman's country estate in 300-year-old Woodstock, the inn has gone through many architectural changes throughout the years, including a period when it had an elaborate Victorian facade. Now restored to its original appearance it is on eighteen acres of rolling farmland. The guestrooms are decorated in the style of an English country house with original antiques and reproductions as well as an abundance of floral chintz. There are two tennis courts, a conference room and restaurant on the estate.

Location: Junction of Rte 169, 20 minutes south of Old Sturbridge Village in Massachusetts, an hour-and-a-half from Boston.
Rates: $60-$115. Season: All year.
Innkeeper(s): Ruth Jensen.
20 Rooms. 20 Private Baths. Swimming Pool. Conference Room. Guest phone in room. Children 12 & up. TV in room. Credit Cards: Visa, MC, AE. Beds: QT. Meals: Continental breakfast.

Delaware

Camden

Jonathan Wallace House
9 South Main St
Camden DE 19934
(302) 697-2921

Circa 1785. The Jonathan Wallace House is an eighteenth-century three-story brick house located in a town with an extensive historic district. Much of the

original woodwork and heart pine floors remain. A courtyard and brick patio are surrounded by mature trees and the second-story screen porch is reminiscent of a summer tree house.

Location: Five miles south of Dover, 40 miles from the beaches.
**Rates: $35-$45. Season: All year.
Innkeeper(s): Sally C. & Chester D. Hollingsworth.
3 Rooms. 1 Private Baths. 1 Shared Baths. Guest phone available. Children 10 & up. TV available. Smoking OK. Beds: QT. Meals: B&B.

"Everything was great, the small details were appreciated, the flowers, amenities in the bathroom and the superb breakfast. We didn't stay long enough."

New Castle

David Finney Inn
216 Delaware St
New Castle DE 19720
(302) 322-6367

Circa 1683. There has been a tavern here since 1683 although the oldest parts of the inn only date back to 1713. Two buildings were put together in 1794 to form the present inn. A courtyard garden shaded by an old walnut tree is in the back of the Dutch Colonial building. Inside, the rooms are decorated with pine antiques and have views of the Delaware River or of the village green.

Location: In the center of New Castle.
Rates: $60-110. Season: All.
Innkeeper(s): Judy & Kurt Piser.
17 Rooms. 17 Private Baths. Credit Cards: All. Meals: Restaurant on the premises.

William Penn Guest House
206 Delaware St
New Castle DE 19720
(302) 328-7736

Circa 1682. William Penn slept here in this old historic home listed in the National Register. In fact, his host Arnoldus de LaGrange witnessed the ceremony in which Penn gained possession of the Three Lower Colonies. Two blocks away is a park that runs along the Delaware River that Penn traveled. Mrs. Burwell who lived next door to the historic house 'gained possession' of it one day about twenty years ago while her husband was away. After recovering from his wife's surprise purchase, Mr. Burwell rolled up his sleeves and set to work restoring the house. Guests may stay in the very room slept in by William Penn or may choose a cozy room under the eaves.

Location: Across from the village green, two blocks from the water.

Rates: $30.
Innkeeper(s): Mr & Mrs Richard Burwell.
4 Rooms. Guest phone available. Children 4 & up. TV available.
Smoking restricted. Meals: Call.

Odessa

Cantwell House
107 High St
Odessa DE 19730
(302) 378-4179

Circa 1840. Odessa was an important trading port on the Delaware River until the 1890s, and the town bears fine examples of Colonial, Federal and Victorian architecture. The Corbit-Sharp House, the David Wilson Mansion and the Brick Hotel have been exquisitely restored and are part of Winterthur Museum. Cantwell House Bed and Breakfast has been completely restored and furnished in country antiques.

Location: On Rt 13, 23 miles south of Wilmington, twenty miles north of Dover.
**Rates: $45-$65. Season: All year.
Innkeeper(s): Carole F. Coleman.
3 Rooms. 1 Private Baths. 1 Shared Baths. Guest phone available. Children 5 & up. TV available. Beds: QD. Meals: Continental breakfast.

Florida

Amelia Island

1735 House
584 S Fletcher Ave
Amelia Island FL 32034
(904) 261-5878

Circa 1928. The 1735 House is perched right at the edge of the Atlantic, just fifteen steps across the sand to the ocean. All the rooms in this New England-style

two-story inn are actually suites. Antiques, wicker and rattan add to the decor and comfort of the rooms. Every morning breakfast is delivered in a basket with a morning paper to each guest.

Location: Amelia Island. Oceanfront.
**Rates: $55-$70. Season: All year.
Innkeeper(s): David & Susan Caples.
5 Rooms. 5 Private Baths. Children. TV in room. Smoking OK.
Credit Cards: Visa, MC, AE. Beds: KQT. Meals: B&B.

"I was a guest for only one night, but the staff's attentiveness was as though I were an especially valued, long-term visitor."

"The breakfasts were delicious and the service excellent."

Key West

Duval House
815 Duval St
Key West FL 33040
(305) 294-1666

Circa 1880. This Victorian inn has long verandas and balconies and is within easy walking distance to the beach.

Location: One-and-a-half blocks off US-1.
Rates: $48-$88.
Innkeeper(s): Ben Connors & Bob Zurbrigen.

Palms of Key West
820 White St
Key West FL 33040
(305) 294-3146, (800) 558-9374.

Circa 1889. The Palms was built by the local saloon keeper. Formerly the old Williams estate, this Victorian is a gingerbread-style mansion with a three-sided porch, bay windows and a cupola tower. The bedroom wings were built in the last decade and offer

all the comforts while retaining the Victorian charm of the main section of the house. A quiet and secluded pool area adds to the comfort of guests.

Location: Old Town, Key West.
**Rates: $55-$100. Season: All year.
Innkeeper(s): Terry Clarkson.
20 Rooms. 20 Private Baths. Swimming Pool. Children Well-be-
haved. TV in room. Smoking OK. Credit Cards: Visa, MC, AE.
Beds: QT. Meals: B&B.

Lake Wales

Chalet Suzanne
Drawer AC
Lake Wales FL 33859-9003
(813) 676-6011

Circa 1928. This inn has been family owned and
operated for over fifty years. In the thirties, Bertha
Hinshaw turned her home into an inn which grew in
reputation for fine food. In World War II the kitchen
and many rooms burned. Building materials were impossible to obtain so portions of existing buildings
were assembled for the whimsical architecture which

rambles along on fourteen levels. There is a soup cannery, plant nursery and landing strip on the inn's 70
acres. Gabled roofs, courts, balconies, spires and
steeples punctuate the fairy-tale orchid, green, pink
and yellow buildings. The restaurant has received the
Craig Clairborne award for one of the 121 best restaurants in the world.

Location: Four miles north of Lake Wales, between Cypress Gar-
dens and Bok Tower.
**Rates: $75-$125. Season: December to April.
Innkeeper(s): Carl and Vita Hinshaw.
30 Rooms. 27 Private Baths. Swimming Pool. Children. Pets OK.
TV in room. Handicap access provided. Smoking OK. Credit
Cards: Visa, MC, AE, DC. Beds: KTC. Meals: Restaurant.

"A thoroughly delightful and charming suite."

*"I now know why everyone always says 'wow!' when
they come up from dinner. Please don't change a thing."*

"Perfect place to celebrate our 10th anniversary."

Orlando

Brown's Bed & Breakfast
529 W Dartmouth St
Orlando FL 32804
(305) 423-8858

Circa 1926. This home is typical of Orlando's two-
story residences of the First World War era. In particular the eyebrow curves of the eaves and porch
reflect the Queen Anne Revival-style of a generation

earlier. The Brown's home overlooks beautiful tree-
lined Lake Ivanhoe in the quaint and quiet section of
College Park. Old fashioned southern hospitality is a
mark of the Brown family. Estelle's hobby is hand
quilting and displays throughout the house are
mingled with the Victorian furnishings.

Location: Twenty minutes to Disney attractions.
**Rates: $35-$50. Season: All year.
Innkeeper(s): Estelle Brown.
3 Rooms. 2 Private Baths. 1 Shared Baths. Guest phone available.
Children By prior arrangement. TV in room. Beds: KQDT. Meals:
Full breakfast.

Chalet Suzanne
See: Lake Wales, FL.

St. Augustine

Casa de Solana
21 Aviles St
St. Augustine FL 32084
(904) 824-3555

Circa 1763. A Spanish military man, Don Manuel
Solana built this home in the early European settle-

ment. The thick coquina-shell walls, high ceilings with dark, hand-hewn beams and polished, bare, hand-

pegged floors are part of the distinctive flavor of the St. Augustine Spanish period. In the carriage house there are two working Majorcan fireplaces. An elegant ten-foot-long mahogany table is the site of an elegant southern breakfast.

Location: Historical district.
**Rates: $100-$125. Season: All year.
Innkeeper(s): Faye L. McMurry.
4 Rooms. 4 Private Baths. Conference Room. Guest phone available. Children Well behaved. TV in room. Handicap access provided. Credit Cards: Visa, MC, AE, DC. Beds: KQT. Meals: Full breakfast.

St. Francis Inn
279 St George St
St. Augustine FL 32084
(904) 824-6068
   Circa 1791. The St. Francis Inn is near the city's oldest house and has long been noted for its hospitality. The inn is a classic example of Old-World architecture. Built by Senor Garcia, who received a

Spanish Grant to the plot of land, "coquina" was used. Coquina is a limestone formed of broken shells and corals cemented together and found on Anastasia Island. Coquina was quarried by convict labor from

Spain. St. Augustine was founded in 1565 and nearby the inn is the oldest building in town.

Location: In the St. Augustine Historic District, our nation's oldest city.
**Rates: $37-$80. Season: All year.
Innkeeper(s): Marie Register.
11 Rooms. 11 Private Baths. Swimming Pool. TV in room. Credit Cards: Visa, MC. Beds: KQTC. Meals: Continental-plus breakfast.
   "We have stayed at many nice hotels but nothing like this. We are really enjoying it."

St. Petersburg

Bayboro House
1719 Beach Dr, SE
St. Petersburg FL 33701
(813) 823-4955
   Circa 1904. Across from Lassing Park in downtown St. Petersburg, the Bayboro has a Victorian flavor to it and was built by one of the founding fathers of the

city, C.A. Harvey. He was the first real estate developer and the first to have the vision to construct the port. The house faces Old Tampa Bay and has an unobstructed view.

Location: Off exit 9 (I-275) downtown St Petersburg.
Rates: $40-$55. Season: All year.
Innkeeper(s): Gordon & Antonia Powers.
3 Rooms. 3 Private Baths. Guest phone available. TV in room. Credit Cards: Visa, MC. Beds: DT. Meals: Continental-plus breakfast.
   "Y'all were real special."
   "A lovely room and the house itself a handsome structure. All of the special touches from the fine linen, pretty quilts, plants, shells and lovely antique furniture made my brief stay enjoyable."
   "Thank you for a fun stay at Bayboro House. Your home is beautiful."

Tampa

Bayshore Terrace
214 Hyde Park Place
Tampa FL 33606
(813) 877-3649
Circa 1903. This guest house is in the Hyde Park Historic District, surrounded by old oak trees. It is a five-minute walk to town and Harbor Island.

Rates: $40 day, $800 month.
Innkeeper(s): Doris Garcia.

Winter Haven

Chalet Suzanne
See: Lake Wales, FL.

Georgia

Atlanta

D.P. Cook House
See: McDonough, GA.

Worley Homestead Inn
See: Dahlonega, GA.

Dahlonega

Worley Homestead Inn
410 W Main
Dahlonega GA 30533
(404) 864-7002

Circa 1845. The Worley Homestead is a unique, antique-filled inn with all the staff in period dress. Dahlonega men are remembered for marching to the Mexican War from this old house in 1846. Again they marched in 1860 to the Civil War. The Chestnut Cottage has its own parlor and canopied bed. The inn is just two blocks to historic Courthouse Square. (The innkeeper is the great-granddaughter of Captain Worley builder of the Worley Homestead.)

Location: Two blocks from Courthouse Square, one hour from Atlanta.
**Rates: $50. Season: All year.
Innkeeper(s): Mick & Mitzi Francis, Joan Schuler.
8 Rooms. 8 Private Baths. Conference Room. Guest phone available. Children. TV in room. Smoking OK. Credit Cards: Visa, MC, AE. Beds: D. Meals: Outsized Captain Worley breakfasts.

McDonough

D.P. Cook House
69 Keys Ferry St
McDonough GA 30253
(404) 957-7562

Circa 1900. The ambience that was Tara lingers still in McDonough. The D.P. Cook House is a beautifully

restored turn of the century Victorian, just one block from the town square. Gracious southern hospitality for which the South is famous is a major feature of the inn. Your innkeeper works for State Senator Starr and is active in community affairs.

Location: Thirty five minutes south of Atlanta off I-75.
**Rates: $55-$65.
Innkeeper(s): Judy Neal.

"We found that the reputation southerners have gained for good manners is well deserved."
"This fairy tale setting and beautifully decorated B&B turned out to be a highlight of our trip. Judy is a very delightful hostess with accommodations that allow dreams to come true. The breakfast & antique place settings were tops."

"I cannot tell you how much we enjoyed your home. During the first hour, all I did was walk around admiring all of your beautiful decorations. I really did feel like Scarlet O'Hara."

Savannah

"417" The Haslam-Fort House

417 East Charlton St
Savannah GA 31401
(912) 233-6380

Circa 1872. The Halsam Fort House, one of the very first houses open for bed and breakfast in Savannah,

is a free-standing three-story brick townhouse built in an Italianate style. The inn is one of only sixteen properties in the Historic District with a full side garden. Most of the original interior details remain in tact. The house has appeared in numerous national publications. The inn is located by a quiet square and features a two-bedroom suite with a living room, full bath and a 'country kitchen' with a stocked refrigerator so that guests may have breakfast at their leisure.

Location: In the heart of Savannah's Historic District.
**Rates: $65-$150. Season: All year.
Innkeeper(s): Alan Fort & Richard McClellan.
2 Rooms. 1 Private Baths. Guest phone in room. Children. Pets OK. TV in room. Handicap access provided. Smoking OK. Beds: KTC. Meals: Continental plus breakfast.

Bed and Breakfast Inn

117 W Gordon St
Savannah GA 31401
(912) 238-0518

Circa 1853. A restored Federal townhouse overlooking beautiful Chatham Square, the inn is in the middle of noble old mansions, museums and restaurants.

Location: In the historic district.

**Rates: $30-$65.
Innkeeper(s): Robert McAlister.

East Bay Inn

225 East Bay Street
Savannah GA 31401
(912) 238-1225

Circa 1800. Overlooking Savannah's Historic Riverfront District, East Bay Inn provides spacious rooms, and warm, elegant surroundings. Four-poster beds are featured in many of the guest rooms. The grand old days are exemplified in the inn's gracious decor.

Location: Historic district.
**Rates: $76-$86. Season: All year.
Innkeeper(s): Jeanne L. Brooks.
28 Rooms. 28 Private Baths. Conference Room. Guest phone in room. Children. TV in room. Handicap access provided. Smoking OK. Credit Cards: All. Beds: Q. Meals: Full breakfast and gourmet restaurant.

Jesse Mount House

209 W Jones St
Savannah GA 31401
(912) 236-1774

Circa 1854. A Greek Revival town house, Jesse Mount has two spacious, luxurious three-bedroom suites complete with gas burning fireplaces. There is a Savannah-style walled garden. Exceptional antiques include a coach used by Tom Thumb to meet Queen Victoria, gilded harps and a grand piano. (The owner is an internationally-known concert harpist.) A pre-Revolutionary London clock chimes gently to urge you to step from your historic lodgings into the compelling charm of Old Savannah. According to the hosts, "The people who search out the small inns and bed and breakfasts are the adventurous ones, the ones who want to experience the real flavor of a place."

Location: In the historic district.
**Rates: $70-$125. Season: All year.
Innkeeper(s): Howard Crawford.
2 Rooms. 2 Private Baths. Guest phone in room. Children. TV in room. Handicap access provided. Smoking OK. Beds: QC. Meals: B&B.

Morel House

117 W Perry St
Savannah GA 31401
(912) 234-4088

Circa 1818. This two-room garden apartment overlooks Orleans Square. The house has four stories and the ground floor is for guests. A continental breakfast is available.

Rates: $59-$90.
Innkeeper(s): Mary Ann Smith. 1 Private Baths. Children. Handicap access provided.

Remshart-Brooks House
106 West Jones Street
Savannah GA 31401
(912) 234-6928
   Circa 1853. Remshart-Brooks House is located in the center of the Historic District, the largest restored historic district in the United States. Guests enjoy the hospitality of a historic home featuring a terrace-garden suite with bedroom, living room, bath and kitchen. Home-baked delicacies enhance the continental breakfast.

Location: In the center of the historic district.
Rates: $60-$70. Season: All year.
Innkeeper(s): Anne Barnett.
1 Rooms. 1 Private Baths. Guest phone in room. Children 6 & up. TV in room. Smoking OK. Beds: Q. Meals: B&B.

Senoia

Culpepper House
Corner of Broad at Morgan, PO Box 462
Senoia GA 30276
(404) 599-8182
   Circa 1871. A Queen Anne Victorian, the Culpepper House has original molding, stained glass windows and original mantelpieces. The house was built by a Confederate veteran, and later occupied for fifty years by Dr. Culpepper. Decorated in cozy Victorian clutter and comfortable whimsy the inn offers guests Southern hospitality at its finest.

Location: Thirty seven miles southwest of Atlanta where 85 & 16 cross.
**Rates: $36.40-$50.
Innkeeper(s): Mary Brown. 4 Rooms. 1 Private Baths. 3 Shared Baths. Guest phone in room. Children 10 & up. TV in room. Smoking Downstairs. Beds: QT. Meals: B&B.

Hawaii

Haiku

Haikuleana
69 Haiku Road
Haiku HI 96708
(808) 575-2890

Circa 1850. This old plantation home features high ceilings and tropical decor. A porch provides views of the exotic gardens. The home is in an area close to beaches and waterfalls. Bring your camera.

Location: Twelve miles east of Kahului.
Rates: $22-$44.
Innkeeper(s): Denise & Clark Champion.
2 Rooms. Meals: Continental breakfast.

Honolulu

John Guild Inn
2001 Vancouver Dr
Honolulu HI 96822
(808) 947-6019

Circa 1919. An Iowa lumber executive built this house. Gables supported by fanciful buttresses add a unique appeal to the inn, now in the National Register. Lanais furnished with white wicker, a game room and a parlor are common rooms. The guest rooms are filled with carefully chosen antiques, reproduction wallpapers and cozy comforters.

Location: In the Manoa Valley.
Rates: $65-$125. Season: All year.
Innkeeper(s): Peter Johnson & Kanoe Cazimero.
8 Rooms. 2 Private Baths. Guest phone available. Children by prior arrangement. Smoking OK. Credit Cards: Visa, MC. Meals: Continental buffet breakfast.

Idaho

Coeur d'Alene

Greenbriar Bed & Breakfast
315 Wallace
Coeur d'Alene ID 83814
(208) 667-9660

Circa 1908. Winding mahogany staircases, woodwork and window seats are one of the features of Greenbriar, now in the National Register. Antiques, imported Irish down comforters with linen covers, sheer curtains and gabled ceilings make the guest rooms inviting. Breakfasts include cheese stratas, Belgian waffles and Swedish pancakes among other choices. The inn is only four blocks from the lake, considered one of the most beautiful in the country. The hosts can assist with canoe and bike rentals and warm up the hot tub when you return from your day's activities.

Location: Thirty miles east of Spokane on the north shore of the lake.
**Rates: $35-$65. Season: All.
Innkeeper(s): Kris McIluenna.
7 Rooms. Hot Tub. Guest phone available. Credit Cards: Visa, MC. Beds: KQD. Meals: Full.

Idaho City

Idaho City Hotel
PO Box 70
Idaho City ID 83631
(208) 392-4290

Circa 1935. This old western-style hotel is located near the hot springs and has a creek flowing in the backyard. The hotel is furnished with antiques and a large flower garden blooms in the backyard. Idaho City is a National Historic Site.

Location: Forty-five minutes from Boise.
Rates: $24-$34.
12 Rooms. Children. Pets OK. TV available. Smoking OK. Credit Cards: Visa, MC, AE. Meals: Full breakfast.

Northfork

Indian Creek Ranch
Rt 2, PO Box 105
Northfork ID 83466
Dial (208) Salmon Idaho operator. Ask for 24F 211
(a ring-down phone number)..

Circa 1905. The main living room in the house was a one-room log cabin called the Red Onion Bar. Now as a small ranch hidden in the middle of the mountains, it is bordered by the Idaho Primitive Area and forest.

Location: Eleven miles below Northfork.
**Rates: $20 per person.
Innkeeper(s): Jack & Lois Briggs.

Illinois

Collinsville

Maggie's Bed & Breakfast
2102 N Keebler Rd
Collinsville IL 62234
(618) 344-8283

Circa 1890. A rustic, two-acre wooded area surrounds Maggie's, a historic former boarding house and mine superintendent's home. The home is furnished with exquisite antiques and art objects collected on world-wide travels. This beautiful, quiet, country Victorian home is enhanced with fourteen-foot high ceilings. Just ten minutes away is downtown St. Louis, the Arch and the Mississippi riverfront.

**Rates: $25-$45. Season: All year.
Innkeeper(s): Margaret Leyda.
4 Rooms. 2 Shared Baths. Hot Tub. Conference Room. Guest phone available. Children. Pets OK. TV available. Smoking OK. Beds: QDTC. Meals: Full breakfast.

Eldred

Hobson's Bluffdale
Rt 1, Hillview Rd
Eldred IL 62027
(217) 983-2854

Circa 1828. A Federal-style farmhouse with Georgian influences, this home was built by John Russell of native limestone from a quarry near the local river bluffs. Russel was a well-known poet whose works were published in *McGuffy's Fifth Reader*. Charles Dickens stayed here as a guest and friend of Mr. Russell, great-great-grandfather of the present owner and innkeeper. The walls are two-feet thick and there is a fireplace large enough to accommodate roasting a deer. An addition and bunk house has been added to allow for eight guest rooms on this working farm. (Chicken, sheep, horses and pigs are raised here.)

Location: Four miles north of Rt 108 on Bluff Rd.
**Rates: $35.
Innkeeper(s): Bill & Lindy Hobson.

Galena

Stillman's Country Inn
513 Bouthillier
Galena IL 61036
(815) 777-0557

Circa 1858. This Victorian mansion was built by Galena merchant, Nelson Stillman. Just up the hill from Ulysses S. Grant's home, it was on a grand scale compared with the plain-style homes and cottages in the area. Grant and his wife often dined with the Stillmans. The tower of the house was often used as a hideout by escaping slaves using the underground railroad system that provided food and shelter. Today the elegant rooms are still furnished with handsome antiques, the guest rooms still have the original working fireplaces and the elegant dining room still provides fine dining. The University of Dubuque, lead mines, historic house museums and the Mississippi Palisades are close by.

Location: Across the street from General U. S. Grant's home.
Rates: $48.50-$55. Season: All year.
Innkeeper(s): Pam & Bill Lozeau.
6 Rooms. 6 Private Baths. Conference Room. Guest phone available. TV available. Smoking OK. Credit Cards: Visa, MC, AE. Beds: D. Meals: Continental breakfast.

Indiana

Indianapolis

Hollingsworth House Inn
6054 Hollingsworth Road
Indianapolis IN 46254
(317) 299-6700

Circa 1854. This Greek Revival farmhouse is in the National Register and is next to a large park. The four acres of the inn add to the restful and elegant atmosphere. Haviland china makes breakfast a special treat.

Rates: $65. Season: All year.
Innkeeper(s): Ann Irvine & Susan Muller.
5 Rooms. 5 Private Baths. Children. Meals: Continental breakfast.

Knightstown

Old Hoosier House
Route 2, PO Box 299-I
Knightstown IN 46148
(317) 345-2969

Circa 1886. High ceilings and tall arched windows immediately give the guest a feeling of being in the nineteenth century. The two-story home is filled with antiques and has a cozy library.

Location: Thirty miles from Indianapolis.
Rates: $55. Season: May 1 to November 1.
Innkeeper(s): Jean & Tom Lewis.
4 Rooms. 1 Private Baths. Meals: Full breakfast.

Morgantown

The Rock House
380 Washington St
Morgantown IN 46160
(812) 597-5100

Circa 1890. Concrete blocks with rocks and stones and even marbles embedded within make this an unusual home.

Location: Thirty-two miles from Indianapolis.
Rates: $55.
Innkeeper(s): Marcella & Daniel Braun.
5 Rooms. 2 Private Baths. Smoking OK.

Muncie

Old Franklin House
704 East Washington St
Muncie IN 47305
(317) 286-0277

Circa 1896.

Location: Two blocks east of highway 67 in center of town, the Emily Kimbrough Historic District.
**Rates: $25-$35.
Innkeeper(s): Arnold & Rebecca Burkart.

Iowa

Avoca

Victorian Bed and Breakfast Inn
425 Walnut St
Avoca IA 51521
(712) 343-6336

Circa 1904. This Victorian was built by Fred Thielsen a local contractor and builder. The house is outstanding for its fishtail shingling and for the golden pine woodwork inside. Detailed columns enhance both the parlor and dining rooms. Midwestern antiques and locally made quilts decorate the guest rooms.

Location: Forty-five miles east of Omaha, Nebraska. Ninety miles west of Des Moines.
Rates: $38-$44.
Innkeeper(s): Rodney & Andrea Murray.

Dubuque

Redstone Inn
504 Bluff St
Dubuque IA 52001
(319) 582-1894

Circa 1894. The Redstone Inn was a twenty-three room duplex built by pioneer industrialist A. A. Cooper as a wedding gift for his daughter Nell. The side occupied by Nell and her husband was a grand Victorian home generously embellished with turrets, porches and nooks. It featured maple and oak woodwork, beveled, leaded and stained glass windows, marble and tiled fireplaces and crystal-shaded gas lamps. In 1984, the Redstone was purchased by a local group of business people and conservationists who converted it into an elegant fifteen-room inn furnished with antiques and steeped in history. The inn is in the National Register.

Location: In northeastern Iowa on the Mississippi River.
**Rates: $55-$120. Season: All year.
Innkeeper(s): Deborah Griesinger, manager.

15 Rooms. 15 Private Baths. Conference Room. Guest phone in room. Children. TV in room. Handicap access provided. Smoking OK. Credit Cards: Visa, MC, AE. Beds: QDTC. Meals: Continental-plus breakfast.

Stout House
1105 Locust
Dubuque IA 52001
(319) 582-1890

Circa 1890. This Richardsonian-Romanesque mansion was built by owner Frank D. Stout for $300,000. Its intricate carving is a showcase for the finest skilled craftsmen of the day working in rosewood, maple, oak and sycamore. One of the ten wealthiest men in Chicago, Mr. Stout entertained Dubuque's upper crust elegantly inside the rough-hewn sandstone house.

Location: In northeastern Iowa on the Mississippi, downtown.
**Rates: $55-$65.
Innkeeper(s): Jan & Dick Clark. Manager: Deborah Griesinger.

Homestead

Die Heimat Country Inn
Main St, Amana Colonies
Homestead IA 52236
(319) 622-3937

Circa 1854. This two-story clapboard house is in the Amana Colonies, a German settlement listed in the National Register. The antiques here are hand-

crafted Amana furnishings of walnut and cherry. Country-style quilts and curtains add personality to each guest room. Nearby are museums, a winery and a woolen mill that imports wool from around the world.

Location: South of Cedar Rapids, west of Iowa City.
Rates: $24.75-$42.75. Season: All year.
Innkeeper(s): Don & Sheila Janda.
19 Rooms. 19 Private Baths. Guest phone available. Children. TV in room. Smoking OK. Credit Cards: Visa, MC. Beds: D. Meals: Continental-plus breakfast.

"Staying at Die Heimat has been one of our life's highlights. We loved the clean rooms, comfortable beds and history connected with your establishment."

"We found your staff very friendly and helpful. As we've never been in this area before they helped us find what and where we needed to go."

"We hope you never change, it's so homey, so welcome while traveling. Thanks for making your parlor available. I can almost see my mother sitting there."

Kansas

Ashland

Hardesty House
712 Main St
Ashland KS 67831
(316) 635-2911
Circa 1900. This two-story brick and concrete hotel is filled with turn-of-the-century furnishings. A bank's cashier's cage, kerosene lamps, pressed tin ceilings and farm implements decorate the inn. There are reproduction wallpapers and old rocking chairs. A restaurant on the premises provides for both dinner and breakfast.

Location: Fifty miles southeast of Dodge City.
Rates: $22.
Innkeeper(s): Kevin Brown.
12 Rooms. 12 Private Baths. Credit Cards: Visa, MC, AE.

Council Grove

The Cottage House
25 North Neosho
Council Grove KS 66846
(316) 767-6828
Circa 1876. A beautifully restored Victorian hotel in the historic section, this inn offers modern comforts in nostalgic surroundings. The rooms are furnished with polished wood antiques and gleaming brass and there are gazebo-style porches in a secluded setting. Just around the corner is the famous Hays House Restaurant, and by special arrangement Cottage House guests are made members of Hays Tavern.

Location: One half block north of Main St, Hwy 56, downtown.
**Rates: $38-$48. Season: All year.
Innkeeper(s): Stephanie Blanton.
42 Rooms. 42 Private Baths. Sauna. Conference Room. Guest phone in room. Children. Pets OK. TV in room. Handicap access provided. Smoking OK. Credit Cards: Visa, MC. Beds: QTWC. Meals: Continental breakfast.

Lawrence

Halcyon House
1000 Ohio
Lawrence KS 66044
(913) 841-0314
Circa 1886. This charming Victorian has been renovated and features a large parlor. Outside is a patio and pleasant yard. The University of Kansas is three blocks from the house.

Location: Twenty-five miles west of Kansas City.
Rates: $55-$69. Season: All year.
Innkeeper(s): Esther Wolfe & Gail Towle.
8 Rooms. 1 Private Baths. Children 10 & up. TV available. Credit Cards: Visa, MC. Meals: Full breakfast.

Melvern

Schoolhouse Inn
106 East Beck, PO Box 175
Melvern KS 66510
(913) 549-3473, 828-3524
Circa 1870. Stone from local quarries and large timbers were used to build the Schoolhouse and it has been carefully restored to make a fine and unusual inn. High ceilings and spacious rooms add elegance to the experience.

Location: Eighty miles southwest of Kansas City.
Rates: $40. Season: All year.
Innkeeper(s): Bill & Mary Fisher.
4 Rooms. 1 Private Baths. Children. Pets OK. Meals: Continental breakfast.

Tonganoxie

Almeda's Bed & Breakfast
220 South Main
Tonganoxie KS 66086
(913) 845-2295

Circa 1917. This inn features a stone bar in a room that was the inspiration for the Marilyn Monroe movie *Bus Stop* and it was actually a bus stop back in the thirties. Antiques, an organ and a country-style decor now make for a welcome stop.

Location: Twenty miles from Kansas City.
Rates: $30.
Innkeeper(s): Alameda & Richard Tinberg.
5 Rooms. Children 5 & up. Smoking OK. Meals: Continental breakfast.

Kentucky

Bardstown

Old Talbott Tavern
Court Square, 107 W Stephen Foster
Bardstown KY 40004
(502) 348-3494

Circa 1779. Old Talbott Tavern claims to be the oldest western stagecoach stop in America that has been continually operating. This old stone inn has antiques, paintings by Prince Philippe of France, fireplaces and the six original rooms. In addition to the pub there are three dining rooms.

Rates: $37. Season: All year.
Innkeeper(s): Peggy Downs.
6 Rooms. 6 Private Baths. Children. Smoking OK. Credit Cards: Visa, MC, AE, DC. Meals: EP.

Bowling Green

Bowling Green Bed & Breakfast
659 East 14th Ave
Bowling Green KY 42101
(502) 781-3861

Circa 1939. This two-story home is very comfortably furnished and offers a cozy at-home feeling. There is an old-fashioned Victrola guests may crank up. Just a short drive away is Mammoth Cave. Your hosts are professors at Western Kentucky University.

Location: South Central Kentucky, midtown in Bowling Green.
**Rates: $30-$40.
Innkeeper(s): Dr. & Mrs. Norman Hunter.

Georgetown

Log Cabin Bed & Breakfast
350 North Broadway
Georgetown KY 40324
(502) 863-3514

Circa 1809. This rustic restored Kentucky log cabin has a shake-shingle roof and chinked logs on the outside. The living room features a huge fieldstone fireplace while other rooms are modern, specifically designed for the comfort of guests.

Location: Two miles off I-75, ten miles from Lexington, Kentucky.
Rates: $45.
Innkeeper(s): Clay & Sanis McKnight.

Harrodsburg

Shakertown at Pleasant Hill
Rt 4
Harrodsburg KY 40330
(606) 734-5411

Circa 1805. A non-profit organization is in charge of preserving and managing this nineteenth-century Shaker settlement. The inn's accommodations are spread out in fourteen of the original Shaker structures. The dirt road running through the village helps to preserve the old-time feeling and is restricted to foot traffic. (There's parking behind each of the buildings.) The rooms are appointed with authentic reproductions of Shaker furnishings, each piece copied from an original that is in the Center Family House Museum. Air conditioning is hidden and all the rooms have private baths but there are no closets. Instead, clothes are hung on the Shaker-style pegs. Dining is available at the village where staff and crafts people are costumed.

Rates: $60-$100.
70 Rooms. 70 Private Baths. Guest phone available. Children. Meals: EP.

Louisiana

Baton Rouge

Nottoway
See: White Castle, LA.

Jeanerette

Albania Plantation Mansion
Highway 182
Jeanerette LA 70544
(318) 276-4816

Circa 1837. Albania is the largest bayou plantation in the country and was built by a French Royalist who received land grants from Louis XVI. The mansion has a magnificent three-story unsupported spiral staircase and some of the finest house antiques in Louisiana. On the third floor is a museum with a world-famous doll collection. The grounds and gardens are draped in a grove of live oaks on the bayou. There are many Civil War artifacts around the property. A gift shop and antique shop is also run by the Albania Foundation.

Location: Highway 182 one mile east of Jeanerette.
**Rates: $55-$85. Season: All year.
Innkeeper(s): Albania Foundation.
Guest phone available. Children. TV in room. Handicap access provided. Smoking OK. Credit Cards: Visa, MC, AE. Beds: Q. Meals: B&B.

New Orleans

Cornstalk Hotel
915 Royal St
New Orleans LA 70116
(504) 523-1515

Circa 1805. This home belonged to Judge Francois Xavier-Martin, the author of the first history of Louisiana and the first Chief Justice of Louisiana's Supreme court. The adjacent property held the Federal Courthouse where Andrew Jackson was tried for contempt of court for imposing martial law in New Orleans. He stayed with Judge Martin while

being tried by Judge Hall. Other famous guests include Harriet Beecher Stowe who wrote *Uncle Tom's Cabin* after viewing the nearby slave markets. The Civil War followed the widely read publication. Surrounding the inn is a 150-year-old wrought-iron cornstalk fence. Stained-glass windows, oriental rugs, fireplaces and antiques grace the inn.

Location: In the heart of the French Quarter.
Rates: $65-$105. Season: All year.
Innkeeper(s): Debbie & David Spencer.
14 Rooms. 14 Private Baths. Guest phone in room. Children. TV available. Smoking OK. Credit Cards: Visa, MC, DC. Beds: KQDT. Meals: Continental breakfast.

Grenoble House
329 Dauphine
New Orleans LA 70112
(504) 522-1331

Circa 1854. Grenoble House consists of several renovated historic buildings in the French Quarter. There are several suites and both a spa and pool are available.

Location: French Quarter.
**Rates: $125-$300.
Innkeeper(s): Carlos Flores.

Maison de Ville
727 Toulouse St
New Orleans LA 70130
(504) 561-5858

Circa 1742. This hotel in the French Quarter was rated by Architectural Digest as the best small hotel in the country. The inn is furnished with eighteenth and nineteenth century antiques. A water fountain is on the patio and there is a swimming pool. Tennessee Williams completed *A Streetcar Named Desire* while a guest at the inn.

Location: French Quarter.
**Rates: $100-$350.
Innkeeper(s): Ronnie Leigh.

Mazant Street Guest House
906 Mazant St
New Orleans LA 70117
(504) 944-2662

Circa 1882. Under the giant magnolia tree at the Mazant, guests often swing in the gentle evening breeze. Both guest rooms and apartments are available in this two-story columned house.

Location: In the neighborhood called "Bywater."
**Rates: $15-$25.
Innkeeper(s): Jane Henderson & Anneke Campbell.

Monmouth Plantation
See: Natchez, MS.

Nine-O-Five Royal Hotel
905 Rue Royal St
New Orleans LA 70116
(504) 523-0219

Circa 1890. A quaint European style hotel, the Nine-O-Five has balconies overlooking the southern charm

of Royal Street. There are eighteen-foot ceilings, antique furnishings and kitchenettes.

Location: French Quarter.
Rates: $45 EP. Season: All year.
Innkeeper(s): J. Morell.
14 Rooms. 14 Private Baths. Jacuzzi Tubs. TV in room. Beds: KQ. Meals: Kitchens in each unit.

Nottoway
See: White Castle, LA.

Prytania Park Hotel
1525 Prytania St
New Orleans LA 70130
(504) 524-0427

Circa 1834. The thirteen rooms in this Victorian-style building are furnished in English Victorian furniture. There are English garden chintzes, fourteen-foot ceilings, and fireplaces throughout the inn. A new section is furnished in English contemporary style. The inn is just one-half block from the historic St. Charles Avenue streetcar.

Location: Lower garden District.
**Rates: $44-$79. Season: All year.
Innkeeper(s): Mrs. Lani Malbrough, Assistant General Manager.
62 Rooms. 62 Private Baths. Guest phone in room. Children. TV in room. Smoking OK. Credit Cards: Visa, MC, AE, DC. Beds: KQT. Meals: Continental-plus breakfast.

Soniat House

1133 Chartres St
New Orleans LA 70116
(504) 522-0570

Circa 1830. Soniat House is a private hotel in a residential section of the French Quarter.

Location: In the French Quarter.
**Rates: $105-$200. Season: All year.
Innkeeper(s): Rodney & Frances Smith. 23 Rooms. 23 Private Baths. Guest phone in room. TV in room. Credit Cards: Visa, MC, AE. Beds: KQT. Meals: Continental breakfast.

The Columns Hotel

3811 St Charles Ave
New Orleans LA 70115
(504) 899-9308

Circa 1883. The Columns was built by Simon Hernsheim, a tobacco merchant, who was the wealthiest philanthropist in New Orleans. The floors are

three layers deep made of oak, mahogany and pine. The two-story columned gallery and portico make for a grand entrance into this restored mansion. The estate was selected by Paramount Studios for the site of the movie *Pretty Baby* with Brook Shields. The hotel has been nominated for the National Register of Historic Places.

Location: Uptown Garden District.
**Rates: $35-$95. Season: All year.
Innkeeper(s): Claire & Jacques Creppeil.
19 Rooms. 10 Private Baths. 3 Shared Baths. Conference Room. Guest phone available. Children. TV available. Handicap access

provided. Smoking OK. Credit Cards: Visa, MC, AE. Beds: KT. Meals: Continental or full breakfast available.

"Staying at the Columns was like experiencing life of the Old South, maybe more like living in a museum."

"We thought about sending you flowers, but flowers wilt; we thought about sending you a box of candy, but candy adds pounds but its best to simply offer our sincere appreciation for your help."

The Frenchman

417 Frenchmen St
New Orleans LA 70116
(800) 831-1781

Circa 1860. The Frenchmen is composed of two 1860s creole townhouses and slave quarters which have been totally renovated to offer the visitor to New Orleans a Victorian experience with all the amenities of today. All rooms are furnished with antiques and a tropical patio features a swimming pool and jacuzzi.

Location: French Quarter.
**Rates: $64-$99. Season: All year.
Innkeeper(s): Mark Soubie.
25 Rooms. 25 Private Baths. Hot Tub. Swimming Pool. Children 14 & up. TV in room. Handicap access provided. Smoking OK. Credit Cards: Visa, MC. Beds: QC. Meals: Full breakfast.

Shreveport

Fairfield Place

2221 Fairfield Ave
Shreveport LA 71104
(318) 222-0048

Circa 1875. Fairfield is a small intimate inn serving a gourmet breakfast.

Location: Near I-20 in the historical district.
**Rates: $55-$80.
Innkeeper(s): Janie Lipscomb.

St. Francisville

St Francisville
118 N Commerce St, PO Drawer 1369
St. Francisville LA 70775
(504) 635-6502

Circa 1880. Morris Wolf, general merchant, built this Victorian gothic-style home often referred to as the Wolf-Schlesinger House. The inn is located in

the center of the business district. Fourteen-foot-ceilings accentuate the character and graciousness of St. Francisville and all the rooms open onto a New Orleans type courtyard.

Location: Between Natchez and New Orleans.
Rates: $35-$55. Season: All year.
Innkeeper(s): Florence & Dick Fillet.
9 Rooms. 9 Private Baths. Conference Room. Guest phone in room. TV available. Smoking OK. Credit Cards: Visa, MC, DC. Beds: KDT. Meals: Continental breakfast.

White Castle

Nottoway
PO Box 160, Mississippi River Road
White Castle LA 70788
(504) 545-2409

Circa 1859. Nottoway is the South's largest plantation home, built for wealthy Virginian John Hampden Randolph. The inn has twenty-two columns supporting the exterior structure and it combines the Greek

Revival and Italianate architectural styles. Listed in the National Register, the mansion is over 53,000 square feet. The White Ballroom is the most famous of Nottoway's sixty-four rooms.

**Rates: $90-$250. Season: All year.
Innkeeper(s): Cindy Hidalgo, Manager.
13 Rooms. 13 Private Baths. Swimming Pool. Guest phone available. Children. TV in room. Smoking OK. Credit Cards: Visa, MC, AE. Beds: QT. Meals: B&B.

"Southern hospitality at its finest."

"Your restaurant has got to be Louisiana's best kept secret."

"We were Rett and Scarlet back in time."

Maine

Bar Harbor

Hearthside Inn
7 High St
Bar Harbor ME 04609
(207) 288-4533

Circa 1907. Built as a physician's home, the inn is located on a quiet street in town. There are four working fireplaces and a porch for guests to enjoy. The parlor has its own library and fireplace and the music room has a studio grand piano. Five minutes away is the Acadia National Park.

Location: In town.
Rates: $68-$85. Season: all.
Innkeeper(s): Barry & Susan Schwartz.
9 Rooms. 7 Private Baths. 2 Shared Baths. Guest phone available. Children 10 & up. Credit Cards: Visa, MC. Beds: D. Meals: Continental-plus breakfast.

Inn at Canoe Point
See: Hulls Cove, ME.

Manor House Inn
West St Historic District
Bar Harbor ME 04609
(207) 288-3759

Circa 1887. Colonel James Foster built this twenty-two-room National Register Victorian mansion. It be-

came part of the tradition of gracious summer living for which Bar Harbor was famous. In addition to the main house there are several charming cottages placed among the many gardens on the property. The innkeeper has authored a fascinating history of the inn and Bar Harbor for their centennial celebration.

Location: Mt Desert Island, Acadia National Park.
Rates: $74-$140. Season: April to November.
Innkeeper(s): Jan Matter.
14 Rooms. 14 Private Baths. Swimming Pool. Conference Room. Guest phone available. Children 12 & up. TV available. Credit Cards: Visa, MC, AE. Beds: KT. Meals: Continental breakfast.

Mira Monte Inn
69 Mt Desert St
Bar Harbor ME 04609
(207) 288-4263, (207) 846-4784 (winter)

Circa 1864. A gracious 18-room Victorian mansion, the Mira Monte has been newly renovated in the

simpler style of early Bar Harbor. It features period furnishings, pleasant common rooms, a library and wraparound porches, all on estate grounds with sweeping lawns, paved terraces and many gardens. The Inn was one of the earliest of Bar Harbor's famous summer cottages.

Location: Five-minute walk from the waterfront, shops and restaurants.
Rates: $65-$95. Season: May 15 to October 30.

Innkeeper(s): Marian Burns.
11 Rooms. 11 Private Baths. Guest phone available. Children. TV available. Smoking OK. Credit Cards: Visa, MC, AE. Beds: KQDT. Meals: Continental breakfast.

"On our third year at your wonderful inn in beautiful Bar Harbor. I think I enjoy it more each year. A perfect place to stay in a perfect environment."

Bath

Elizabeth's Bed & Breakfast
360 Front St
Bath ME 04530
(207) 443-1146
Circa 1820. This historic home is right on the Kennebec River and yet still a convenient in-town location. Elizabeth's is furnished in country antiques.

Location: Off Rte 1, 40 miles north of Portland.
Rates: $35-$50.
Innkeeper(s): Elizabeth Lindsay.

Belfast

Hiram Alden Inn
19 Church St
Belfast ME 04915
(703) 338-2151
Circa 1840. This early Victorian on one acre in the historic district is walking distance to the restored

downtown and the bay. The interior boasts six imported marble mantels, tin ceilings, and a slate roof. The original brass and German silver fixtures, solid cherrywood spiral staircase, and wraparound porch add to the elegance and charm of the Hiram Alden.

Location: Coastal Rt 1 between Camden & Acadia National Park.
**Rates: $40-$45. Season: All year.
Innkeeper(s): Jim & Jackie Lovejoy, Jennifer, Jon & Jeffrey.
8 Rooms. 4 Shared Baths. Conference Room. Guest phone available. Children. TV available. Smoking OK. Beds: KQDTC. Meals: Full breakfast.

"A four star stay with a four star family."
"Not just a comfortable room, but a delightful experience."
"A touch of class."

Bethel

Hammons House
Broad St
Bethel ME 04217
(207) 824-3170
Circa 1859. An elegant Greek Revival side-hall-plan mansion, embellished with colonial touches, the Ham-

mons House was built by the Hon. David Hammons, U.S. Congressman. The adjacent barn was converted to a small summer theater in the early 1920s by William Upson. Occasionally a murder-mystery weekend is held at the inn. Every day a gourmet breakfast is served.

Location: Centrally located on the village common in the Bethel Historic District.
**Rates: $75. Season: All year.
4 Rooms. 2 Private Baths. Conference Room. Guest phone available. Children. TV available. Smoking OK. Credit Cards: Visa, MC. Beds: Extra-long doubles. Meals: Full breakfast.

"One of the nicest B&B's we've stayed in."
"Charm of your home a highlight of our New England tour."
"Wonderful hospitality and a beautiful home."

Norseman Inn
Rt 2 Rumford Rd
Bethel ME 04217
(207) 824-2002
Circa 1800. One of Bethel's most historic structures, part of the present inn was built in 1800 and became the Riverside Hotel years later. From 1912-1918 it

was the Dr. William Rogers Chapman estate. Two outstanding fieldstone fireplaces contain stones from around the world. The inn is situated on four landscaped acres surrounded by foothills and the Androscoggin River.

Location: One mile east of Bethel Center.
Rates: $32-$42. Season: All year.
Innkeeper(s): Natalie & Dick Fain.
10 Rooms. 3 Shared Baths. Guest phone available. Children 8 & up. TV available. Smoking OK. Credit Cards: Visa, MC, AE. Beds: QT. Meals: B&B.

Boothbay

Kenniston Hill Inn
Route 27
Boothbay ME 04537
(207) 633-2159

  Circa 1786. Six fireplaces warm this white clapboard, center chimney colonial set amidst four acres of gardens and woodlands. It was built by David Ken-

niston, a prominent shipbuilder and landowner and was occupied by the Kennistons for over one hundred years. The parlor has a huge open hearth fireplace. For several years the inn was used as a country club and later as a restaurant. A full country breakfast is served in the dining room.

Location: Mid-coast Maine.
**Rates: $55-$75. Season: April to December.
Innkeeper(s): Ellen & Paul Morissette.
8 Rooms. 8 Private Baths. Guest phone available. Children 10 & up. TV available. Smoking OK. Credit Cards: Visa, MC. Beds: KQ. Meals: B&B.

  "England may be the home of the original bed and breakfast, but Kenniston Hill Inn is where it has been perfected! Thanks for the gourmet breakfast, cozy room and a wonderful two days."

Boothbay Harbor

Admiral's Quarters & Captain Sawyer's Place
Commercial St
Boothbay Harbor ME 04538
(207) 633-2474

  Circa 1820. Two large old sea captain's houses make up the inn. Captain Sawyer built his house with a prominent widow's watch. It features rounded windows and views of Boothbay Harbor and the town.

Location: In the Harbor District by the water.
Rates: $40-$60.
Innkeeper(s): Jean E. and George T. Duffy.

Bridgton

Noble House
PO Box 180
Bridgton ME 04009
(207) 647-3733

  Circa 1903. Once a senator's private residence, this stately manor on three acres, is surrounded by tall old oaks and a grove of towering pines. All the guest rooms and porches feature this park-like view. Most guests meander down to the lakeside hammock to take views of Mt. Washington. In the evening, at the water's edge, folk stay to watch an unforgettable Maine sunset. Tastefully furnished rooms, a grand piano and a library set the tone for a gracious stay.

Location: On Highland Lake.
Rates: $55-$75.
Innkeeper(s): Dick & Jane Starets. Meals: Full breakfast.

Brunswick

Brunswick Bed & Breakfast
165 Park Row
Brunswick ME 04011
(207) 729-4914

  Circa 1860. This completely restored Greek Revival home overlooks the park in the Brunswick Historic District. The inn features twin front parlors furnished with antiques and providing views of the park. There is a guest house apartment complete with brick floors and skylights. Bowdoin College is two blocks away, L.L. Bean and Freeport are a ten minute drive.

Rates: $50-$60. Season: All.
Innkeeper(s): Travis B. & Nancy Keliner.
5 Rooms. 3 Private Baths. 1 Shared Baths. Guest phone available. TV available. Smoking OK. Beds: DT. Meals: Full breakfast.

Samuel Newman House

7 South St
Brunswick ME 04011
(207) 729-6959

Circa 1821. This Federal-style inn was built by noted architect Samuel Melcher.

Location: Adjacent to Bowdoin College, walking distance to Summer Music Theater, shops.
**Rates: $30-$50.
Innkeeper(s): Jona & John Pierce. 7 Rooms. Meals: Continental breakfast.

Camden

Blue Harbor House

67 Elm St, Rt 1
Camden ME 04843
(207) 236-3196

Circa 1835. This country Cape home was built on the 1768 homesite of Camden's first settler, James Richards, who was granted the land by the king, as

the first person to fulfill all the conditions of a settler. An 1806 carriage house has been refurbished to offer private suites. The bustling harbor is a five-minute walk.

Location: In the village.
Rates: $60-$100. Season: All year.
Innkeeper(s): Bob & Connie Hood.
6 Rooms. 4 Private Baths. 2 Shared Baths. Children 12 & up. Credit Cards: MC, AE. Beds: QD. Meals: Full breakfasts on the sunporch.

"The canopy bed, stenciled walls, antique crocks and baskets all lend to the ambience of the friendliest inn we have visited in years. It's so New England!!"

Camden Harbour Inn

83 Bayview St
Camden ME 04843
(207) 236-4200

Circa 1874. This inn was first visited by steamship passengers as a stop from Boston to Bangor. Guests were picked up by the inn's horse-drawn carriages

and driven along the harbor's edge, through the village and up the hill to the inn. There they were delighted by the spectacular panoramic views of both harbor and mountains.

Location: Mid-coast of Maine, Penobscot Bay.
Rates: $45-$90. Season: All year.
Innkeeper(s): Sal Vella & Patti Babii.
20 Rooms. 17 Private Baths. 3 Shared Baths. Conference Room. Guest phone available. Children 12 & up. TV available. Handicap access provided. Smoking OK. Credit Cards: Visa, MC, AE. Beds: QDT. Meals: Full breakfast.

"One of the six best seafood restaurants on the Maine Coast." Yankee Magazine.

Craignair Inn

See: Clark Island, ME.

Maine Stay Bed & Breakfast

22 High St
Camden ME 04843
(207) 236-9636

Circa 1813. One of Camden's treasured colonials, the Maine Stay is just a five-minute walk from the center of the village and the Camden Harbor. Eight schooners from Maine's popular Windjammer Fleet have their home port here and may be tracked from nearby Mt. Battle. The inn is decorated with period furnishings and has a large country dining room with an adjoining deck. Spacious guest rooms, baths and parlors set the stage for a memorable stay.

Location: Ninety-seven miles from Portland, 200 miles from Boston.
Rates: $40-$60. Season: All year.
Innkeeper(s): Sally & Bob Tierney.

8 Rooms. 2 Private Baths. 5 Shared Baths. Conference Room. Guest phone available. Children 8 & up. Smoking Limited to deck. Beds: DT. Meals: Full substantial breakfast.

Castine

The Manor
Battle Ave, PO Box 276
Castine ME 04421
(207) 326-4861
 Circa 1895. A stunning shingle-style "cottage" of grand proportions, the home was built for Commodore Fuller of the New York Yacht Club. The club

still begins its summer cruise in Castine every year. On five acres of lawns and gardens, the inn reflects the magnificent summer holidays enjoyed in Bar Harbor at the turn of the century. Public rooms include the Hunting Room, the Billiard Room and the Library.

Rates: $55-$95.
Innkeeper(s): Paul & Sara Brouillard.
Meals: Continental breakfast.
 "Beautiful and elegant - a very special place. We will return!! With friends!"
 "Great to be back."

Center Lovell

Center Lovell Inn
Rt 5
Center Lovell ME 04016
(207) 925-1575
 Circa 1805. The Cape-style annex was added in 1830 and attached by a wraparound porch to an 1805 farmhouse. It was owned by the governor of Florida, Eckley Stearns, who transformed the house into its present Mississippi steamboat appearance by the addition of the mansard-roofed third floor. Acclaimed by

Architectural Digest, the inn overlooks Kezar Lake Valley and has a panoramic view of the White Mountains.

Location: Western Maine.
**Rates: $50-$60. Season: May 1 to October 20.
Innkeeper(s): Bil & Susie Mosca.
11 Rooms. 7 Private Baths. 4 Shared Baths. Jacuzzi Tubs. Guest phone available. Children. TV available. Smoking OK. Credit Cards: Visa, MC. Beds: DT. Meals: B&B or EP, gourmet and continental cuisine.

 "Finest food I have ever eaten in 40 states and 30 countries, located in one of the most beautiful areas anywhere."

Clark Island

Craignair Inn
Clark Island Rd
Clark Island ME 04859
(207) 594-7644
 Circa 1930. Originally Craignair was built to accommodate stonecutters working for the nearby granite quarries. Overlooking the loading docks of the Clark Island Quarry, where granite schooners once were loaded, this roomy three-story building lends itself well as a quaint and cozy inn tastefully decorated with local antiques.

Location: Spruce Head, Maine.
Rates: $51-$70. Season: All year.
Innkeeper(s): Norman Smith.
23 Rooms. 5 Private Baths. 7 Shared Baths. Conference Room. Guest phone available. Children. Smoking OK. Credit Cards: Visa, MC. Beds: DTC. Meals: B&B and restaurant.

Cornish

Cornish Inn
PO Box 266, Rt 25
Cornish ME 04020
(207) 625-8501
 Circa 1826. The Cornish Inn has provided a respite from the hustle and bustle of everyday life for over a century. In the foothills of the White Mountains, this New England village inn features fourteen hand-sten-

ciled rooms abounding with antiques and handcrafted items. The library, parlors, dining room and wraparound veranda exude a homey country elegance.

Location: Thirty miles west of Portland in the Lakes Region of southwest Maine.
**Rates: $35-$50. Season: May to October then December to March.
Innkeeper(s): Sandy & Gary Holstein.
14 Rooms. 8 Private Baths. 2 Shared Baths. Guest phone available. Children. TV available. Smoking OK. Credit Cards: Visa, MC. Beds: DT. Meals: Full breakfast.

Damariscotta

Elfinhill
See: Newcastle, ME.

Newcastle Inn
See: Newcastle, ME.

Eastport

Artists Retreat
29 Washington St
Eastport ME 04631
(207) 853-4239
Circa 1846. A stately Victorian home with gracious, elegant interiors, the inn is furnished with its original ornately-carved, marble-topped furniture and knick-knacks. Victoriana buffs will be delighted to enjoy the nineteenth-century ambience of this island city.

Location: Two blocks up from the waterfront.
Rates: $30-$40. Season: All year.
Innkeeper(s): Joyce Weber.
5 Rooms. 2 Shared Baths. Conference Room. Guest phone available. Children. TV available. Smoking OK. Credit Cards: Visa, MC. Beds: QT. Meals: Full breakfast.

Todd House
Todd's Head
Eastport ME 04631
(207) 853-2328
Circa 1775. Todd House is a typical full Cape with huge center chimney. In 1801, Eastern Lodge No. 7 of the Masonic Order was chartered here. It became a temporary barracks when Todd's Head was fortified. Guests may use barbecue facilities overlooking Passamaquoddy Bay.

Location: On ocean.
Rates: $25-$40. Season: All year.
Innkeeper(s): Ruth M. McInnis.

6 Rooms. Guest phone available. Children. Pets OK. TV in room. Handicap access provided. Smoking OK. Beds: DT. Meals: Continental breakfast.

Weston House
26 Boynton St
Eastport ME 04631
(207) 853-2907
Circa 1810. Jonathan Weston, an 1802 graduate of Harvard, built his Federal-style house on a hill over-

looking Passamaquoddy Bay. John Audubon stayed here as a guest of the Westons while awaiting passage to Labrador in 1833.

Rates: $35-$50. Season: All year.
Innkeeper(s): Jett & John Peterson.
5 Rooms. 3 Shared Baths. Conference Room. Guest phone available. TV available. Beds: KQT. Meals: Full breakfast.
"The best of an eight day six state New England stay."
"Breakfasts are a gastronomic delight. We can't wait to return!"

Eliot

High Meadows Bed & Breakfast
Rt 101
Eliot ME 03903
(207) 439-0590
Circa 1736. A ship's captain built this home filled with charming remembrances of the old colonial days. All the convenience of modern facilities are available, however. It is close to factory outlets, great dining and historic Portsmouth's beaches and theater.

Location: Six-and-one-half miles from historic Portsmouth, New Hampshire, 1 hour from Boston.
Rates: $50-$60. Season: April to December.
Innkeeper(s): Elaine Raymond.
4 Rooms. 1 Private Baths. 3 Shared Baths. Conference Room. Guest phone available. TV available. Smoking OK. Beds: QT. Meals: Continental-plus breakfast.

Freeport

Captain Josiah Mitchell House
188 Main St
Freeport ME 04032
(207) 865-3289

Circa 1779. The Captain Josiah Mitchell House is one of the most famous historical houses in Freeport and the state of Maine. Captain Mitchell was commander of the clipper ship *Hornet* which sailed in the 1800s. In 1865, as it sailed from New York to San Francisco, it caught fire, burned and was lost. The passengers and crew survived in three longboats and drifted for forty-five days. It is the longest survival at sea in an open boat that has been recorded. When the boats drifted into one of the South Pacific Islands, Mark Twain was there. He befriended the Captain and sailed back to the Mainland with him. Many of his sea stories were dedicated to him and the diary of Captain Mitchell was used in writing the *Mutiny on the Bounty*. Flower gardens and a porch swing on the veranda now welcome guests to Freeport and the Captain's House.

Location: In town on Main St.
Rates: $60-$70. Season: All.
Innkeeper(s): Alan & Loretta Bradley.
7 Rooms. 7 Private Baths. Guest phone available. Children. TV available. Credit Cards: Visa, MC. Beds: DT. Meals: Full breakfast.

"Your wonderful stories brought all of us together. You have created a special place that nurtures and brings happiness and love for each to experience."

"This has been a dream. Your house is warm and full of hospitality. Be proud of all you have accomplished; this house, your art, your trips and successful, loving children."

"We stayed here the coldest night of the winter (ten below zero), yet we never felt more warmth."

Isaac Randall House
Independence Drive
Freeport ME 04032
(207) 865-9295

Circa 1823. Isaac Randall's Federal-style farmhouse was once a dairy farm, then a stop on the Underground Railway for slaves escaping into Canada. Mr. Randall was a direct descendant of John Alden and Priscilla Mullins of the *Mayflower* whose romance was immortalized by Longfellow's *The Courtship of Miles Standish*.

Location: Walking distance to downtown.
Rates: $40-$65. Season: All year.
Innkeeper(s): Glyn & Jim Friedlander.

8 Rooms. 6 Private Baths. 1 Shared Baths. Guest phone available. Children. Pets OK. TV available. Handicap access provided. Smoking OK. Beds: QTC. Meals: Hearty breakfasts.

"Staying in your home was the highlight of our vacation."
"Enchanted to find ourselves surrounded by all your charming antiques and beautiful furnishings."
"A delightful get-away weekend."

Hulls Cove

Inn at Canoe Point
PO Box 216, Rt 3
Hulls Cove ME 04644
(207) 288-9511

Circa 1889. This oceanfront inn has served as a summer residence for several generations of families escaping the heat of the cities. Guests are pampered in the gracious hospitality of the past, surrounded by ocean and pine forests. They relax on the deck overlooking Frenchman's Bay or actively pursue outdoor activities at the National Park.

Location: On the ocean, 1/4 mile to Acadia National Park, 2 miles from Bar Harbor.
Rates: $75-$135. Season: All year.
Innkeeper(s): D. L. Johnson.
5 Rooms. 5 Private Baths. Conference Room. Guest phone available. Children 12 & up. TV available. Handicap access provided. Smoking OK. Beds: QT. Meals: B&B.

Kennebunkport

Captain Lord Mansion
Pleasant & Green, PO Box 800
Kennebunkport ME 04046
(207) 967-3141

Circa 1812. In the National Register, the Captain Lord Mansion, built during the War of 1812, is one of the finest examples of Federal architecture on the coast of Maine. A four-story spiral staircase winds up the cupola where one may view the town and the Kennebunk River and Yacht Club. When the mansion was originally built, it provided a street entrance so the villagers could climb the stairs to the cupola and

view inbound ships without bothering the family. The inn features eleven rooms with fireplaces.

Location: Historic District of the village.
Rates: $99-$149. Season: All year.
Innkeeper(s): Bev Davis & Rick Litchfield.
16 Rooms. 16 Private Baths. Conference Room. Guest phone available. Credit Cards: Visa, MC, AE. Beds: QK. Meals: Full breakfast.

"A showcase of elegant architecture, with lovely remembrances of the past. Meticulously clean and splendidly appointed. I can't remember a more relaxing afternoon. It's a shame to have to leave."

Harbor Inn
PO Box 538A
Kennebunkport ME 04046
(207) 967-2074

Circa 1903. Tucked behind the white iron Victorian fence is the Harbor Inn. A yellow canopy covers the

stairs leading to the old-fashioned veranda and the double Dutch door. You may hear the quiet purring of the fishing boats or smell the fresh, salty air right there at the door. Inside, all the guest rooms are furnished with canopied or four-poster beds, period

lighting, oriental rugs and antique coverlets. The inn's kitchen has blue iris stained glass windows and an old wood stove set on a brick hearth. The parlor features an old grandfather clock and fireplace. Just past the inn, further down Ocean Avenue where the Kennebunk River runs to the sea, is Spouting Rock and Blowing Cave. Mainers say the sky is bluer here than anywhere else in the world.

Location: Ocean Avenue, along the Kennebunk River.
Rates: $70-$135. Season: May to November.
Innkeeper(s): Charlotte & Bill Massmann.
9 Rooms. 9 Private Baths. Guest phone available. Children 12 & up. TV available. Smoking OK. Beds: QT. Meals: Hearty breakfast.

"Everything is beautifully done. It's the best we've ever been to."
"Feeling of peace and calm."

Inn at Harbor Head
RR 2, PO Box 1180
Kennebunkport ME 04046
(207) 967-5564

Circa 1898. The inn is a rambling, shingled saltwater farmhouse on the water in historic Cape Porpoise - the quiet side of Kennebunkport. The inn has been completely restored and offers elegance as well as outstanding views of the harbor, ocean and islands. Ancient apple trees shield the inn from the road and a back terrace leads down to the shore.

Location: Pier Road, Cape Porpoise.
**Rates: $65-$95. Season: All year.
Innkeeper(s): Noan & Dave Sutter.
4 Rooms. 4 Private Baths. Guest phone available. Children 12 & up. Credit Cards: Visa, MC, AE, Discover. Beds: KQD. Meals: Full breakfast.

Inn on South Street
PO Box 478A
Kennebunkport ME 04046
(207) 967-4539, 5151.

Circa 1807. Built in the Greek Revival style, the Inn on South Street now stands on a quiet side street. It was towed there by oxen from its original location right on the village green, because a wealthy citizen complained that it was cutting off her river view. The inn boasts a handsome "good-morning" staircase, original pine plank floors, hand-planed wainscoting and a new old-fashioned herb garden.

Location: Southern coast of Maine, 2 hours from Boston, 3/4 hour from Portland.
Rates: $60-$85. Season: February to January 1st.
Innkeeper(s): Jacques & Eva Downs.
3 Rooms. 3 Private Baths. Guest phone available. Children 10 & up. Credit Cards: AE. Beds: QDT. Meals: B&B.

"The Inn on South Street *was the first place we stayed in Maine and was by far the best in our two weeks in Maine.*"

Kylemere House 1818
South St, PO Box 1333
Kennebunkport ME 04046
(207) 967-2780

Circa 1818. Located in Maine's largest historic district, the home was built by Daniel Walker, a descendant of one of the original families in the Port. In 1895, the well-known Maine artist and architect, Abbot Graves, purchased the house and used the barn as his studio. He named the house 'Crosstrees' for the two husband and wife maple trees planted on either side of the front door. Today only one maple remains at the entrance to this center-chimney colonial.

Rates: $55-$65. Season: April 1 to December 31.
Innkeeper(s): Bill & Mary Kyle.
5 Rooms. 3 Private Baths. 1 Shared Baths. Guest phone available. Children 12 & up. Credit Cards: AE. Beds: KQT. Meals: B&B.

Maine Stay Inn and Cottages
Maine St, PO Box 500A
Kennebunkport ME 04046
(207) 967-2117

Circa 1860. The Maine Stay Inn is listed in the National Historic Register and is elegantly decorated with antiques. Though considered to be a square-

block Italianate contoured in a low hip-roof design, later additions of the Queen Anne period include a

suspended spiral staircase, crystal windows, ornately carved mantels and moldings, bay windows and porches. One of the former owners, a sea captain, built the handsome cupola. It became a favorite spot for making taffy! In the twenties it was also used to spot rumrunners off the shore. Cottages have been added to the property and all guests enjoy afternoon tea and stories of the Maine Stay's heritage.

Location: In the Kennebunkport National Historic District, within walking distance of the village.
**Rates: $63-$104. Season: April to November.
Innkeeper(s): Jacques & Carol Gagnon.
17 Rooms. 17 Private Baths. Conference Room. Guest phone available. Children. Handicap access provided. Smoking OK. Credit Cards: Visa, MC, AE. Beds: QC. Meals: EP & B&B available.

"*Beautifully decorated home, clean, clean accommodations, cute cottages.*"
"*Loved coming home for tea every afternoon.*"
"*Thank you for the special attention you gave us.*"

Old Fort Inn
Old Fort Ave, PO Box M 24
Kennebunkport ME 04046
(207) 967-5353

Circa 1880. The Old Fort Inn is a luxurious mini-resort nestled in a secluded setting. It has a tennis court, fresh water swimming pool and shuffleboard. Bikes are also available. The inn has its own antique shop filled with country furniture, primitives and china. There is a tennis court and shuffleboard court for guests. The ocean is just a block's walk away.

Location: One block from the ocean.
**Rates: $78-$125. Season: Mid-April to mid-December.
Innkeeper(s): David & Sheela Aldrich.
14 Rooms. 14 Private Baths. Swimming Pool. Conference Room. Guest phone available. Children 8 & up. TV available. Smoking OK. Credit Cards: Visa, MC, AE, Discover. Beds: KQT. Meals: Continental-plus breakfast.

Port Gallery Inn
Corner of Spring & Maine, PO Box 1367
Kennebunkport ME 04046
(207) 967-3728

Circa 1891. This Victorian mansion was given to Captain Titcomb, builder of the largest ships on the Kennebunk River. Kennebunkport, summer home of the rich and famous, is in the National Register of Historical Places with twenty-six different architectural styles. The inn features a Marine Art Gallery specializing in paintings of old seafaring days.

Location: Center Village.
Rates: $79-$98. Season: All year.
Innkeeper(s): Francis & Lucy Morphy.

7 Rooms. 7 Private Baths. Children 12 & up. TV in room. Smoking OK. Credit Cards: Visa, MC, DC. Beds: Q.

"It's like coming home. You make your guests feel warm."

Welby Inn
Ocean Avenue, PO Box 774
Kennebunkport ME 04046
(207) 967-4655

Circa 1900. This merchant sea captain's home is in the gambrel style which is much like a ship's hull

turned upside down. The extensive wood-paneled walls covering most of the first floor are of cypress wood personally carried by the captain during a southern trading expedition.

Location: One-half mile from Dock Square.
Rates: $60-$70. Season: All year.
Innkeeper(s): David Knox & Betsy Rogers-Knox.
7 Rooms. 5 Private Baths. 2 Shared Baths. Guest phone available. Children 10 & up. Credit Cards: AE. Beds: QDT. Meals: Full breakfast.

York Harbor Inn
See: York Harbor, ME.

New Harbor

Gosnold Arms
Northside Rd, Rt 32
New Harbor ME 04554
(207) 677-3727

Circa 1870. A remodeled, sparkling-white saltwater farmhouse with its own steamboat wharf, this inn has a glassed-in dining porch overlooking the water. The congenial family atmosphere was first initiated by a Smith College dorm mother who assembled several cottages in addition to the rooms in the house. One cottage, in fact, is a rustic pilot house picked up, helm and all, off a steamboat and nestled bayside.

Location: Mid-coast Maine on the Pemaquid peninsula.
Rates: $44-$110. Season: June to November.
Innkeeper(s): Lucy Phinney.
26 Rooms. 19 Private Baths. 7 Shared Baths. Conference Room. Guest phone available. Children. Smoking OK. Credit Cards: Visa, MC. Beds: QDTC. Meals: Full breakfast and noted restaurant.

Newcastle

Elfinhill
20 River Rd, PO Box 497
Newcastle ME 04553
(207) 563-1886

Circa 1851. Elfinhill is a beautiful unspoiled Greek Revival home that looks out to the river. There are wide pumpkin pine floors and pleasant furnishings. The home is convenient to village shops and restaurants. The hosts were recently written up in *Yankee Magazine* for their excellent fruitcake and cheesecake mail order business.

**Rates: $40-$50.
Innkeeper(s): Emma Stephenson & Don Smith. Meals: Full breakfast.

Glidden House
Glidden St, RR1, Box 740
Newcastle ME 04553
(207) 563-1859

Circa 1850. This Victorian guest house overlooks the Damariscotta River and is close to the twin village, Newcastle/Damariscotta. A separate apartment is available as well as regular guest rooms.

**Rates: $35-$55.
Innkeeper(s): Doris E. Miller.

Newcastle Inn
River Rd
Newcastle ME 04553
(207) 563-5685

Circa 1860. The Newcastle Inn has been an inn since the early twenties. Located on the Damariscotta River, the neighbors just behind the inn are ninety-seven sail boats. The river separates the twin towns of Damariscotta and Newcastle. A five-course dinner is now available at the inn. Honeymooners will enjoy the room with the old-fashioned canopy bed.

**Rates: $45-$65. Season: April to December.
Innkeeper(s): Sylvia & Frank Kelley.
19 Rooms. Guest phone available. Children. Pets OK. TV available. Handicap access provided. Smoking OK. Credit Cards: Visa, MC. Beds: KQT. Meals: Hearty, homecooked breakfast. Restaurant.

"We have peddled the entire coast of Maine in fourteen days and are happy to report that this area is one of the two prettiest between New Hampshire and Canada."

"When I think of the Newcastle Inn I think of: on the water, bald eagles, lighthouse, Rachel Carson, sanctuary, lobster, Beethoven, seals, Maine Blueberry Blintzes, Geraniums, Schnauzers, Puffins, new friends, antiques and welcome."

North Waterford

Olde Rowley Inn
Route 35 North
North Waterford ME 04267
(207) 583-4143

Circa 1790. A stagecoach stop with a rich colonial heritage, the Olde Rowley features an open hearth fireplace in the keeping room and an excellent restaurant.

Location: Wester Lakes and Mountain Region.
Rates: $55.
Innkeeper(s): L. Peter & Pamela R. Leja.

Ogunquit

Captain Lorenz Perkins House
Rt 1, PO Box 2130
Ogunquit ME 03907
(207) 646-7825

Circa 1800. An 18th-century colonial home, the fireplace is faced with tile acquired by Captain Perkins during his travels. The inn is near one of the best beaches on the coast.

Location: Rt 1, 1/4 mile north of the village.

Rates: $50-$70.
Innkeeper(s): The Shelleys.

Morning Dove Bed & Breakfast
5 Bourne Lane, PO Box 1940
Ogunquit ME 03907
(207) 646-3891

Circa 1865. A classic New Englander, this home was previously owned by the prominent Moses Littlefield family for 115 years. The owners lovingly restored the original architectural details of the period. The inn features airy rooms with original art, antiques, and lace curtains. Its spectacular gardens are just a walk to beaches, Marginal Way & Perkins Cove.

Location: Adjacent to Barn Gallery at Shore Rd.
Rates: $40-$70. Season: All year.
Innkeeper(s): Eeta & Peter Sachon.
7 Rooms. 3 Private Baths. 2 Shared Baths. Guest phone available. Children 12 & up. Smoking OK. Credit Cards: Visa, MC, AE. Beds: QT. Meals: Continental breakfast.

York Harbor Inn
See: York Harbor, ME.

Portland

The Inn at Park Spring
135 Spring St
Portland ME 04101
(207) 774-1059

Circa 1835. This three-story brick Portland-style building features a large bay with floor-to-ceiling windows There are several uniquely decorated rooms with such amenities as crystal chandeliers, marble fireplaces, four poster beds, and pedestal baths that will provide just the right touch of luxury. Within walking distance is the old Port District, Portland Museum of Art and the working waterfront.

Rates: $55-$85. Season: All year.
Innkeeper(s): Wendy Wickstrom.
7 Rooms. 5 Private Baths. 2 Shared Baths. Conference Room. Guest phone available. Children 5 & up. TV available. Handicap access provided. Credit Cards: Visa, MC, AE, DC, Discovery. Beds: Q. Meals: Continental-plus breakfast.

York Harbor Inn
See: York Harbor, ME.

Waldoboro

Broad Bay Inn & Gallery
Main St
Waldoboro ME 04572
(207) 832-6668

Circa 1905. In the heart of an unspoiled coastal village, the Old Broad Bay features canopy beds and Victorian furnishings.

Location: Mid-coast Maine in residential area on Main St.
**Rates: $35-$55.
Innkeeper(s): Jim & Libby Hopkins.

Walpole

The Bittersweet Inn
HCR 64, PO Box 013
Walpole ME 04573
(207) 563-5552

Circa 1840. The original farm house was built in the early 1800s with a Victorian addition constructed in the early 1900s. A large barn is connected to the house and is available to store bikes or ski equipment. There is a right-of-way through the woods to the Damariscotta River.

Rates: $45. Season: All year.
Innkeeper(s): Ruth Hurd.
5 Rooms. 2 Shared Baths. Guest phone available. Children 12 & up. Credit Cards: Visa, MC. Beds: QT. Meals: Full breakfast.

York Harbor

York Harbor Inn
Rte 1 A, PO Box 573
York Harbor ME 03911
(207) 363-5119

Circa 1637. This is an inn with classic coastal charm, seven working fireplaces, and ocean views. There is an English-style pub in the cellar and an ocean view dining room serving continental cuisine and New England seafood. It's listed in the National Register.

Location: On the Shore Road at the entrance to York Harbor.
**Rates: $45-$120. Season: All year.
Innkeeper(s): Joe, Jean & Garry Dominguez.
20 Rooms. 10 Private Baths. Guest phone available. Children. TV available. Handicap access provided. Smoking OK. Credit Cards: Visa, MC, AE. Beds: D. Meals: MAP, B&B, Gourmet restaurant.

Maryland

Annapolis

Charles Inn
74 Charles St
Annapolis MD 21401
(301) 268-1451
  Circa 1860.

Location: Historic downtown Annapolis.
**Rates: $50.
Innkeeper(s): Marian O'Brien & Eugene.

Prince George Inn
232 Prince George St
Annapolis MD 21401
(301) 263-6418
  Circa 1884. The Prince George Inn is a three-story brick townhouse comfortably furnished with an emphasis on Victorian decor. The guest parlor, breakfast room, porch and courtyard offer areas for relaxing. In the heart of the colonial city, the inn is near restaurants, museums, shops, the city dock and the Naval Academy. Your hostess operates a walking tour service.

Location: Historic district of Annapolis.
**Rates: $40-$50. Season: All year.
Innkeeper(s): William & Norma Grovermann.
4 Rooms. 2 Shared Baths. Guest phone available. TV available. Smoking OK. Beds: QDT. Meals: B&B.

Baltimore

Admiral Fell Inn
888 S Broadway
Baltimore MD 21231
(301) 522-7377
  Circa 1850. The Admiral Fell Inn consists of three buildings constructed between 1850 and 1910, the oldest of which is a three-story columned building of red brick with a Victorian-style facade. These build-

ings were at one time a boarding house for sailors. Each room is now tastefully furnished with period

pieces and antiques and bears the name and biography of a person noted in Baltimore history.

Location: Fell's Point, one mile five minutes from the convention center and business district.
**Rates: $90-$135. Season: All year.
Innkeeper(s): Jim Widman.
37 Rooms. 37 Private Baths. Conference Room. Guest phone available. Children. TV available. Handicap access provided. Smoking OK. Credit Cards: Visa, MC, AE. Beds: KQ. Meals: Continental breakfast. Restaurant.

Betsy's Bed & Breakfast
1428 Park Ave
Baltimore MD 21217
(301) 383-1274
  Circa 1895. With thirteen-foot ceilings, this four-story turn-of-the-century townhouse features many elegant architectural touches. The hallway floor, for instance, is laid in alternating strips of oak and walnut. There are six carved marble fireplaces. The most elaborate of these is in the dining room, carved in fruit designs. The inn is decorated with handsome brass rubbings executed by the owner during a stay in England.

Location: Balton Hill, downtown Baltimore.

**Rates: $50-$60. Season: All year.
Innkeeper(s): Betsy Corater.
3 Rooms. 1 Private Baths. 1 Shared Baths. Hot Tub. Children. TV in room. Credit Cards: Visa, MC, AE. Beds: KQT. Meals: Continental-plus breakfast.

"What a wonderful time we've had while lodging with you. Your home is lovely. You have been a beautiful and gracious host."

Mensana Inn
See: Stevenson, MD

Mulberry House
**111 West Mulberry St
Baltimore MD 21201
(301) 576-0111**

Circa 1830. This dwelling was built on land purchased from John Eager Howard (an officer in Washington's army.) It was originally built as a three-story Federal period townhouse. A fourth floor was added during the Victorian period with the addition of a cornice, giving the building an Italianate appearance. The old mansion has been restored including the original fine Belgian gold marble fireplace and leaded-glass mullioned windows.

Location: Downtown Baltimore.
Rates: $65. Season: All year.
Innkeeper(s): Charlotte & Curt Jeschke.
4 Rooms. 2 Shared Baths. Guest phone available. Children 16 & up. Smoking OK. Beds: Q. Meals: Full breakfast.

Shirley Guest House
**205 W Madison St
Baltimore MD 21201
(301) 728-6550**

Circa 1880. An elegant Victorian mansion located in a downtown historic neighborhood, the Shirley Guest House has an English stairway of polished ash that winds up four stories. The original 100-year-old lift still carries up to three guests. The inn is decorated with Victorian and Edwardian antiques and turn-of-the-century artwork. The Inner Harbor, business district and cultural centers are all just a short walk away.

Location: Mt Vernon historical neighborhood; ten blocks from the Inner Harbor.
**Rates: $50-$75. Season: All year.
Innkeeper(s): Zippy Goldman, Ellen Steininger, Monica Gesue.
27 Rooms. 27 Private Baths. Conference Room. Guest phone available. Children. TV available. Smoking OK. Credit Cards: Visa, MC, AE. Beds: QT. Meals: Continental-plus breakfast.

Chestertown

White Swan Tavern
**231 High St
Chestertown MD 21620
(301) 778-2300**

Circa 1730. During the 1978 restoration of the Inn, an archaeological dig discovered that the site was used prior to 1733 as a tannery, operated by the

"Shoemaker of Chestertown". His one-room dwelling is now converted to one of the guest rooms. After additions to the building it became a tavern in 1793 when it was described as *"situated in the center of business..with every attention given to render comfort and pleasure to such as favor it with their patronage."*

Location: Eastern shore of Maryland. Downtown historic district.
Rates: $75-$100. Season: All year.
Innkeeper(s): Mary Clarkson.
5 Rooms. 5 Private Baths. Conference Room. Guest phone available. Children. TV available. Handicap access provided. Smoking OK. Beds: DTC. Meals: B&B.

"It is again considered to be 'the best tavern stand in town.'"

New Market

National Pike Inn
**9 West Main Street
New Market MD 21774
(301) 865-5055**

Circa 1796. A Federal-style house, National Pike Inn is in historic New Market. A unique widows watch was added in 1900. Massive woodworking adorns the inside of this elegant inn. National Pike was the East-West connection between Baltimore to Cumberland and points west. The towns along the pike were located approximately eight miles apart which was as far as the drivers could drive their herds in one day. New Market is one hour from Washington, DC and Baltimore, MD.

Location: Six miles east of Frederick. Exit 62 off I-70.
Rates: $50-$80.
Innkeeper(s): Tom & Terry Rimel.

Strawberry Inn
17 Main St, PO Box 237
New Market MD 21774
(301) 865-3318
Circa 1860. Strawberry Inn is a restored Maryland farmhouse located in the center of a 200-year old Na-

tional Historic Register town. The white Victorian clapboard house is furnished with antiques, of course, since New Market is the antique capital of Maryland.

Rates: $55-$65. Season: All year.
Innkeeper(s): Jane & Ed Rossig.
5 Rooms. 5 Private Baths. Conference Room. Guest phone available. Children 8 & up. Handicap access provided. Smoking OK. Beds: QT. Meals: B&B.
"A tiny jewel in a Victorian setting." NY Times.

Princess Anne

Elmwood C. 1770 Bed & Breakfast
Locust Point, PO Box 220
Princess Anne MD 21853
(301) 651-1066
Circa 1770. This Federal-style brick home was once the home of Confederate General Arnold Elzey. Later Norman Taylor, botanist, and head of the Botanical Gardens of Brooklyn lived here. The property is on one mile of waterfront, an inviting spot for fishing, crabbing and hiking.

Location: Lower eastern shore.
Rates: $60-$95.

Innkeeper(s): Mr & Mrs Stephen Monick.

Stevenson

Mensana Inn
1718 Greenspring Valley Rd
Stevenson MD 21153
(301) 653-2403
Circa 1900. This home was built by Edmund Burke, one of Teddy Roosevelt's "Rough Riders". It is furnished with antiques and oriental rugs. Trophies from

African hunting expeditions are hung on the living room wall and include a rhino, cape buffalo and wart hog. High on a hill and on eighteen acres, the inn affords a commanding view of the Green Spring Valley.

Location: Ten minutes to Pikesville, Towson, Owings Mills and 15 minutes to Baltimore.
**Rates: $140. Season: Closed December 18 to January 3.
Innkeeper(s): Lee Hendler.
8 Rooms. 8 Private Baths. Hot Tub. Sauna. Conference Room. Guest phone in room. Children. TV in room. Smoking OK. Credit Cards: Visa, MC, AE, DC. Beds: T.
"I feel like Scarlet O'Hara, living at Tara. Where's Rhett?"
"It's like staying at Teddy Roosevelt's House."

Vienna

Tavern House
111 Water St, PO Box 98
Vienna MD 21869
(301) 376-3347
Circa 1760. River views are available from the guest rooms of this old Tavern, popular during Colonial days. The inn has been renovated and the polished wood floors and white plaster walls provide the backdrop for simple antique furnishings and reproductions. Five fireplaces at the inn include a cooking hearth down in the cellar.

Location: On Nanticoke River on Maryland's Eastern Shore.
**Rates: $45-$60.
Innkeeper(s): Harvey & Elise Altergott.

Massachusetts

Ashfield

Ashfield Inn
Main St
Ashfield MA 01330
(413) 628-4571

Circa 1919. This Georgian mansion was originally built as a summer home for Milo Belding. Enormous

porches overlook spectacular perennial and herb gardens. The romantic interior includes a reception hall, grand stairway and fireplaced living room. For all seasons, the Ashfield Inn is an elegant and secluded estate.

Location: Berkshire foothills, five-college area.
**Rates: $70. Season: All year.
Innkeeper(s): Roger & Linda Hebert.
5 Rooms. 1 Private Baths. 2 Shared Baths. Conference Room. Guest phone available. Children 10 & up and infants. TV available. Smoking OK. Credit Cards: Visa, MC, AE. Beds: KQTWC. Meals: Full gourmet breakfast.

"Ashfield Inn has everything: privacy, elegance, fabulous food, amenities (like terry robes, flowers & fruit) that made me feel pampered. Wonderful hospitality in a spectacular romantic setting."

Barnstable

Ashley Manor
3660 Olde Kings Highway, PO Box 856
Barnstable MA 02630
(617) 362-8044

Circa 1699. Besides the wide board flooring (usually reserved for the king) and huge open-hearth

fireplaces with beehive ovens there is a secret passageway connecting the upstairs and downstairs suites. It was thought to be a hiding place for Tories during the Revolutionary War. The inn now rests gracefully on two acres of manicured lawns sprinkled with cherry and apple trees.

Location: In the heart of Cape Cod's Historic District.
Rates: $85-$125.
Innkeeper(s): Donald & Fay Bain.
6 Rooms. 6 Private Baths. Beds: Q. Meals: Full breakfast in front of the fireplace.

"Enchanting."

"This is absolutely perfect! So many very special, lovely touches."

"Can't wait to come back."

Honeysuckle Hill
See: West Barnstable, MA.

Thomas Huckins House

2701 Main St, Rt 6A
Barnstable MA 02630
(617) 362-6379

Circa 1705. A family of merchants and shippers, the Huckinses settled in Barnstable in 1639. Thomas, a skilled furniture maker, built his home across the road from Calves Pasture Lane, part of the common grazing land used by the colonists. The home has a

ten-foot fireplace and its original paneling, windows, hinges and latches. Just down the road from this Cape half-house is a graveyard where slate headstones bear the names of early residents. American antique furnishings with canopy beds add to the gracious feeling of the inn.

Location: Cape Cod.
Rates: $55-$95. Season: All year.
Innkeeper(s): Burt & Eleanor Eddy.
3 Rooms. 3 Private Baths. Guest phone available. TV available. Smoking OK. Credit Cards: Visa, MC. Beds: D. Meals: B&B.

"*Your home is even warmer and more charming in person than the lovely pictures in* Early American Life Magazine."

Barnstable Village

Beechwood

2839 Main St
Barnstable Village MA 02630
(617) 362-6618

Circa 1853. Beechwood is a carefully restored example of Queen Anne-style architecture. It offers period furnishings, fireplaces, ocean views with warmth and elegance. A favorite hideaway among

couples who look forward to a gentle return to the Victorian nineteenth century. The inn takes its name from the rare old beech trees that shade the veranda.

Location: Along the Old King's Highway Historic District.
Rates: $85-$115. Season: All year.
Innkeeper(s): Miles & Sandra Corey.
6 Rooms. 6 Private Baths. Guest phone available. Smoking OK.
Credit Cards: Visa, MC, AE. Beds: QTK. Meals: Full breakfast.

Charles Hinckley House

Olde Kings Highway, PO Box 723
Barnstable Village MA 02630
(617) 362-9924

Circa 1809. Built by shipwright Charles Hinckley, direct descendant of the last governor of Plymouth Colony, the inn is a fine example of Federal colonial architecture. A twin chimney, hip-roofed post and beam structure, the Charles Hinckley House is an

award-winning restoration. There are four working fireplaces at the inn. It stands watch over one of Cape Cod's most photographed wildflower gardens. A short walk down the quiet lane out front brings you to the bay.

**Rates: $89-$125. Season: All year.
Innkeeper(s): Les & Miya Patrick.
4 Rooms. 4 Private Baths. Guest phone available. Handicap access provided. Beds: Q. Meals: Full breakfast.

"Country Living *magazine didn't do you justice! ...your inn is even more wonderful.*"

"*Sometimes you can tell a book by its cover...wildflower gardens overflowing onto the lawn and lining the path...suggests the old-fashioned country homeness within.*" Interiors.

Bass River

Belvedere Bed & Breakfast Inn
167 Main St
Bass River MA 02664
(617) 398-6674

Circa 1820. This Federal Colonial home was built by a local sea captain, Elisha Baker. He was a prominent local figure in the War of 1812 and owned and com-

manded three schooners. The home has a dominate belvedere, lovely gardens and a white picket fence along the lane.

Location: Cape Cod, Mid-Cape.
**Rates: $36-$48. Season: All year.
Innkeeper(s): Judy & Dick Fenuccio.
4 Rooms. 1 Private Baths. 3 Shared Baths. Guest phone available. Children 12 & up. TV available. Beds: QDT. Meals: B&B.

"Masters of the art of giving guests a true vacation. The home is superb and cleaner than any high quality hotel."

"Sitting at the window made me feel like being in a Victorian novel."

"Impeccable, a wonderful place to stay on beautiful Cape Cod."

Becket

Canterbury Farm
Fred Snow Rd
Becket MA 01223
(413) 623-8765

Circa 1780. A late Colonial, early Federal home, Canterbury Farm is on 200 acres of woodlands. It is one of the oldest and best preserved properties in the area. Authentically restored, the inn has several fireplaces and is decorated with antiques, fireplaces, and homemade braided rugs.

Location: Berkshire Mountains.
**Rates: $50-$70.

Innkeeper(s): Linda & Dave Bacon.

Bernardston

Bernardston Inn
Church St
Bernardston MA 01337
(413) 648-9282

Circa 1905. The present building was erected on the site of an old established coaching inn. Recently

renovated, the Bernardston Inn has ceiling fans, claw-foot bathtubs, and guest rooms with traditional and antique furnishings.

Location: Junction Rts 5 & 10.
**Rates: $48. Season: All year.
Innkeeper(s): Toby A. D. Holmes & Steven Pardue.
7 Rooms. 7 Private Baths. Guest phone available. Children. TV available. Smoking OK. Credit Cards: Visa, MC. Beds: QT. Meals: B&B and restaurant.

"Delighted with the charming atmosphere, excellent accommodations and outstanding service."

"A perfect spot for our honeymoon - we hope to return."

Brewster

Old Sea Pines Inn
2553 Main St
Brewster MA 02631
(617) 896-6114

Circa 1900. This turn-of-the century mansion has recently been redecorated. It is located conveniently near restaurants and small shops and is close to beaches and bike paths. The inn has thirteen rooms, most with private baths. There is a restaurant on the premises.

Location: Cape Cod.
Rates: $32-$65.
Innkeeper(s): Michele & Steve Rowan.

Buckland

1797 House
Charlemont Rd
Buckland MA 01338
(413) 625-2975

Circa 1797. The house was built by Zenas Graham who married the same year and went on to have twelve children. The Graham family retained the house well into the 1940s. At one time it served as the Winter School for Young Ladies, run by Mary Lyon, founder of Mount Holyoke College. Features include

12-over-12 windows, four fireplaces, and a peaceful screened porch. Comfort is everywhere and very enticing after a day of sightseeing.

Location: Foothills of Berkshires.
Rates: $40-$55. Season: January 15 to October 31.
Innkeeper(s): Janet Turley.
3 Rooms. 3 Private Baths. Conference Room. Guest phone available. TV available. Smoking OK. Beds: TD. Meals: Full breakfast.

"When I become stressed, I send my mind to your porch."

"These are the most restful nights I've ever spent away from home."

Cape Cod

Nashua House
See: Oak Bluffs, MA.

Note: For Cape Cod see also these cities: Barnstable, Barnstable Village, Bass River, Brewster, Dennis, East Orleans, East Sandwich, Falmouth, Harwich Port, Provincetown, Sandwich, West Barnstable, Woods Hole, Yarmouth Port.

Centerville

Copper Beech Inn
497 Main St
Centerville MA 02632
(617) 771-5488

Circa 1820. At the sight of the largest copper beech tree on Cape Cod, you'll find the Copper Beech Inn, built by Captain Hillman Crosby as a gift to his wife when they were married. The Crosby name has long

been associated with boat builders and particularly, fast sailing ships. Preserved and restored, the Cape-style home is situated amid other white clapboard houses shaded by elms and surrounded by hedges. Summer theater, fine restaurants, and the beach are nearby.

Location: Cape Cod.
Rates: $65. Season: All year.
Innkeeper(s): Anita J. Diehl (Joyce).
3 Rooms. 3 Private Baths. Conference Room. Guest phone available. Children 12 & up. Pets OK. TV available. Handicap access provided. Credit Cards: Visa, MC, AE. Beds: K. Meals: Full breakfast.

"Everything we were looking for, clean & private, but best of all was our wonderful hosts. They made us feel very much at home and made delicious breakfasts."

Concord

Anderson-Wheeler Homestead
154 Fitchburg Turnpike
Concord MA 01742
(617) 369-3756

Circa 1890. When route 117 was the main road between Boston and Fitchburg, the Lee family ran a stage coach stop here. They provided room and board and a change of horses. There was a even a leather and blacksmith shop. In 1890 it burned and a

Victorian home was built by Frank Wheeler, developer of rust-free asparagus. Since that time the

home has always remained in the family. A veranda overlooks an extensive lawn and Sudbury River. The area is popular for bird-watching and cross-country skiing. Inside, the inn is tastefully decorated with antiques accentuated with five working fireplaces and several inviting window seats.

**Rates: $50-$60. Season: All year.
Innkeeper(s): David & Charlotte Anderson.
5 Rooms. 1 Private Baths. 2 Shared Baths. Conference Room. Guest phone available. Children. TV available. Smoking OK. Credit Cards: Visa, MC. Beds: KDT. Meals: Continental plus.

"The five nights spent with you were the most comfortable and most congenial of the whole cross-country trip. We'll be back."

"This visit has been absolutely splendid. Your personal warmth should insure success."

"We enjoyed every moment of our visit."

Hawthorne Inn
462 Lexington Rd
Concord MA 01742
(617) 369-5610

Circa 1870. The Hawthorne Inn is situated on land that once belonged to Ralph Waldo Emerson, the Alcotts and Nathaniel Hawthorne. It was here Bronson Alcott planted his fruit trees, made pathways to the Mill Brook and erected his Bath House. On the field the Alcott family tended their crops of vegetables and herbs. Hawthorne purchased the land and repaired a path leading to his home with trees planted on either side. Two of these trees yet stand. Directly across the road is Hawthorne's House, the Wayside. Next door to it is the Alcott's Orchard House. On the other side is Grapevine Cottage where the concord grape was developed. Nearby is the Old North Bridge where the "shot heard round the world" was fired. Also close is Walden Pond and Sleepy Hollow Cemetery where Emerson, the Alcotts, the Thoreaus and Hawthorne were laid to rest. The inn is filled with original art and handsome antiques, wood floors and books of poetry.

**Rates: $90-$125.
Innkeeper(s): G. Burch & Marilyn Mudry. Meals: Continental plus breakfast.

Dennis

Four Chimneys Inn
946 Main St, Rt 6A
Dennis MA 02638
(617) 385-6317

Circa 1881. This spacious Victorian stands across from Lake Scargo, which legend says was created at the command of an Indian chief whose daughter needed a larger fishbowl for her goldfish. The village maidens dug the lake with clam shells and all the fish happily multiplied. The inn has eight-foot-high windows, high ceilings, a cozy library and parlor, and a gracious summer porch from which to view the "fishbowl".

Location: Centrally located on Cape Cod, directly across from Scargo Lake.
Rates: $35-$62. Season: March to December.
Innkeeper(s): Christina Jervant & Diane Robinson.
9 Rooms. 7 Private Baths. 1 Shared Baths. Conference Room. Guest phone available. Children 10 & up. TV available. Smoking OK. Beds: QDT. Meals: Continental breakfast.

Isaiah B. Hall House
152 Whig St
Dennis MA 02638
(617) 385-9928

Circa 1857. Right next to the Cape's oldest cranberry bog is this Greek Revival farmhouse built by Isaiah Hall, a barrel maker (cooper) and builder. Isaiah

designed and patented the original barrel invented for shipping cranberries. In 1948, Dorothy Ripp, an artist, established the inn. Many pieces of her work remain at the inn.

Location: North Shore (Bayside) of Cape Cod.
**Rates: $42-$65. Season: All year.
Innkeeper(s): Marie & Dick Brophy.

11 Rooms. 10 Private Baths. 1 Shared Baths. Conference Room. Guest phone available. Children 8 & up. TV available. Smoking OK. Credit Cards: Visa, MC, AE. Beds: QD. Meals: B&B.

East Orleans

Parsonage
202 Main St, PO Box 1016
East Orleans MA 02643
(617) 255-8217

Circa 1770. On a street filled with old sea captains' homes, the Parsonage is a Cape home, complete with ancient wavy glass in the windows and antique furnishings throughout. Main Street, the road to Nauset Beach, is lined with lovely old homes of sea captains and other early settlers. Breakfast is served in the courtyard or in your room.

Location: Halfway between Hyannis & Provincetown on the Cape.
Rates: $40-$60.
Innkeeper(s): Chris & Lloyd Shand.

Ships Knees Inn
Beach Rd
East Orleans MA 02643
(617) 255-1312

Circa 1817. Guests enjoy a unique lodging experience in this 190-year-old restored sea captain's house. This New England inn is located just a short

walk to the ocean and Nauset Beach. Guest rooms have beamed ceilings and feature four-poster beds piled with quilts. The rooms are appointed with a special colonial color scheme. A few of the accommodations overlook Orleans Cove.

Location: One and a half hours from Boston.
Rates: $38-$80. Season: All year.
Innkeeper(s): Carol & Dick Hurlburt.

22 Rooms. 9 Private Baths. 13 Shared Baths. Swimming Pool. Guest phone available. Children. TV in room. Smoking OK. Beds: KQDTC. Meals: Continental breakfast.

"Enjoyed the short stroll to the ocean. Beautiful grounds, peaceful environment."

"Warm, homey and very friendly atmosphere. a very unique inn with authentic antiques. Very impressed with the beamed ceilings in some of the rooms."

East Sandwich

Wingscorton Farm Inn
11 Wing Blvd
East Sandwich MA 02537
(617) 888-0534

Circa 1757. Wingscorton is a working farm on seven green acres of lawns, gardens and orchards that adjoin a short walk to a private ocean beach. The cen-

turies-old Cape Cod manse is a historical landmark on what was once known as the King's Highway, the oldest historical district in the United States. All the rooms have working fireplaces, fully restored antique furnishings and private baths. A private carriage house makes for a special retreat for couples and newlyweds. Breakfast features fresh produce with eggs, meats and vegetables from the farm's livestock and gardens.

Location: Cape Cod.
**Rates: $95-$125. Season: All year.
Innkeeper(s): Dick Loring & Sheila Weyers.
Guest phone available. Children. TV in room. Smoking OK. Credit Cards: Visa, MC. Beds: QTC. Meals: Full farm breakfast. B&B, MAP.

Edgartown

Charlotte Inn
South Summer St
Edgartown MA 02539
(617) 627-4751

Circa 1860. A widow's walk sits atop this white clapboard sea captain's house. Inside the inn are a restaurant, unusual gift shop, and the Edgartown Art

Gallery. Traditional early American antiques, down comforters, and four poster beds add to the romance and elegance of this beautiful Martha's Vineyard inn.

Rates: $32-$195. Season: All year.
Innkeeper(s): Gery & Paula Conover.
24 Rooms. 22 Private Baths. Guest phone available. Smoking OK.
Meals: Full breakfast.

Dr. Shiverick House
Pent Lane, PO Box 640
Edgartown MA 02539
(617) 627-8497

Circa 1840. You could have knocked on any door in town in 1855 and have been given swift directions to Dr. Shiverick's house. In the attic, away from his patients, the doctor kept two skeletons, hanging side-by-side, and his surgical paraphernalia. Over the years the house was continually added onto, rotated, or restyled. The white picket fences, daintily manicured gardens, and spreading linden trees are just what the doctor ordered.

Rates: $65-$300. Season: All year.
Innkeeper(s): Tina Mclaughlin-Ramsdell.
10 Rooms. 10 Private Baths. Guest phone available. Children. TV available. Smoking OK. Credit Cards: MC, AE. Beds: QTC. Meals: Continental breakfast.
"Incredible breakfast, much more than continental!"
"Warm and wonderful."

Edgartown Inn
56 N Water
Edgartown MA 02539
(617) 627-4794

Circa 1798. The Edgartown Inn was originally built as a home for whaling Captain Worth. (Fort Worth, Texas, was later named for his son.) The house was converted to an inn around 1820 when Daniel Webster was a guest. Later, Nathaniel Hawthorne

> **D**uring the Edgartown Inn's long and distinguised career as one of the fine colonial inns of the New England coast, it has played host to many notable guests. At the height of his career, Daniel Webster was denied admittance because he was dark-skinned and thought to be an Indian, but later returned as a guest. The inn owner admonished his children not to "sop the platter" in Webster's presence, that is, not to dip their bread into the gravy. But to the delight of the children, Webster himself "sopped the platter". This earthy gesture prompted the children to follow suit, and put everyone at ease in his company.

stayed here and proposed to the innkeeper's daughter Eliza Gibbs (who turned him down). Fully restored, it hosted John Kennedy.

Location: Town center, one block from the harbor.
Rates: $42-$120. Season: April 1 to November 1.
Innkeeper(s): Suzanne.
21 Rooms. 13 Private Baths. 8 Shared Baths. Guest phone available. Children 6 & up. TV available. Smoking OK. Beds: KQT.
Meals: Full country breakfast.

The Arbor
222 Upper Main St
Edgartown MA 02539
(617) 627-8137

Circa 1890. This turn-of-the-century guest house is on the bicycle path in historic Edgartown. The house is walking distance from downtown and the harbor. Guests may relax in the hammock, have tea on the porch or walk the unspoiled island beaches of Martha's Vineyard.

Location: Seven miles east of ferry landing at Woods Hole on Martha's Vineyard.
**Rates: $45-$90.
Innkeeper(s): Peggy Hall.
6 Rooms. 4 Private Baths. 2 Shared Baths. Guest phone available. Children 12 & up. Smoking OK. Credit Cards: Visa, MC. Beds: QDT. Meals: Continental breakfast.

Victorian Inn
South Water St, PO Box 947
Edgartown MA 02539
(617) 627-4784

Circa 1890. The Victorian Inn is situated on a street where many sea captains built their mansions here on the Island of Martha's Vineyard. Most of the guest rooms open onto a balcony overlooking the harbor or the inn's English Garden, where a full gourmet breakfast is served in sunny weather.

Location: One block from the harbor across from the famous Pagoda Tree.
**Rates: $85-$165.
Innkeeper(s): Lewis & Arlene Kiester.

Fairhaven

Edgewater Bed & Breakfast
2 Oxford St
Fairhaven MA 02719
(617) 997-5512

Circa 1760. On the historic Moby Dick Trail, Edgewater overlooks the harbor from the grassy slopes of Poverty Point. The inn is a recently restored home of the charming and rambling, eclectic-style of the area. Across the harbor in New Bedford, is Herman Melville's "dearest place in all New England" where visitors immerse themselves in the history and lore of whaling. Near the inn is the Gothic Revival-style Unitarian Church with stained glass by Tiffany.

Location: On the water overlooking historic New Bedford Harbor.
Rates: $30-$65.
Innkeeper(s): Kathy Reed. Meals: Continental breakfast.

Fall River

Simeon's Mansion House
See: Seekonk, MA.

Falmouth

Captain Tom Lawrence House
75 Locust St
Falmouth MA 02540
(617) 540-1445

Circa 1861. Tom Lawrence was a captain of a whaling crew and retired here to Falmouth, building his home that today offers hospitality as an inn. Freshly ground grain is used much as it was in the 1800s with blueberry pancakes now a frequent specialty of the inn. The beach is half a mile away.

Location: Historic district of Falmouth.
Rates: $45-$69.
Innkeeper(s): Barbara Sabo-Feller.

Mostly Hall
27 Main St
Falmouth MA 02540
(617) 548-3786

Circa 1849. Mostly Hall was built as Falmouth's first summer home by a Yankee sea captain for his New Orleans bride. It features a wraparound porch, thirteen-foot ceilings and a widow's walk. It is built in the southern plantation style.

Location: Across from the historic village green.
Rates: $60-$85. Season: All but two weeks in January & February.
Innkeeper(s): Caroline & Jim Lloyd.
6 Rooms. 6 Private Baths. Conference Room. Guest phone available. Children 16 & up. TV available. Beds: Q. Meals: Full breakfast.

"Of all the inns we stayed at during our trip, we enjoyed Mostly Hall the most....Imagine, southern hospitality on Cape Cod!!"

Palmer House Inn
81 Palmer Ave
Falmouth MA 02540
(617) 548-1230

Circa 1901. It's just a short walk to the village com-

mon from this turn-of-the-century Victorian. The original stained glass windows and the rich woodwork are all typical of the gracious homes in the historic district of Falmouth.

Location: Cape Cod.
Rates: $80-$90. Season: All year.
Innkeeper(s): Phyllis Niemi & Bud Peacock.
8 Rooms. 8 Private Baths. Guest phone available. TV available. Smoking OK. Credit Cards: Visa, MC. Beds: DT. Meals: Full gourmet breakfast.

"Exactly what a New England inn should be!"

"The meals were fantastic, I hope I can do justice to the recipes at home."

"Two of the nicest and caring people we've met on the Cape. The Palmer House is lovely."

Wyndemere House at Suppewissett
718 Palmer Ave
Falmouth MA 02193
(617) 540-7069

Circa 1797. In 1797 Lord Wyndemere left Sussex, England under mysterious circumstances relating to his wife's death and disappearance. He built this

Paul-Revere style colonial home and became known for his reclusive lifestyle and his many political and civil liberties writings. After additions and renovations, it has become a country inn full of amenities and adventures. Try one of the frequent English mystery weekends.

Location: One block from exit 5 South Rt 28.
**Rates: $75-$95. Season: May to October.
Innkeeper(s): Carole Railsback.
6 Rooms. 4 Private Baths. 2 Shared Baths. Guest phone available. Children 12 & up. TV available. Smoking OK. Beds: KQTC. Meals: Full breakfast.

Great Barrington

Bread and Roses
Star Rt 65, PO Box 50
Great Barrington MA 01230
(413) 528-1099

Circa 1810. According to legend, this farmhouse was built by the Indians early in the last century. Over the years many additions have been completed giving the inn a rambling shape.

Rates: Call.
Innkeeper(s): Elliot & Julie Lowell.

Seekonk Pines Inn
142 Seekonk Cross Rd
Great Barrington MA 01230
(413) 528-4192

Circa 1832. Known as the Crippen Farm from 1835-1879, Seekonk Pines Inn now includes both the

original farmhouse and a Dutch Colonial wing. Through the years many of the owners of the house were wealthy and made major alterations to the original New England frame house. Green lawns, gardens and meadows surround the inn. The name *Seekonk* was the local Indian name for the Canadian geese which migrate through this part of the Berkshires.

Location: Berkshire Hills corner of Rt 23 & Seekonk Cross Rd.
Rates: $50-$80. Season: All year.
Innkeeper(s): Linda & Chris Best.
7 Rooms. 2 Private Baths. 2 Shared Baths. Swimming Pool. Conference Room. Guest phone available. Children. TV available. Beds: QTC. Meals: Full breakfast.

"Sharing your home has enriched my life and etched many lovely memories to draw on."

Harwich Port

Captain's Quarters
85 Bank St
Harwich Port MA 02646
(617) 432-0337, (800) 992-6550 (Outside the state).

Circa 1850. This Victorian home features a classic wraparound porch, nostalgic gingerbread trim, an

authentic turret room and a graceful curving front stairway. It lies on an acre of sunny lawns, broad shade trees and colorful gardens. The inn is a five-minute walk to sandy Bank Street Beach and is close to town.

Location: Lovely residential area, 3/10 mile from Nantucket Sound.
**Rates: $50-$75. Season: April to October.
Innkeeper(s): The Van Gelder family.
6 Rooms. 6 Private Baths. Swimming Pool. Guest phone available. Children 12 & up. TV available. Smoking OK. Credit Cards: Visa, MC, AE. Beds: Q. Meals: Continental plus buffet breakfast.

"Perfect place to get away from it all."

"We enjoy the warm hospitality every summer and fall."

"Accommodations are very comfortable and attractive - this is our favorite inn!"

Hyannis

Honeysuckle Hill
See: West Barnstable, MA.

Liberty Hill Inn
See: Yarmouth Port, MA.

Hyannisport

Copper Beech Inn
See: Centerville, MA.

Lenox

Apple Tree Inn
224 West St
Lenox MA 01240
(413) 637-1477
Circa 1885. Situated on twenty-two panoramic hilltop acres, this completely refurbished 100-year-old

inn is across from the Tanglewood Music Festival. A 400-variety rose garden is a favorite spot. Inside is an oak-beamed and paneled tavern and a circular dining

room with excellent cuisine. The guest rooms in the main house upstairs are the most romantic, with fireplaces, views and skylights. A clay tennis court and a large pool are on the grounds.

Location: Western Massachusetts.
**Rates: $45-$240. Season: Closed March & April.
Innkeeper(s): Greg & Aurora Smith.
33 Rooms. 27 Private Baths. 6 Shared Baths. Swimming Pool. Conference Room. Guest phone available. Children 12 & up. TV in room. Smoking OK. Credit Cards: All. Beds: KQT. Meals: Continental breakfast. Restaurant.

"The greatest warmth I have experienced in New England, Old England, or anywhere else."

"The best place in the world for a honeymoon."

"Nicest staff, host and hostess we have ever met."

Candlelight Inn
53 Walker St
Lenox MA 01240
(413) 637-1555
Circa 1885. The Candlelight Inn is on the main corner in historic Lenox, near all the Berkshire's outstanding cultural events. Five ski areas are nearby.

There are four separate dining rooms, all elegantly appointed. A fabulous cozy bar and lounge provides entertainment. In the winter, romantic fireside dining is popular but any time is right for the superb cuisine of Chef Heller.

Rates: $50-$150. Season: All year.
Innkeeper(s): Robert Artig & Marsha Heller (chef).
8 Rooms. 8 Private Baths. Guest phone available. TV available. Smoking OK. Credit Cards: All. Beds: KQT. Meals: EP, continental breakfast.

"...culinary genius" June 1982, Gourmet Magazine.

"The most romantic inn we've ever seen."

"A wonderful inn and beautiful people working there."

"Dinner and the room were perfect in every way."

East Country Berry Farm

830 East St
Lenox MA 01240
(413) 442-2057

Circa 1798. Around the time of the French and Indian War a land grant was given to the widow and children of Captain Stevens. Now, two historic restored farmhouses on twenty-three acres of lawn, fields, trees and wildflowers are open for bed and breakfast.

Location: Berkshire Mountains, Western Massachusetts.
Rates: $40-$95.
Innkeeper(s): Rita Fribush Miller.

Rookwood Inn

19 Stockbridge Rd
Lenox MA 02140
(413) 637-9750

Circa 1830. Within easy walking distance to Tanglewood, home of the Boston Symphony Orchestra, Rookwood is a Victorian inn that was once the town tavern. It was moved to its present site and rebuilt as a Victorian cottage at the turn of the century.

Location: One block from the town center.
Rates: $44-$125. Season: All year.
Innkeeper(s): Tom & Betsy Sherman.
17 Rooms. 17 Private Baths. Children. TV available. Handicap access provided. Beds: QDTC. Meals: Full breakfast.

The Gables Inn

103 Walker St, Rt 183
Lenox MA 01240
(413) 637-3416

Circa 1885. At one time this was the home of Pulitzer Prize-winning novelist, Edith Jones Wharton. This Queen Anne-style Berkshire cottage features a handsome eight-sided library and Mrs. Wharton's own four-poster bed. The inn has an unusual indoor swimming pool with jacuzzi and tennis courts, and a popular gourmet restaurant.

Location: One mile to Tanglewood.
Rates: $65-$125. Season: All year.
Innkeeper(s): Mary & Frank Newton.
13 Rooms. 13 Private Baths. Hot Tub. Swimming Pool. Conference Room. Guest phone available. Children 12 & up. Smoking OK. Credit Cards: Visa, MC. Beds: QT. Meals: Continental plus breakfast, restaurant.

Underledge Inn

76 Cliffwood St
Lenox MA 01240
(413) 637-0236

Circa 1876. A drive along Cliffwood Street under the archway of greenery and then up Underledge's

winding drive takes you to a peaceful setting looking out to the serene Berkshire Hills. The inn sits resplendently atop four acres and gives almost every room a sunset view. (It was at one time the summer home of two wealthy sisters.) In the foyer is an exquisite oak staircase and a floor-to-ceiling oak fireplace. A unique solarium provides a special atmosphere for breakfast. Just down the street are elegant boutiques, quaint shops and fine restaurants.

Rates: $60-$125. Season: All year.
Innkeeper(s): Marcie & Cheryl Lanoue.
10 Rooms. 10 Private Baths. Guest phone available. Children 10 & up. TV available. Smoking OK. Credit Cards: Visa, AE. Beds: KQ. Meals: B&B.

"Your homemade breakfasts with the sound of classical music in the background start the morning off in a happy mood. After our day's outing it was a joy to come back to your porch overlooking the large lawn and the tranquillity of the rooms."

Whistler's Inn

5 Greenwood St
Lenox MA 01240
(413) 637 0975

Circa 1820. Whistler's Inn is an English Tudor-style home surrounded by eight acres of woodland and gardens. Inside, elegance is abundant in the impressive Louis XVI music room with its Steinway piano, chandeliers, and gilt palace furniture. There is an English library with chintz covered sofas. Here guests are served sherry and tea. A baronial dining room features a Baroque candelabrum.

Location: Across the street from the famous "Church on the Hill".
Rates: $65-$165.
Innkeeper(s): Joan & Richard Mears.

Lowell

Sherman-Berry House
163 Dartmouth St
Lowell MA 01851
(617) 459-4760
  Circa 1893.

Location: I-495 & Rt 3, 24 miles northwest of Boston.
**Rates: $40-$45.
Innkeeper(s): Susan Scott & David Strohmeyer.

Marblehead

Spray Cliff on the Ocean
251 Spray Ave
Marblehead MA 01945
(617) 631-6789
  Circa 1910. Panoramic views stretch out in grand
proportions from this old English Tudor mansion set
high above the Atlantic. The inn provides a spacious
and elegant atmosphere inside. Outside the inn, a
brick terrace is surrounded by lush flower gardens
where eider ducks, black cormorants and sea gulls
abound.

Location: Oceanfront, 15 minutes to Boston.
**Rates: $85. Season: All year.
Innkeeper(s): Richard & Diane Pabich.
5 Rooms. 5 Private Baths. Guest phone available. Children 12 &
up. Smoking OK. Credit Cards: Visa, MC, AE, DC, CB. Beds:
QTK. Meals: B&B.

Martha's Vineyard

Nashua House
See: Oak Bluffs, MA.

Thorncroft Inn
See: Vineyard Haven, MA.

Nantucket Island

Corner House
49 Centre St
Nantucket Island MA 02554
(617) 228-1530
  Circa 1723. An especially charming and attractive
eighteenth-century inn, the Corner House has been

brought very gently into the twentieth century.
Original architectural details such as old pine floors,

original paneling and fireplaces remain. The screened
porch overlooks an English perennial garden where
guests often take afternoon tea. More than 400 buildings are in the historic district. The main street of
town was laid out in 1697 and paved in 1837 with cobblestones from Gloucester.

Location: Five-minute walk to the ferry, shops, museums, res-
taurants and galleries. No car necessary.
Rates: $75-$110. Season: April to January 4th.
Innkeeper(s): Sandy & John Knox-Johnston.
12 Rooms. 12 Private Baths. Children 8 & up. Smoking OK. Credit
Cards: Visa, MC. Beds: KQT. Meals: Continental-plus breakfast.
  *"Thanks for taking wonderful care of us. We expected
Corner House to be charming from all we had read, but
in addition you two and your staff are extraordinary.
You do everything just right for guests comfort and en-
joyment."*
  *"You have a delightfully quaint home and we had a
grand time examining your antique pieces of furniture.
We enjoyed your breakfast and your afternoon tea."*
  *"Thank you for making our honeymoon a memorable
time! Everything about our Nantucket vacation was per-
fect after we moved to the Corner House."*
  *"Your house is inviting and comfortable and your
Corner House Muffins the best ever! I hope Gourmet
does it justice and that their stay went smoothly."*

Four Chimneys
38 Orange St
Nantucket Island MA 02554
(617) 228-1912
  Circa 1835. The Four Chimneys is situated on famed
Orange Street where 126 sea captains built their mansions. Captain Frederick Gardner built this Greek

Revival house, one of the largest on Nantucket Island. The "Publick Room" is a double parlor with twin

fireplaces. Outdoors there are porches across three levels of the house which provide views of the harbor and beyond.

Location: A short walk from cobblestoned Main Street.
Rates: $90-$115. Season: April to December.
Innkeeper(s): Betty York.
10 Rooms. 10 Private Baths. Conference Room. Guest phone available. TV available. Smoking OK. Credit Cards: Visa, MC, AE, DC, CB. Beds: Q. Meals: B&B.

The Woodbox
29 Earl St
Nantucket MA 02554
(617) 228-0587
Circa 1709. Captain Bunker built this home and followed it with an adjoining house two years later. Eventually the houses were made into one by cutting into

the sides of both. As Nantucket's oldest inn, the Woodbox also provides a dining room with low-

beamed ceilings, pine-paneled walls and Early American atmosphere.

Rates: $90-$140.
Innkeeper(s): Dexter Tutein.
9 Rooms. 9 Private Baths. Children. Handicap access provided. Smoking OK. Beds: DTK.
"The best place to stay on Nantucket!"
"One of the best breakfasts on the island."

New Bedford

Edgewater Bed & Breakfast
See: Fairhaven, MA.

Oak Bluffs

Nashua House
30 Kennebec Ave
Oak Bluffs MA 02557
(617) 693-0043
Circa 1873. Methodist Camp Grounds first occupied Oak Bluffs as a religious retreat starting in 1835. After the Civil War the area from the Camp Grounds to the ocean was developed according to a design that provided "curving ways around open spaces that lent themselves to a meandering stroll, casual encounters between neighbors, a sense of grace, ease, leisure and appreciation of natural beauty abetted by intentional charm." The Nashua House is an original Victorian guest house remaining from Copeland's overall design. Its century-old rooms and shared baths harken back to simpler times.

Location: Martha's Vineyard Island.
Rates: $29-$55.
Innkeeper(s): Harry & Son.

Petersham

Winterwood at Petersham
North Main St
Petersham MA 01366
(617) 724-8885
Circa 1842. The town of Petersham is sometimes called a museum of Greek Revival-style architecture. One of the grand homes facing the town common is Winterwood. Originally a summer home it boasts fireplaces in almost every room and the two-room suite even has twin fireplaces. Private dining is available for small groups.

Location: Central Massachusetts.
Rates: $60-$85. Season: All year.

Innkeeper(s): Jean & Robert Day.
5 Rooms. 5 Private Baths. Conference Room. Guest phone available. Children. Smoking OK. Credit Cards: Visa, MC. Beds: TD. Meals: Continental plus breakfast.

"Between your physical facilities and Jean's cooking, our return to normal has been made even more difficult. Your hospitality was just a fantastic extra to our total experience."

"We were enchanted with the inn and were treated like honored guests by all the staff."

"A truly splendid job."

Provincetown

Land's End Inn
22 Commercial St
Provincetown MA 02657
(617) 487-0706

Circa 1908. Built as a shingle-style summer cottage for Charles Higgins, a Boston merchant, Land's End stands high on a hill overlooking Provincetown and all of Cape Cod Bay. Part of the Higgins' collection of oriental wood carvings and stained glass is housed at the inn. Furnished lavishly in Victorian style the inn offers a comforting atmosphere for relaxation and beauty.

Rates: $52-$88. Season: All year.
Innkeeper(s): David Schoolman.
15 Rooms. 10 Private Baths. 4 Shared Baths. Guest phone available. Children 9 & up and infants. Smoking OK. Beds: D. Meals: B&B.

Somerset House
378 Commercial St
Provincetown MA 02657
(617) 487-0383

Circa 1850. Just a few yards from the beach, Somerset House has large guest rooms filled with both Victorian and modern furnishings. It was built by a ship chandler and then sold to Dr. Birge and his wife, both medical doctors. After housing several families of doctors, it became a guest house in 1928. Now a historic seashore inn, Somerset House can be easily identified by its profusely planted front garden. The inn is near the heart of town and convenient to restaurants and the Provincetown Playhouse.

Location: Village Center.
Rates: $36-$65.
Innkeeper(s): Jon Gerrity.

Rockport

Inn on Cove Hill
37 Mt Pleasant St
Rockport MA 01966
(617) 546-2701

Circa 1791. This 200-year-old Classic Federal home was built from the proceeds of pirates' gold found at Gully Point. The fine colonial is graced with the irreplaceable workmanship of the day. A beautifully-crafted spiral staircase, random-width pumpkin pine floors, and hand-forged hinges display the artisan's handiwork. A picket fence and granite walkway invite guests to experience one of the truly historical inns of Rockport.

Location: Rt 127 A, 1 block from town center.
Rates: $35-$70. Season: April to October.
Innkeeper(s): John & Marjorie Pratt.
11 Rooms. 9 Private Baths. 2 Shared Baths. Guest phone available. TV in room. Smoking OK. Beds: QT. Meals: Continental breakfast.

Old Farm Inn
291 Granite St
Rockport MA 01966
(617) 546-3237

Circa 1799. One of the earliest saltwater towns on Cape Ann. The red farmhouse is representative of the simple country-farm style of the period. The rustic beams, paneling, wide-pine flooring and six fireplaces are original. The initials of James, grandson of the earliest owner of the property, can be found chiseled on the old granite gatepost along with the date, 1799. A novel *The Yankee Bodleys* by Naomi Babson is based on the lives of the people who actually lived on the farm in the 1830s.

Location: At Halibut Point in Rockport on Cape Ann.
Rates: $53-$75. Season: April to December.
Innkeeper(s): The Balzarinin family.
7 Rooms. 5 Private Baths. 2 Shared Baths. Guest phone available. Children. TV available. Smoking OK. Beds: KQTC. Meals: Continental-plus breakfast.

Salem

Coach House Inn
284 Lafayette St
Salem MA 01970
(617) 744-4092

Circa 1879. Decorated with an elegant charm, this European-type inn is warmed by many Victorian fireplaces. The Coach House operates with a European plan providing coffee and tea in the morning.

Location: On Rt 1A & 114 in the historic district.
Rates: $50-$68.
Innkeeper(s): Patricia Kessler.

Salem Inn
7 Summer St
Salem MA 01970
(617) 741-0680

Circa 1834. Captain Nathaniel West, first owner of this historical building, believed that his home should be maintained in readiness for him after returning to shore at his journey's end. Today that same philosophy is practiced for guests of the Salem Inn.

Location: Historic downtown.
**Rates: $69-$90. Season: All year.
Innkeeper(s): Richard & Diane Pabich.
23 Rooms. 23 Private Baths. Guest phone available. Children. TV available. Smoking OK. Credit Cards: All. Beds: KQT. Meals: B&B.

Sandisfield

New Boston Inn
Jct Rt 8 & 57
Sandisfield MA 01255-0120
(413) 258-4477

Circa 1737. In the taproom, adjacent to the dining room of the Berkshire's oldest inn, are oak boards twenty-two inches wide called "king's wood" because colonists illegally kept it from the King of England's saw mills. A comprehensive renovation from 1985-1987 has kept all the building's eccentricities intact, such as the 20' x 40' ballroom with its barrel-vaulted

ceiling and double fireplaces. It is said an Irish ghost, a young girl dressed in black wedding attire, roams the inn. (Brides wore black back then.)

Location: Berkshire County, on CT line, four towns in from the NY line.
Rates: $85-$110. Season: All year.
Innkeeper(s): Ann & Bill McCarthy.
6 Rooms. 6 Private Baths. Conference Room. Guest phone available. Children. TV available. Credit Cards: Visa, MC, AE. Beds: QTK. Meals: B&B.

Sandwich

Captain Ezra Nye House
152 Main St
Sandwich MA 02563
(617) 888-6142

Circa 1829. Captain Ezra Nye built his first home in 1826, but coming home from the sea where the sky was his ceiling, he found his first home far too confining. Therefore, he built this much larger Federal style home across the street. The inn is within walking distance to the Doll & Glass Museum, the famous Heritage Plantation, the Scenic Railroad, and the Dexter Grist Mill. There are hand-stenciled walls, museum-quality antiques, and art - all in the heart of the village.

**Rates: $40-$65. Season: All year.
Innkeeper(s): Elaine & Harry Dickson.
6 Rooms. 4 Private Baths. 1 Shared Baths. Conference Room. Guest phone available. Children 6 & up. TV available. Smoking OK. Credit Cards: Visa, MC. Beds: DT. Meals: Continental breakfast.

Seekonk

Simeon's Mansion House
940 County St
Seekonk MA 02771
(617) 336-6674

Circa 1798. Simeon, an officer in the Revolutionary War and later a wealthy merchant, then Lt. Governor of Rhode Island, built this Federal home in a style that was typical of the great houses of Newport and Providence, R.I. nearby. The home is on a nine-acre knoll overlooking the pastoral fields and banks of the Palmer River. Guests are invited to tend the farm animals at the barn, gather eggs or take to the road on a bicycle to see the ancient mill ruins and waterfall. Breakfast is served in the kitchen where the massive cooking fireplace is still used in season. The inn is in the National Register due to Simeon's illustrious war record and the architectural importance of the house.

Location: East of Junction 114A & County St.
**Rates: $60. Season: All year.
Innkeeper(s): Daniel & Linda Horton.
3 Rooms. 1 Shared Baths. Guest phone available. Children. TV available. Smoking limited. Beds: DC. Meals: Full breakfast.

"Great weekend! New experiences, very enjoyable stay. Though short, good memories last forever."

Sheffield

Colonel Ashley Inn
Bow Wow Road, RR 1, PO Box 142
Sheffield MA 01257
(413) 229-2929

Circa 1814. Colonel John Ashley, founder of Sheffield, wrote a declaration of independence in 1774. His slave Mum Beth overheard the declaration and

proceeded to sue for her own independence. She was the first slave in America to win freedom through the courts. Col. Ashley was also noted for putting down the Battle of Shay's Rebellion. The innkeeper is a

direct descendant of Colonel Ashley, and presides graciously over the center-chimney colonial farmhouse, now an enchanting inn.

Location: Picturesque setting at the intersection of two rural roads.
Rates: $70-$85. Season: Closed during March & April (mud season).
Innkeeper(s): Nancy & Gery Turborg.
4 Rooms. 4 Private Baths. Swimming Pool. Guest phone available. Children 9 & up. TV available. Smoking OK. Beds: QT. Meals: B&B.

"Hospitality doesn't begin to describe what goes on here."

Staveleigh House
Rt 7, PO Box 608
Sheffield MA 01257
(413) 229-2129

Circa 1821. Next to the town green, under the shade of century-old trees is a choice retreat with a cheerful dining room, five attractive guest rooms and a library where afternoon tea is served.

Rates: $60-$75.
Innkeeper(s): Marion Whitman.

South Sudbury

Longfellow's Wayside Inn
Wayside Inn Rd
South Sudbury MA 01776
(617) 443-8846

Circa 1702. The first known license for a hotel or tavern was obtained here in 1716. Henry Ford endowed the non-profit corporation that manages the Wayside Inn in 1944 to preserve it as a historical and literary shrine. The inn's second owner is known to have led the colonists of Sudbury on the march to Concord on April 19, 1775 toward the Old North Bridge. Originally opened as How's Tavern in 1702, it later became the Red Horse Tavern and finally in 1897 a new owner, acknowledging the popular association with Longfellow's Poem, *Tales of a Wayside Inn* named it Longfellow's Wayside Inn. The Old Barroom, Longfellow's Parlor, the piano forte and grandfather clock are all here. A reproduction 18-century Grist Mill, the Redstone Schoolhouse, the Martha-Mary Chapel and many of the inn's original antiques are all on the property. Allow six to twelve months ahead for reservations. The inn is open for touring and dining.

Location: Forty-five minutes from Boston, 20 minutes from the Old North Bridge in Concord.
Rates: $52.50. Season: All year.

10 Rooms. 10 Private Baths. Conference Room. Children. Smoking OK. Credit Cards: All major. Beds: TD. Meals: EP.

Sturbridge

Commonwealth Inn
11 Summit Ave
Sturbridge MA 01518
(617) 347-7603
  Circa 1890.

Location: One mile from Old Sturbridge Village.
**Rates: $35-$50.
Innkeeper(s): Kevin MacConnell.

Publick House Historic Inn
On the Common
Sturbridge MA 01566
(617) 347-3313
  Circa 1771. Colonel Ebenezer Crafts, the original innkeeper, is known for having recruited Sturbridge's Revolutionary militia at his own expense. He drilled

the cavalry on the common and rewarded them afterwards with his hearty Yankee cooking. The inn still uses 1771 recipes for lobster pie and breakfast muffins.

**Rates: $70-$125.
Innkeeper(s): Buddy Adler.

  "Excellent - worth a trip from anywhere."
  "A trip back in time to the Colonial Days."
  "Friendliness among staff members - overwhelming - see you next year!"
  "It is wonderful to have a place where time can stand still for an evening and link us to those special roots we have in our country."

Vineyard Haven

Thorncroft Inn
278 Main St, PO Box 1022
Vineyard Haven MA 02568
(617) 693-3333
  Circa 1918. The Thorncroft Estate is a classic craftsman bungalow with a dominant roof and neo-colonial details. It was built by Chicago grain mer-

chant John Herbert Ware. Now, with the renovation work completed, guests can experience an authentic turn-of-the-century ambience with canopied beds, walnut Victorian suites, and balconies - all situated on three and one-half acres.

Location: Martha's Vineyard, one mile from the ferry.
**Rates: $55-$110. Season: All year.
12 Rooms. 12 Private Baths. Guest phone available. Children. TV available. Smoking OK. Credit Cards: Visa, MC, AE. Beds: QT. Meals: Full breakfast.

West Barnstable

Honeysuckle Hill
591 Main St
West Barnstable MA 02668
(617) 362-8418
  Circa 1825. A part of the Old King's Highway Historic District and in the National Register of Historic Places is this Queen Anne Victorian built by Josiah Goodspeed. The inn features many antiques. All of the guest rooms have cozy featherbeds and tins of homemade cookies at bedside.

Location: Cape Cod.
**Rates: $80-$95. Season: All year.
Innkeeper(s): Barbara & Bob Rosenthal.
3 Rooms. 3 Private Baths. Conference Room. Guest phone available. Children 12 & up. TV available. Smoking OK. Credit Cards: Visa, MC, AE. Beds: KQ. Meals: Full breakfast.

"Your warm hospitality and cozy accommodations were the highlight of our trip. I refer anyone who is heading for New England on to you."

West Newton

Withington House
274 Otis St
West Newton MA 02165
(617) 332-8422

Circa 1830. This private homestay is on one acre in the West Newton Hill Historic District and was at one time the home of Increase Sumner Withington. Decorated with antiques, the twenty-two-room Italinate house has a Georgian-style porch and seven fireplaces. A special collection of antique cribs add to the decor. The airport and many of Boston's colleges are nearby. The owners will sometimes entertain guests at their private club. A small poodle is in residence.

Location: Greater Boston.
**Rates: $45. Season: All year.
Innkeeper(s): Marise Tracey Zellmann.
2 Rooms. Guest phone available. TV available. Beds: DT. Meals: Full American breakfast.

Woods Hole

Grey Whale Inn
565 Woods Hole Rd
Woods Hole MA 02543
(617) 548-7692
Circa 1804.

Location: Overlooking Vineyard Sound on Cape Cod.
Rates: $69-$95.
Innkeeper(s): Bill & Joy Norris.

Yarmouth Port

Liberty Hill Inn
77 Main St
Yarmouth Port MA 02675
(617) 362-3976

Circa 1825. Situated on the site of the original Liberty Pole dating from Revolutionary times, Liberty Hill Inn is an 1825 Greek Revival mansion furnished with

Early American antiques. Its setting on the hill affords views of Cape Cod Bay and the magnificent English gardens at the inn. On historic Old King's Highway, it's just a brief walk to antique shops, auctions and restaurants.

Location: Cape Cod.
Rates: $55-$75. Season: All year.
Innkeeper(s): Beth & Jack Flanagan.
6 Rooms. 4 Private Baths. 1 Shared Baths. Conference Room. Guest phone available. Children 17 & up. TV available. Smoking OK. Credit Cards: Visa, MC. Beds: KQT. Meals: Continental breakfast.

"I really felt pampered."
"A wonderfully quiet get-a-way, peaceful and romantic."
"Everything was perfect, from the homemade breads to the fluffy towels provided every day."
"I loved the large airy room and the bay view."

Olde Captain's Inn

101 Main St
Yarmouth Port MA 02675
(617) 362-4496

Circa 1835. In the National Register, the Olde Captain's House was formerly known as the Merrymac Inn. The inn is a restored sea captain's house close to the area's restaurants. Yarmouth Port is a central Cape Cod town with ferries to Martha's Vineyard and Nantucket just eight miles away.

Location: "Captain's Mile" on Old King's Highway on Cape Cod.
Rates: $40-$85.
Innkeeper(s): Betsy O'Connor & Sven Tilly.

What's a Dollar Worth? -- Year 1852

From the probate records of the estate of Elisha Baker we can get a glimpse of the dollar's value during the mid-1800s. After his death in 1852, certain items of the estate were appraised. A cow was valued at $18, a horse and wagon at $57, a wheelbarrow and other farm tools at $59, the house and its furniture at $195.50. Elisha Baker had stocks worth $1,600 and three ships, the *W. G. Hall*, the *Boston* and the *Florilla*, in which he owned 1/16 shares. These shares were valued at not more than $300. In all, according to the probate records, he left his family $4,747 when he died at age 64.

The house is now **The Belvedere Bed and Breakfast.** See Bass River, Massachusetts.

Michigan

Ann Arbor

The Homestead
See: Saline, MI.

De Tour Village

Hubbard's Bonnevue Lodge
206 S Huron Box 65
De Tour Village MI 49725
(906) 297-2391
  Circa 1912. Each room in Bonnevue Lodge has a picturesque view of St Mary's River and Drummond

Island. Guests enjoy boat watching from the wicker furnishings on the front porch.

Rates: $30. Season: All year.
Innkeeper(s): Ruth & Carl Hubbard.
2 Rooms. 3 Shared Baths. Guest phone available. Children by special arrangement. TV available. Smoking OK. Credit Cards: Visa, MC. Beds: TC. Meals: B&B.

Douglas

Rosemont Inn
83 Lake Shore Dr
Douglas MI 49406
(616) 857-2637
  Circa 1886. Rosemont with its gingerbread and Victorian facade has been welcoming guests ever since it was constructed. Its ideal location across from the beach on Lake Michigan makes porch sitting a favorite pastime here. Most of the fourteen guest rooms have fireplaces and the inn has its own swimming pool.

Location: At the shore of Lake Michigan.
Rates: $50-$75.
Innkeeper(s): Ric & Cathy Gillette.

Holland

Old Wing Inn
5298 E 147th Ave
Holland MI 49423
(616) 392-7362
  Circa 1844. This home was built for Rev. George Smith, a missionary for an Ottawa Indian colony here. In the National Register, it is the oldest house in town. In May, Holland's tulip festival draws many gardeners into the area. A Dutch village and wooden shoe factories are nearby.

Location: One and a half miles east of US 31 on East 40th St.
**Rates: $40-$55.
Innkeeper(s): Chuck and Chris Lorenz.

The Parsonage
6 E 24th St
Holland MI 49423
(616) 396-1316
  Circa 1908. Built in 1908 for $3,371.93 by members of Prospect Park Christian Reformed church, this

Queen Ann-style home was the parsonage for the church. Over the years it housed nine different pastors and their families. The Holland Garden Club chose the Parsonage to decorate for their Christmas tour, inspired by the rich oak woodwork, antique furnishings and leaded glass throughout the inn. Two sitting rooms, a formal dining room, garden patio and summer porch add to the spacious feeling. The hosts have developed what they hope will become the official identity flag for the B&B industry.

Location: Ten miles north of Saugatuck, 35 miles southwest of Grand Rapids.
Rates: $40-$65. Season: May 1 to November 1.
Innkeeper(s): Bonnie Westrate.
4 Rooms. 1 Shared Baths. Guest phone available. TV available.
Credit Cards: MC. Beds: D. Meals: Continental-plus breakfast.

Niles

Yesterdays Inn
518 N 4th
Niles MI 49120
(616) 683-6079
  Circa 1875. Nearly every style of architecture used in the last one hundred years is represented on the street where Yesterdays Inn stands. Distinctive paired brackets and dentils under the eaves mark the Italianate design of the inn and there are tall shuttered and curved windows. There are four guest rooms. The hosts have golf, sailing and skiing packages available.

Location: Eight miles from Notre Dame University.
**Rates: $45.
Innkeeper(s): Dawn & Phil Semler.

Pentwater

Pentwater Inn
180 E Lowell Box 98
Pentwater MI 49449
(616) 869-5909
  Circa 1880. A tandem bike and full breakfast are special treats at the Pentwater, a favorite location for family reunions. The nearby beach provides fishing, water skiing and boating.

Location: Two blocks from the shopping area in a quiet residential neighborhood.
Rates: $25-$55.
Innkeeper(s): Janet Gunn.

Saline

The Homestead
9279 Macon Rd
Saline MI 48176
(313) 429-9625
  Circa 1851. Saline was named for the old salt wells here. The Homestead land was a favorite camping spot for Indians while they salted their fish and many

arrowheads have been found on the farm. Furnished with antiques and very comfortable beds, this 1851 brick farmhouse is a mixture of comfort with country and elegant Victorian decor. There are fifty acres of fields, woods and river for walking or cross-country skiing. A good antiquing country, it's fifteen minutes from Ann Arbor and Ypsilanti, forty from Detroit and Toledo.

Location: Southeast Michigan, within six miles of I-94 & US 23, 8 miles south of Ann Arbor.
Rates: $40-$50. Season: All year.
Innkeeper(s): Shirley Grossman.
5 Rooms. 2 Shared Baths. Conference Room. Guest phone in room. Children 12 & up. TV available. Smoking OK. Credit Cards: Visa, MC, DC, CB. Beds: DT. Meals: B&B.
  "The best B&B in the world! Another super wonderful visit here."
  "Thank you for being 'home' to us and sharing your insights of Saline."
  "Glad we spent our special time away with you and your home."

Saugatuck

Maplewood
428 Butler St Box 1059
Saugatuck MI 49453
(616) 857-2788
  Circa 1860. On the quiet village green in the center of Saugatuck stands the Maplewood Hotel. Built during Michigan's lumber era, it is a gleaming tribute

to the nineteenth century workmen. The architecture is unmistakably Greek Revival and the elegant three-story inn boasts four massive wooden pillars. Crystal chandeliers, period furniture made in Grand Rapids and well-appointed lounge areas make the Maplewood a perennial favorite.

Rates: $45-$135. Season: All year.
Innkeeper(s): Donald & Harriet Mitchell.
13 Rooms. 13 Private Baths. Swimming Pool. Conference Room. Guest phone available. Children with prior arrangement. TV in room. Handicap access provided. Smoking OK. Credit Cards: Visa, MC, AE. Beds: KQC. Meals: Continental, gourmet dining room.

"Staying at the Maplewood provided the pleasure of listening to classical music on the player grand piano in the Mitchell Lounge. It was so easy vacationing...steps from boutiques, art galleries and antique shops."

Rosemont Inn
See: Douglas, MI.

Singapore Country Inn
900 Lake St
Saugatuck MI 49453
(616) 857-4346
Circa 1865. At one time the Singapore Country Inn served as an ice house, then a tannery, a barrel stave mill, boat building factory and since the turn of the century, a fine hotel. The hotel was originally built on the waterfront and later moved to its present site overlooking Kalamazoo Lake. Recently restored, the inn features guest rooms in different country themes.

Location: Three blocks from downtown Saugatuck.
**Rates: $34-$84. Season: All year.
Innkeeper(s): Michael & Denise Simcik.
12 Rooms. 12 Private Baths. Hot Tub. Guest phone available. Children 12 & up. TV available. Handicap access provided. Smoking OK. Credit Cards: Visa, MC. Beds: KDT. Meals: Hearty continental breakfast.

The Kirby House
294 W Center St, PO Box 1174
Saugatuck MI 49453
(616) 857-2904
Circa 1890. The Kirby House is a large, gracious Victorian home built by Sarah Kirby with the

proceeds of her ginseng farm that surrounded the property. The ambience is warm and the house boasts four fireplaces and a grand staircase. The house is wrapped by an expansive veranda on three sides.

Location: West Michigan near Lake Michigan.
**Rates: $55-$75. Season: All year.
Innkeeper(s): Marsha & Loren Kontie.
10 Rooms. 4 Private Baths. 4 Shared Baths. Sauna. Swimming Pool. Guest phone available. Children. Smoking OK. Credit Cards: Visa, MC. Beds: QDT. Meals: B&B.

"Not wishing to return home from a vacation is rather typical, but crying when one leaves their hosts is unheard of - until The Kirby House."

The Park House
888 Holland St
Saugatuck MI 49453
(616) 857-4535
Circa 1857. The Park House, a Greek Revival home, has had overnight guests such as Susan B. Anthony during its long history of hospitality. A country theme pervades the inn with antiques and old woodwork and pine floors.

Location: Thirty five miles southwest of Grand Rapids.
**Rates: $40-$75
Innkeeper(s): Lynda & Joe Petty.

Traverse City

Warwickshire Inn
5037 Barney Rd
Traverse City MI 49684
(616) 946-7176

Circa 1902. The Warwickshire has a panoramic view of Traverse City and both the East and West Bay. The rooms feature turn-of-the-century Victorian furnishings.

Location: Two miles west of City Center.
**Rates: $50-$60.
Innkeeper(s): Dan & Pat Warwick.

Minnesota

Brainerd

Pleasant Acres
Rt 6, PO Box 313
Brainerd MN 56401
(218) 963-2482

Circa 1918. *"We got great place. Cheep but nice. Looks at lake. Lots of fish. Try us you like us."*

Location: Gull Lake.
**Rates: $35. Season: All year.
Innkeeper(s): Alan "the Chief" Gunsbury.
12 Rooms. Conference Room. Children. Pets OK. Smoking OK. Credit Cards: All. Beds: TC. Meals: B&B.

Red Wing

Pratt-Taber Inn
706 West Fourth
Red Wing MN 55066
(612) 388-5945

Circa 1876. In the heart of this restored Mississippi River town, banker and city treasurer, A. W. Pratt, had this home built during the centennial. The star-studded porch detail celebrates the event. Other fine details of this Italianate-style home include feather-painted slate fireplaces, butternut and walnut woods, and the gingerbread woodwork on the exterior. Furnishings are in both early Renaissance Revival style and country Victorian. A patriotic library in deep reds and navy has a murphy bed hidden in a buffet and a collection of over 1,000 optican slides and a victrola. Secret bureau drawers, authentic Victorian wallpapers, dress-up clothes, and hand stenciling are all part of the experience.

Location: Fifty-five miles south of the Twin Cities.
Rates: $49-$89. Season: All year.
Innkeeper(s): Jane & Charles Walker.
6 Rooms. 2 Private Baths. 2 Shared Baths. Conference Room. Guest phone available. Children 7 & up. TV available. Handicap access provided. Smoking OK. Credit Cards: Visa, MC. Beds: QT. Meals: B&B.

"The knack for illusion makes the inn seem lost in time." Mid West Living.

"Wherever I am and I need a peaceful moment, I will sit down and imagine sitting on the restful porch, listening to the chimes of the nearby churches and enjoying the soft summer breezes." Garrison Keillor, Prairie Home Companion.

Stillwater

Driscolls for Guests
1103 South 3rd St
Stillwater MN 55082
(612) 439-7486

Circa 1869. A wicker-filled porch is the first welcoming sight to this historic inn in downtown Stillwater. A parlor fireplace and piano, period furnishings and an elegant breakfast in bed are luxuries provided by Driscolls.

Location: Residential section of the village.
**Rates: $44-$49.
Innkeeper(s): Mina C. Ingersoll.

Mississippi

Columbus

Alexander's Inn
408 7th South
Columbus MS 39701
(601) 327-4259

Circa 1828. Alexander's is the oldest brick home in Northern Mississippi. It has been been totally reconstructed and is now available for guests.

Location: Historic district of Columbus.
**Rates: $45-$55.
Innkeeper(s): Alexander Amaxopulos.

Fayette

Historic Springfield Plantation
Hwy 553
Fayette MS 39069
(601) 786-3802

Circa 1791. The first mansion in Mississippi, Springfield Plantation was the setting for the wedding

of Andrew Jackson in 1791. It has been continuously operated as a plantation for almost 200 years and 1000 acres still remain. The mansion is graced with magnificent hand-carved cornices and mantels.

Location: Twenty miles north of Natchez, via US 61, 8 miles west of Fayette.
**Rates: $35-$55. Season: All year.
Innkeeper(s): Arthur E. La Salle.
3 Rooms. 1 Shared Baths. Conference Room. Guest phone available. Children. Pets OK. TV available. Smoking OK. Beds: DT. Meals: Continental breakfast.

Holly Springs

Hamilton Place
105 E Mason Ave
Holly Springs MS 38635
(601) 252-4368

Circa 1838. This raised Louisiana cottage is listed in the National Register. Guest rooms are furnished with antiques and there is an antique shop in the carriage house. Enjoy breakfast in the formal dining room or on the deck overlooking the pool or the gazebo.

Location: Thirty-five miles southeast of Memphis off US 78.
**Rates: $65. Season: All year.
Innkeeper(s): Linda & Jack Stubbs.
3 Rooms. 3 Private Baths. Swimming Pool. Guest phone available. Children. TV available. Handicap access provided. Smoking OK. Credit Cards: Visa, MC. Beds: QT. Meals: B&B.

Lorman

Rosswood Plantation
Hwy 552
Lorman MS 39095
(601) 437-4215

Circa 1857. Rosswood is a stately columned mansion in an original plantation setting. Here guests may find antiques, buried treasure, ghosts, a slave revolt, a Civil War battle, the first owner's diary and genuine southern hospitality. Voted the "prettiest place in the country" by *Farm & Ranch Living*, the manor is a Mississippi Landmark and is in the National Register.

Location: Original plantation setting.
**Rates: $65-$75. Season: All year.
4 Rooms. 2 Private Baths. 2 Shared Baths. Conference Room.
Guest phone available. Children. TV available. Smoking OK.
Credit Cards: Visa, MC. Beds: Q. Meals: B&B.

"The plantation to see if you can only see one."
"A warm, real lived-in home, not a museum."
"This is everyone's Tara."

Natchez

Monmouth Plantation
36 Melrose
Natchez MS 39120
(800) 828-4531

Circa 1818. Monmouth was the home of General
John A. Quitman, who stormed the castle of Chapul-
tepec and took Mexico City in 1847, during the War

with Mexico. He later become acting Governor of
Mexico, Governor of Mississippi and a U.S. Congressman. At the time of his death he was called the
"most popular man in America". The plantation is in
the National Register of Historic Places and has an

AAA four-diamond rating. Early guests who enjoyed
the acres of gardens, pond and walking paths were
Jefferson Davis and Henry Clay. The inn has both
four-poster and canopy beds, turn-down service and
an evening cocktail hour.

Location: One mile from downtown Natchez.
**Rates: $75-$135. Season: All year.
Innkeeper(s): Bob Kenna & Marguerite Guerio.
14 Rooms. 14 Private Baths. Conference Room. Guest phone in
room. Children 10 & up. TV in room. Handicap access provided.
Credit Cards: Visa, MC, AE. Beds: KQT. Meals: Full breakfast.
*"We felt we were part of the family, yet we had all the
privacy we wanted."*
"The best historical inn we have stayed at anywhere."
"The staff was great!"
*"Thank you for doing the fine restoration and sharing
it with us."*

Rosswood Plantation
See: Lorman, MS.

Port Gibson

Oak Square
1207 Church St
Port Gibson MS 39150
(601) 437-4350, 437-5771

Circa 1850. Six fluted Corinthian columns, each
twenty-two feet tall, support the front gallery and
grace the entrance to Oak Square, a graceful Greek
Revival mansion. There is a large front gallery and an
unusual divided staircase with matching columns on
the landing of the entrance hall. General Ulysses S.
Grant said that this was the town "too beautiful to
burn." This inn has a rare collection of Civil War
memorabilia and a four-diamond rating from the
AAA.

Location: On US 61, midway between Natchez and Vicksburg, 1
mile from Natchez Trace Parkway.
Rates: $65-$75. Season: All year.
Innkeeper(s): Mr & Mrs William D. Lum.
7 Rooms. 7 Private Baths. Guest phone available. Children. TV
available. Smoking restricted to certain areas. Credit Cards: Visa,
MC, AE. Beds: QT. Meals: B&B.

Vicksburg

Anchuca
1010 First East
Vicksburg MS 39180
(601) 636-4931, (800) 262-4822 outside Miss.

Circa 1830. Anchuca is a Greek Revival Mansion
rising resplendently above the brick-paved streets of

Vicksburg. It houses magnificent period antiques and artifacts, and is complete with gas burning chandeliers and landscaped grounds. From the balcony here Jefferson Davis delivered a famous speech during the Civil War. The former slave quarters and a more recent 1900s cottage house have been transformed into enchanting hideaways with formal decor and four-poster beds.

Rates: $75-$105. Season: All year.
Innkeeper(s): Kathy McKay.
9 Rooms. 9 Private Baths. Sauna. Swimming Pool. Guest phone available. Children. Pets OK. TV in room. Smoking OK. Credit Cards: Visa, MC, AE, Discover. Beds: QDTC. Meals: B&B.

Cedar Grove Mansion Inn
2200 Oak St
Vicksburg MS 39180
(601) 636-1605

Circa 1840. Vicksburg's grand antebellum estate, Cedar Grove lets guest relive *Gone With the Wind*. There are five acres of gardens, fountains and gazebos. Gas chandeliers flicker reminding guests of the splendor and elegance of an earlier time. The mansion was built by John Klein as a wedding present for his bride, and although Cedar Grove survived the Civil War, a Union cannonball is still lodged in the parlor wall.

**Rates: $65 & up. Season: All year.
Innkeeper(s): Estelle MacKay.
18 Rooms. 18 Private Baths. Hot Tub. Swimming Pool. Guest phone available. Children 8 & up. TV in room. Credit Cards: Visa, MC. Beds: KQ. Meals: EP.

The Corners
601 Klein St
Vicksburg MS 39180
(601) 636-7421

Circa 1872. The Corners, listed in the National Register, was built as a wedding present. It is the only inn in Vicksburg with original Porterre gardens and a view of the Mississippi River from the front gallery. An interesting combination of Italianate and Greek Revival styles, there are twelve-foot-high jib windows and rococo medallions and molding. Some of the guest rooms have fireplaces.

Location: Corner of Klein & Oak St.
**Rates: $65-$85. Season: All year.
Innkeeper(s): Bette & Cliff Whitney.
9 Rooms. 7 Private Baths. 1 Shared Baths. Guest phone in room. Children. TV in room. Handicap access provided. Smoking OK. Credit Cards: Visa, MC. Beds: QT. Meals: B&B.

"Our stay at The Corners was dreamy. I now want a cozy fireplace in my next house! Thanks to the Whitneys for their hospitality. I look forward to a return visit." C. Griffith, Southern Living Magazine.

Tomil Manor
2430 Drummond St
Vicksburg MS 39180
(601) 638-8893

Circa 1906. The original Tomil Manor was built by Mr. Johnson in a Spanish design, as a replica of his Panther Burn plantation in the Delta region of Mississippi. Unfortunately, both Mr. Johnson and the plan-

tation were lost in a tornado in 1918. The present inn is of French and English design and decor. A spectacular staircase and double-entry foyers set the tone. There are thirty-two stained glass windows. Tomil Manor is decorated with unusual antique furnishings, tester beds and cypress, oak, pine and blue poplar woodworking.

**Rates: $40-$60. Season: All year.
5 Rooms. 1 Private Baths. 2 Shared Baths. Hot Tub. Sauna. Guest phone available. TV available. Credit Cards: Visa, MC. Beds: KQD. Meals: Full southern breakfast.

"Fantastic, great, especially the hospitality."

"The greatest, friendly warm people. Breakfast was super."

"Enjoyed everything very much especially the antique beds."

Missouri

Hartville

Frisco House
PO Box 118
Hartville MO 65667
(417) 741-7304, 833-0650

Circa 1895. This faithfully restored Victorian house is furnished with period antiques and is in the National Register.

Location: Northwest corner of Church and Rolla.
**Rates: $30-$35.
Innkeeper(s): Charley & Betty Roberts.

Lebanon

Historic Oakland Mansion
Rt 1, PO Box 179
Lebanon MO 65536
(417) 588-3291

Circa 1887. An old man's dream, this three-story Victorian sits on seventy-eight acres. For the retirement home of Jacob Blickensderfer, the setting in the beautiful Ozark countryside was perfect. Unheard of at the time was his air-lock entrance in the front hall which used two sets of tightly fitting doors. Another "unusual feature" of the home that had the neighbors talking was his duct system that ran through the house with heat generated from a basement furnace. To the enjoyment of guests, the walnut staircase winds three stories high and an observatory with a rotating dome tops the house.

Location: Six miles from Lebanon.
Rates: $40-$55. Season: February through December.
Innkeeper(s): Wes & Connie Allbritton.
6 Rooms. 3 Shared Baths. Conference Room. Guest phone available. Children 10 & up. TV available. Smoking OK. Credit Cards: Visa, MC, AE. Beds: QD. Meals: B&B.

St Joseph

Harding House
219 North 20th St
St Joseph MO 64501
(816) 232-7020

Circa 1903. This turn-of-the-century American Foursquare home was built by George Johnson, owner of the world's largest hardware store (in 1903), Wyrth Hardware Company. The home has fourteen beveled and leaded glass windows, oak woodwork and gracious pocket doors. Annual events in St. Joseph include the Apple Blossom, Pony Express, Jesse James, and Prairie View festivals.

Location: Fifty miles north of Kansas City.
Rates: $30-$45.
Innkeeper(s): Mary Harding.
Children. Meals: Full breakfast.

St. Genevieve

The Inn St. Gemme Beauvais
78 North Main, PO Box 231
St. Genevieve MO 63670
(314) 883-5744

Circa 1848. The Inn St. Gemme Beauvais is Historic District Building #1 and is in the National Register of Historic Places. This stately old home is decorated with period pieces from the nineteenth century. Interesting pieces include the inn's office outfitted with cubbyholes from a post office in Illinois and an old spool cabinet obtained from a store in River Aux Vases. A beautiful marble mantelpiece graces the fireplace. Two-story white pillars mark the gracious entrance to the red brick inn.

Location: In Missouri's oldest settlement.
Rates: $35-$45. Season: All year.
Innkeeper(s): Frankie & N. B. Donze
13 Rooms. 13 Private Baths. Guest phone available. Credit Cards: MC. Beds: D. Meals: B&B.

St. Louis

Maggie's Bed & Breakfast
See: Collinsville, IL.

Zachariah Foss Guest House
See: Washington, MO.

Washington

Zachariah Foss Guest House
#4 Lafayette
Washington MO 63090
(314) 239-6499

Circa 1846. Zachariah Foss and his wife, Amelia, arrived here from Maine with their five children and selected this lovely spot on the Missouri River, across from the busy steamboat landing, for their new home. Zachariah was a cabinet maker and Amelia a school teacher so the first private English-speaking school house in the county was opened in this German settlement. The house is three stories of clapboard and stone constructed in a Federal style. Washington is a quaint historic rivertown in the heart of the Missouri wine country providing a picturesque setting for the inn. Guests enjoy the fragrance of drying herbs and

the old fashioned porch, antique-filled rooms and a his-and-hers clawfoot bathtub. The house has been nominated for the National Register. Missouri wine is served at the Zachariah Foss house. A tandem bike is at hand and carriage rides are available from the house.

Location: Forty-five minutes west of St. Louis, 15 minutes off I-44 & I-70.
Rates: $95 double, $135 for 4.
Innkeeper(s): Sunny & Joy Drewel, Janet Berlener.
7 Rooms. Children 12 & up. Credit Cards: Visa, MC. Beds: D. Meals: B&B.

Montana

Big Sky

Lone Mountain Ranch
PO Box 145
Big Sky MT 59716
(406) 995-4644

Circa 1920. This lodge is situated in 13 log cabins and has common rooms that include a hot tub, dining room, game room and sitting room. The inn is furnished with Indian artifacts. In the winter guests may take advantage of the sleigh rides offered if not enjoying the skiing that day. Ski rentals are provided at the lodge. Summer activities include fly fishing and horseback riding.

Rates: $88. Season: Closed May and November.
Innkeeper(s): Bob & Vivian Schaap.
13 Rooms. 13 Private Baths. Jacuzzi Tubs. Children. Smoking OK.
Credit Cards: Visa, MC, AE. Meals: All meals included.

Bozeman

Voss Inn
319 S Willson
Bozeman MT 59715
(406) 587-0982

Circa 1883. A lovely restored Victorian mansion, the Voss Inn offers six elegant guest rooms.

Location: Four blocks south of downtown on the way to Montana State University.
**Rates: $50-$60.
Innkeeper(s): Ken & Ruthmary Tonn.

Stevensville

Country Caboose
852 Willoughby Road
Stevensville MT 59870
(406) 777-3145

Circa 1923. This little red caboose is set on the old railroad tracks out in the country in view of Bitterroot Mountains.

Location: South of Missoula.
Rates: $30. Season: May to October.
Innkeeper(s): Lisa & Kirk Thompson.
1 Rooms. 1 Private Baths. Children. Meals: Full breakfast.

Nebraska

Alliance

Prairie House
602 Box Butte
Alliance NE 69301
(308) 762-1461
Circa 1903. Decorated with turn-of-the-century antique furnishings, the Prairie House is one of Alliance's oldest homes.

Location: In town.
Rates: $22-$30.
Innkeeper(s): Cecilia & John Sturm.

Bartley

Pheasant Hill
HC 68, PO Box 12
Bartley NE 69020
(308) 692-3278
Circa 1937.

Location: Six miles north of Bartley.
**Rates: $30.
Innkeeper(s): Dona Nelms.

Lincoln

The Grand
2109 South 24th St
Lincoln NE 68502
(402) 476-7873
Circa 1910. This private home is open only to senior citizens. Once inside the entry with its grand Corinthian columns, ceilings of stained glass, and the wide sweeping stairway you'll understand the name of the inn. Outside, a veranda provides views of the lawns, gardens, and gas lanterns. The innkeepers speak Norwegian, Swedish, and Danish.

Rates: $35. Season: All year.
7 Rooms. 5 Private Baths. Guest phone available. Smoking OK.
Meals: Full breakfast.

McCook

Pheasant Hill
See: Bartley, NE.

North Platte

Watson Manor Inn
410 S Sycamore, PO Box 458
North Platte NE 69103
(308) 532-1124
Circa 1880. This home was originally built in Wallace but was later cut into four sections and moved by team and hayrack to its present location. Another home was attached to it at the rear.

**Rates: $35-$60.
Innkeeper(s): Ron & Patty Watson.

Nevada

Carson City

Winters Creek Ranch
1201 US 395 North
Carson City NV 89701
(702) 849-1020

Circa 1865. This old ranch was established back in 1865. There are fifty acres of meadows and ponderosa pines as well as spectacular views of the Sierra Nevada Mountains. Horseback riding, cycling, fishing, hiking or just sitting in the hot tub are favorite activities of guests and can be done without leaving the ranch. Four guest rooms are available but families and honeymooners often prefer the guest cottage.

Rates: $75-$85.
Innkeeper(s): Myron Sayan & Susan Hannah.

Imlay

Old Pioneer Garden
Star Rt, Unionville #79
Imlay NV 89418
(702) 538-7585

Circa 1861. There is a trout stream through this old ranch. Home movies are shown in the parlor and the host will prepare a picnic lunch for guests.

Rates: $25-$45. Season: All year.
8 Rooms. 3 Private Baths. Children by prior arrangement. Handicap access provided. Smoking OK. Meals: Full breakfast.

Virginia City

Edith Palmer's Country Inn
South B Street, PO Box 756
Virginia City NV 89440
(702) 847-0707

Circa 1862. Within easy walking distance to the historic district of Virginia City, this inn is an old country home. Guests enjoy the gourmet breakfast and the wine cellar. There are five rooms.

Rates: $55-$75.

Savage Mansion
146 South D St, PO Box 445
Virginia City NV 89440
(702) 847-0574

Circa 1861. This house was constructed by the Savage Mining Company to serve as both a home for the mine superintendent and as offices. There are six rooms and a suite. The inn is usually closed in the winter but will open if enough advance notice is given.

Rates: $45-$70.
Innkeeper(s): Bob Kugler.
6 Rooms. 2 Private Baths. Guest phone available. TV available. Credit Cards: Visa, MC. Meals: Continental breakfast.

New Hampshire

Bedford

Bedford Village Inn
2 Old Bedford Road
Bedford NH 03102
(603) 472-2602
   Circa 1810. Built by Josiah Gordon, the inn stands as a landmark restoration of a farm estate. It features wide pumpkin-pine boards, Indian shutters, exposed chestnut beams and working fireplaces. Outside in

the adjacent pastures a herd of French Charolais cows graze with their calves. The inn's guest rooms have king-size beds and canopied four-posters and are situated in the converted barn. Public spaces at the Bedford Village Inn include the Milk Room Lounge and the unique viewing porches perched in the original barn silos.

Rates: Call. Season: All year.
14 Rooms. 14 Private Baths. Conference Room. Guest phone available. Children. TV available. Smoking OK. Beds: K.
   "Thank you for the gracious hospitality you showed me and my staff on Sunday evening. I was extremely happy with the accommodations and the food and wine were exquisite."

   "One of the most memorable weekends we can remember. Please compliment Neal and yourself for a beautiful facility and the gracious manner in which you treated your guests. Each of us felt very relaxed and special!"

Bradford

Bradford Inn
Main Street
Bradford NH 03221
(603) 938-5309
   Circa 1898. The Bradford Hotel was the most elaborate lodging in town in 1898 when it boasted of electricity, a coal furnace and a large dining room. Now the inn is restored to its turn-of-the-century

charm and ambience. Guests once again enjoy the grand staircase, the wide halls, parlors, high ceilings, and sunny and spacious rooms.

Location: Rural country village.
**Rates: $40-$100. Season: All year.
Innkeeper(s): Connie & Tom Mazol.
14 Rooms. 14 Private Baths. Conference Room. Guest phone available. Children. Pets OK. TV in room. Handicap access provided. Smoking OK. Credit Cards: Visa, MC, Discover. Beds: DTC. Meals: B&B, MAP, EP, continental breakfast or full breakfast.
   "We enjoyed excellent breakfasts and dinners while at the Bradford Inn as well as a clean and spacious suite and a most pleasant host and hostess. Have recommended it to our friends."

Mountain Lake Inn

Rt 114
Bradford NH 03221
(603) 938-2136

Circa 1760. This white Colonial center-door-plan home is situated on 167 acres, seventeen of which are lakefront. A sandy beach is inviting for sunning but guests often prefer to take out the canoe and the rowboat. The Pine Room has floor-to-ceiling windows that look out to the garden. A seventy-five-year-old Brunswick pool table is in the lounge, along with a wood-burning fireplace.

Location: Three miles south of Bradford.
**Rates: $65.50-$76.50.
Innkeeper(s): Carol & Phil Fullerton.

Bridgewater

Pasquaney Inn

Rt 3 A
Bridgewater NH 03222
(603) 744-2712

Circa 1840. At the turn of the century, the Pasquaney was originally a stopover point on the Old Star Route from Boston to Montreal. The inn was built in the classic style of a New England resort with white clapboard siding, tall windows, and a broad veranda stretching the length of the inn and facing the lake with its sandy beaches. The mountains are just beyond.

Rates: $46-$58 per person, double occupancy. Season: All year.
Innkeeper(s): The Ballard family.
26 Rooms. 18 Private Baths. 8 Shared Baths. Conference Room. Guest phone available. Children all ages. TV available. Smoking OK. Credit Cards: Visa, MC. Beds: KQDT. Meals: MAP, country breakfast & full dinner.

Campton

Mountain Fare Inn

Mad River Road
Campton NH 03223
(603) 726-4283

Circa 1850. A white farmhouse, the Mountain Fare Inn attracts skiers and other sports enthusiasts as well as families who enjoy the outdoors. The inn is decorated in a casual New Hampshire-style country decor. There are flower gardens in the summer and unparalleled foliage in the fall. Often, ski teams, family reunions and other groups are found enjoying the outdoors here with Mountain Fare as a base. In the winter everyone here seems to be a skier and the gables are piled high with snow, chimneys smoking. The Mountain Fare is a convenient and fun stop between Vermont and Maine.

Location: In the White Mountain area, 40 miles north of Concord. Exit 28 of I-93.
**Rates: $24-$35. Season: All year.
Innkeeper(s): Susan & Nicholas Preston.
9 Rooms. 5 Private Baths. 2 Shared Baths. Guest phone available. Children. TV available. Smoking OK. Beds: DT. Meals: Hearty skier's breakfast.

Centre Harbor

Red Hill Inn

RD 1, PO Box 99M
Centre Harbor NH 03226
(603) 279-7001

Circa 1904. The mansion was once the centerpiece of a thousand-acre estate. It was called "keewaydin" after the strong north wind that blows across Sunset Hill. When the depression was over the inn was sold and was subsequently owned by many families including European royalty escaping from Nazi Germany. Now the mansion is a lovely restored country inn with

spectacular views of the area's lakes and mountains. From your room you can see the site of the filming of *"On Golden Pond."*

Location: Central New Hampshire in the Lakes Region.
**Rates: $65-$115. Season: All year.
Innkeeper(s): Don Leavitt & Rick Miller.
13 Rooms. 13 Private Baths. Conference Room. Guest phone available. Children. TV available. Smoking OK. Credit Cards: Visa, MC, AE. Beds: QT. Meals: B&B.

Conway

Darby Field Inn
Bald Hill, PO Box D
Conway NH 03818
(603) 447-2181

Circa 1826. The Darby Field Inn is a rambling, converted farmhouse, characterized by its huge fieldstone fireplace, stone patio and outstanding views of the Mt. Washington Valley and the Presidential Mountains. For many years it was called the Bald Hill Grand View lodge but was renamed to honor the first man to climb Mt. Washington, Darby Field.

Location: Off Rt 16, 1/2 mile south of Conway.
**Rates: $55-$82.50 per person, double occupancy. Season: All year.
Innkeeper(s): Marc & Marily Donaldson.
16 Rooms. 14 Private Baths. 2 Shared Baths. Swimming Pool. Guest phone available. Children 2 & up. TV available. Smoking OK. Credit Cards: Visa, MC, AE. Beds: QDT. Meals: MAP, restaurant.

"Dripping with country charm."

Cornish

Chase House Bed & Breakfast
Rt 12 A
Cornish NH 03745
(603) 675-5391

Circa 1766. The original house was built by Cornish's first English settler, Dudley Chase. It was moved in 1845 to accommodate the Sullivan County Railroad. Now designated a National Landmark, it

was the birthplace of Salmon Chase, Governor of Ohio, Secretary of the Treasury for President Lincoln

and Chief Justice of the Supreme Court. The Chase Manhattan Bank was named for him. The inn is noted as a fine example of federal architecture.

Location: Upper Valley Region.
**Rates: $65-$85. Season: All year.
Innkeeper(s): Hal & Marilyn Wallace.
6 Rooms. 4 Private Baths. Guest phone available. Children by prior arrangement. TV available. Credit Cards: Visa, MC. Beds: QT. Meals: B&B.

Holderness

Manor On Golden Pond
Rt 3, PO Box T
Holderness NH 03245
(603) 968-3348

Circa 1903. This English-style country mansion is set on thirteen manicured acres. It was built by a Florida land developer, fulfilling his boyhood dream of having

a beautiful mansion high on a hill overlooking lakes and mountains. No expense was spared in bringing craftsmen from around the world to make the home a work of art. This is reflected in the quarter oak in the dining room and billiard room, the marble fireplaces and the hand-carved mahogany lobby.

Location: On Squam Lake, 40 minutes north of Concord, NH.
**Rates: $59-$125. Season: All year.
Innkeeper(s): Andy Lamoureux.
29 Rooms. 29 Private Baths. Swimming Pool. Conference Room. Guest phone available. Children. TV available. Smoking OK. Credit Cards: Visa, MC, AE, DC, CB. Beds: KQTC. Meals: B&B and restaurant with gourmet dining.

"Just a note to tell you that every part of our stay was memorable: the setting, the inn itself, the dining, the staff, the fascinating boat tour. Everything was outstanding!"

"The Manor has an indescribable beauty that makes you feel warm and welcomed."

Jackson

Village House
Rt 16 A, PO Box 359
Jackson NH 03846
(603) 383-6666

Circa 1860. The Village House was built as the annex to the larger Hawthorne Inn. A colonial-style building with a porch winding around three sides, it was originally built to house employees and overflow

patrons who arrived in the summer for two-month-long stays at the turn of the century. When the main inn burned, the annex became an operating bed and breakfast inn.

Location: White Mountains, Mt Washington Valley.
Rates: $55-$85. Season: All year.
Innkeeper(s): Robin Crocker, Lori Allen.
10 Rooms. 8 Private Baths. 2 Shared Baths. Swimming Pool. Guest phone available. Children 10 & up. TV available. Smoking OK. Credit Cards: Visa, MC. Beds: DT. Meals: B&B.

"Your hospitality and warmth made us feel right at home. The little extras, such as turn-down service, flowers and baked goods are all nice touches and greatly appreciated."

Jaffrey

Benjamin Prescott Inn
Rt 124 East
Jaffrey NH 03452
(603) 532-6637

Circa 1853. Colonel Prescott arrived on foot in Jaffrey in 1775 with an ax in his hand and a bag of beans on his back. The family built the classic Greek revival

home many years later in 1853. Now candles light each window and can be seen from the stonewall-lined lane that passes by the inn. Each room bears the name of a Prescott family member.

**Rates: $45-$100. Season: All year.
Innkeeper(s): Richard Rettig.
8 Rooms. 8 Private Baths. Guest phone available. Children 10 & up. Credit Cards: Visa, MC. Beds: KQT. Meals: B&B.

Littleton

Beal House Inn
247 West Main St
Littleton NH 03561
(603) 444-2661

Circa 1833. This federal renaissance-style farmhouse has been an inn for fifty-four years. The original barn

still stands, though it is now covered with white clapboard and converted to an antique shop. The inn itself is furnished with antiques which are for sale, a living antique shop. The Beal House is a Main Street Landmark as well as being the area's first bed and breakfast inn.

Location: Junction of Rt 18, 302, and 10, in Littleton.
**Rates: $35-$75. Season: All year.
Innkeeper(s): Doug & Brenda Clickenger.

14 Rooms. 12 Private Baths. 2 Shared Baths. Guest phone available. Children. Smoking OK. Credit Cards: Visa, MC, AE, DC. Beds: KQTC. Meals: B&B.

"My observation of other guests assures me that these innkeepers know and understand people, their needs and wants. Attention to cleanliness and amenities from check-in to check-out is a treasure."

Thayers Inn
136 Main St
Littleton NH 03561
(603) 444-6469

Circa 1843. Thayers Inn opened January, 1850, as Thayer's White Mountain Hotel. In those days the inn built its reputation on service. Guests had fresh firewood and fresh candles delivered to their rooms each day and a pitcher of water for washing as well as a personal "thunderjug" (chamberpot.) Ulysses Grant

is said to have spoken from the inn's balcony to the Littleton townsfolk during a federal court hearing. Thayers Inn has a handsome facade, featuring four thirty-foot hand-carved pillars and a charming cupola. From the cupola guests may view the surrounding mountains, after climbing the stairs to the top. The inn is in the National Register and holds the triple diamond award from the Auto Club.

**Rates: $20.95-$28.95. Season: All year.
Innkeeper(s): Don & Carolyn Lambert.
40 Rooms. 36 Private Baths. 4 Shared Baths. Guest phone in room. Children. TV in room. Smoking OK. Credit Cards: All. Beds: DC. Meals: EP, restaurant.

"I felt as if I woke up in my favorite aunt's bedroom this morning. Thank you!"

"The true tradition of New England hospitality is ...practiced at this inn."

"This Thanksgiving holiday just passed, Russ and I spent a lot of time thinking about the things that are most important to us. It seemed appropriate that we should write to thank you for your warm hospitality as innkeepers."

Lyme

Loch Lyme Lodge
Rt 10 RFD 278
Lyme NH 03768
(603) 795-2141

Circa 1784. Both a library and a tavern may be found at the Loch Lyme Lodge. International cuisine is served and on Sundays guests look forward to a special lakeside buffet in the evening.

Location: Connecticut River Valley.
Rates: $24.50 per person.
Innkeeper(s): Paul & Judy Barker.

Newport

Backside Inn
RFD 2, PO Box 213
Newport NH 03773
(603) 863-5161

Circa 1835. On four acres of lawns, stone fences and towering pines, Backside Inn is a handsome Cape-style plank house in the National Register. This four-season country inn on the 'backside' of Mt. Sunapee, has ten uniquely furnished guest rooms.

Location: Backside of Mt. Sunapee.
Rates: $48-$58 per person, double occupancy.
Innkeeper(s): Bruce & Mackie Hefka. Meals: Full breakfast.

North Conway

1785 Inn
Rt 16 at The Scenic Vista
North Conway NH 03860
(603) 356-9025

Circa 1785. This central chimney home was built by Elijah Dinsmore, a veteran of the American Revolution and the French and Indian War. The old original chimney and fireplaces and the brick oven in the dining room form a beehive construction, the size of an entire room, in the middle of the house. Hand-hewn beams and roof rafters display the construction techniques of the era. The inn has a three diamond Auto club award.

**Rates: $55-$100. Season: All year.

Innkeeper(s): Charlie & Becky Mallar.
13 Rooms. 8 Private Baths. 5 Shared Baths. Guest phone available. TV available. Handicap access provided. Smoking OK. Credit Cards: Visa, MC, AE, DC, CB. Beds: QDTC. Meals: Full breakfast, restaurant.

"Occasionally in our lifetimes is a moment so unexpectedly perfect that we use it as our measure for our unforgettable moments. We just had such an experience at the 1785 Inn."

"What a thoroughly enjoyable, relaxing haven you've made. Our stay reminded me of long weekends spent with my grandparents in upstate New York..."

Buttonwood Inn

Mt Surprise Rd, PO Box 3297
North Conway NH 03860
(603) 356-2625

Circa 1820. Built as a four-room, center chimney, New England-style Cape Cod, the Dearborn Farm, as it was then known, was a working farm. Nestled at the

base of the majestic summit of Mount Surprise it had over 100 acres on the mountain. Of the outbuildings only the granite barn foundation remains. Through the years the house has been extended to twenty rooms.

**Rates: $40-$65. Season: All year.
Innkeeper(s): Ann & Hugh Begley.
9 Rooms. 2 Private Baths. 3 Shared Baths. Swimming Pool. Guest phone available. Children. TV available. Smoking OK. Credit Cards: Visa, MC, AE. Beds: DTC. Meals: Full breakfast.

"The moment we spotted your lovely inn nestled midway on the mountainside we knew we had found a winner."

"You have a unique way of making people feel at home."

Cranmore Mt Lodge

Kearsarge Rd, PO Box 1194
North Conway NH 03860
(603) 356-2044

Circa 1850. In the Four Season Resort area of the White Mountains, the lodge was once home to Babe Ruth's daughter. Ruth was a frequent guest for years and one guest room is decorated with his furnishings. The old barn is held together with wooden pegs. It features exposed barn beams in the dorm rooms created there.

Location: Village of Kearsarge in North Conway.
Rates: $53-$92. Season: All year.
Innkeeper(s): Dennis & Judy Helfand.
17 Rooms. 5 Private Baths. 6 Shared Baths. Hot Tub. Swimming Pool. Guest phone available. Children. TV in room. Smoking OK. Credit Cards: Visa, MC, AE. Beds: QTC. Meals: Full breakfast.

Darby Field Inn

See: Conway, NH.

Stonehurst Manor

Rt 16
North Conway NH 03860
(603) 356-3271

Circa 1876. Built as the summer home for the Bigelow family, founder of the Bigelow Carpet Company, the graciousness of the manor can be experienced even before you walk through the huge

front door. The English-style manor stands on lush, landscaped lawns and thirty acres of pine trees. Inside, the inn is graced by leaded and stained glass windows, rich old oak, a winding staircase and a massive, hand-carved oak fireplace.

Location: One mile north of the village.
Rates: $50-$135. Season: All year.
Innkeeper(s): Peter Rattay.
24 Rooms. 22 Private Baths. 2 Shared Baths. Hot Tub. Sauna. Conference Room. Guest phone available. Children. TV in room. Handicap access provided. Smoking OK. Credit Cards: Visa, AE, DC. Beds: QT. Meals: MAP, gourmet restaurant.

"An architecturally preserved replica of an English country house, a perfect retreat for the nostalgic-at-heart." Phil Berthiaume, Country Almanac.

Village House
See: Jackson, NH.

North Woodstock

Mt. Adams Inn
Rt 3 South Main St
North Woodstock NH 03262
(603) 745-2711
  Circa 1875. This historic nineteenth-century Victorian inn is situated along the banks of the Moosaiauki River. Original tin ceilings and cobblestone fireplaces make a comfortable atmosphere that

was first enjoyed when people came for the whole summer, taking carriage rides through the mountains. There are unique rock formations along the river in the back of the inn called the "mummies". Tourists have enjoyed them for over a century. The restaurant in the inn serves authentic Polish cuisine.

Location: The heart of the White Mountains.
Rates: $36-$42. Season: All year.
Innkeeper(s): Billy Etchells & John White.
22 Rooms. 2 Private Baths. 5 Shared Baths. Guest phone available. Children 12 & up. TV in room. Credit Cards: Visa, MC. Beds: QT. Meals: Full breakfast, MAP.
  "It's just like being home."
  "Enjoyed having breakfast and dinner all in the same building."
  "Last of the grand inns from the late 1800s when guests were dropped off by train right across the road."

Portsmouth

High Meadows Bed & Breakfast
See: Eliot, ME.

Morning Dove Bed & Breakfast
See: Ogunquit, ME.

York Harbor Inn
See: York Harbor, ME.

Sugar Hill

Hilltop Inn
Main Street (Rt 117)
Sugar Hill NH 03585
(603) 823-5695
  Circa 1895. Near North Conway and Franconia Notch, this spacious, rambling Victorian provides a comfortable and relaxing stay. The home is furnished throughout with antiques. Even the kitchen has the Victorian touch with its old-fashioned cooking stove.

Location: White Mountain National Forest area.
Rates: $45.
Innkeeper(s): Meri & Mike Hern.

Sunset Hill House
Sunset Road
Sugar Hill NH 03585
(603) 823-5522
  Circa 1880. Sunset Hill House is in the Heart of the White Mountains in Sugar Hill, the site of the first ski school in America. Cannon Mountain can be seen from the dining-room windows of the inn. It is New Hampshire's biggest ski mountain with twenty-one miles of trails, a vertical drop of 2,146 feet, and an 80-passenger tram. The Sunset Hill Golf Course is one of the oldest golf courses in New England. Maple syrup flows in the spring and just a mile away from Sunset Hill is Stewart's Sugar House where visitors can learn about sugaring and sample farm fresh maple products. The inn still boasts the most tremendous view of the Presidential Range.

Location: White Mountains of New Hampshire.
Rates: $50-$63, MAP. Season: All year.
Innkeeper(s): Betty Lou Carmichel.
30 Rooms. 30 Private Baths. Swimming Pool. Conference Room. Guest phone available. Children. TV available. Smoking OK. Credit Cards: Visa, MC, AE. Beds: DT. Meals: MAP.

Suncook

Suncook House
62 Main St
Suncook NH 03275
(603) 485-8141
  Circa 1920. Suncook is a newly renovated Georgian Country Home of brick on a quiet corner of Suncook, on the main road to the mountains and lakes. The

rooms are decorated with period furnishings. A full breakfast is served.

Location: Corner of Main & Whitten Street.
**Rates: $34-$48.
Innkeeper(s): Gerry & Evelyn Lavoie. Meals: Full breakfast.

Sunnapee

Backside Inn
See: Newport, NH.

Tamworth

Tamworth Inn
Main Street
Tamworth NH 03886
(603) 323-7721
Circa 1833. An authentic New England village inn on two acres of lawn bordered by a sparkling trout stream. The Tamworth Inn is located across from the Barnstormers Theater, one of the country's oldest summer stock theaters, now in its fifty-seventh year

under the direction of Francis Cleveland, son of President Grover Cleveland. The Tamworth Pub is on the premises of the inn.

Location: In the village.
**Rates: $50-$75. Season: All year.
Innkeeper(s): Ron & Nancy Brembt.
22 Rooms. 10 Private Baths. 12 Shared Baths. Swimming Pool. Guest phone available. Children 7 & up. TV available. Credit Cards: Visa, MC, AE. Beds: KQT. Meals: EP, restaurant.

"It was great spending the day touring the beautiful countryside, shopping in the bustle of North Conway and returning to the quiet village of Tamworth and your wonderful inn."

Wakefield

Wakefield Inn
Mountain Laurel Rd, Rt 1, PO Box 2185
Wakefield NH 03872
(603) 522-8272
Circa 1803. Early travelers pulled up to the front door of the Wakefield Inn by stagecoach. While the passengers disembarked, their luggage was handed up to the second floor. It was brought in through the door which is still visible over the porch roof. In the Historic District of Wakefield, the inn was originally opened in 1803. A spiral staircase, ruffled curtains, wallpapers and a wraparound porch all create that special romantic ambience of days gone by. In the dining room an original three-sided fireplace casts a warm glow on dining guests just as it did back in 1803.

Rates: $55-$59.
Innkeeper(s): Harry & Lou Sisson.

Waterville Valley

Snowy Owl Inn
Waterville Valley Resort
Waterville Valley NH 03215
(603) 236-8371
Circa: 1830. The Snowy Owl Inn burned a number of years ago, but today it stands again dedicated to the hospitality of days gone by. Natural wood and native stone make for handsome architecture in keeping with the scenic Waterville Valley. Inside, a massive fieldstone fireplace rises three stories in the lobby atrium. A complete resort experience is provided with an indoor sports center including a pool, tennis courts, jogging track and exercise room. Next door is an indoor ice skating rink! The inn is bordered by quiet woods and rippling Snow's Brook.

Location: In New Hampshire's White Mountain National Forest.
Rates: Call.
Innkeeper(s): Mark Anderson.

Westmoreland

Partridge Brook Inn
Hatt Rd, PO Box 151
Westmoreland NH 03467
(603) 399-4994
Circa 1790. Once a tavern and a stopover for the Underground Railroad, the home was originally built by Captain Abiathar Shaw, a prosperous nailmaker. The exquisite hand-carved woodwork on the mantel

took Theophilus Hoyt over 100 days to complete. By the end of that time he had also won the heart and

hand of Sabrana Shaw, the captain's daughter. The home features stenciled parlor floors, Indian shutters and mortise-and-tenon doors.

Location: Between Keene, New Hampshire & Brattleboro, Vermont.
Rates: $55-$65. Season: All year.
Innkeeper(s): Donald & Renee Strong.
5 Rooms. 5 Private Baths. Guest phone available. Children. TV available. Credit Cards: Visa. Beds: KQD. Meals: EP or full breakfast.

"Your wonderfully comfortable bed helped plant my feet firmly on the ground and your delicious breakfast sent us out into the world, ready. What a warm and beautiful place to stay. We'll be back."

"What a passage back in time to a beautiful era. You have redone it so well, all the charm and grace so evident."

Wolfeboro

Isaac Springfield House
Rt 28 South
Wolfeboro NH 03894
(603) 569-3529

Circa 1871. This yellow Victorian with its picket fence out front was built by Isaac Springfield, known for incorporating the South Wolfeboro Blanket and Manufacturing Company. Springfield Point was later named after him. Wolfboro is said to be America's

oldest summer resort. The countryside offers lovely views anytime and brilliant foliage in the fall. The lake

is just five minutes away from the inn. Inside the inn, which has recently been restored after years of abandonment, is a spacious dining room and a cozy parlor with fireplace and piano. Antique and brass furnishings add to the ambience.

Rates: $55. Season: All year.
Innkeeper(s): Rose LeBlanc & Andrew Terragni.
4 Rooms. Children. Smoking OK. Credit Cards: MC, Visa. Beds: QD. Meals: Full country breakfast.

New Jersey

Cape May

Barnard-Good House
238 Perry St
Cape May NJ 08204
(609) 884-5381
 Circa 1865. A Second Empire Victorian, the Bernard-Good House is graced by a mansard roof with its original shingles, and a wraparound veranda adds

to the charm of this lavender, blue and tan cottage. Other features include an original picket fence and a concrete-formed flower garden. This inn was selected by *New Jersey Magazine* as the #1 spot for breakfast in New Jersey.

Rates: $65-$85. Season: April 1 to November 15.
Innkeeper(s): Nan & Tom Hawkins.
6 Rooms. 2 Private Baths. 3 Shared Baths. Guest phone available. Credit Cards: Visa and MC for deposit only. Beds: KD. Meals: Full breakfast.
 "Even the cozy bed can't hold you down when the smell of Nan's breakfast makes its way upstairs. I love

her rhubarb-walnut bread, while my husband's favorite is her Texas shellfish pie...much camaraderie shared around the table."

Colvmns By the Sea
1513 Beach Dr
Cape May NJ 08204
(609) 884-2228
 Circa 1905. Dr. C.N. Davis, Philadelphia physician and inventor of calamine lotion, built this home back in the days when a summer "cottage" might have twen-

ty rooms, twelve-foot ceilings, three-story staircases, and hand-carved ceilings. Large, airy rooms with an abundance of windows provide magnificent views of the ocean. To make an even more pleasant stay, the innkeepers provide beach tags and towels as well as bikes. Afternoon tea is served.

Rates: $69-$89.
Innkeeper(s): Barry & Cathy Rein.
11 Rooms. 11 Private Baths. Guest phone available. Children 12 & up. TV available. Credit Cards: Visa, MC. Beds: QT. Meals: Full gourmet breakfast.

Dormer House, International
800 Columbia Ave
Cape May NJ 08204
(609) 884-7446

Circa 1899. A turn-of-the-century 'summer cottage' the Dormer House features complete suites, all private. This colonial revival estate is three blocks from the ocean and three blocks from the historic walking mall. The house was built by marble dealer John Jacoby and retains much of the original marble and furniture. Several years ago the inn was converted into guest suites with kitchens.

Location: On the corner of Franklin & Columbia in the historic district.
Rates: $40-$102. Season: All year.
Innkeeper(s): Bill & Peg Madden.
8 Rooms. 8 Private Baths. Guest phone available. Children. TV available. Smoking OK. Credit Cards: Visa, MC. Beds: QDT. Meals: EP.

Duke of Windsor Inn
817 Washington St
Cape May NJ 08204
(609) 884-1355

Circa 1896. This Queen Anne Victorian has a three-story tower that houses two guest rooms and a conversation area. The inn has a carved natural oak open

staircase with stained glass windows at top and bottom. An exquisite original plaster ceiling and five antique chandeliers grace the dining room, while sliding oak doors open to the library with its corner fireplace.

Location: Southernmost tip of New Jersey, 2 blocks from main shopping, 4 blocks from the ocean.
Rates: $45-$85. Season: February to December.

Innkeeper(s): Bruce & Fran Prichard.
9 Rooms. 7 Private Baths. 2 Shared Baths. Guest phone available. Children 12 & up. Credit Cards: Visa, MC. Beds: D. Meals: B&B.

"Your warmth and gracious hospitality will be long remembered as I think back on the lovely weekend spent in your home. It was just what I needed."

"Thanks for your warm hospitality. Tom and I loved staying in your home! We certainly appreciate all the hard work you both put into renovating the house and decorating each room so uniquely."

Gingerbread House
28 Gurney St
Cape May NJ 08204
(609) 884-0211

Circa 1869. Gingerbread House is a restored Victorian cottage decorated with period antiques and a fine collection of paintings. The inn is a half-block from the ocean, and its breezes are often enjoyed from the wicker-filled porch. The Gingerbread is one of eight original Stockton Row Cottages, summer retreats built for wealthy families from Philadelphia and Virginia.

Location: Ocean resort on southern tip of New Jersey.
Rates: $65-$90. Season: All year.
Innkeeper(s): Fred & Joan Echevarria.
6 Rooms. 3 Private Baths. 3 Shared Baths. Children 7 & up. TV available. Smoking OK. Beds: D. Meals: Continental-plus breakfast.

Heirloom Bed & Breakfast
601 Columbia Ave
Cape May NJ 08204
(609) 884-1666

Circa 1876. In the heart of Cape May's historic district, and only one block from the beach is this former gambling casino and brothel. All the rooms have been decorated with fine antiques and many boast balconies with views of the Atlantic.

**Rates: $65. Season: April 1 to November 30.
Innkeeper(s): Frank & Anthony Ruggiero.
9 Rooms. 9 Private Baths. Guest phone available. Children 12 & up. TV available. Beds: Q. Meals: Continental-plus breakfast.

Holly House

20 Jackson St
Cape May NJ 08204
(609) 884-7365

Circa 1891. Holly House is one of the seven Renaissance Revival cottages famous as Cape May's 'Seven Sisters'. The inn was designed by Stephen Decatur Button as a Victorian beach house and is in the National Register. A three-story circular staircase and the original coal-grate fireplaces are architectural highlights. The innkeeper is a former mayor of Cape May.

Location: On the beach in the center of the historic district.
Rates: $40-$60. Season: All year.
Innkeeper(s): Corinne & Bruce Minnix.
6 Rooms. 2 Shared Baths. Guest phone available. Children 3 & up.
Credit Cards: Visa, MC. Meals: EP.

"Informal, comfortable mix of old and new."
"I just feel at home."
"Friendly people."

Mainstay Inn

635 Columbia Ave
Cape May NJ 08204
(609) 884-8690

Circa 1872. The Mainstay Inn was once the elegant and exclusive Jackson's Clubhouse in the days when it

was popular with gamblers. This grand villa was designed by a famous architect, and many of the guest rooms, as well as the grand parlor, look much as they did in the 1870s. Fourteen-foot ceilings, elaborate chandeliers, a sweeping veranda and a cupola are among the many features of the mansion.

Location: Center of the Cape May National Landmark District.
Rates: $55-$98. Season: April to mid-December.

Innkeeper(s): Tom and Sue Carroll.
13 Rooms. 9 Private Baths. 4 Shared Baths. Conference Room. Guest phone available. Children 12 & up. Beds: KQ. Meals: Full breakfast.

"By far the most lavishly and faithfully restored guesthouse...run by two arch-preservationists." **Travel and Leisure.**

Seventh Sister Guesthouse

10 Jackson St
Cape May NJ 08204
(609) 884-2280

Circa 1888. Most of the Seventh Sister's guest rooms have ocean views. The inn is in the National Register of Historic Places. Extensive wicker and original art collections are featured, and three floors are joined by a spectacular central circular staircase. The inn is only a block from the town center.

Location: One hundred feet from the beach in the center of the Cape May Historic District.
Rates: $60.
Innkeeper(s): Bob and Jo-Anne Myers.
6 Rooms. 2 Shared Baths. Guest phone available. Smoking OK. Beds: D.

"A breeze-kissed sweetheart of a house." **1001 Decorating Ideas.**

The Abbey

Columbia Ave & Gurney St
Cape May NJ 08204
(609) 884-4506

Circa 1869. Pennsylvania coal baron John McCreary built this elaborate home, a gothic villa with an imposing sixty-foot tower. It is now an opulent country inn.

Location: On the shores of the Atlantic Ocean.
Rates: $60-$95.
Innkeeper(s): Jay & Marianne Schatz.

Ocean Grove

Cordova
26 Webb Ave
Ocean Grove NJ 07756
(201) 774-3084, (212) 751-9577 (winter).
Circa 1886. The Cordova, a century-old Victorian inn, has been recommended in *New Jersey Magazine* as "one of seven places to stay on the Jersey shore."

The inn is in the historic area of Ocean Grove. Many presidents including Wilson, Cleveland and Roosevelt slept here and spoke at the Great Auditorium with its 7,000 seats. Nearby is a white, sandy beach and a wooden boardwalk. Founded as a Methodist retreat, the town did not allow ocean bathing or even cars until a few years ago. At the Cordova, guests feel like part of the family and have use of the kitchen, lounge, barbecue and picnic tables.

**Rates: $20-$56. Season: Memorial Day to Labor Day.
Innkeeper(s): Doris & Vlad and son, Eric Chernik.
10 Rooms. 1 Private Baths. Guest phone available. Children. TV available. Beds: DTC. Meals: B&B.
"Just like an extended family, warm, hospitable."
"Great place!"
"Warm, helpful and inviting, homey and lived-in atmosphere."
"European charm."

Princeton

Peacock Inn
20 Bayard Lane
Princeton NJ 08540
(609) 924-1707
Circa 1775. Built as the private home of John Deare, the inn is an elegant gambrel-roofed lodging with high

dormers and many rooms with fireplaces. There is a wide front porch, two comfortable bars and a large dining room. The house is a Princeton landmark, host to many luminaries during its close association with Princeton University.

Location: Central Jersey, in the center of Princeton.
Rates: $55-$90. Season: All year.
Innkeeper(s): Deirdre Higgins.
16 Rooms. 6 Private Baths. 10 Shared Baths. Conference Room. Guest phone in room. Children. Smoking OK. Credit Cards: Visa, MC, DC. Beds: DT. Meals: Hearty country breakfast.

Spring Lake

Sandpiper Hotel
7 Atlantic Ave
Spring Lake NJ 07762
(201) 449-6060
Circa 1888. This historic Victorian inn is just one-quarter block from the ocean. Approaching its centennial, the Sandpiper offers romantically appointed rooms, a large wraparound porch and old-fashioned hospitality. Spring Lake is a lovely Victorian-era community with an uncluttered two-mile-long oceanfront boardwalk.

Location: Atlantic at Ocean Ave.
**Rates: $65-$125. Season: All year.
15 Rooms. 15 Private Baths. Guest phone in room. Children. TV in room. Smoking OK. Credit Cards: All. Beds: KQDT. Meals: Continental breakfast, restaurant.

The Normandy Inn
21 Tuttle Ave
Spring Lake NJ 07762
(201) 449-7172
Circa 1888. An Italianate villa with Queen Anne influences, the Normandy Inn features interesting sun-

burst designs and neo-classical interiors. Its Victorian antiques are accentuated by Victorian colors docu-

mented and researched by Roger Moss. The house was moved onto the present site around 1910.

Location: Five houses from the Atlantic Ocean.
Rates: $75-$100. Season: All year.
Innkeeper(s): Michael and Susan Ingino.
20 Rooms. 15 Private Baths. 3 Shared Baths. Guest phone available. Children. TV available. Smoking OK. Beds: DTC. Meals: B&B.

Woodbine

Henry Ludlam Inn
124 S Delsea Dr, Rd 1, PO Box 41
Woodbine NJ 08270
(609) 861-5847

Circa 1760. Each of the six guest rooms features a fireplace and view of Ludlam Lake. Canoeing and fishing are popular activities and the innkeepers make

sure you enjoy these at your peak by providing you with a full country breakfast.

Location: Twelve miles west of Stone Harbor, 31 miles south of Atlantic City.
Rates: $55-$75. Season: All year.
Innkeeper(s): Ann & Marty Thurlow.
6 Rooms. 2 Private Baths. 2 Shared Baths. Guest phone available. Children 12 & up. TV available. Smoking OK. Beds: DT. Meals: Full gourmet breakfast. Dinner available on Saturday nights October through April.

"We have stayed in many bed and breakfasts but none compare to the wonderful gourmet breakfast you serve!"

"You have a lovely home filled with so much warmth...we are truly looking forward to our next stay with you! Everything was great!"

"Enclosed is a token of our appreciation for the delicious dinner you served us the night we were snow bound at your home. We thoroughly enjoyed our first bed and breakfast."

"By the time we left we felt like old friends!...I'm afraid that staying with you spoiled us!"

New Mexico

Albuquerque

Casita Chamisa
850 Chamisal Rd NW
Albuquerque NM 87107
(404) 897-4644
   Circa 1850. Casita Chamisa is an old-nineteenth century adobe that is on top of the ruins of an Indian village. When the host, an archaeologist, decided to dig a pool she did a test of the area and discovered a deeply stratified village attributed to the Pueblo IV Period of 1300-1650. Later an archaic campsite was discovered and attributed to 720 BC by carbon dating. After a two-year excavation the findings are being analyzed. The inn has an addition that now includes an indoor swimming pool.

Location: Fifteen minutes from town.
**Rates: $60. Season: a.
Innkeeper(s): Kit & Arnold Sargeant.
2 Rooms. 2 Private Baths. Swimming Pool. Children. Smoking OK. Credit Cards: Visa, MC. Beds: KQT. Meals: Continental-plus.

Pilar

The Plum Tree
PO Box 1-A, Rt 68
Pilar NM 87571
(505) 758-4696, (800) 552-0070, x822
   Circa 1900. This pueblo-style adobe is surrounded by peach, apple and plum trees in a century-old Indian village. Nearby are petroglyphs, Indian books etched into the rocks. An old water system used by the Indians when the village area was farmed is said to have been discovered by the Conquistadors. They followed it to the warm springs from which it originated. There they discovered an Indian maiden. After slaying her and throwing her body into the water, the stream turned cold and remains so today.

Location: On Rt 68 between Santa Fe and Taos.

**Rates: $29.50
Innkeeper(s): Karen & Dick Thibodeau.

Santa Fe

Grant Corner Inn
122 Grant Ave
Santa Fe NM 87501
(505) 983-6678
   Circa 1905. A restored Colonial manor, the Grant Corner Inn was originally built by the Wisor family. It is secluded by a garden with willow trees and surrounded by a white picket fence. Each of the rooms is professionally appointed with antique furnishings, and personal art collections of the Walter family.

**Rates: $45-$110 Season: All year.
Innkeeper(s): Louise Stewart & Pat Walter.
13 Rooms. 7 Private Baths. 6 Shared Baths. Sauna. Swimming Pool. Guest phone in room. Children 5 & up. TV in room. Handicap access provided. Smoking OK. Credit Cards: Visa, MC. Beds: KQTC. Meals: B&B.
   "Charming and cozy, loaded with friendliness."
   "The attention to detail is superb."
   "The very best of everything - comfort, hospitality, food, and T.L.C."

Preston House
106 Faithway St
Santa Fe NM 87501
(505) 982-3465
   Circa 1886. Previous owners of the Preston House included a man who helped 'divvy up' the southwest territories at the end of the Civil War and a cure-all doctor. Many historic tales of the area may be found in the innkeeper's library.

**Rates: $45-$125.
Innkeeper(s): Signe Bergman.

Taos

Hacienda del Sol
PO Box 177
Taos NM 87571
(505) 758-0287

Circa 1800. This ancient hacienda was purchased by a local art patroness Mabel Dodge as a hide-away for her Indian husband, Tony Luhan. This spacious adobe hacienda is set amid huge cottonwoods, blue spruce, and ponderosa pines and has an uninterrupted view of the Taos Mountains across 95,000 acres of Indian land. A tradition of hospitality includes Georgia O'Keefe who painted here and D. H. Lawrence as guests. The mood is that of tranquility, a step back in time and place. On moonlit nights guests hear Indian drums and coyotes.

Location: North of Santa Fe in a high valley at the base of Saugri de Cristo Mountains.
**Rates: $24-$78 Season: All year.
Innkeeper(s): Mari & Jim Ulmer.
3 Rooms. 3 Private Baths. Guest phone available. TV available. Smoking OK. Credit Cards: Visa, MC. Beds: QD. Meals: Continental-plus breakfast.

"Your warm friendliness and gracious hospitality have made this week an experience we will never forget! Thank you so much for making the first week so very special."

La Posada De Taos
309 Juanita Lane, PO Box 1118
Taos NM 87571
(505) 758-8164

Circa 1850. La Posada is an old adobe with five guest rooms. The inn serves a full breakfast before guests leave for visiting the art galleries, Indian pueblos or more athletic activities such as kayaking, skiing and hiking.

Rates: $42-$75.

The Taos Inn
PO Drawer N
Taos NM 87571
(505) 758-2233, (800) TAOS-INN

Circa 1660. The Taos Inn is a historic landmark with sections dating back to the 1600s. The inn offers a rustic wood and adobe setting with wood-burning fireplaces, vigas, and wrought iron. A sense of the exotic tri-cultural heritage of the Spanish, Anglo, and Indian is picked up easily in the inn with its hand-loomed Indian bedspreads, antique armoires, custom Taos-style furniture and Pueblo Indian style fireplaces.

Rates: $50-$85. Season: All year.
Innkeeper(s): Bruce, Feeny & Scot.
40 Rooms. 40 Private Baths. Conference Room. Guest phone in room. Children. TV in room. Handicap access provided. Smoking OK. Credit Cards: Visa, MC, AE. Beds: KQTC. Meals: AP. Restaurant with Grand Spectator award wine list and full bar.

New York

Binghamton

Merryhart Victorian Inn
See: Marathon, NY.

Burdett

The Red House Country Inn
Picnic Area Rd
Burdett NY 14818
(607) 546-8566
  Circa 1844. This original farmstead is nestled within the 13,000-acre Finger Lakes National Forest. There

is a large veranda, groomed lawns, flower gardens and picnic areas. Pet Samoyeds, goats, and horses share the seven acres and next to the property are acres of wild blueberry patches and stocked fishing ponds. The Red House is near Seneca Lake and world-famous Glen Gorge. The Corning Glass Museum and Cornell University are nearby.

Location: Within Finger Lakes National Forest near Watkin's Glen.
Rates: $32-$65. Season: All year.
Innkeeper(s): Sandy Schmanke & Joan Martin.
6 Rooms. 4 Shared Baths. Guest phone available. Children 12 & up. TV available. Smoking OK. Credit Cards: Visa, MC. Beds: D. Meals: Full country breakfast.
  "Delightful. Beautifully located, hiking, cross-country skiing. Guest rooms are charming."
  "Breakfast unbelievably good. Absolutely superior in all ways."

Corning

Rosewood Inn
134 E First St
Corning NY 14830
(607) 962-3253
  Circa 1855. Rosewood Inn is a 130-year-old home retaining the charm of the Victorian era in its original Greek Revival style. There are four two-story, square columns and arched windows and doors. In 1917 the interior and exterior were renovated into an English Tudor style. Other majestic homes line the street by the Rosewood Inn.

Location: Downtown.
Rates: $40-$80.
Innkeeper(s): Winnie & Dick Peer.

Frankfort

Blueberry Hill
389 Brockway Rd
Frankfort NY 13340
(315) 733-0040
  Circa 1828. Tons of blueberries grow on this sixty-acre property of woodlands, ponds and streams. Behind the rose-covered stone fences is a Greek Revival home, decorated with traditional furnishings. Guests are served a full breakfast in the kitchen next to the brick hearth fireplace and underneath exposed oak beams.

Location: In the Mohawk Valley.
**Rates: $35.
Innkeeper(s): Bob & Flo McCraith.

Ithaca

Merryhart Victorian Inn
See: Marathon, NY.

Rose Inn

813 Auburn Rd, Rt 34 N, PO Box 6576
Ithaca NY 14851-6576
(607) 533-4202

Circa 1851. The Rose Inn is located on twenty landscaped acres fifteen minutes from Ithaca and Cornell University. The property is part of a land grant awarded to members of a regiment who fought in the Sullivan Campaign against the Iroquois Indians. A classic Italianate Mansion, it has long been famous

for its fabulous circular staircase made of Honduran mahogany. Charles Rosemann is a hotelier from Germany with a degree from the Hotel School in Heidelberg. Sherry is a noted interior designer specializing in pre-Victorian architecture and furniture.

Location: Finger Lakes region of Central New York.
**Rates: $95-$175. Season: All year.
Innkeeper(s): Sherry & Charles Rosemann.
10 Rooms. 8 Private Baths. 2 Shared Baths. Conference Room. Guest phone available. Children 12 & up. TV available. Handicap access provided. Credit Cards: Visa, MC, AE. Beds: KQT. Meals: Full gourmet breakfast.

"Your efforts represent the blending of two outstanding talents, which when combined with your warmth, produce the ultimate experience in being away from home. Staying at the Rose Inn is like staying with friends in their beautiful home."

Keene

The Bark Eater

Alstead Mill Rd
Keene NY 12942
(518) 576-2221

Circa 1830. Originally a stagecoach stopover on the old road for Lake Placid, The Bark Eater has been in nearly continuous operation since the 1800s. In those early days it was a full day's journey over rugged mountainous terrain with two teams of horses. It has

been in the Wilson family since the 1930s. The atmosphere still reflects those early times with the wide

board floors, fireplaces, and rooms filled with antiques. Located on a spacious farm, there is hiking, swimming, sunning or downhill skiing, skating, bobsledding and tobogganing. The *Bark Eater* is the English translation of the Indian word Adirondacks.

Location: One mile from town.
**Rates: $72. Season: All year.
Innkeeper(s): Joe Pete Wilson.
17 Rooms. 4 Private Baths. Guest phone available. Children. Pets OK. Smoking OK. Meals: Full gourmet breakfast.

"Staying at a Country Inn is an old tradition in Europe, and is rapidly catching on in the United States...A stay here is a pleasant surprise for anyone who travels." William Lederer, Ugly American.

Marathon

Merryhart Victorian Inn

12 Front St, PO Box 363
Marathon NY 13803
(607) 849-3951

Circa 1895. This Queen Anne Victorian rests on the banks of the Tioughnioga River. John Salmon, a local merchant, built the home and installed stained glass windows throughout, including a stunning set of double stained glass windows that adorn the carved staircase. Outside, the tree-lined street has several other Victorian homes in this picturesque old-fashioned village.

Location: On I-81 between Binghamton and Syracuse, 20 miles from Ithaca.
Rates: $25-$37. Season: All year.
Innkeeper(s): Lou & Bobbie Sisco.
4 Rooms. 1 Private Baths. Conference Room. Guest phone available. Children by special arrangement. Beds: KDC. Meals: Full buffet-style breakfast.

Oneida

The Pollyanna
302 Main St
Oneida NY 13421
(315) 363-0524

Circa 1860. The Oneida community settled near here during the Transcendentalist Movement. Roses and iris grace the gardens of this Italian villa. The inn

is filled with special collections and antiques and there are three Italian-marble fireplaces. Of the two crystal chandeliers, one is still piped for original gas. A hand-crafted white wool and mohair rug runs up the staircase to the rooms where guests are pampered with bed warmers and down quilts. Mrs. Chapin is an artist-craftsman who teaches spinning, felting, bobbin lace and other crafts. Both hosts are well traveled. Nearby Broad and Main Streets are noted for the pure architectural styles of the many gracious homes.

Location: In the historic section of downtown.
**Rates: $30-$65. Season: All year.
Innkeeper(s): Deloria & Kenneth Chapin.
5 Rooms. 1 Shared Baths. Conference Room. Children if well-behaved. TV available. Beds: QT. Meals: Full breakfast.

"Housekeeping is immaculate. Your flowers are the talk of the town."

"Can we take your bed with us?"

"Yours is one of our favorite houses." Madison County Historical Society.

Penfield

Strawberry Castle Bed & Breakfast
1883 Penfield Rd, Rt 441
Penfield NY 14526
(716) 385-3266

Circa 1875. A rosy brick Italianate villa, Strawberry Castle was once known for the grapes and strawber-

ries grown on the property. Ornate plaster ceilings and original inside shutters are special features of the inn. There are six roof levels, carved ornamental brackets, and columned porches topped by a white cupola.

Location: East of Rochester on Rt 441.
Rates: $55-$65. Season: All year.
Innkeeper(s): Charles & Cynthia Whited.
3 Rooms. 2 Shared Baths. Swimming Pool. Conference Room. Guest phone available. TV available. Smoking OK. Credit Cards: Visa, MC, AE. Meals: B&B.

"You have a most unusual place. We applaud your restoration efforts and are thankful you've made it available to travelers."

Rochester

Strawberry Castle Bed & Breakfast
See: Penfield, NY.

Rome

Blueberry Hill
See: Frankfort, NY.

The Pollyanna
See: Oneida, NY.

Saranac Lake

The Point
Star Route
Saranac Lake NY 12983
(518) 891-5678
Circa 1930. Designed by renowned architect, William Distin, and built for William A. Rockefeller, this Adirondack 'Great Camp' has hosted fashionable

house parties for the Vanderbuilts, Whitneys and Morgans. No expense was spared in the creation of this elegant and rustic lakefront estate. Walk-in-granite fireplaces, rare Adirondack antiques and massive hand-hewn beams are distinctive elements of the inn. A cord of wood is needed to fuel all the fireplaces each day. This lavish camp welcomes those who prefer to 'rough it' with extravagance and style.

Location: Adirondack region, Upstate New York, lake front.
**Rates: $350-$550. Season: All year.
Innkeeper(s): Robert & Winifred Carter.
11 Rooms. 11 Private Baths. Sauna. Swimming Pool. Conference Room. Guest phone available. Children by prior arrangement. Pets OK. TV available. Handicap access provided. Smoking OK. Beds: KQT. Meals: AP, gourmet.

"An incredibly beautiful setting with the warm ambience of your own home, but away from home, thankfully. A very special place to return to again and again. Thanks especially to our gracious hosts for their humor and camaraderie."

Saratoga Springs

The Westchester House
102 Lincoln Ave, PO Box 944
Saratoga Springs NY 12866
(518) 587-7613
Circa 1880. Perhaps Saratoga's oldest guest house, the Westchester has been welcoming vacationers for more than one hundred years. This gracious Queen Anne Victorian features two elaborate fireplaces and

distinctive wainscoting. Saratoga was at one time America's favorite resort. Victorian vacationers packed their Saratoga trunks and headed off for a

summer near the Adirondacks. The tradition of high living, culture, romance and health ran strong during the 1880s. Strains of Victor Herbert's music filled the air and Mark Twain, Diamond Jim Brady, and Lily Langtree all participated in the Saratoga summer. The inn has recently been purchased by new owners who are working hard to recreate that atmosphere.

Location: Thirty miles north of Albany in the Adirondack foothills.
Rates: $40-$125. Season: All year.
Innkeeper(s): Bob & Stephanie Melvin.
8 Rooms. 2 Private Baths. 2 Shared Baths. Guest phone available. Children by prior arrangement. Beds: KDT. Meals: Continental-plus breakfast.

Southold

Goose Creek Guesthouse
1475 Waterview Drive
Southold NY 11971
(516) 765-3356
Circa 1860. Grover Pease left for the Civil War from this house, and after his death his widow Harriet ran a summer boarding house here. The basement actually dates from the 1780s and is constructed of large rocks. Southold has many old historic homes and a guidebook is provided for visitors.

Location: North Fork of Long Island, New York.
**Rates: $35-$50. Season: All year.
Innkeeper(s): Mary Mooney-Getoff.
3 Rooms. 1 Shared Baths. Guest phone available. Children. Beds: QT. Meals: B&B.

"A lovely country home quiet and secluded. Homey atmosphere. I could really relax and unwind here. Hostess is a great cook."

Syracuse

The Pollyanna
See: Oneida, NY.

Utica

Blueberry Hill
See: Frankfort, NY.

The Pollyanna
See: Oneida, NY.

Watkins Glen

The Red House Country Inn
See: Burdett, NY.

Westfield

The William Seward Inn
RD 2, South Portage Rd, Rt 394
Westfield NY 14787
(716) 326-4151
 Circa 1821. The William Seward Inn is a two-story Greek Revival estate standing on a knoll overlooking

Lake Erie. Seward was a Holland Land Company agent before becoming governor of New York. He

later became Lincoln's Secretary of State and is well known for his involvement in the Alaska Purchase of 1867. Seward sold his home to George Patterson, who also became governor of New York. Most of the inn's furnishings are dated from 1790 to 1870 from the Sheraton-Victorian period. One room has a canopy bed and private porch with a lake view, but all rooms are well furnished and attractive. A gourmet breakfast is served in the dining room.

Location: Three to five hours from Pittsburgh and Cleveland.
**Rates: $55-$75. Season: All year.
Innkeeper(s): Peter & Joyce Wood.
10 Rooms. 10 Private Baths. Guest phone available. Children 12 & up. TV available. Handicap access provided. Smoking OK. Credit Cards: Visa, MC. Beds: KQT. Meals: Full Breakfast.
 "Compliment the cook, the breakfasts are delicious."
 "We don't want to tell anybody about this place. We want to keep it all to ourselves."
 "The solitude and your hospitality are what the doctor ordered."

Windham

Albergo Allegria Bed & Breakfast
Rt 296
Windham NY 12496
(518) 734-5560
 Circa 1876. A pretty porch filled with wicker furniture welcomes guests to the gothic grace and beauty of another century. This Victorian inn is garnished with many decorative details and enriched by period wallpapers and Victorian accessories. The library has floor-to-ceiling bookcases, inviting Queen Anne chairs and tufted chesterfields. The owners have restored two of the original cottages of the former Osborn House, once a boarding house complex.

Rates: $45-$105. Season: All year.
Innkeeper(s): Lenore & Vito Radelich.
28 Rooms. 28 Private Baths. Guest phone available. Children. TV available. Handicap access provided. Credit Cards: Visa, MC, AE, DC. Beds: QDC. Meals: Full hearty breakfast.
 "Full of warmth and character...one of the best northern Italian restaurants this side of Milan."

North Carolina

Asheville

Cedar Crest Victorian Inn
674 Biltmore Ave
Asheville NC 28803
(704) 252-1389

Circa 1890. In the National Register, the inn offers eleven gracious rooms. The splendid leaded glass entrance sets the pace for a romantic Victorian stay.

Location: Asheville, 1 1/4 miles from exit 50 I-40.
**Rates: $50-$85.
Innkeeper(s): Jack & Barbara McEwan. Meals: Continental breakfast.

Flint Street Inn
100 & 116 Flint St
Asheville NC 28801
(704) 253-6723

Circa 1915. Side by side, these two lovely old family homes are located in Asheville's oldest neighborhood

and are within comfortable walking distance of downtown. Two-hundred-year-old oaks, old-fashioned gardens and a fish pond adds to the ambience of this beautiful Blue Ridge Mountain inn.

Location: Montford Historic District, downtown.
**Rates: $50-$60. Season: All year.
Innkeeper(s): Rick Lynne & Marion Vogel.
8 Rooms. 8 Private Baths. Guest phone available. TV available. Smoking OK. Credit Cards: Visa, MC, AE. Beds: D. Meals: Hearty southern-style breakfast.

"Our home away from home."

Reed House Bed & Breakfast
119 Dodge St
Asheville NC 28803
(704) 274-1604

Circa 1892. This Victorian home, complete with a view tower, sits on a hill above Biltmore Village. Guests enjoy a porch that surrounds half the house and is filled with swings and rockers.

Location: South Asheville near Biltmore House.
Rates: $40.
Innkeeper(s): Marge Turcot. Meals: Continental.

The Old Reynolds Mansion
100 Reynolds Heights
Asheville NC 28804
(704) 254-0496

Circa 1855. A three-story brick antebellum mansion listed in the National Registry of Historic Places, this beautifully restored inn, is furnished in the style of a by-gone era. There are mountain views from all

rooms, wood-burning fireplaces, two-story veranda and a swimming pool. The Old Reynolds Mansion is situated on a four-acre knoll of Reynolds Mountain.

Rates: $35-$60. Season: All year, weekends only December-April.
Innkeeper(s): Fred & Helen Faber.

"This was one of the nicest places we have ever stayed, convenient to Asheville but secluded in the mountains. We spent every sundown on the porch waiting for the fox's daily visit."

Bryson City

Randolph House
PO Box 816
Bryson City NC 28713
(704) 488-3472

Circa 1895. Randolph House is a nostalgic mountain estate tucked among pine trees and dogwoods, near the entrance of Great Smoky Mountain National Park. Listed in the National Register, the inn provides an unforgettable experience, not the least of which is the gourmet dining provided on the terrace or in the dining room.

Location: Western North Carolina, Smoky Mountains.
**Rates: $50 - $55. Season: April 1 to November 1.
Innkeeper(s): Bill & Ruth Adams.
6 Rooms. 3 Private Baths. 3 Shared Baths. Guest phone available. Children 12 & up. TV available. Handicap access provided. Smoking OK. Credit Cards: Visa, MC, AE. Meals: MAP.

Chapel Hill

The Inn at Bingham School
PO Box 267
Chapel Hill NC 27514
(919) 563-5583

Circa 1791. Once a prestigious preparatory school, this is the former home of headmaster William Bingham. The original structure dates from 1791 and the inn is a combination of Greek Revival and Federal styles featuring much of the original faux wood grainings and marble. Eighteenth-century English is the decor for some rooms while others feature country antiques.

Location: NC 54W at Mebane Oaks Rd.
**Rates: $75-$85. Season: All year.
Innkeeper(s): Jane & Bob Kelly.
6 Rooms. 6 Private Baths. Hot Tub. Conference Room. Guest phone available. TV available. Smoking OK. Beds: QT. Meals: Full English breakfast.

Charlotte

The Homeplace B&B
5901 Sardis Rd
Charlotte NC 28226
(704) 365-1936

Circa 1902. This completely restored Victorian home sports ten-foot beaded ceilings, heart-of-pine floors, a handcrafted staircase and a tin roof.

Location: Southeast Charlotte, near I-85, I-77, and Hwy 74.
**Rates: $40-$60.
Innkeeper(s): Peggy & Frank Dearien. Meals: Full breakfast.

Durham

Arrowhead Inn
106 Mason Rd
Durham NC 27712
(919) 477-8430

Circa 1775. The Lipscombe family and later owners made additions to the original manor house but none destroyed the fanlight, molding, wainscoting, mantelpieces, and heart-of-pine floors. Past its doors, Catawba and Waxhaw Indians traveled the "Great Path" to Virginia. A stone arrowhead and marker at the inn's front door designate the path. Current visitors enjoy the home's long tradition of hospitality.

**Rates: $45-$85. Season: January to December 22.
Innkeeper(s): Jerry & Barb Ryan.
6 Rooms. 2 Private Baths. 1 Shared Baths. Conference Room. Guest phone available. Children. Smoking OK. Credit Cards: Visa, MC. Beds: KQTC. Meals: Full breakfast.

Colonial Inn
See: Hillsborough, NC.

Edenton

The Lords Proprietors' Inn
300 North Broad St
Edenton NC 27932
(919) 482-3641

Circa 1787. Edenton, on Albemarle Sound, was one of the colonial capitals of North Carolina. The inn consists of three houses providing elegant accommodations within walking distance of everything in town. A guided walking tour from the Visitors' Center offers opportunities to see museum homes and other points of interest.

Location: Three adjacent houses on the main street of town.
Rates: $45-65. Season: All year.

Innkeeper(s): Arch & Jane Edwards & Sandy Hendee.
17 Rooms. 17 Private Baths. Swimming Pool. Conference Room.
Guest phone available. Children. TV available. Smoking OK. Beds:
KQT. Meals: B&B.

"Your inn is without doubt the most elegant and comfortable place I've ever stayed."

"This is really a professional operation which actually lives up to and exceeds its billing! You really are to be congratulated."

Greensboro

Greenwood Bed & Breakfast
205 N. Park Dr
Greensboro NC 27401
(919) 274-6350

Circa 1905. Greenwood is a fully restored, "stick-style" chalet on the park in the historic district. The inn is decorated with wood carvings and art from around the world and the living room boasts two fireplaces. Air conditioning and a swimming pool in the back yard are other amenities.

Location: Fisher Park Historic District.
**Rates: $30-$55.
Innkeeper(s): Jo Anne Green.

Hendersonville

Claddagh Inn at Hendersonville
7655 North Main St
Hendersonville NC 28739
(704) 693-9368

Circa 1900. Nominated for the National Register of Historical Places, Claddagh has been host for eighty-five years to visitors staying in Hendersonville. The wide wraparound porch invites a soothing rest with its plethora of rocking chairs. Many of North Carolina's finest craft and antique shops are just two blocks

from the inn. A short drive from town provides spectacular sights in the Great Smoky Mountains and the

Blue Ridge Parkway. Carl Sandburg's home and the Biltmore Estate are nearby.

Location: Downtown, corner of Main and Seventh Ave.
**Rates: $18-$55. Season: All year.
Innkeeper(s): Marie & Fred Carberry.
24 Rooms. Guest phone available. TV available. Meals: Full home cooked country breakfast.

"Home-like atmosphere and good food."
"Feel like family."

Hickory

The Hickory Bed & Breakfast
464 7th St SW
Hickory NC 28602
(704) 324-0548

Circa 1908. Vineyards, azaleas, holly bushes, dogwoods and pin oaks frame the inn and its swimming pool.

Location: Off I-40, exit 123.
Rates: $25-$35.
Innkeeper(s): Jane & Bill Mohoney. Meals: Full breakfast.

Highlands

Colonial Pines Inn
Hickory St, PO Box 2309
Highlands NC 28741
(704) 526-2060

Circa 1930. This old Colonial-style country home has been open for guests since the 1950s. Set on two acres of lawn and trees at an elevation of 4,200 feet, the inn provides mountain scenery often enjoyed from the expansive porch. Nearby are gourmet restaurants and excellent shopping.

Location: One-half mile from Main Street.
Rates: $45-$65. Season: All year.
Innkeeper(s): Chris & Donna Alley.
7 Rooms. 7 Private Baths. Guest phone available. Children. TV available. Credit Cards: Visa, MC. Beds: KQT. Meals: Full breakfast.

"We feel so at home here!"
"Great sour dough bread."

Hillsborough

Colonial Inn
159 W King St
Hillsborough NC 27278
(919) 732-2461

Circa 1759. This historic inn is probably one of the most venerable in the United States. The oldest part

was built on the site of a tavern and hospitality house originally constructed in 1752 but destroyed by fire in 1758. Cornwallis stayed at the inn and used it as his headquarters. Aaron Burr, who fought a duel with Alexander Hamilton and was Vice President of the United States was also a guest at the inn.

**Rates: $45-$65. Season: All year except the first week in January.
Innkeeper(s): Carolyn Welsh & Evelyn Atkins.
15 Rooms. 15 Private Baths. Children. Smoking OK. Credit Cards: Visa, MC, AE.

New Bern

Harmony House Inn
215 Pollock St
New Bern NC 28560
(919) 636-3810

Circa 1850. Originally a four-room two-story home in the Greek Revival style, this home was enlarged in 1860 and 1880. Finally in 1900, the house was sawed in half. The west side was moved nine feet and new hallways, rooms and a staircase were added. A wall was then built to divide the home into two sections.

Location: In the New Bern Historic District.
Rates: $45-$65.

Innkeeper(s): A.E. & Diane Hansen.
9 Rooms. 9 Private Baths. Guest phone available. Children. TV available. Smoking OK. Beds: QTC. Meals: Full breakfast.

"It feels like coming home, so spacious and elegant. Delicious breakfast and restful decor."

King's Arms Inn
217 Pollock St
New Bern NC 28560
(919) 638-4409

Circa 1848. Four blocks from the Tryon Palace, in the heart of the New Bern Historic District, this colonial-style inn features a mansard roof and touches of Victorian architecture. Guest rooms are decorated with antiques, canopy and four-poster beds and fireplaces. An old tavern in town was the inspiration for the name of the inn. It was said to have been visited by members of the First Continental Congress.

Rates: $52-$58. Season: All year.
Innkeeper(s): David Packs.
8 Rooms. 8 Private Baths. Guest phone available. Children. TV in room. Smoking OK. Credit Cards: Visa, MC, AE. Beds: QTC. Meals: Continental plus breakfast.

New Berne House
709 Broad St
New Bern NC 28560
(919) 636-2250

Circa 1921. This stately red brick colonial revival replica was built by the Taylor family, well known for their historic preservation work in North Carolina. Located in the historic district it is only one block to the historic governor's mansion, Tryon Palace, now a Williamsburg type living museum. The formal parlor has been splendidly refurbished and is the setting for afternoon tea. A gracefully sweeping staircase leads to the guest rooms with canopy beds and antique furnishings. Canadian quiche and crunchy pecan tarts are among the breakfast offerings.

Rates: $50-$58. Season: All year.
Innkeeper(s): Joel & Shan Wilkins.
6 Rooms. 3 Shared Baths. Guest phone available. Children. TV available. Smoking limited. Credit Cards: Visa, MC, AE. Beds: QDT. Meals: Full breakfast.

New Chapel

Colonial Inn
See: Hillsborough, NC.

Raleigh

The Oakwood Inn
411 North Bloodworth St
Raleigh NC 27604
(919) 832-9712
Circa 1871. Presiding over Raleigh's Oakwood Historic District, this lavender and gray Victorian beauty is in the National Register. A formal parlor is graced by rosewood and red velvet while the ballroom features an alabaster chandelier. The inn is an easy walk to the Governor's Mansion.

Location: Historic district of downtown Capitol area.
**Rates: $55-$70. Season: All year.
Innkeeper(s): Diana Newton.
6 Rooms. 2 Private Baths. 2 Shared Baths. Guest phone available. Children 12 & up. TV available. Smoking OK. Credit Cards: Visa, MC, AE. Beds: KQ. Meals: Full elegant breakfast.

Southern Pines

Jefferson Inn
150 W New Hampshire Ave
Southern Pines NC 28387
(919) 692-6400
Circa 1902. An elegant restaurant is located at the Jefferson Inn and there's also a covered courtyard and lounge. Guests are provided with a continental breakfast when they stay at this turn-of-the-century inn.

Location: In the Sand Hills.
Rates: $40-$45.
Innkeeper(s): Evert & Twilah Maks.

Tryon

Mill Farm Inn
PO Box 1251
Tryon NC 28782
(704) 859-6992

This stone house is on three acres of lawns and pastures. The Pacolet River borders part of the property. The porches of the inn provide both breezes and views of the surrounding countryside.

Location: Highway 108, 2 1/2 miles from I-26.
Rates: $40-$90.
Innkeeper(s): Chip & Penny Kessler. Meals: Continental breakfast.

Stone Hedge Inn
Howard Gap Road, PO Box 366
Tryon NC 28782
(704) 859-9114
Circa 1932. The Stone Hedge Inn was built entirely out of local fieldstone. Thirty acres of fields, woods, streams and gardens surround the inn. The property is on what used to be the main road from Asheville to Charlotte in the 1800s. Trained chefs prepare a gourmet dinner for those choosing the Modified American Plan.

Location: Western North Carolina Mountains.
Rates: $50-$74. Season: March 1 to December 29.
Innkeeper(s): John & Lucille Weiner.
4 Rooms. 4 Private Baths. Swimming Pool. Guest phone available. Children. TV available. Handicap access provided. Smoking OK. Credit Cards: Visa, MC, AE. Beds: QD. Meals: MAP & B&B, gourmet restaurant.

Waynesville

Hallcrest Inn
299 Halltop Rd
Waynesville NC 28786
(704) 456-6457
Circa 1880. This simple white frame farmhouse was the home of the owner of the first commercial apple orchard in western North Carolina. It sits on a choice

location atop Hall Mountain with a breathtaking view of Waynesville and the Balsam Mountain Range. The main house has a gathering room, a dining room and eight guest rooms furnished with family antiques. The 'Side Porch' features four rooms with balconies and other porches are available for rocking and talking. Family-style dining is offered around lazy-susan tables.

Location: US 276 N.
Rates: $60 MAP. Season: Memorial Day till the end of October.
Innkeeper(s): Russell & Margaret Burson.
12 Rooms. 12 Private Baths. Guest phone available. Children. TV available. Smoking OK. Beds: D. Meals: MAP.

"Just like a visit to Grandmothers."
"Country charm with a touch of class."
"The food is wonderful."

The Palmer House Bed & Breakfast
108 Pigeon St
Waynesville NC 28786
(704) 456-7521

Circa 1885. This rambling old inn retains the small-town charm so often found in the mountains. A full breakfast is served and suppers are available. Nearby activities include hiking, golfing and skiing. The hosts

are book lovers as is evidenced by the stocked library and the bookstore at the rear of the inn.

Location: One quarter block from Main St.
Rates: $40-$45.
Innkeeper(s): Kris Gillet & Jeff Minick.

Wilmington

Anderson Guest House
520 Orange St
Wilmington NC 28401
(919) 343-8128

Circa 1851. A separate guest house overlooks the lawn and garden of this townhouse built in the 1800s. Just a few minutes away are some of North Carolina's famous sandy beaches.

Location: Downtown historic Wilmington.
Rates: $55.
Innkeeper(s): Landon & Connie Anderson.

Andrew Jackson's birthplace, Mecklenburg County, N.C.

North Dakota

Medora

The Rough Riders
Medora ND 58645
(701) 623-4444

Circa 1865. This old hotel has the branding marks of Teddy Roosevelt's cattle ranch as well as other brands stamped into the rough-board facade out front. A wooden sidewalk helps to maintain the turn-of-the-century cow town feeling. There are seven guest rooms furnished with antiques upstairs above the restaurant. In the summer an outdoor pageant is held complete with horses and stagecoaches.

Location: On I-94, 120 miles west of Bismarck.
Rates: $45-$55. Season: May 1 to October 1.
9 Rooms. 9 Private Baths. Children. Smoking OK. Credit Cards: Visa, MC, AE. Meals: Continental breakfast.

Ohio

Chillicothe

Vanmeter Bed & Breakfast
178 Church St
Chillicothe OH 45601
(614) 774-3510

  Circa 1830. This Greek Revival homestay has an old boxwood garden and is in the National Register of Historic Places.

Rates: $35. Season: All year.
Innkeeper(s): Helen Vanmeter.
5 Rooms. Conference Room. Children. Meals: Self-catering breakfast.

Cleveland

Private Lodgings, Inc.
PO Box 18590
Cleveland OH 44118
(216) 321-3213

  Circa 1920. Jane McCarrol's *Private Lodgings, Inc.* is a reservation service organization that has listings of historic homes in Cleveland. Private apartments for short term lodging are also available from this company.

Location: Greater Cleveland area.
Rates: $30-$65.

Dayton

Willowtree Inn
See: Tipp City, OH.

Granville

Buxton Inn
313 East Broadway
Granville OH 43023
(614) 587-0001

  Circa 1812. In the National Register, the Granville was built as a tavern and served as a stagecoach stop on the way from Newark, Ohio to Columbus. Black walnut was used to construct the inn, including the frame, siding and even the pillars. There are five dining rooms, an upstairs ballroom, and in the backyard, a smokehouse.

Rates: $45. Season: All year.
Innkeeper(s): Orville & Audrey Orr.
15 Rooms. 15 Private Baths. TV available. Credit Cards: Visa, MC, AE. Meals: B&B.

Kelley's Island

The Beatty House
South Shore Dr, PO Box 402
Kelley's Island OH 43438
(419) 746 2379

  Circa 1861. In the National Register, this fourteen-room limestone house was built by Ludwig Bette, a

Russian immigrant who became a grape grower and wine maker. Vast wine cellars are found beneath the house where more than 75,000 gallons of wine were stored. Guests arrive via a ferry from Marblehead every hour on weekdays and every half hour on weekends in the summer. The ride is twenty minutes. All the guest rooms have both the views and the breezes of Lake Erie. Grape vineyards, a wine company, and a state park are all nearby on the three-mile by five-mile island.

Location: Lake Erie.
Rates: $50-$55. Season: April to November.
Innkeeper(s): Martha & Jim Seaman.
3 Rooms. Guest phone available. Children. Beds: DC. Meals: B&B.

Lebanon

Golden Lamb
27 South Broadway
Lebanon OH 45036
(513) 932-5065
Circa 1815. Jonas Seaman obtained a license to operate a "house of public entertainment" and created the Golden Lamb. Much of the inn's furnishings are Shaker items, and the Shaker collection is so substantial that the inn has set aside two museum-type rooms to house it. The Black Horse Tavern is a part of the inn and is kept in its original style. Flintlock rifles and horse racing mementoes decorate the Tavern. Eleven presidents and Charles Dickens stayed at the Golden Lamb.

Rates: $52. Season: Every day but Christmas.
Innkeeper(s): Jackson Reynolds.
19 Rooms. 19 Private Baths. Guest phone available. TV available. Credit Cards: All. Meals: EP.

Loudonville

Blackfork Inn
303 North Water St, PO Box 149
Loudonville OH 44842
(419) 994-3252
Circa 1865. A Civil War businessman Philip Black, brought the railroad to town and built the inn. Blackfork is in the National Register because of its well-preserved Second Empire style. Carefully restored with the help of noted preservationists, the inn is filled with a collection of Ohio antiques. Located in a scenic Amish area, the three-course breakfasts feature local produce.

Rates: $72. Season: All year.
Innkeeper(s): Sue & Al Gorisek.

6 Rooms. 6 Private Baths. Guest phone available. Children. Smoking OK. Credit Cards: Visa, MC. Meals: Continental-plus breakfast.

Marblehead

Old Stone House Inn
133 Clemons St
Marblehead OH 43440
(419) 798-5922
Circa 1861. Possessing one of the best locations in the area, this lakefront mansion was built by Alexander Clemons who ran the stone quarry in the area. Views of Kelley's Island and 128 feet of lake frontage are enjoyed by guests. A widow's walk atop the house was used during war time by Union soldiers and an old Civil War cannon sits as sculpture at the front of the inn. Breakfast is served beside an expansive lake view.

Rates: $55. Season: Closed December.
Innkeeper(s): Don & Nilene Cranmer.
12 Rooms. 6 Shared Baths. Children 6 & up. Smoking OK. Credit Cards: Visa, MC. Beds: D. Meals: B&B.

Old Washington

Zane Trace Bed & Breakfast
Main St, PO Box 115
Old Washington OH 43768
(614) 489-5970
Circa 1859. An Italianate Victorian, Zane Trace Bed and Breakfast is on the Old National Trail in Zane Grey country. The inn is a charming two-story brick with tall many-paned windows and louvered shutters. Inside are fourteen-foot ceilings, a wide sweeping staircase, several fireplaces, an elegant parlor, and crystal chandeliers. Zanesville, with its Zane Grey Museum is close by.

Location: One mile off I-70 between Wheeling, West Virginia and Columbus, near Zanesville.
Rates: $35-$60. Season: May to mid-November.
Innkeeper(s): Ruth Wade.
4 Rooms. 2 Shared Baths. Swimming Pool. Children. Smoking OK. Beds: D. Meals: Continental-plus breakfast.

Poland

Inn at the Green
500 South Main St
Poland OH 44514
(216) 757-4688

Circa 1876. This Victorian 'Baltimore' townhouse is on a slight rise, allowing a sweeping view down the street. Many fine historic homes line the street such as Connecticut Western Reserve colonials, Federal and Greek Revival homes. All are a reminder of the prosperous days of the last century when Poland built up around the beautiful Yellow Creek as it wound through a sycamore forest. William McKinley lived here as a youth and later began a law practice in town. The inn features twelve-foot ceilings, five Italian marble fireplaces and original poplar floors. A greeting room is often the site for breakfast and guests. Guests also enjoy the library and porch.

Location: At the south end of the Poland Village Green.
Rates: $35-$45. Season: All year.
Innkeeper(s): Ginny & Steve Meloy.
4 Rooms. 2 Private Baths. 1 Shared Baths. TV available. Beds: DT. Meals: Continental breakfast.

Tipp City

Willowtree Inn
1900 W State Rt 571
Tipp City OH 45371
(513) 667-2957

Circa 1827. This Federal-style mansion was built between 1827-1830. It was a copy of a similar home in North Carolina, the former home of the builders. Antique furnishings of the period and polished wood floors add to the ambience of the rambling homestead. The inn is just eight miles north of the I-75 and I-70 intersections.

Location: Two-and-a-half miles west of I-75 at exit 68.
**Rates: $55-$65. Season: All year.
Innkeeper(s): Mrs. John DeBold.
6 Rooms. 1 Private Baths. 5 Shared Baths. Guest phone available. Children 12 & up. TV available. Credit Cards: Visa, MC, AE. Beds: DT. Meals: Full breakfast.

Worthington

Worthington Inn
649 High St
Worthington OH 43085
(614) 885-2600

Circa 1831. The Worthington Inn was built as a stagecoach stop by R. D. Coles, local entrepreneur. It was restored as a Victorian in 1983, yet the original ballroom, main entry, dining rooms and upper sitting rooms remain. A door from an old courthouse and ceiling rosettes from a local train station are examples of the care taken during the reconstruction. Period wallpapers and stenciling, Victorian furnishings and a Pub Room all make for an enjoyable experience.

Location: Eight miles north of Columbus.
Rates: $69-$125. Season: All year.
26 Rooms. 26 Private Baths. Children. Smoking OK. Credit Cards: All. Meals: B&B.

Zoar Village

Cobbler Shop Inn
Corner of 2nd and Main St.
Zoar Village OH 44697
(216) 874-2600

Circa 1828. The original structure, a cobbler shop, was built in 1828 with an enlargement which doubled the size of the building in 1860. The inn is situated in

the center of the historic district of Zoar Village, the setting of a Christian communal society established in 1817. A favorite at the inn is a waist-high rope bed, spread with an 1835 coverlet.

Location: Ten miles south of Canton, three miles east of I-77, exit 95.
Rates: $40-$50. Season: All year.
Innkeeper(s): Marian "Sandy" Worley.
4 Rooms. 2 Shared Baths. Guest phone available. Children 7 & up. TV available. Smoking OK. Credit Cards: Visa, MC, AE. Beds: T. Meals: B&B.

"Just wanted to tell you again what a delightful time I had...your inn and shop are lovely. You go that extra mile to make your guests feel very welcome."

"Your kindness and generosity was outstanding. I gained ten pounds, but what the heck! My husband loved your sticky buns."

Oklahoma

Guthrie

Harrison House
124 West Harrison
Guthrie OK 73044
(405) 282-1000

Circa 1890. This inn was an old bank building for the Guthrie Savings Bank. The original vault is still in the inn, now furnished in Victorian antiques. The Harrison House is Oklahoma's first bed and breakfast inn, and the rooms are named after famous citizens such as Tom Mix, a Guthrie bartender who became a real Hollywood cowboy. Guests here enjoy hiking and horseback riding at Horse Thief Canyon Ranch, and hayrides and cookouts at the 5 W Sunrise Ranch. Transportation is sometimes by surrey and covered wagons.

Rates: $40-$100. Season: All year.
Innkeeper(s): Phyllis Murray.
23 Rooms. 23 Private Baths. Guest phone available. TV available. Beds: KQT. Meals: B&B.

Oregon

Ashland

Cowslip's Belle
159 N Main St
Ashland OR 97520
(503) 488-2901
   Circa 1913. Cowslip's Belle is a Craftsman-era bungalow, its simple design reflecting a rebellion against

the ornate, and often over-decorated Victorian. The inn is named for a flower mentioned in *Midsummer Night's Dream*, and each of the guest rooms is named after one of Shakespeare's favorite flowers.

Location: Three blocks from theaters and the plaza.
**Rates: $48-$68. Season: All year.
Innkeeper(s): Jon & Carmen Reinhardt.
4 Rooms. 4 Private Baths. Guest phone available. Children 10 & up. Credit Cards: Visa, MC. Beds: QT. Meals: Full breakfast.

   "The atmosphere was delightful, the decor charming, the food delicious and the company grand. Tony says he's spoiled forever."

   "Our room was perfect. The breakfasts were delicious and the conversations lively. The Cowslip's Belle adds to the ambience of Ashland. We thoroughly enjoyed our visit."

   "Thank you for the special joy you brought to our vacation.!"

   "You two are really wonderful people and really made us see how unique and special Ashland and her people are."

Edinburgh Lodge Bed & Breakfast
586 East Main Street
Ashland OR 97520
(503) 488-1050
   Circa 1908. The Edinburgh, built by a miner, became the J. T. Currie Boarding House for teachers and railroad workers. Handmade quilts and period furnishings adorn each guest room. In the afternoon, tea is served and in the morning, a full breakfast.

**Rates: $49-$62.
Innkeeper(s): Linda Thirlwall.

Hersey House
451 North Main Street
Ashland OR 97520
(503) 482-4563
   Circa 1904. A saltbox Victorian built with leaded glass windows, the inn also features an L-shaped stair-

case. James Hersey, Ashland City Councilman, was the first of five generations of Herseys to occupy the house.

Rates: $65. Season: May to November.
Innkeeper(s): Gail E. Orell, K. Lynn Savage.
4 Rooms. 4 Private Baths. Guest phone available. Children 12 & up. Beds: Q. Meals: B&B

"We couldn't have asked for anything more, the delicious breakfasts and thoughtful social hour. Your house and gardens are beautiful."

"I truly consider your home, my home, away from home."

"We remember with fondness, our stay earlier this year. We have had Eggs Hersey several times and look forward to another stay in July."

McCully House Inn
See: Jacksonville, OR.

Royal Carter House
514 Siskiyou Blvd
Ashland OR 97520
(503) 482-5623

Circa 1909. Listed in the National Register, the Royal Carter House is surrounded by tall trees and lovely gardens. The inn has a secluded deck and two guest rooms.

Location: Southern Oregon, four blocks from the Shakespeare theater.
**Rates: $44-$60.
Innkeeper(s): Roy & Alyce Levy.
"Thank you! I really feel special here!"
"Loved your hospitality."
"Warm, quiet, restful! We'll be back!"

Astoria

Rosebriar Inn
636 Fourteenth St
Astoria OR 97103
(503) 325-7427

Circa 1902. Commanding a spectacular view of the harbor, Rosebriar, a neoclassical Greek clapboard house is situated on a hill overlooking the village. Built by banker Frank Patton the house boasts hand stenciling, carved ceilings, leaded glass and polished woodwork. With an addition in 1950, the building grew to 7,000 square feet and housed the "Holy Name Convent". The former chapel is now used for groups and receptions. Astoria is the oldest American settlement west of the Rockies, dating from a fur trading post established in 1811. Over 400 historical homes and buildings make walking tours popular. Museums in the area include the Flavel House, Heritage Museum and the outstanding Columbia River Maritime Museum. Astoria is also busy with fishing, logging and shipping.

Location: One hundred miles from Portland.
**Rates: $38-$50. Season: All year.

Innkeeper(s): Ann Leenstra & Judith Papendick.
9 Rooms. 2 Private Baths. 3 Shared Baths. Conference Room. Guest phone available. Children 6 & up. Pets OK. Credit Cards: Visa, MC. Beds: QT. Meals: B&B.

"I really feel special here. Loved your hospitality."
"Warm, quiet, restful! We'll be back."

Eugene

Country Garden Bed & Breakfast Inn
245 Pearl St
Eugene OR 97401
(503) 345-7417

Circa 1909. A Swiss bungalow-style house, Country Garden is embellished with curved brackets, stick work, interior boxed window seats, a gable roof,

dormer windows and cedar shingle siding. The garden is filled with perennials, rock garden species and shade trees. The house originally belonged to Eugene

Skinner for whom the city of Eugene was named, and is located at Skinner's Butte.

Location: East Skinner Butte Historical Neighborhood.
Rates: $49. Season: All year.
Innkeeper(s): Lori & Rochy Warner.
2 Rooms. 2 Private Baths. Guest phone available. Children. TV available. Handicap access provided. Credit Cards: Discounts for extended stays. Beds: DT. Meals: Continental breakfast.

"There are some places where you feel at home right when you walk in. These places are few, but your bungalow is certainly one of them. We were charmed!"

House in the Woods
814 Lorane Highway
Eugene OR 97405
(503) 343-3234

Circa 1910. Rhododendrons and azaleas provide the perfect backdrop for the House in the Woods. Bicycle trails near the home lead to shops, art galleries, museums and wineries.

Location: Southwest Eugene, Willamette Valley.
**Rates: $38-$55.
Innkeeper(s): Eunice & George Kjaer.

Independence

Out of the Blue
386 Monmouth St
Independence OR 97351
(503) 838-3636

Circa 1880. A Queen Anne Victorian now in the National Register, the inn is appropriately appointed by its antique dealer host. Independence is a small historic town in the mid-Willamette Valley and was the end of the trail for covered wagons traveling overland from Independence, Missouri. The inn is within walking distance of downtown, the Marine Park on the Willamette River, and the Heritage Museum.

Location: Two miles from Western Oregon State College, 12 miles from Salem.
**Rates: $28-$38. Season: All year.
Innkeeper(s): Morris & Mona.
2 Rooms. 1 Shared Baths. Swimming Pool. Guest phone available. Children 10 & up. TV available. Smoking OK. Credit Cards: Visa, MC. Beds: D. Meals: Full breakfast.

Jacksonville

Livingston Mansion Inn
4132 Livingston Road, PO Box 1476
Jacksonville OR 97530
(503) 899-7107

Circa 1915. This stately home was built for Charles Connor, orchardist. The town of Jacksonville was

founded in 1851, following the discovery of gold in Rich Gulch, and is now a National Historic Landmark.

Location: Off Rt 5, 5 miles west of Medford.
**Rates: $70-$80. Season: All year.
Innkeeper(s): Sherry Lossing.
3 Rooms. 3 Private Baths. Swimming Pool. Guest phone available. Children occasionally accepted. Credit Cards: Visa, MC. Beds: KQT.

McCully House Inn
240 East California
Jacksonville OR 97530
(503) 899-1656

Circa 1861. The Dr. J.W. McCully mansion was one of the most expensive and palatial residences in the area. According to legend, after taking a wagon train across the plains, he and his four brothers were successful in the gold fields. The mansion is an elegant and graceful inn now in the National Register of Historic Places. A magnificent square grand piano that Dr. McCully had shipped around the Horn, still graces the parlor.

Location: Southern Oregon, Ashland & Jacksonville area.
**Rates: $60-$70. Season: All year.
Innkeeper(s): Renee & Kirk Gibson.
4 Rooms. 4 Private Baths. Credit Cards: Visa, MC. Beds: QT. Meals: Country continental breakfast.

Medford

Under the Greenwood Tree
3045 Bellinger Lane
Medford OR 97501
(503) 776-0000

Circa 1861. Orchards, acres of pasture and lawn, gardens and huge old oaks provide the lush green setting for the inn. 'Under the Greenwood Tree' is a name taken from Shakespeare's *As You Like It.* It referred to a retreat to a country farm setting. The Walz family first settled the area before Medford became a town. Handhewn buildings on the property include an old barn, a carriage house with original farm tools and wagons, and a ten-ton weigh station that still works. It was used for weighing hay wagons. Elegantly appointed guest rooms, classical music, leather-bound volumes and afternoon tea typify the inn's amenities.

Rates: $55-$75. Season: All year.
Innkeeper(s): Renate Ellam.
4 Rooms. 4 Private Baths. Children 13 & up. Credit Cards: Visa, MC. Meals: Full breakfast.

Newport

Blackberry Inn
See: Seal Rock, OR.

Portland

General Hooker's House
125 SW Hooker
Portland OR 97219
(503) 222-4435

Circa 1900. This turn-of-the-century Queen Anne townhouse has been exquisitely restored by a fourth-generation Portlander. From the roof garden guests may enjoy an enchanting view of the city below, the river, bridges and Mount Hood. Convenient to everything, the inn also has a business suite with private entrance and sitting room. The host's cat, General Hooker, sleeps here.

Location: Downtown Portland in Lair Hill Historic Conservation District.
Rates: $45-$60. Season: All year.
Innkeeper(s): Lorry Hall.
3 Rooms. 1 Private Baths. 2 Shared Baths. Conference Room. Guest phone in room. Children 15 & up. TV available. Credit Cards: Visa, MC. Beds: KQT. Meals: Continental breakfast.

"What a pleasure to walk into your bright and airy house with its engaging mix of the best of two centuries. You really know your city Lorry, and your welcoming home is Portland at its best!"

Portland's White House
1914 NE 22
Portland OR 97212
(503) 287-7131

Circa 1912. A magnificently elegant turn-of-the-century mansion, the White House has been restored to its former splendor. As a National Historic Landmark the inn is generally referred to as the White House because of its tall impressive Greek columns, fountain and circular drive.

Location: Two blocks north of Broadway Ave.
**Rates: $40-$65. Season: All year.
Innkeeper(s): Mary & Larry Hough.
6 Rooms. 2 Private Baths. 2 Shared Baths. Conference Room. Guest phone in room. Children 12 & up. TV in room. Credit Cards: Visa, MC. Beds: Q. Meals: Full breakfast.

Salem

State House Bed & Breakfast
2146 State St
Salem OR 97301
(503) 588-1340

Circa 1920. This three-story home is situated on the banks of Mill Creek. Amid the green lawns and roses, ducks and geese meander past the huge old oak and down to the water. Tero and Eva Hicks purchased this home almost new. He became a state leader of the Republican party. Their son Loren was thrilled to be so close to Mill Creek, just south of the lawn. When he was nine he discovered an abandoned baby girl on the side porch. The mother of the baby apparently selected the house because it looked "just right" and "surely had nice people there". The baby was adopted by Loren's aunt. He grew up and became legal counsel to Governor Mark Hatfield, a Circuit Judge, and held other offices for the state. The inn allows guests an opportunity to feed the ducks and geese and enjoy the garden stretched along the banks of Mill Creek. The inn is close to everything in Salem.

Location: One mile from I-5 Santiam turn-off, twelve blocks from the Capital.
Rates: $40-$60. Season: All year.
Innkeeper(s): Mike Winsett & Judy Uselman.
Beds: Q. Meals: B&B.

Seal Rock

Blackberry Inn
6575 NW Pacific Coast Highway
Seal Rock OR 97376
(503) 563-2259

Circa 1938. Easy access to the beach and lovely nature trails make the special setting of the Blackberry Inn, rebuilt after a fire.

Location: Twelve miles south of Newport.
**Rates: $45-$49.
Innkeeper(s): Barbara Tarter.

The Dalles

Williams House Inn
608 W 6th St
The Dalles OR 97058
(503) 296-2889

Circa 1899. At the end of the famous Oregon Trail in the beautiful Columbia River Gorge is The Dalles. The Columbia River is the only river in the world that completely bisects a major mountain range. The river level at The Dalles is only sixty-four feet above sea level, flowing through solid basalt walls and the Cascade Mountains. The location once served as a meeting point for ten Indian nations who gathered for games, trading, and salmon fishing. Because it was impossible to take a wagon through the long Cascade gap, the only passage to the west was by barge and later by stern wheelers. The Dalles became a key location for transportation and shipping between the east and west.

One of the most well known houses in the town is the Williams House. This National Register inn is a handsome green and white Victorian with lots of gingerbread, a veranda and gazebo, as well as a belvedere tower. Lush green lawns extend from a wrought iron fence at the street up to the inn. A natural arboretum slopes down to Mill Creek on the west. A favorite room is Harriet's Room with its own private balcony overlooking the Klickitat Hills and the Columbia River; a canopied four-poster bed, chaise lounge and a period writing desk offer all the creature comforts. Breakfast is served in the formal dining room or outdoors in the secluded gazebo. Barbara's homemade granola muffins, delicious fruits and the inn's own cherry honey are specialties. The hosts own twenty-five acres of cherry trees. For more history on this area, be sure to ask Don. He is very active in historic preservation and knows the local history well.

Note: This inn is featured on the front cover.

**Rates: $45-$60. Season: All year.
Innkeeper(s): Don & Barbara Williams.
3 Rooms. 2 Private Baths. 2 Shared Baths. Guest phone in room. Children. TV available. Smoking In common rooms only. Credit Cards: Visa, MC. Beds: Q. Meals: Continental-plus breakfast.

"We have had such a beautiful stay. A fantasy come true, including the most gracious, delightful company in conversation, Barb and Don Williams!"

"Especially enjoyed being able to take a candlelight bubblebath."

"Once I return to New York City, I am recommending this inn to every one I know."

"This has been a perfectly extraordinary experience. This home is the warmest I have ever been in and the hosts were most generous."

Pennsylvania

Airville

Spring House
Muddy Creek Forks
Airville PA 17302
(717) 927-6906

Circa 1798. Spring House was built of local fieldstone by a Pennsylvania legislator. He owned a

nail factory in this pre-Revolutionary War village. The house sits in a valley cut by scenic Muddy Creek and it surrounded by trees and hills. Restored to its original stenciling and whitewashed walls, the house is filled with memories of a simpler rural life of pure water and fire for heat.

Location: York County near Lancaster County.
**Rates: $50-$75. Season: All year.
Innkeeper(s): Ray Constance Hearne.
5 Rooms. 2 Private Baths. 3 Shared Baths. Guest phone available. Children. Handicap access provided. Credit Cards: Visa, MC. Beds: Q. Meals: B&B.

"In a world that has so much plastic, microwaved food, canned entertainment and trained courtesy, we entered into a brief moment of the unique and unusual. It was like time rushed back and stood still."

"It allowed us to experience all sorts of realism - warm conversation, great food and interesting surroundings. Thank you!"

Allentown

Salisbury House
910 East Emmaus Ave
Allentown PA 18103
(215) 791-4225

Circa 1810. Built in the plantation style, this stone house was operated as an inn for over a century and

then became a private home. A formal boxwood garden and lotus pond blend with pleasant woodland to provide an enchanting and peaceful setting for Salisbury House. Inside are spacious rooms including an elegant dining room and a well-stocked, paneled library warmed with its own fireplace. The guest rooms are filled with family heirlooms, fireplaces, plank floors and wallpapers. Some guests choose to breakfast in the greenhouse while others opt for the formal dining room or the cozy sunporch.

Location: Two and 8/10 miles from Pennsylvania 309.

**Rates: $85. Season: All year.
Innkeeper(s): Judith and Ollie Orth.
5 Rooms. 1 Private Baths. 4 Shared Baths. Conference Room.
Guest phone available. TV available. Smoking OK. Credit Cards:
Visa, MC, AE. Beds: DT. Meals: Full gourmet breakfast.

Bethlehem

Salisbury House
See: Allentown, PA.

Bird-In-Hand

Greystone Motor Lodge
2658 Old Philadelphia Pike, PO Box 270
Bird-In-Hand PA 17505
(717) 393-4233
  Circa 1883. In the mid-1800s a farmhouse was built.
Later, in 1883, it was transformed into a French-Vic-

torian mansion. There are seven guest rooms with
stained glass windows, cut crystal doors, original
woodwork and antique bath fixtures. The carriage
house, originally a barn, was converted to five additional rooms.

Location: Rt 340, 1 block west of railroad overpass.
Rates: $44-$62. Season: March 15 to November 15.
Innkeeper(s): Jim & Phyllis Reed.
12 Rooms. 12 Private Baths. Guest phone available. Children.
Smoking OK. Credit Cards: Visa, MC, AE. Beds: DC. Meals: Con-
tinental breakfast.

*"Enjoying the beauty, fresh air and quietness was a
refreshing change from some large sterile motor inn.
The rooms are beautiful and clean, the beds very comfortable and everyone was friendly."*

Bloomsburg

The Inn at Turkey Hill
991 Central Road
Bloomsburg PA 17815
(717) 387-1500
  Circa 1839. Turkey Hill is an elegant white brick
farmhouse with white clapboard guest rooms, all with
a view of the duck pond and the gazebo. In the dining
room are hand painted scenes of the rolling Pennsylvania countryside.

Location: Exit 35 on I-80.
**Rates: $50-$120. Season: All year.
Innkeeper(s): Elizabeth Eyerly Pruden.
18 Rooms. 18 Private Baths. Conference Room. Guest phone available. Children. Pets OK. TV available. Handicap access provided.
Smoking OK. Credit Cards: All. Beds: KQC. Meals: Continental
breakfast and gourmet restaurant.

Boiling Springs

The Garmanhaus
217 Front St
Boiling Springs PA 17007
(717) 258-3980
  Circa 1860. Daniel Kaufman, builder of the Garman-
haus, laid out the village of Boiling Springs in 1845.
This gracious Victorian home was later purchased by
R. R. Webbert, a lieutenant in the Civil War. The village was well-known for its iron industry. Nearby activities include visiting historic Boiling Springs
Tavern, excellent fishing, or attending live theater.

Location: Historic village of Boiling Springs.
**Rates: $47. Season: April to December.
Innkeeper(s): John & Molly Garman.
4 Rooms. 2 Shared Baths. Sauna. Swimming Pool. Guest phone
available. Children. Pets OK. TV available. Handicap access
provided. Beds: DT. Meals: Continental-plus breakfast.

Christiana

Winding Glen Farm Tourist Home
107 Noble Rd
Christiana PA 17509
(215) 593-5535
  Circa 1730.

Rates: $30.
Innkeeper(s): Minnie Metzler.

Cooksburg

Gateway Lodge & Cabins
Rt 36, PO Box 125
Cooksburg PA 16217
(814) 744-8017, (800) 843-6862 (PA only).
  Circa 1934. A log cabin inn, the Gateway Lodge is appointed in colonial decor with antiques throughout. It is constructed of pine and hemlock logs with wormy chestnut walls and trim. A heavy-beamed ceiling and weathered stone fireplace dominate the lounge. Dining room lighting is by kerosene lamps. The first reservation of each day has the privilege of selecting the menu for that evening's dinner.

Location: Fourteen miles north on Rt 36 from I-80 exit 13, Brookville.
Rates: $50-$60. Season: All year.
Innkeeper(s): Joseph & Linda Burney.
8 Rooms. 3 Private Baths. 2 Shared Baths. Swimming Pool. Conference Room. Guest phone available. Children. TV available. Smoking OK. Credit Cards: Visa, MC. Beds: DT. Meals: Full breakfast.

Danville

The Pine Barn Inn
#1 Pine Barn Place
Danville PA 17821
(717) 275-2071
  Circa 1860. The inn is a restored nineteenth-century Pennsylvania German barn. Original stone walls and

beams accent the restaurant and a large stone fireplace warms the tavern. It was the first all-electric residence in the state.

**Rates: $35-$45.
Innkeeper(s): Susan Dressler.
51 Rooms. 45 Private Baths. 6 Shared Baths. Conference Room. Children 16 & up. Pets OK. TV available. Smoking OK. Credit Cards: All. Meals: EP.
  "For four years we have stayed at the Pine Barn Inn. I thought then, and still think, it is truly the nicest inn I have been in and I've been in many. Everything was just right."

East Berlin

Leas-Bechtel Mansion Inn
400 West King St
East Berlin PA 17316
(717) 259-7760
  Circa 1897. This many-gabled Queen Anne Mansion was built by William Leas, a wealthy banker. It is

listed in the National Register of Historic Places and is in the National Historic District of East Berlin, Pennsylvania. The town of East Berlin was founded by Pennsylvania Germans prior to the American Revolution. The inn is furnished with an abundance of Victorian antiques and collections. Ask about the winter ski package.

Location: Western frontier of the Pennsylvania Dutch Country.
**Rates: $60-$95. Season: All year.
Innkeeper(s): Ruth Spangler.
7 Rooms. 7 Private Baths. Children. TV available. Credit Cards: Visa, MC, AE. Beds: QDT. Meals: B&B.
  "Ruth Spangler was a most gracious hostess and took the time to describe the history of your handsome museum-quality antiques and the special architectural

details of your magnificent inn. We deeply appreciate her hospitality."

Ephrata

Covered Bridge Inn
990 Rettew Mill Road
Ephrata PA 17522
(717) 733-1592
Circa 1814. This Federal-style limestone farmhouse features original hand-carved woodwork, rare Indian

doors, corner cupboard floorboards, and old glass panes. Three herb gardens and views of the covered bridge, old mill, and barn all add to the rustic setting to enjoy from the summer porch.

Location: Lancaster County and Pennsylvania Amish Country.
**Rates: $45-$50. Season: All year.
Innkeeper(s): Betty Lee Maxey.
4 Rooms. 2 Shared Baths. Guest phone available. Children 9 & up. TV available. Beds: QD. Meals: Full Pennsylvania Dutch breakfast. Picnic basket available.

"We've been to quite a few B&B's and by far yours out ranks them all. You both are as special as the inn is. Now the only problem we have is that we loved the place so much we're not sure we want to share it with anyone else!"

The Smithton Inn
900 West Main Street
Ephrata PA 17522
(717) 733-6094
Circa 1763. On a hill overlooking the Ephrata Cloister, this pre-Revolutionary War inn and stagecoach stop was built by Henry Miller. He was a member of the Cloister, a unique Protestant religious society also known as Seventh Day Baptists. They constructed several medieval German buildings that are now operated as a museum by the Pennsylvania Museum Commission. The inn's rooms have working

fireplaces, canopy beds, and night shirts for each guest!

Location: Lancaster (the Pennsylvania Dutch) County.
**Rates: $55-$105. Season: All year.
Innkeeper(s): Dorothy Graybill.
7 Rooms. 7 Private Baths. Guest phone available. Children. Pets OK. Handicap access provided. Smoking OK. Credit Cards: Visa, MC, AE. Beds: KQTC. Meals: MAP & B&B, full breakfast.

"After visiting over 50 inns in four countries Smithton has to be one of the most romantic picturesque inns in America. I have never seen its equal!!"

Gettysburg

Cozy Comfort Inn
264 Baltimore St
Gettysburg PA 17325
(717) 337-3997
Circa 1870.

Location: Historic district midway between Lincoln Square & National Visitor's Center.
Rates: $30-$40. Season: March 1 to December 1.
Innkeeper(s): Joel C. Nimon.

Hickory Bridge Farm
See: Orrtanna, PA.

Leas-Bechtel Mansion Inn
See: East Berlin, PA.

New Salem House
See: McKnightstown, PA.

The Brafferton Inn
44 York Street
Gettysburg PA 17325
(717) 337-3423

Circa 1786. This inn, the earliest deeded house in Gettysburg, was designed by James Gettys. It is listed

in the National Registry of Historic Places. The huge brownstone home has walls that range from eighteen inches to two-and-one-half feet thick. All guest rooms have skylights, and the dining room has a four-wall primitive mural of famous scenes in the area.

Location: In center square.
Rates: $50-$65.
Innkeeper(s): Mimi & Jim Agard.
5 Rooms. Meals: B&B.

Glen Moore

Conestoga Horse Bed & Breakfast
Hollow Rd, PO Box 256
Glen Moore PA 19343
(215) 458-8535

Circa 1750. Quiet horse pastures, old farm houses, barns, and some of the most beautiful countryside in

Chester County attract guests to Conestoga Horse. All rooms are located in the oldest part of the farmhouse or in the tenant's cottage, now furnished

with antiques and period furniture. This picturesque stone house was named for the six-bell teams of Conestoga horses and wagons on their journeys between Philadelphia and points west.

Location: Northwestern Chester County.
Rates: $45-$80. Season: All year.
Innkeeper(s): Richard and Patricia Moore.
5 Rooms. 2 Private Baths. 3 Shared Baths. Guest phone available.
Children. Beds: DT. Meals: B&B.

Gordonville

The Osceola Mill House
313 Osceola Mill Road
Gordonville PA 17529
(717) 768-3758

Circa 1766. This limestone mill house rests on the banks of Peckwa Creek and is surrounded by Amish farms in a quaint historic setting. Fireplaces in the

keeping room and in the bedrooms provide warmth and charm.

Location: Lancaster County, 15 miles east of Lancaster near Intercourse, PA.
Rates: $40-$65. Season: All year but Christmas Eve and New Year's Eve
Innkeeper(s): Barry & Joy Sawyer.
3 Rooms. 1 Shared Baths. Guest phone available. Children 12 & up. Beds: QD. Meals: Continental breakfast.

"It was wonderful! The inn is beautiful and your hospitality overwhelming. We can't wait to return."

"One for my book of memories, charming, beautiful place; beautiful people."

Holicong

Barley Sheaf Farm
Rt 202, PO Box 10
Holicong PA 18928
(215) 794-5104

Circa 1740. The Barley Sheaf is on property that was part of the original William Penn land grant. This

beautiful stone house with its white shuttered windows and mansard roof is set on thirty acres of farmland. Once owned by the noted playwright George S. Kaufman, it was the gathering place for some of the brightest stars of the performing arts world including the Marx Brothers, Lillian Hellman, and S. J. Perlman. The 'bank barn', pond, and majestic old trees round out a beautiful setting.

Location: Fifty minutes north of Philadelphia in Bucks County.
Rates: $80-$125. Season: February 13 to December 20.
Innkeeper(s): Ann and Don Mills; Amy Donohoe, Manager.
9 Rooms. 9 Private Baths. Swimming Pool. Guest phone available. Children 8 & up. TV available. Handicap access provided. Smoking OK. Beds: QT. Meals: Full farm-fresh breakfast.

Honesdale

Tyler Hill Bed & Breakfast
See: Tyler Hill, PA.

Intercourse

The Osceola Mill House
See: Gordonville, PA.

Kane

Kane Manor Country Inn
230 Clay St
Kane PA 16735
(814) 837-6522

Circa 1896. This Georgian Revival mansion, on 250 acres of woods and trails, was built for Dr. Elizabeth

Kane, the first female doctor to practice in the area. Many of the family's possessions, dating back to the American Revolution and the Civil War, remain in the mansion. (Ask to see the attic!) President Ulysses S. Grant spent a vacation here with the Kanes and was arrested briefly for fishing out of season because he and his party mistakenly took a shortcut through Elk County.

Location: Northwestern Pennsylvania.
Rates: $49-$69. Season: All year.
Innkeeper(s): Laurie Anne Dalton.
10 Rooms. 6 Private Baths. 4 Shared Baths. Guest phone available. Children. Pets OK. TV in room. Handicap access provided. Smoking OK. Credit Cards: Visa, MC. Beds: D. Meals: B&B.

Kennett Square

Meadow Spring Farm
201 East Street Rd
Kennett Square PA 19348
(215) 444-3903

Circa 1836. Three generations of Hicks have run this working 245-acre farm with dairy cows, pigs, chickens, a dog, and cats. Guests are welcome to watch the milking, gather eggs, or pick vegetables from the garden. The white brick farmhouse also has a hot tub in the country kitchen and surrounded by skylights and views of the garden. Rows of Victorian dolls line the doll room and three-story doll house.

Location: Forty-five minutes from Philadelphia.
Rates: $45. Season: All year.
Innkeeper(s): Anne Hicks.
4 Rooms. 2 Shared Baths. Jacuzzi Tubs. Hot Tub. Swimming Pool.
Conference Room. Guest phone available. Children. TV available.
Smoking OK. Beds: QTC. Meals: Real country breakfast.

"A home away from home."
*"The highlight of our experience was your warm self...
A great pleasure to be at this beautifully decorated
farmhouse."*

Lahaska

Bucks County Inn
Street Rd, Peddlers Village
Lahaska PA 18931
(215) 794-7055
   Circa 1860. Charmingly furnished rooms in an old
stone farmhouse, the inn is located in Peddler's Village, a colonial village of quality specialty shops.

Location: Central Bucks County.
Rates: $65-$125. Season: All year.
Innkeeper(s): Donna Jamison.
6 Rooms. 6 Private Baths. Conference Room. Guest phone available. TV in room. Smoking OK. Credit Cards: Visa, MC, AE.
Beds: KQ. Meals: B&B.

The Buttonwood Inn
Rt 202
Lahaska PA 18931
(215) 794-7438
   Circa 1792.

Location: Bucks County.
Rates: $65.
Innkeeper(s): Cindy Gurn.

Lancaster

Hollinger House
2336 Hollinger Road
Lancaster PA 17602
(717) 464-3050
   Circa 1876. The seventeen house was built for the
Hollinger family, whose excellent harness leather won
them an international reputation. The red brick house
has a spacious front veranda and an unusual triple-
tier porch at the side. Recently, it was a "Decorator
Showcase House" as part of an annual fund-raising
event for the local hospital.

Rates: Call. Season: All year.
Innkeeper(s): Leon & Jean Thomas.
4 Rooms. 2 Private Baths. 2 Shared Baths. Guest phone available.
Children. TV available. Beds: DTC. Meals: Full Lancaster County-
style breakfast.

Leas-Bechtel Mansion Inn
See: East Berlin, PA.

Spring House
See: Airville, PA.

The Osceola Mill House
See: Gordonville, PA.

Witmer's Tavern - Historic 1725 Inn
2014 Old Philadelphia Pike
Lancaster PA 17602
(717) 299-5305
   Circa 1725. This authentic pre-Revolutionary War
inn was built by an agent for the London Land Company, Benjamin Weitmer (the original spelling of the
family name). Witmer's Tavern is filled with

eighteenth-century nine-over-six windows, corner cupboards, locks, and hinges. It is the sole survivor of some 62 inns that once lined the nation's first turnpike between Lancaster and Philadelphia. Ask for the little book on its history compiled by the owners.

Location: One mile east of Lancaster on Rt 340 at beginning of farmland.
**Rates: $55-$75. Season: All year.
Innkeeper(s): Brant Hartung and his sister, Pamela Hartung.
5 Rooms. 2 Shared Baths. Children if well behaved are welcome. Smoking OK. Beds: D. Meals: Continental breakfast.

Leesport

The Loom Room
RD 1, PO Box 1420
Leesport PA 19533
(215) 926-3217
  Circa 1812.

Location: Six miles north of Reading, Pennsylvania, two miles north of the airport.
Rates: $45.
Innkeeper(s): Gene & Mary Smith.

Ligonier

Grant House Bed & Breakfast
244 W Church St
Ligonier PA 15658
(412) 238-5135
  Circa 1875. This completely restored late Victorian farmhouse is within walking distance of the reconstructed historic French and Indian Fort Ligonier. Nearby is the Compass Inn Museum, where volunteers, dressed in colonial garb conduct tours through the inn, log barn and blacksmith shop.

Location: Laure Mountain area, 50 miles east of Pittsburgh.
Rates: $40-$45. Season: All year.
3 Rooms. 1 Private Baths. 2 Shared Baths. Conference Room. Guest phone available. TV available. Smoking OK. Beds: QT. Meals: B&B.

McKnightstown

New Salem House
275 Old Rt 30, PO Box 24
McKnightstown PA 17343
(717) 337-3520
  Circa 1875. In the quiet rural village of New Salem, five minutes from historic Gettysburg, is this Civil War vintage home. It is situated in orchard country on two acres of gardens. The innkeepers operate a specialty perennial nursery, and the inn has a shade garden, a rock garden, a pond, and long perennial borders. Your hosts are well-traveled and knowledgeable about the antiquing, biking and battlefield touring available in the area.

Location: Five miles west of Gettysburg.
**Rates: $35-$50. Season: All year.
Innkeeper(s): Alan & Gretchen Mead.
4 Rooms. 2 Private Baths. 2 Shared Baths. Conference Room. Guest phone available. Children 12 & up. Credit Cards: Visa, MC. Beds: DT. Meals: Full hearty breakfast.
  "Mary loved the New Salem. And she knows her hotels! She is foreign editor of Hotels and Restaurants International. We stay at the Waldorf-Astoria, the best of Europe. We'll stay at the New Salem any time in preference."

Mercer

Magoffin Guest House Bed & Breakfast
129 S Pitt St
Mercer PA 16137
(412) 662-4611
  Circa 1884. This house was built by Dr. Magoffin for his Pittsburgh bride, Henrietta Bouvard. Its Queen

Anne style is characterized by patterned brick masonry, gable detailing, bay windows and a wraparound porch. The technique of "marbleizing" is evident on six of the nine fireplaces. Homemade cinnamon rolls are featured each morning. From Monday through Saturday a lunch room is featured at the inn.

Location: Next door to the Mercer County Historical Society Museum near I-79 & I-80.
Rates: $35-$55. Season: All year.

Innkeeper(s): Janet McClelland.
6 Rooms. 4 Private Baths. 1 Shared Baths. Guest phone available. Children. TV available. Smoking OK. Credit Cards: Visa, MC. Beds: DTC. Meals: Continental breakfast.

"While in Arizona we met a family from Africa. They had driven near your beautiful little town and stopped at the Magoffin House. After crossing the United States they said the Magoffin House was quite the nicest place they had stayed."

Mertztown

Longswamp Bed & Breakfast
RD 2, PO Box 26
Mertztown PA 19539
(215) 682-6197

Circa 1789. Colonel Trexler, a country gentleman, added a mansard roof in 1860 to this large farmhouse. The inn is now a stately Federal-style mansion with a magnificent walnut staircase and pegged wood floors. It is said that the Colonel discovered his unmarried daughter having an affair, and he shot her lover. Because he was well-known in the community, he escaped hanging. But after his death his ghost could be seen from the upstairs bedroom watching the road. In 1905, an exorcism was reported to have sent his spirit to a nearby mountaintop.

Location: On five acres adjacent to 40 acres of woods.
Rates: $60-$65. Season: All year.
Innkeeper(s): Elsa Dimick.
7 Rooms. 3 Private Baths. Guest phone available. Children. TV available. Credit Cards: Visa, MC. Beds: Q. Meals: Gourmet breakfast.

"Warm country atmosphere turns strangers into friends."

Monticello

Tyler Hill Bed & Breakfast
See: Tyler Hill, PA.

New Hope

The Backstreet Inn
144 Old York Rd
New Hope PA 18939
(215) 862-9571

Circa 1750. Situated on three acres of lush landscaping and gardens, the inn features some unusual rooms. One, called The Secret Room or Anne Frank

Room, is down a small hallway that is hidden by a sliding bookcase. Other rooms reveal the stone walls and are decorated with antiques and frills. Breakfast is often graciously served with crystal stemware, fine imported china, and a silver tea service.

Rates: $69-$110. Season: All year.
Innkeeper(s): Rolf Braun & Nicholas Laurinolas.
7 Rooms. 2 Private Baths. 2 Shared Baths. Swimming Pool. Conference Room. Guest phone available. TV available. Smoking OK. Credit Cards: Visa, AE, DC. Beds: D. Meals: Full gourmet breakfast.

"Look up charm and hospitality in Websters; you'll find the definition to be Nick & Rolf!"

"You made us feel like we've been staying with friends. Everything is perfect!"

"You guys were great. I think we're in love! Could just be the cookies!"

"The room and its surroundings were absolutely beautiful."

The Wedgewood Inn
111 W Bridge
New Hope PA 18938
(215) 862-2570

Circa 1870. The present house was built on the foundations of the old "Hiproof House" where Lord Stirling stayed during an encampment in 1776 just prior to George Washington's famous crossing of the Delaware River. The gracious 1870 Victorian that was later built is adjacent to a Classic Revival house built in 1833. Both houses comprise the Wedgewood Inn. In the stone house, there are twenty-six-inch stone walls. Brick walkways meander through the flower beds to the carriage house. In both houses, lofty windows, hardwood floors, and antique furnishings add to the warmth and style of the Wedgewood's hospitality. Pennsylvania Dutch surreys arrive and depart from the inn providing nostalgic carriage rides through town.

Location: On two acres in the heart of New Hope's Historic District.
**Rates: $60-$90. Season: All year.
Innkeeper(s): Nadine Silnutzer & Carl Glassman.
12 Rooms. Guest phone available. Meals: Continental-plus breakfast.

"After several years of researching the inns of Bucks county, we halted our quest when we found The Wedgewood. The Wedgewood has all the comforts of a highly professional accommodation yet with all the warmth a personal friend would extend."

"Having come years ago to New Hope as a child, I remembered a veranda wrapped around a Victorian home with a gazebo. Twenty years later I researched New Hope and found descriptions of an inn that seemed to match my memory. I am delighted to find "my" Victorian home, and today, twenty years later for my husband's thirtieth birthday, we are here."

North Wales

Joseph Ambler Inn
1005 Horsham Rd
North Wales PA 19454
(215) 362-7500

Circa 1734. This beautiful fieldstone-and-wood house was built over a period of three centuries and in three separate stages. Originally, it was part of a grant that Joseph Ambler, a wheelwright and a Quaker, obtained from William Penn in 1688. A large stone bank barn and tenant cottage on twelve acres make up the rest of the property. Inside, guests enjoy the cherry wainscoting and walk-in fireplace in the schoolroom.

Location: In the town of Montgomeryville.
Rates: $67-$97. Season: All year.
Innkeeper(s): Steve & Terry Kratz.
15 Rooms. 15 Private Baths. Children. Credit Cards: All. Beds: QDT.

"What a wonderful night my husband and I spent at the Joseph Ambler Inn. It was special because of the great pains taken by yourselves to make the inn quaint and unique. We are already planning to come back to your wonderful get-away."

"Thanks for the lovely and comfortable room, the serenity and beauty of the stone house and the friendly, warm welcome of the innkeepers."

Orrtanna

Hickory Bridge Farm
96 Hickory Bridge Rd
Orrtanna PA 17353
(717) 642-5261

Circa 1750. Flower beds surround this farmhouse, the oldest part of which was constructed of "mud

bricks" and straw. The land once belonged to Charles Carroll, father of a signer of the Declaration of Independence. Inside is a beautiful stone fireplace for cooking and a back porch where guests often enjoy breakfast in the summer. This family of innkeepers has been in the country inn business for nearly 20 years. Guest accommodations include several country cottages as well as rooms in the farmhouse.

Location: Eight miles west of Gettysburg.
Rates: $59-$65. Season: All year.
Innkeeper(s): Dr. & Mrs. James Hamett, Robert and Mary Lynn Martin.
7 Rooms. 6 Private Baths. 2 Shared Baths. TV available. Credit Cards: Visa, MC. Beds: Q. Meals: Continental breakfast.

"It is so peaceful here!"
"Everything is beautiful and well taken care of."

Philadelphia

Bed & Breakfast of Valley Forge
See: Valley Forge, PA.

Bucks County Inn
See: Lahaska, PA.

Conestoga Horse B & B
See: Glen Moore, PA.

The Buttonwood Inn
See: Lahaska, PA.

Schellsburg

Millstone Inn
PO Box 279
Schellsburg PA 15559
(814) 733-4864

  Circa 1922. This Georgian-style stone inn has a pillared side porch that has its own stone fireplace. The interior features crowned molding, brass fixtures, and brass hardware. The living room fireplace displays an ornate mantel crafted by Robert Wellford in the 1800s. (A mantel also attributed to Wellford appears in the White House.)

Location: Nine miles west of Bedford on Rt 30.
**Rates: $40-$65. Season: All year.
Innkeeper(s): Mike & Patti Murphy.
4 Rooms. 2 Private Baths. 2 Shared Baths. Guest phone available. Children. TV available. Smoking OK. Beds: DC. Meals: Continental breakfast.

Thornton

Pace One Restaurant and Country Inn
Thornton Rd
Thornton PA 19373
(215) 459-9784

  Circa 1740. This beautifully renovated stone barn has two-and-a-half-foot thick walls, hand-hewn wood

beams, and many small-paned windows. Just in front of the inn was the Gray family home used as a hospital during the Revolutionary War when Washington's army crossed nearby Chadd's Ford.

**Rates: $65-$75. Season: All year.
Innkeeper(s): Ted Pace.

8 Rooms. 7 Private Baths. Conference Room. Children. Smoking OK. Credit Cards: All. Beds: Q. Meals: Continental breakfast.

  "Dear Ted & Staff, We loved it here!! The accommodations were great! And the brunch on Sunday, fantastic. Thanks for making it a beautiful weekend for us."

Tyler Hill

Tyler Hill Bed & Breakfast
Rt 371, PO Box 62
Tyler Hill PA 18469
(717) 224-6418

  Circa 1847. Tyler Hill is a 19th-century farmhouse surrounded by an acre of fruit trees, flowers, vegetable and herb gardens.

Location: Sixteen miles northeast of Honesdale, 20 miles west of Monticello, NY.
**Rates: $55-$65.
Innkeeper(s): Wayne Braffman & Roberta Crane.

Valley Forge

Bed & Breakfast of Valley Forge, RSO
PO Box 562
Valley Forge PA 19481
(215) 783-7838

  Circa 1709. Carolyn Williams is in charge of this reservation service that represents eight private historic homes as well as other interesting bed and breakfast properties in the area. One example of a Valley Forge private host home is the gracious mansion that in 1777 was taken over as General Weedon's Headquarters. A cave on the property housed an aide-de-camp of the general's successor. The house itself was begun in 1709 as a a corner box on the eastern approach to Valley Forge National Park. With beautiful stately columns added later, the house conveys the feel of a southern mansion. Today, three acres of wooded land remain of the estate. A formal garden with an in-ground pool and a gazebo complete the gracious setting.

Rates: $35-$70. Season: All year.
Innkeeper(s): Carolyn J. Williams, Coordinator.
Swimming Pool. Guest phone available. TV available. Credit Cards: Visa, MC. Beds: KQDT. Meals: Full or continental breakfast.

  "I'll never go back to a hotel. Bed and breakfasts are comfortable and pleasant and you get a real feel for the people, a chance to really discover the area. You often get the bonus of making lasting friends."

"My transfer to this area was much smoother than I anticipated. My hosts helped me to feel right at home...the friendship that was established will last well beyond my stay at their home."

Waterville

The Point House
Church St
Waterville PA 17776
(717) 299-5305

Circa 1800. An overnight logger's inn, The Point House has been restored from the days of the big lumber drives in northern Pennsylvania. Mr. Witmer, the builder, had a contract to cut and ship to England "the tallest, straightest pines that could be found" to be used in English sailing ships. The inn looks out over Little and Big Pine Creeks. Guests may swim and boat from the front lawn.

Location: Just off Rt 44 at the end of the little village of Waterville's Lane, north of Rt 220.
**Rates: $35.
Innkeeper(s): Brant Hartung.
5 Rooms. 2 Shared Baths. Children Well behaved children welcome. TV available. Smoking OK. Beds: D. Meals: Continental breakfast. Guest kitchen available.

Rhode Island

Block Island

New Shoreham House
PO Box 356, Water St
Block Island RI 02807
(401) 466-2651

Circa 1870. Complete with resident ghost and cracked stairs, the New Shoreham House retains a fresh

newly papered and painted Victorian seaside charm. A deck faces out to sea and there's a mystical herb garden in the backyard called the Sea Star.

Location: Overlooking the harbor and the Atlantic Ocean.
**Rates: $55-$83. Season: All year.
Innkeeper(s): Kathy & Bob Schleimer.
15 Rooms. 5 Shared Baths. Guest phone available. Children. TV available. Credit Cards: Visa, MC, AE, DC. Beds: DC. Meals: B&B.

Bristol

The Joseph Reynolds House
956 Hope St
Bristol RI 02809
(401) 254-0230

Circa 1693. The Joseph Reynolds house is a National Historic Landmark and is set in a beautiful New England town on Narragansett Bay. The house is the

only known three-story structure from the seventeenth century in New England. It served as the military headquarters of General Lafayette during his several week stay in Bristol in 1778. Many homes were destroyed by the British when they shelled the town during the Revolutionary War but the Reynolds house survived. The hosts here are knowledgeable about historic preservation.

Location: Twenty-five minutes from Newport.
**Rates: $55-$120. Season: All year.
Innkeeper(s): Richard & Wendy Anderson.
4 Rooms. Children. Beds: KDT. Meals: B&B.

Narragansett

Mon Reve
41 Gibson Ave
Narragansett RI 02882
(401) 783-2846

Circa 1890. Your hostess, a French professor, welcomes guests to her home which is in the National Register of Historic Places. The inn is decorated with Victorian furnishings.

Location: Near Ocean and Newport.
Rates: $45.
Innkeeper(s): Eva Doran.

Newport

Aboard Commander's Quarters
54 Dixon St
Newport RI 02840
(401) 849-8393

Circa 1885. This fourteen-room Newport colonial is tastefully furnished with antiques to exemplify the charm of nineteenth-century Newport. The hosts enjoy sharing information about favorite things to do

Newport and special restaurants. The inn is within walking distance to mansions, ships and restaurants.

Location: On a quaint street one block from the harbor.
Rates: $60-$85. Season: June to September.
Innkeeper(s): Dr. & Mrs. Joseph L. Tracy.
4 Rooms. 4 Private Baths. Guest phone available. Children 7 & up. TV available. Smoking OK. Credit Cards: Visa, MC. Beds: KT. Meals: Continental breakfast.

Brinley Victorian Inn
23 Brinley St
Newport RI 02840
(401) 849-7645

Circa 1870. With two Victorian parlors and a library, the Brinley provides a quiet haven from the bustle of the Newport wharves. Each room is decorated with period antiques and many romantic touches. Guests are pampered with fresh flowers in their rooms and mints on their pillows when they return from touring the historic sites or sailing Narragansett Bay.

Location: Central to historic sites, shopping and dining.
Rates: $45-$95.
Innkeeper(s): Philip Sisson.
16 Rooms. 10 Private Baths. 6 Shared Baths. Conference Room. Guest phone available. TV available. Smoking OK. Credit Cards: Visa, MC. Beds: DT. Meals: Continental breakfast.

Pilgrim House
123 Spring St
Newport RI 02840
(401) 846-0040

Circa 1900. This turn-of-the-century Victorian offers a panoramic view of Newport Harbor from its third

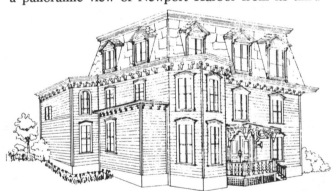

floor deck. Breakfast is served here and guests enjoy lingering. The inn is in the wharf area and is next to historic Trinity Church and just a short walk to fine shops and restaurants. Newport's mansions and beaches are nearby and one can easily stroll to quaint antique shops on Spring Street.

Rates: $40-$80. Season: April to December.
Innkeeper(s): Bruce & Pam Bayuk.
10 Rooms. 6 Private Baths. 4 Shared Baths. Guest phone available. Children 14 & up. TV available. Smoking OK. Credit Cards: Visa, MC. Beds: QT. Meals: B&B.

"Wonderful warm hospitality."
"Overwhelming view."
"Lovely family who can cook the best muffins in Rhode Island."
"A warm, comfortable inn in the heart of everything."

Queen Anne Inn
16 Clarke St
Newport RI 02840
(401) 846-5676

Circa 1890. This Victorian farmhouse has a garden sitting room for the visitors who stay here in the twelve guest rooms. A continental breakfast is served.

Location: Two blocks from the harbor in Historic Hill.
**Rates: $40-$60.
Innkeeper(s): Peg McCabe.

Simeon's Mansion
See: Seekonk, MA.

The Old Dennis House
59 Washington St
Newport RI 02840
(401) 846-1324

Circa 1740. Situated on the oldest residential street in Newport, the Old Dennis House was built about 1740. Its elaborate "pineapple" doorway is among the

most attractive in Newport. It was built by a sea captain and boasts the city's only flat widow's walk. This marvelous house now provides several inviting rooms for those who want to experience historic Newport at its best.

**Rates: $55-$190. Season: All year.
Innkeeper(s): Rev. Henry G. Turnbull.
10 Rooms. 9 Private Baths. 1 Shared Baths. Guest phone available. Children. TV available. Smoking OK.

The Thames Street Inn
400 Thames St
Newport RI 02840
(401) 847-4459

Circa 1865. The Thames Street Inn is a newly restored Victorian landmark designed by architect Dudley Newton. For 120 years the historic structure was located on Spring Street where it served as a convent. In an effort to save it and preserve part of Newport's

architectural character, the building was moved to its present location in 1985, when it was converted to the Thames Street Inn. Now guests can enjoy Victorian charm in the middle of Newport's wide array of shops and fine restaurants. The inn is air conditioned.

Location: In the heart of Newport's Yachting Village.
Rates: $45-$125.
Innkeeper(s): Beth Hoban.
Guest phone in room. TV in room. Credit Cards: a Meals: Continental breakfast.

Providence

Simeon's Mansion
See: Seekonk, MA.

South Carolina

Anderson

Evergreen Inn
1109 South Main
Anderson SC 29621
(803) 225-1109

Circa 1834. The inn was built by the Ackers-Broyle family. They brought in dirt from the Savannah River

to elevate the home six feet higher than the surrounding properties. The family was known for their fabulous vegetable and rose gardens. Unusual trees such as a pencil cedar and the largest crepe myrtle in South Carolina still grace the gardens.

Location: Halfway between Atlanta and Charlotte.
Rates: $52-$70.
Innkeeper(s): Myrna Ryter.
7 Rooms. 6 Private Baths.

"I only have one complaint with this place, sooner or later you have to leave. It's fantastic."

"Very fun, great for family. A fine use for a fine house."

"Nothing like this in England!"

Beaufort

Bay Street Inn
601 Bay St
Beaufort SC 29902
(803) 524-7720

Circa 1850. Built by one of Beaufort's major cotton planters, cracks can still be seen on the front steps

where trunks were thrown from the upper gallery by the family and slaves when the Union fleet was approaching in 1861. A fine example of Greek Revival Architecture, there are fourteen-foot ceilings, marble fireplaces, and two-story veranda. All the rooms have unobstructed water views and fireplaces. Joel Pointsett planted the original poinsettia plants while visiting the builder.

Location: On the water in the historic district.
**Rates: $50-$65. Season: All year.
Innkeeper(s): Gene & Kathleen Roc.
6 Rooms. 6 Private Baths. Conference Room. Guest phone available. Children 12 & up. TV available. Smoking OK. Credit Cards: Visa, MC. Beds: QT. Meals: EP.

Old Point Inn

212 New Street
Beaufort SC 29902
(803) 524-3177, 525-6104

Circa 1898. Two-story porches on this Queen Anne Victorian overlook portions of the historic district. Views of the Intracoastal Waterway enable guests to watch the boats sail by. The town is where *The Big Chill* was filmed. The marina, waterfront park, beaches, marsh walk and many historic properties are nearby.

Location: Forty-five miles north of Savannah, 35 miles from Hilton Head.
Rates: $50-$60. Season: All year.
Innkeeper(s): Sandra & Charlie Williams.
3 Rooms. 3 Private Baths. Guest phone available. Children. Credit Cards: Visa, MC, AE. Beds: KQT. Meals: Continental-plus breakfast.

Charleston

Bed & Breakfast in Summerville

See: Summerville, SC.

Charleston Society Bed & Breakfast

84 Murray Blvd
Charleston SC 29401
(803) 723-4948

Circa 1800. This reservation service represents fifteen private homes in Historic Charleston These include eighteenth-century homes that characterize the life-style of the aristocrats who lived here during the pre-Revolutionary, post-Revolutionary and antebellum days. All the homes are located in Charleston's Historic District.

Location: Historic Charleston.
Rates: $60-$150.
Innkeeper(s): Eleanor Rogers.

Olde Towne Inn

184 Ashley Ave
Charleston SC 29403
(803) 723-8572

Circa 1810.

Location: Near the hospital in the Charleston Historic District.
Rates: $35-$55.
Innkeeper(s): Smith & Davis.

Johnston

The Cox House Inn

602 Lee St, PO Box 486
Johnston SC 29832
(803) 275-3234

Circa 1910.

Location: Highway 121, 2 blocks from the center of town.
**Rates: $38-$50.
Innkeeper(s): Mr. & Mrs. Scott Derrick.

Summerville

Bed & Breakfast in Summerville

304 South Hamilton St
Summerville SC 29483
(803) 871-5275

Circa 1865.

Location: Off 17A and I26 in the Historic District.
Rates: $50-$75
Innkeeper(s): Dusty & Emmagene Rhodes

South Dakota

Yankton

The Mulberry Inn
512 Mulberry St
Yankton SD 57078
(605) 665-7116
  Circa 1873. Located in a historic neighborhood of fine old homes, the Mulberry is an eighteen-room brick house in the National Register. Marble fireplaces and polished parquet floors set the tone for an elegant environment highlighted with antiques and featuring prints by Laura Ashley. The Missouri River is nearby.

Location: Ninety miles southwest of Sioux Falls.
Rates: $25-$42.
Innkeeper(s): Linda Cameron.

Tennessee

Chattanooga

Mentone Inn
See: Mentone, AL.

Gatlinburg

Buckhorn Inn
Rt 3 PO Box 393
Gatlinburg TN 37738
(615) 436-4668
  Circa 1937. Buckhorn, set high on a hilltop, is surrounded by over thirty acres of woodlands and green lawns. Inspiring mountain views and a spring-fed lake right on the grounds are special treats. Paintings by area artists enhance the antique-filled guest rooms, most with working fireplaces. In the morning a full breakfast is served.

Location: One mile from the Great Smoky Mountains National Park.
Rates: $55-$78.
Innkeeper(s): Kathy Welch.

Greenville

Big Spring Inn
315 North Main St
Greenville TN 37743
(615) 638-2917
  Circa 1905. Big Spring Inn is a three-story brick manor house with huge porches, leaded and stained glass windows, a grand entrance hall and an upstairs library. Original wallpaper illustrating a park with willow trees and men, women and children strolling by is still in the dining room. The dining room is also graced with a 1790 Hepplewhite table. The house is in the Main Street Historical District of Greenville.

The smallest state in the United States was formed here, Franklin, when local pioneers seceded from North Carolina. It later became a part of Tennessee, having lasted only three years.

Rates: $45-$70. Season: All year.
Innkeeper(s): Jeanne Driese & Cheryl Van Dyck.
5 Rooms. 3 Private Baths. 2 Shared Baths. Swimming Pool. Conference Room. Children 12 & up. TV available. Smoking OK.
Credit Cards: Visa, MC. Beds: KT. Meals: B&B.

Hendersonville

Monthaven
1154 W Main
Hendersonville TN 37075
(615) 824-6319
  Circa 1810. In the National Register, Monthaven was once used during the Civil War by soldiers recuperating from battle wounds and illness. A two-story frame and brick house, painted white, the inn offers an afternoon tea as well as a continental-plus breakfast.

Location: Twelve miles north of downtown Nashville.
**Rates: $40.
Innkeeper(s): Hugh & Jackie Waddell.

Loudon

River Road Inn
River Road
Loudon TN 37774
(615) 458-4861
  Circa 1857. River Road Inn, a Federal-style home, is in the National Register. Furnished with antiques, the inn features a teakwood circular staircase that winds up three floors. Extensive gardens provide additional enjoyment as well as a bushy screen for fishing.

Location: Thirty miles southwest of Knoxville. One-and-one-half miles from I-75.
**Rates: $50. Season: All year.
Innkeeper(s): Dan, Dave & Kaky Smith.
6 Rooms. 4 Private Baths. 2 Shared Baths. Guest phone available. Children. TV available. Smoking OK. Credit Cards: Visa, MC. Beds: QC. Meals: Full or continental breakfast, guest's choice.

Memphis

The Great Southern Hotel
See: Brinkley, AR

Nashville

Monthaven
See: Hendersonville, TN.

Rogersville

Hale Springs Inn
110 West Main St
Rogersville TN 37857
(615) 272-5171
  Circa 1824. Hale Springs Inn is the oldest continually operating inn in the state. Presidents Andrew Jackson, James K. Polk, and Andrew Johnson stayed here.

The *McKinney Tavern*, as Hale Springs was known then, was Union headquarters during the war. Canopy beds, working fireplaces and an evening meal by candlelight in the elegant dining room all make for a romantic stay.

Location: East Tennessee.
**Rates: $35 = $60. Season: All year.
Innkeeper(s): Stan & Kim Pace.
10 Rooms. 10 Private Baths. Guest phone available. Children. TV available. Smoking OK. Credit Cards: Visa, MC, AE. Beds: QTC. Meals: Continental breakfast.

Rugby

Newbury House at Historic Rugby
Hwy 52, PO Box 8
Rugby TN 37733
(615) 628-2441
  Circa 1880. Mansard-roofed Newbury House Inn first lodged visitors to this unique English village in 1880, when famous author and social reformer, Thomas Huges, founded Rugby. Filled with authentic Victorian antiques, the inn even includes some furnishings that are original to the colony. The entire village is in the National Register of Historic Places.

Rates: $37-$47. Season: February 1 to December 15.
Innkeeper(s): Historic Rugby Staff.
5 Rooms. 3 Private Baths. 2 Shared Baths. Conference Room. Guest phone available. Children 6 & up. Smoking OK. Beds: D. Meals: EP, restaurant on premises.

Texas

Austin

Bed & Breakfast Texas Style
See: Dallas, TX.

Big Sandy

Annie's Bed & Breakfast
106 N Tyler
Big Sandy TX 75755
(214) 636-4307

Circa 1901. Annie's Attic, a well-known craft and pattern company, renovated this Victorian house and created a showplace for fine antiques, imported rugs, outstanding handmade quilts and other sewing and stitchery items. The house is surrounded by a white picket fence and detailed gingerbread decorates the porches and balconies.

Location: Ten miles from I-20 in northeast Texas.
Rates: $45-$100. Season: All year.
Innkeeper(s): Les & Martha Lane.
13 Rooms. 8 Private Baths. 2 Shared Baths. Guest phone available. Children. Credit Cards: Visa, MC. Meals: Full breakfast.

Cuero

Reiffert-Mugge Inn
304 W Prairie
Cuero TX 77954
(512) 275-2626

Circa 1886. Emil Reiffert originally built his home at Indianola, a major seaport on Matagorda Bay. The home stood through two hurricanes and in 1886, 100 people who entered the home were saved from the storm which destroyed the city and caused its abandonment. The house was dismantled and moved to Cuero. A reminder of its Victorian past and coastal origins, the house stands proudly with its 1887 wallpapers still hanging in the elegant parlors. Twenty-

eight oak trees shade the grounds and servants' quarters. Guests are encouraged to enjoy the large parlor and sitting rooms, the balcony, verandas, and patios. The inn is located in a historic residential district of many older homes.

Location: Corner of Prairie & Indianola, two blocks east of US 183.
Rates: $35-$50. Season: All year.
Innkeeper(s): Gil & Lisa Becker.
6 Rooms. 6 Private Baths. Conference Room. Guest phone available. Children 12 & up. TV available. Handicap access provided. Smoking OK. Beds: KQT. Meals: Continental-plus breakfast.
"The bisquits are little bits of heaven."

Dallas

Bed & Breakfast Texas Style, RSO
4224 W Red Bird Lane
Dallas TX 75237
(214) 298-8586

The only state-wide bed and breakfast reservation service in Texas, Bed and Breakfast Texas Style features over 100 inspected and approved homes throughout the state.

**Rates: $25-$60.

Innkeeper(s): Ruth Wilson.
Meals: Continental to full Texas spread, depending on each individual host home.

Frank Lloyd Wright Bed & Breakfast Home
RSO Address: 4224 W Red Bird Lane
Dallas TX 75237
(214) 298-8586 (RSO)

Circa 1920. A historical marker points to this bungalow, a Frank Lloyd Wright Prairie home in an area of restored historical mansions. There are three floors which include a music room, upstairs sunroom, dining room, and living room all available to guests. There is a canopy bed in the Iris room and many antiques throughout. This historic home is convenient to the Convention Center and Arts District.

Location: Historical area of Dallas.
**Rates: $50-$60. Season: All year.
Innkeeper(s): Doris & Bill.
2 Rooms. 1 Private Baths. 1 Shared Baths. Swimming Pool. Guest phone available. Children 12 & up. TV available. Credit Cards: Visa, MC. Beds: KD. Meals: Continental plus breakfast.

Ft. Worth

Bed & Breakfast Texas Style
See: Dallas, TX.

Fredericksburg

Country Cottage Inn
405 E Main St
Fredericksburg TX 78624
(512) 997-8549

Circa 1850. The inn is the first two-story limestone house built in town and has twenty-four-inch thick walls and an old Texas-style front porch.

Rates: $50-$70.
Innkeeper(s): Darleen Schneidewent.

Houston

Bed & Breakfast Texas Style
See: Dallas, TX.

Jefferson

Hotel Jefferson Historic Inn
124 W Austin
Jefferson TX 75657
(214) 665-2631

Circa 1851. The building was erected for use as a cotton warehouse at a time when Jefferson was a

large inland port and the building was on the river front. After becoming a hotel, the inn was owned and operated at different times by three different women, before women even had the right to vote. The inn is within walking distance to many antebellum and Victorian homes as well as fine antique shops, museums, and restaurants. On occasion Lady Bird Johnson is a guest here.

Location: Heart of Jefferson's Historic Riverfront District.
**Rates: $45-$75. Season: All year.
Innkeeper(s): Neely & Tanya Plumb.
23 Rooms. 23 Private Baths. Guest phone available. Children. Pets OK. TV in room. Handicap access provided. Smoking OK. Credit Cards: Visa, MC. Beds: KQ. Meals: EP.

"Thanks for opening the Hotel Jefferson - and for your labor of love to the Big D Little Classic T Bird Club. We'll never forget your hospitality!"

San Antonio

Bed & Breakfast Texas Style
See: Dallas, TX.

Stephenville

The Oxford House
563 N Graham
Stephenville TX 76401
(817) 965-6885 or 968-8171

Circa 1898. A lawyer's $3,000 fee provided the funds for the construction of the Oxford House. The money in silver was brought back to town in a buckboard from the boomtown of Thurber by W. J. Oxford, Esq.

The home was a family residence until the death of Elizabeth, the Judge's first wife. He remarried but thirty days later his second wife died. The home then served as a bank and as a boarding house for six prominent Stephenville bachelors. The home was occupied by Myrtle White Oxford, the Judge's third wife, until 1983. The house was built of cypress with porches reaching three-quarters of the way around the home. Hand-turned gingerbread trim and a carved wooden ridgerow make the house stand out. Now, graciously restored, the inn welcomes guests who enjoy a quality bed and breakfast.

Rates: $60-$80.
Innkeeper(s): Paula & Bill Oxford.

"Thank you for making us feel so comfortable in our new weekend-home! We enjoyed our stay with you so much and look forward to seeing you again very soon."

"Thank you for making our "snowy" stay so pleasant."

"The Oxford House was a special treat. I have wanted to stay at a bed and breakfast house for sometime and found it very enjoyable. The pink room was my pick with its window seat and pretty iron bed."

"Thanks for letting me experience the comfort and history of Oxford House."

Utah

Cedar City

Paxman's Summer House
170 North 400 West
Cedar City UT 84720
(801) 586-3755

Circa 1900. A turn-of-the-century Victorian house two blocks from the Shakespearean Festival, Paxman's is tastefully decorated with antiques. Three bedrooms on the upper level surround a small sitting room.

**Rates: $28-$50.
Innkeeper(s): Karlene Paxman.

Woodbury Guest House
237 South 300 West
Cedar City UT 84720
(801) 586-6696

Circa 1898. Roses line a driveway winding through spacious lawns to this peaceful setting. The Shakespeare festival is just a three-minute walk away. A full breakfast is served.

Location: Three-minute walk from the Utah Shakespearean Festival, in Southern Utah.
**Rates: $45-$65.
Innkeeper(s): Leon & MaryAnne Green.

Park City

The Imperial Hotel
221 Main St, PO Box 1628
Park City UT 84060
(801) 649-1904

Circa 1904. Built for silver miners by the Bogen Mine Company, this four-story clapboard is a country Victorian with a modified gambrel roof. It has been beautifully restored and is in the National Historical Register. Inside, a cozy elegance has been created with lace curtains, Utah country-pine antiques and turn-of-the-century wallpapers. Outside, wide porches

span two levels of the inn. Because the mountain air whets the appetites of those who come to enjoy the beautiful scenery, the inn provides a hearty full breakfast. Items such as blueberry pancakes made with 105-year-old starter, Utah raspberries, frittatas and homemade sausage (cured without nitrate) are on the menu.

Location: Close to restaurants, shops, galleries, ski slopes and hiking areas.
Rates: $40-$80 Summer. $75-$150 Winter. Season: All year.
Innkeeper(s): Peggie Collins.
11 Rooms. 11 Private Baths. Guest phone available. TV available. Meals: Full breakfast.

"Like visiting friends or Grandma's house."

"The Imperial is worth a visit itself with its cozy, friendly, homey atmosphere. It's both beautiful and convenient."

"Like childhood but better."

"It sounded like a good place to stay; but we found it to be fabulous. The after-ski snack was enough to be dinner. In fact, we deliberately skipped the snack three times in order to go out to dinner!"

The Old Miners' Lodge - A Bed & Breakfast Inn

615 Woodside Ave, PO Box 2639
Park City UT 84060-2639
(801) 645-8068

Circa 1893. Originally established as a miners' boarding house, the Old Miners' Lodge is a significant structure in the Park City, Utah National Historic District. It is a two-story Victorian with a western flavor, and just on the edge of the woods beyond the house is a deck and a steaming hot tub. Park City is well known both as a historic silver-mining town and a modern ski and golf resort.

Location: National Historic District of Park City, 35 miles east of Salt Lake City.
**Rates: $40-$135. Season: All year.
Innkeeper(s): Hugh Daniels, Jeff Sadowsky & Susan Wynne.
7 Rooms. 5 Private Baths. 2 Shared Baths. Hot Tub. Conference Room. Guest phone available. Children. Credit Cards: Visa, MC, AE, Discover. Beds: KQT. Meals: Full breakfast.

Washington School Inn

544 Park Ave, PO Box 536
Park City UT 84060
(801) 649-3800

Circa 1889. Made of local limestone, this inn is the former school for Park City children. With its classic bell tower, the four-story inn is listed in the National Register of Historic Places. There are twelve guest rooms, some with fireplaces.

Location: Park City's Historic Old Towne District.
**Rates: $75-$225.
Innkeeper(s): Faye Evans & Delphine Covington.

Salt Lake City

Brigham Street Inn

1135 East South Temple
Salt Lake City UT 84102
(801) 364-4461

Circa 1896. The Brigham Street Inn is a luxurious and stunning home, one of many historic mansions that dot South Temple Street (formerly Brigham Street). With skylights, fireplaces or perhaps a jacuzzi, each of the nine rooms was created by a different designer as a benefit for the Utah Heritage Foundation. The formal dining room features an elegant chandelier while the parlor is graced with a grand piano and gleaming oak floors. The American In-

stitute of Architects, the American Society of Interior Designers, the Utah Heritage Foundation and the Utah Historical Society have all presented the Brigham Street Inn with architectural awards.

Location: Twenty minutes from the airport, three minutes from the University, two minutes from the center of the city.
**Rates: $65-$140. Season: All year.
Innkeeper(s): On-site managers 24 hours a day.
9 Rooms. 9 Private Baths. Guest phone available. TV available. Credit Cards: Visa, MC, AE. Meals: Continental breakfast.

Pinecrest Bed & Breakfast Inn

6211 Emigration Canyon Rd
Salt Lake City UT 84108
(801) 583-6663

Circa 1915. Nestled in the towering pines beside Emigration Creek, Pinecrest Bed & Breakfast Inn was constructed of local stone quarried by the Emigration Railroad in 1915. This beautifully preserved inn of European design is located on an estate complete with trails, trout pond, and waterfall.

Location: Six miles east of Salt Lake City, 20 miles to Park City.
**Rates: $55-$125. Season: All year.
Innkeeper(s): Phil & Donnetta Davis.
7 Rooms. 6 Private Baths. 1 Shared Baths. Hot Tub. Sauna. Conference Room. Guest phone available. TV available. Smoking OK. Credit Cards: Visa, MC, AE. Beds: K. Meals: Continental-plus breakfast.

"I have traveled throughout the world and never have I felt so much warmth as at Pinecrest. I have only one complaint, our stay wasn't long enough!"

The National Historic Bed & Breakfast
936 E 1700 South
Salt Lake City UT 84105
(801) 485-3535

Circa 1891. This inn is a newly restored San Francisco-style, three-story Victorian built by Byron Cummings, a famous archaeologist and the University of Utah's first Dean of Arts and Sciences.

Location: Seven minutes from downtown, the airport and the Latter Day Saints Temple. Minutes to ski resorts.
**Rates: $37-$87.
Innkeeper(s): Mike & Katie Bartholome.

The Spruces Bed and Breakfast
6151 South 900 East
Salt Lake City UT 84121
(801) 268-8762

Circa 1903. The Spruces was built as a residence for the Martin Gunnerson family. Gunnerson was a cabinetmaker and carpenter by trade and had eleven children. This Gothic Victorian house was recently renovated to serve as an inn and is gracefully set amidst sixteen tall spruce trees transplanted in 1915 from Big Cottonwood Canyon. Surrounded by a small quarter horse breeding operation, the inn is north of Wheeler Historic Farm.

Location: Country setting.
**Rates: $38-$50.
Innkeeper(s): Glenn & Lisa Dutton.
4 Rooms. 2 Private Baths. 1 Shared Baths. Guest phone available. Children. Meals: Continental breakfast.

Vermont

Arlington

Hill Farm Inn
RR 2, PO Box 2015
Arlington VT 05250
(802) 375-2269

Circa 1790. One of Vermont's original land grant farmsteads, Hill Farm Inn has welcomed guests since 1905, when the widow Mettie Hill opened her home

to summer vacationers. It consists of two farmhouses, one section of which was moved to its present location by forty yokes of oxen. The original Hill Farm Inn sign hangs in the living room while a new reproduction sign hangs outside. The farm has recently benefited from a community conservancy group's efforts to save it from subdivision.

Location: One half mile off Route 7 A, between Arlington & Manchester.
**Rates: $38-$42 per person double occupancy. Season: All year.
Innkeeper(s): George & Joanne Hardy, Cathy Harper.
12 Rooms. 6 Private Baths. 6 Shared Baths. Guest phone available. Children. TV available. Smoking OK. Credit Cards: Visa, MC, AE. Beds: KQTC. Meals: MAP, full country breakfast.

"The inn has everything you would expect. A superb location with lots to do indoors and out. Beautifully kept rooms and excellent home cooking with home-grown vegetables."

The Arlington Inn
Historic Rt 7 A
Arlington VT 05250
(802) 375-6532

Circa 1848. The Arlington Inn is a faithfully restored Greek Revival mansion that is set on lushly landscaped grounds. Martin Chester Deming, builder of the home, was the owner of the Vermont Railroad.

According to legend, his father Sylvester Deming attempted to burn the building down just prior to completion because he felt the structure was too ostentatious. Local folks say Sylvester still moves within the inn today.

Location: Rt 7 A between Bennington & Manchester.
**Rates: $48-$125. Season: All year.
Innkeeper(s): Paul & Madeline Kruzel.
13 Rooms. 13 Private Baths. Swimming Pool. Conference Room. Guest phone available. Children. TV available. Handicap access provided. Smoking OK. Credit Cards: Visa, MC. Beds: D. Meals: B&B, restaurant.

"So wonderful! We hate to leave. A pleasurable experience."

"Charming, the dining was the best we ever experienced in Vermont."

"What a romantic place and such outrageous food!!"
"Fantastic fairy tale inn."

The Inn at Sunderland
See: Sunderland, VT.

Barre

Woodruff House
13 East St
Barre VT 05641
(802) 476-7745

Circa 1883. This blue Queen Anne Victorian with cranberry shutters was built by an area granite

manufacturer. (Barre is the "Granite Center of the World" and has the world's largest granite quarries.) The Woodruff House has an eclectic atmosphere and a friendly family.

Location: Halfway between Boston & Montreal, in the heart of Barre.
Rates: $35-$45. Season: All year.
Innkeeper(s): Robert & Terry Somani.
2 Rooms. 1 Shared Baths. Guest phone available. Children. TV available. Beds: DT. Meals: Full breakfast.
"Friendly and warm. Like going home to Grandma's."

Belmont

The Parmenter House
Church St
Belmont VT 05730
(802) 259-2009

Circa 1874. This twelve-room Victorian was the private home of three generations of Parmenters. The living room is decorated in the beautiful Eastlake style amid paintings and screens by Alfred Rasmussen, Cynthia's grandfather. Her mother carved the walnut dining room set and her uncles painted the

trunk in which her grandmother brought her belongings from Denmark.

Rates: $50-$70. Season: All year.
Innkeeper(s): Lester & Cynthia Firschein.
5 Rooms. 5 Private Baths. Guest phone available. Children 8 & up.
Credit Cards: Visa, MC. Meals: B&B.

"It's the prettiest inn I've ever seen."
"We couldn't ask for a friendlier more beautiful place to stay. We'll be back."
"Just like it's supposed to be."

Bennington

The Arlington Inn
See: Arlington, VT.

Bethel

Eastwood House
Rt 107
Bethel VT 05032
(802) 234-9686

Circa 1816. Eastwood House is a brick Federal-style house built in 1816 as a stagecoach stop and tavern.

There are five fireplaces, hand-stenciled walls and wide-plank floors. A view of the river, surrounding cornfields and the mountains beyond, can be seen from the inn's porch.

Rates: $30, $40 & $50. Season: All year.
Innkeeper(s): Christine & Ron Diamond.
6 Rooms. 2 Shared Baths. Guest phone available. Children. TV available. Credit Cards: Visa, MC, AE. Beds: DTC Meals: Full breakfast.

"A beautifully restored old stagecoach stop, so immaculate, with ample and delicious breakfasts, and the most gracious and friendly of hosts."

Brandon

Beauchamp Place
31 Franklin St, US Rt 7
Brandon VT 05733
(802) 247-3905
Circa 1830. The Beauchamp Place is an elegant Victorian in a magnificently restored Second Empire

mansard-style mansion. The owner designed the metal ceilings and had them cast from original Victorian dies in Missouri. The inn is in the National Register of Historic Places.

Location: Central Vermont.
Rates: $60-$85 plus 15% gratuity. Season: All year.
Innkeeper(s): Georgia & Roy Beauchamp.
8 Rooms. 5 Shared Baths. Guest phone available. TV available. Credit Cards: Visa, MC, AE. Beds: KQT. Meals: Full breakfast.

"A Victorian gem of lavish comfort, exquisite."

"Outstanding inn of our entire trip."

"The consummate hosts."

"Furnishings of museum quality."

Chester

The Stone Hearth Inn
Rt 11 West
Chester VT 05143
(802) 875-2525
Circa 1810. Exposed beams, wide-pine floors and Vermont-stone fireplaces abound in this restored

1810 country inn near Chester's historic Stone Village. Guests may relax in the parlor, library or the attached barn which has been converted into a comfortable common room with a fieldstone fireplace. A fully stocked pub is on the property.

Location: One mile west of the village green.
**Rates: $24-$38 per person. Season: All year.
Innkeeper(s): Janet & Don Strohmeyer.
10 Rooms. 8 Private Baths. 2 Shared Baths. Hot Tub. Conference Room. Guest phone available. Children. TV available. Smoking OK. Credit Cards: Visa, MC, AE, Discover. Beds: KQTC. Meals: AP, MAP, full breakfast.

"The perfect inn for families - be it summer or winter. Love the food and the player piano. We'll be back."

Gassets

Old Town Farm Inn
Rt 10
Gassets VT 05143
(802) 875-2346
Circa 1861. Called the "Town Farm" because people were given food and lodging in return for a day's work on the farm, it is now a comfortable New England inn with a beautiful spiral staircase. Town Farm is noted for having once been the home of 6'10"

"Uncle Sam" Braddish. The inn has its own pond and features vegetables from its own garden. Maple syrup

taken from the farm's trees is served and the family sells its popular *Country Inn Spring Water* in Boston.

Location: One quarter mile east of Rt 10 & 103.
**Rates: $45-$50 MAP. Season: All year.
Innkeeper(s): Richard & Ruth Lewis.
10 Rooms. 2 Private Baths. 4 Shared Baths. Guest phone available. Children. TV available. Credit Cards: Visa, MC, AE. Beds: QTC. Meals: B&B.
  "A warm haven! Very friendly and comfortable."
  "Beautiful! Just like home."
  "Excellent food and lodging. You have a nice family and a nice inn!"

Jeffersonville

Windridge Inn
Main St
Jeffersonville VT 05464
(802) 644-8281
  Circa 1860. When the unspoiled village of Jefferson-ville was recently added to the National Register of

Historic Places, the construction of the Windridge Inn on Main Street was estimated to be in 1860. Now, its interior of century-old pine paneling and exposed

hewn beams, includes all the modern conveniences. The atmosphere here is like Vermont itself, a mixture of early American, English and French Canadian styles. The artist-host has a gallery next door to the inn.

Location: Rt 15 & 108.
Rates: $25 per person, double occupancy. Season: All year.
5 Rooms. 5 Private Baths. Swimming Pool. Conference Room. Guest phone available. Children. Pets OK. TV available. Smoking OK. Credit Cards: Visa, MC. Beds: T. Meals: Breakfast and lunch.
  "Super excellent. Good and delicious food."
  "Great as always."

Ludlow

Castle Inn
See: Proctorsville, VT.

Manchester

The Arlington Inn
See: Arlington, VT.

The Inn at Sunderland
See: Sunderland, VT.

Manchester Village

1811 House
Historic Rt 7 A
Manchester Village VT 05254
(802) 362-1811
  Circa 1775. The historic Lincoln Home has been operated as an inn since 1811, except for a time when it was the private residence of Mary Lincoln Isham, granddaughter of President Lincoln. It has been authentically restored to the Federal period with anti-ques and canopy beds. The gardens look out over a golf course and it's just a short walk to tennis or swim-mming.

Location: On the Green in Manchester Village.
Rates: $80-$120.
Innkeeper(s): Jack & Mary Hirst; Jeremy & Pat David.
11 Rooms. 11 Private Baths. Guest phone available. Children 16 & up TV available. Smoking OK. Credit Cards: Visa, MC, AE. Beds: KQD. Meals: Full breakfast.

Poultney

Stonebridge Inn
Rt 30
Poultney VT 05764
(802) 287-9849

Circa 1808. The inn's land was part of a grant from Lord Poultney, first Earl of Bath. In 1841 an addition

was added with a five-foot-thick foundation, designed as the First Bank of Poultney. The cellar was the bank's vault. The house was built in the Federal style and a later addition added the Greek Revival front to the building.

Rates: $54-$84. Season: All year.
Innkeeper(s): Jane Davidson & Lenore Lyons.
5 Rooms. 2 Private Baths. 3 Shared Baths. Smoking OK. Credit Cards: Visa, MC. Beds: QD. Meals: Full breakfast with restaurant on the premises.

Proctorsville

Castle Inn
Rt 103 & 131, P.O. Box 157
Proctorsville VT 05153
(802) 226-7222

Circa 1904. The Fletcher family settled in the Ludlow area in the 1700s. Allen Fletcher was brought up

in Indiana but returned to Vermont, tearing down a Victorian house to build this English-style mansion overlooking the Okemo Valley. It features an oval dining room, a mahogany-paneled library and spacious guest accommodations complete with individual sitting areas. In 1911, Mr. Fletcher became Governor of Vermont.

Location: Three and one half miles south of Ludlow.
Season: Closed April & November.
Innkeeper(s): Michael & Sheryl Fratino.
13 Rooms. 9 Private Baths. 2 Shared Baths. Conference Room. Guest phone available. Children 6 & up. TV available. Smoking OK. Credit Cards: Visa, MC, AE. Beds: QD. Meals: MAP, restaurant on the premises.

"Castle Inn has to be the very best place in Vermont."
"A rainbow at the end of a very long drive."
"A fantasy weekend."

The Golden Stage Inn
Depot St, PO Box 218
Proctorsville VT 05153
(802) 226-7744

Circa 1780. The Golden Stage Inn served as a stagecoach stop shortly after Vermont's founding. It

was also a link in the Underground Railroad and the home of Cornelia and Otis Skinner. Extensive gardens surround the wrap-around porch as well as the swimming pool. The hosts were flavor experts for Dole but now put their tasting skills to work for their guests.

Location: Near Ludlow on four acres.
Rates: $60 per person, double occupancy.
Innkeeper(s): Kirsten Murphy & Marcel Perret.
10 Rooms. 6 Private Baths. 2 Shared Baths. Swimming Pool. Guest phone available. Children 2 & up. Smoking OK. Credit Cards: Visa, MC, AE. Beds: QT. Meals: MAP dinner and breakfast.

"I'm moving in."
"The food is so good, it's a sin!"
"The essence of a country inn!
"Four stars."

Shrewsbury

Buckmaster Inn
Lincoln Hill Rd, RR1, PO Box 118, Cuttingsville
Shrewsbury VT 05738
(802) 492-3485

Circa 1801. John Buckmaster was given a tavern license in 1820, and the inn became a well-known

stopping place on the Woodstock Road. It was originally a stagecoach stop in the Green Mountains. Standing majestically on a knoll, the Buckmaster overlooks a typical red-barn scene and picturesque valley. Its center hall, grand staircase and wide-pine floors are typical of colonial charm. Wood burning fireplaces, a library, huge porches and a country kitchen are special spots at this stately inn. Cross-country skiing and hiking is right at the door.

Rates: $30-$55. Season: All year.
Innkeeper(s): Sam & Grace Husselman.
4 Rooms. 1 Private Baths. 1 Shared Baths. Conference Room. Guest phone available. Children 10 & up. TV available. Beds: KQDT. Meals: Hearty breakfast.

"Honeymoon heaven."

"Fantastic views. Very relaxing atmosphere. I could stay here forever."

"I've been in many B&B's but the accommodations and hospitality is best here."

"Quiet and peaceful."

South Strafford

Watercourse Way Bed & Breakfast
Rt 132, PO Box 101
South Strafford VT 05070
(802) 765-4314

Circa 1850. The Ompompanoosuc River is the setting for Watercourse Way and provides an appealing spot for kayaking, fishing and picnicking.

Location: Central Vermont, north of the White River Junction.
**Rates: $20-$40.
Innkeeper(s): Lincoln & Anna Alden.

Sunderland

The Inn at Sunderland
Historic 7A
Sunderland VT 05250
(802) 362-4213

Circa 1840. Farmer and merchant William Bradley, built this home as a wedding present for his wife. This is commemorated in the heart medallions under each window and incorporated in the roof trim. The inn maintains its original chestnut interior trim and six

panel-chestnut doors as well as a lovely walnut staircase with a turned newel post. There is an unusual sculpted slate mantelpiece as well. The goal of the innkeepers is to surround guests with luxury and caring comfort to renew both body and spirit.

Location: At the base of Mt. Equinox, midway between Manchester & Arlington.
Rates: $65-$85 per room. Season: All year.
Innkeeper(s): Tom & Peggy Wolf.
10 Rooms. 8 Private Baths. 1 Shared Baths. Children. Handicap access provided. Smoking OK. Credit Cards: Visa, MC, AE. Beds: QDTC. Meals: B&B.

"We traveled many inns, this is the best!"

"A great escape from the everyday bustle."

"A veritable treasure."

"Heaven can wait, we've got to come back here first."

Waitsfield

Lareau Farm Country Inn
PO Box 563, Rt 100
Waitsfield VT 05673
(802) 496-4949

Circa 1832. Settled in 1790 by the first doctor in Waitsfield, this Greek Revival house was completed

in 1832. The original settlers are buried on a beautiful knoll by the river. The gardens are full of old-fashioned roses, lilacs, delphiniums, iris and peonies. The Lareau Farm is in a wide meadow next to the crystal-clear Mad River, inviting a canoe trip or a refreshing swim.

Location: Central Vermont, Sugarbush Valley.
**Rates: $25-$45 per person. Season: All year.
Innkeeper(s): Dan & Susan Easley.
10 Rooms. 6 Private Baths. 4 Shared Baths. Guest phone available. Children 5 & up. TV available. Credit Cards: Visa, MC, AE. Beds: TDC. Meals: Full Vermont breakfast.

"Hospitality is a gift. Thank you for sharing your gift so freely with us."

Weathersfield

The Inn at Weathersfield
Rt 106
Weathersfield VT 05151
(802) 263-9217

Circa 1795. Built by Thomas Prentis, a Revolutionary War veteran, this inn was originally a four-room farmhouse set on 237 acres of wilderness. Two rooms were added in 1796 and a carriage house in 1830. During the Civil War the inn served as a station for the Underground Railroad. The six pillars that give the inn its southern colonial look were built in 1900. There are eleven fireplaces, a beehive oven, wide-plank floors and period antiques throughout.

Location: Near Perkinsville on Rt 106.
**Rates: $130 MAP for two. Season: All year.
Innkeeper(s): Mary Louise & Ron Thorburn.

12 Rooms. 12 Private Baths. Sauna. Conference Room. Guest phone available. Children 8 & up. TV available. Handicap access provided. Smoking OK. Credit Cards: Visa, MC, AE. Beds: TD. Meals: MAP, restaurant.

"To 'INN'scribe the Inn at Weathersfield is to 'Inn'dorse a truly remarkable experience! Ron and Mary Louise, so 'Inn'dustrious a twosome, are 'Inn'comparable. We were 'Inn'fatuated with the fireplaces and canopied beds.

"Thanks for contributing to the success of our carriage ride. Your idea of serving lunch along the carriage trail was a big hit."

"Delighted with the atmosphere, facilities and food. Our next reunion is four years hence."

"There isn't one thing we didn't enjoy about our weekend with you and we are constantly reliving it with much happiness."

Weston

1830 Inn on the Green
Main St, Rt 100, PO Box 104
Weston VT 05161
(802) 824-6789

Circa 1830. Built as a wheelwright shop, the building later saw duty as the town hall and an undertaking parlor. Moved to its present site, it became a home graced by a beautiful curving staircase from the home of Hetty Green, "The Witch of Wall Street". In the Weston Historic district and tucked in the hollow of the Green Mountains, the inn sits across the village green from the oldest summer theater in the state.

Location: South Central Vermont on Rt 100.

Rates: $55-$70. Season: Memorial Day to Oct. 31, plus Thanksgiving
Innkeeper(s): Susan & Arthur Burke.
4 Rooms. 2 Private Baths. 2 Shared Baths. Guest phone available.
Children 14 & up. Smoking OK. Beds: KQT. Meals: Full breakfast.

"A romantic and relaxing atmosphere which made our weekend feel like a real vacation."
"Everything so perfectly and lovingly put together!"
"A special memory we'll treasure."

Woodstock

The Charleston House
21 Pleasant St
Woodstock VT 05091
(802) 457-3843
  Circa 1835. This Greek Revival townhouse has been authentically restored. Listed in the National

Register, the house is furnished with antiques and reflects fine craftsmanship combined with a

hospitality reminiscent of a family homecoming. The picturesque village of Woodstock has been called one of the most beautiful villages in America by *National Geographic Magazine.*

**Rates: $70-$90. Season: May to April.
Innkeeper(s): Barb & Bill Hough.
7 Rooms. 7 Private Baths. Guest phone available. Children. TV available. Smoking OK. Credit Cards: Visa, MC. Beds: QT. Meals: Full breakfast.
  "Wonderful experience, unbelievable breakfast."
  "I felt like I was a king, elegant but extremely comfortable."
  "Great hosts."

The Inn at Weathersfield
See: Weathersfield, VT.

Virginia

Alexandria

Princely Bed & Breakfast, Ltd.
819 Prince St
Alexandria VA 22314
(703) 683-2159

This is a reservation service that represents a wide variety of private historic homes built from 1750 to 1840. Most are located in Old Town and are furnished with fine antiques. The new subway to Washington DC is fast and frequent with trips every fifteen minutes.

Location: Eight miles to the White House and 8 miles to Mt. Vernon.
Rates: $68 double (average).
Guest phone available. Children 16 & up. TV available. Credit Cards: All.

Bowling Green

Bensonhouse of Bowling Green
Contact Bensonhouse of Richmond to make Reservations.
Bowling Green VA 22427
(804) 648-7560

Circa 1699. Part of a large land grant issued to Major Thomas Hoomes in 1667, this is the oldest home in Caroline County and one of the most well preserved Georgian houses in Virginia. Built of Flemish bond brick the house features a center-hall plan, gambrel roof and wide pine-plank floors. Covering more than 125 acres, the property reflects the hosts enthusiasm for wildflowers. There are boxwoods, holly trees and cedars in abundance. For reservations, contact Bensonhouse, 2036 Monument Avenue, Richmond, VA 23220.

**Rates: $46-$55. Season: All year.
3 Rooms. 1 Private Baths. 1 Shared Baths. Guest phone available. Children. Credit Cards: Visa, MC, AE. Beds: QD. Meals: Hearty Virginia breakfast.

""We just had to tell you how perfect our accommodations were! You knew just what we were looking for, we couldn't have been happier...will certainly call again and tell our friends about Bensonhouse!"

Charles City

Edgewood Plantation
Rt 5 Historic (James River Plantation)
Charles City VA 23030
(804) 829-2962

Circa 1849. Edgewood is a Gothic style home. It was built by Northerner Spencer Rowland, thirty years before the style was popular in the South. The build-

ing has been used as a restaurant, church, post office, telephone exchange, and nursing home. Guests can visit a nearby 1725 mill with an unusual inside mill wheel. General Jeb Stuart of the Confederate Army stopped here for coffee on his way to Richmond to warn Lee of the Union strength.

Location: Twenty-three miles east of Richmond, west of Williamsburg.
Rates: $70-$85. Season: All year.
Innkeeper(s): Julian & Dot Boulware.

6 Rooms. 1 Private Baths. 2 Shared Baths. Guest phone available. TV available. Handicap access provided. Credit Cards: Visa, MC, AE. Beds: KD. Meals: Full breakfast.

Charlottesville

Carrsbrook
Guesthouses, Po Box 5737
Charlottesville VA 22905
(804) 979-7264

Circa 1794. Once the heart of a thriving plantation, this manor house is now in the National Register and is thought to have been designed by Thomas Jefferson, who often dined here. It was built by Jefferson's

nephew and ward, Peter Carr who was raised at Monticello and was Jefferson's private secretary until his death. Carr is buried in the family cemetery at Monticello. Behind the house is an old Indian burial ground referred to by Jefferson as an archaeological dig which he studied. He also convinced Carr to plant a vineyard on the hill sloping towards the river. There is a lovely formal boxwood garden on the property.

Rates: $48-$68. Season: All year.
Innkeeper(s): Stanley & Jaime .
1 Rooms. 1 Private Baths. Guest phone in room. Children. TV available. Beds: Q. Meals: B&B.

Franklin-Halifax House
Guesthouses, PO Box 5737
Charlottesville VA 22905
(804) 979-7264

Circa 1750. The reconstructed Franklin Halifax House is a combination of a 220-year-old log building and a 150-year-old log "dog trot", that once served as a hunting cabin for Teddy Roosevelt. Its double room

and queen suite with hearth provide a combination of old-world charm and modern comfort located in a beautiful country setting in the foothills of the Blue Ridge Mountains.

Rates: $56-$68. Season: All year.
Innkeeper(s): Lynn & Michael.
2 Rooms. 1 Private Baths. Guest phone available. Children. Beds: QD. Meals: Continental plus.

"Your house was beyond my expectations and beyond the description. It was exactly (and more so) what I thought a B&B place should be like."

"Quarters were lovely and comfortable - a memorable holiday."

Guesthouses
PO Box 5737
Charlottesville VA 22905
(804) 979-7264

Guesthouses is America's first reservation service for bed and breakfast accommodations, appropriately began in an area with a centuries-old tradition of outstanding hospitality. It was founded in 1976 to serve the Bicentennial visitors to Monticello and the University of Virginia. Hosts in the program are well informed and hospitable. All the homes, whether budget, moderate, or deluxe, have been inspected carefully to assure a pleasant stay. A descriptive list of seventy homes may be ordered for $1 from Guesthouses.

Rates: $45-$85.

Longhouse
Guesthouses, PO Box 5737
Charlottesville VA 22905
(804) 979-7264

Circa 1812. This two-story wood-frame house was originally a stagecoach tavern called Yancey's Tavern then later, Cocke's Tavern. During the Civil War it served as a convalescent station for wounded Confederate soldiers. Located on scenic Rt 250 West near the Blue Ridge Parkway and Skyline, the Longhouse now provides hospitality to a growing circle of new friends.

Rates: $40-$60. Season: All year.
Innkeeper(s): Jim & Lalah.
2 Rooms. 1 Private Baths. Swimming Pool. Guest phone available. Children. TV available. Handicap access provided. Beds: QDTC. Meals: Continental-plus breakfast.

Mayhurst Inn
See: Orange, VA.

Westbury
Guesthouses, PO Box 5737
Charlottesville VA 22905
(804) 979-8327
   Circa 1820. Westbury is a red brick, Federal-style plantation house situated on what was once a major East-West route traveled by Thomas Jefferson and later by Union Civil War prisoners. A major feature

of the manor is a two-story columned portico festooned with Victorian gingerbread. Inside, the two-story reception hall displays a graceful staircase and every room has a fireplace.

Rates: $48-$56. Season: All year.
Innkeeper(s): Jay & Sara.
1 Rooms. 1 Private Baths. Guest phone available. Children. TV available. Beds: D. Meals: B&B.
   "Such a wonderful home. The perfect house for someone who loves history as I do, and you've made me feel so at home."

Chincoteague

Miss Molly's Inn
Chincoteague VA 23336
(804) 336-6686
   Circa 1886. This Victorian home was built by J.T. Rowley, the "Clam King of the World" and his

daughter, Miss Molly, lived in it for 84 years. The house has been beautifully restored and furnished in period antiques. Marguerite Henry wrote *Misty of Chincoteague* here while rocking on the front porch with Miss Molly and Captain Jack.

Rates: $65-$85. Season: April 1 to December 1.
7 Rooms. 1 Private Baths. 6 Shared Baths. Conference Room. Guest phone available. Children 12 & up. TV available. Beds: KQT. Meals: Full breakfast and afternoon tea.

Gordonsville

Sleepy Hollow Farm
Rt 3, Box 43 on VA 231
Gordonsville VA 22942
(703) 832-5555
   Circa 1775. Generations have built the brick farmhouse around the eighteenth century dining room

and upstairs bedrooms. The pink and white room in fact, was frequently visited by a friendly ghost (a woman who lived here during the Civil War) according to local stories. She hasn't been seen for several years since the innkeeper, a former missionary, had the house blessed. The grounds feature a herb garden, a pond with gazebo, terraces, and abundant wildlife. A recent addition has added guest rooms to the chestnut slave cabin on the property.

Location: On VA-231 3 miles north of Gordonsville.
**Rates: $50-$75. Season: All year.
Innkeeper(s): Beverley Allison.
6 Rooms. 6 Private Baths. 1 Shared Baths. Conference Room. Guest phone available. Children. TV available. Credit Cards: Visa, MC. Beds: QTC. Meals: Full country breakfast.

"It's like coming to visit family, a lovely place."

"This house is truly blessed."

Gwynn's Island

Bensonhouse of Gwynn's Island
Contact Bensonhouse of Richmond to make Reservations.
Gwynn's Island VA 23066
(804) 648-7560
  Circa 1730. Built by a sea captain, the Captain Keeble House stands on Cherry Point overlooking Chesapeake Bay. Constructed of clapboard in the true Williamsburg style, many of the original windows, fireplace mantels, floors and doors remain in the house. The host family enjoys fishing, collecting antiques, history and writing. For reservations, contact Bensonhouse, 2036 Monument Avenue, Richmond, VA 23220.

Location: On the Northern Neck of Virginia, just 45 minutes from Williamsburg.
**Rates: $40-$75. Season: All year.
5 Rooms. 2 Private Baths. 3 Shared Baths. Guest phone available. Children 8 & up, well behaved. TV available. Credit Cards: Visa, MC, AE. Beds: QT. Meals: B&B.

Hot Springs

Vine Cottage Inn
Rt 220
Hot Springs VA 24445
(703) 839-2422
  Circa 1900. Nestled among the Allegheny Ridges in a mountain spa stands this turn-of-the-century, multi-gabled home. Rocking chairs line a long veranda welcoming prospective sportsman or nature lovers. Hot Springs (close to Warm Springs, Virginia) has 106-degree baths located in the Homestead Spa nearby where visitors can experience the spa vacations enjoyed back in 1761. The inn is steps away from horse-

back and carriage riding and there are many hiking trails, golf courses and hunting and fishing spots. Ask the innkeepers for their secret fishing spot.

Location: In the village, along Rt 220.
Rates: $40-$55. Season: All year.
Innkeeper(s): Wendell & Pat Lucas.
14 Rooms. 8 Private Baths. 6 Shared Baths. Guest phone available. Children. TV available. Smoking OK. Credit Cards: Visa, MC. Beds: DT. Meals: Country continental breakfast.

"Pat and Wendell are exceptionally considerate innkeepers; we've visited several times, each a pleasure!"

"Comfortable rooms; tastefully and beautifully decorated."

"Clean and extra friendly. I felt like I was home."

Lancaster

The Inn at Levelfields
Star Rt 3, PO Box 216
Lancaster VA 22503
(804) 435-6887
  Circa 1857. This is an authentic hip-roofed Georgian-style Colonial home standing at the head of an

entrance drive. The inn's notable features are its lofty and graceful proportions, the spaciousness of dining and guest rooms, and an impressive double-tiered portico. Once the center of a plantation of more than 1,200 acres, Levelfields is one of the last mansions to be built in the Commonwealth. It has been completely refurbished and filled with family antiques and oriental rugs, offering the finest in Virginia tradition.

Location: Northern Neck of Virginia.
Rates: $55-$65.
Innkeeper(s): Doris and Warren Sadler.
4 Rooms. 4 Private Baths. Swimming Pool. Guest phone available. Children. TV available. Smoking OK. Credit Cards: Visa, MC. Beds: KQT. Meals: Full breakfast, restaurant.

"We wanted to let you know how very much we enjoyed ourselves. Your hospitality far exceeds any we've experienced and truly made our evening and stay one we'll treasure."

Leesburg

Norris House Inn
108 Loudoun St SW
Leesburg VA 22075
(703) 777-1806

Circa 1806. Northern Virginia's foremost architects and builders, the Norris brothers purchased this brick building in 1850, and began extensive renovations

several years later. Using only the finest wood and brick available, they remodeled the exterior of this

Federal-style house in the Eastlake style. Dentil work was added to the cornice and the portico was framed with turned spindles. Beautifully restored, the inn features built-in bookcases in the library and a cherry fireplace mantel.

Location: Northern Virginia, 40 miles west of Washington, DC, 15 miles from Dulles Airport.
Rates: $55-$115. Season: All year.
Innkeeper(s): Barbara Vlcek.
7 Rooms. 2 Private Baths. 5 Shared Baths. Guest phone available. Children 12 & up. Beds: QT. Meals: Full breakfast.

"Thank you for your gracious hospitality. We enjoyed everything about your lovely home, especially the extra little touches that really make the difference."

Lexington

Fassifern Bed & Breakfast
Rt 5, PO Box 87
Lexington VA 24450
(703) 463-1013

Circa 1867. Fassifern, which draws its name from the seat of the Cameron Clan in Scotland, was built on the site of older dwellings just after the Civil War. It's located on three-and-a-half acres surrounded by

stately trees and graced with a pond. In 1864, the home was burned during a raid on Lexington, and a major renovation had to be undertaken.

Location: On Rt 39, 3/4 mi from I-64, Exit 13.
**Rates: $35-$65. Season: All year.
Innkeeper(s): Pat & Jim Tichenor.
6 Rooms. 4 Private Baths. 2 Shared Baths. Conference Room. Guest phone available. Children 16 & up. TV available. Credit Cards: Visa, MC. Beds: DQT. Meals: B&B.

"The perfect host and hostess and the perfect house for a memorable bed and breakfast."

"Excellent - best B&B ever. Exquisite room, excellent hospitality."

Mathews

Riverfront House Bed & Breakfast
Rt 14 East, PO Box 310
Mathews VA 23109
(804) 725-9975

Circa 1840. This farmhouse is situated on seven acres along Put-In-Creek and has a wraparound veranda overlooking the river.

Location: Near Williamsburg
**Rates: $38-$52.
Innkeeper(s): Annette & Ira Goldreyer. Meals: Deluxe continental breakfast.

Middleburg

Welbourne
Middleburg VA 22117
(703) 687-3201

Circa 1775. This seventh-generation antebellum mansion in Virginia's fox-hunting country once presided over a 10,000-acre estate. With family members start-

ing their own estates, Welbourne now stands at 600 acres. Furnishings had been collected by family members as they traveled all over the world during the past two hundred years. Many Civil War stories fill the family history book. (Ask to see it!) In the 1930s, F. Scott Fitzgerald and Thomas Wolfe frequented the house and used it as a setting for their writings.

Location: Fifty miles west of Washington, DC.
**Rates: $80-$100. Season: All year.
Innkeeper(s): Mrs. N. H. Morison.
10 Rooms. 10 Private Baths. Conference Room. Guest phone available. Children. Pets OK. TV available. Smoking OK. Credit Cards: AE. Beds: QT. Meals: Full breakfast.

"...the furnishings portray a house and home that's been around for a long, long time. And none of it is held back from the guests. Life today at Welbourne is quiet and unobtrusive. It's genteel..." Philip Hayward, Country Magazine.

Montross

The Inn at Montross
Courthouse Square
Montross VA 22520
(804) 493-9097

Circa 1683. On the site of a seventeenth-century tavern, Montross was rebuilt in 1800. Operating as an "ordinary" tavern since 1683, parts of the structure

have been in continuous use for more than 300 years. It was visited by burgesses and Justices of the Court (Washington, Lee and Jefferson). The guest rooms feature canopy beds and colonial furnishings.

Location: Seven miles from Stratford Hall, 46 miles east of Fredericksburg on VA Rt 3 (Historyland Hwy).
**Rates: $55-$65. Season: All year.
Innkeeper(s): Eileen & Michael Longman.
6 Rooms. 6 Private Baths. Conference Room. Guest phone available. Children By prior arrangement. TV available. Smoking OK. Credit Cards: All. Beds: QT. Meals: Continental plus breakfast. Restaurant.

Mt Jackson

The Widow Kip's Country Inn
Rt 1, PO Box 117
Mt Jackson VA 22842
(202) 477-2400

Circa 1830. This grand farmhouse with early 1900 add-ons, is situated on 200 acres just a stone's throw

from the beautiful Shenandoah River. Seven working fireplaces, (one in each bedroom), a "Lillian Gish" veranda, a root cellar, and a farmhand bunkhouse complete the picture. Four-poster, Lincoln, and spindle beds are topped with hand-crafted quilts. The house is filled with antiques.

Location: Exit 69 off E *81 to Rt 11, south 1.3 miles.
Rates: $50. Season: All year.
Innkeeper(s): Rosemary Kip.
6 Rooms. 5 Private Baths. 2 Shared Baths. Swimming Pool. Children. TV available. Handicap access provided. Smoking In public room only. Beds: QD. Meals: Full breakfast.

"Its ambience, charm and warmth made our stay a memorable one. Decorated with flair and imagination, nostalgia greeted us in every room."

Orange

Hidden Inn
249 Caroline St
Orange VA 22960
(703) 672-3625
Circa 1895. Acres of huge old trees can be seen from the wraparound veranda of this Victorian inn nestled in the Virginia countryside. Meticulous attention has been given to every detail of the restoration right down to the white lace and fresh cut flowers. Montpelier, James Madison's famous estate, is just five miles from the inn. Civil War sites and many fine wineries are located nearby.

**Rates: $59-$89. Season: All year.
Innkeeper(s): Ray & Barbara Lonick.
5 Rooms. 5 Private Baths. Guest phone available. Children. TV available. Smoking OK. Credit Cards: Visa, MC. Beds: KQTC. Meals: Full country breakfast. MAP also available.

Mayhurst Inn
US-15, South, PO Box 707
Orange VA 22960
(703) 672-5597
Circa 1859. An extravagant and playful Italianate Victorian villa, Mayhurst is listed in the National Register of Historic Places. It is considered one of the finest examples of Virginia architecture of this period. During the Civil War it served as the Northern Virginia army headquarters. There are twenty-two rooms, a cupola on the fourth floor that provides views of the surrounding area, and a dual-spiral staircase. Thirty-six acres of old oaks, cedars, and magnolias surround the inn. There is also a pond for swimming and fishing.

Location: One mile south of Orange.
**Rates: $45-$85.

Innkeeper(s): Stephen & Shirley Ramsey.

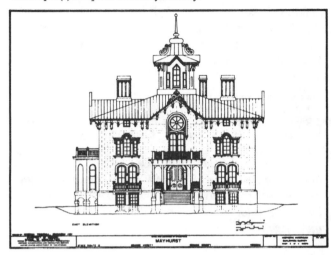

"Sooo comfortable."
"I felt like we had been away for much longer than two days."
"The best. Our dream Victorian."
"A delicious Victorian fantasy." W. B. O'Neal, Architecture in Virginia.

Sleepy Hollow Farm
See: Gordonsville, VA.

Petersburg

Bensonhouse of Petersburg
Contact Bensonhouse of Richmond to make Reservations.
Petersburg VA 23803
(804) 648-7560
Circa 1890. Reflective of the Queen Anne style, this yellow brick inn features a corner turret, Tuscan

columns and a color-patterned slate roof. The elegance and splendor of the original home is evident in the many original lighting fixtures and fireplace mantels. It is within walking distance of museums and the Trapezium House, built without right angles or parallel sides in the 1800s. For reservations, contact Bensonhouse, 2036 Monument Avenue, Richmond, VA 23220.

Location: Petersburg, VA.
**Rates: $45-$70. Season: All year.
5 Rooms. 3 Private Baths. 2 Shared Baths. Guest phone available. Children 12 & up. TV available. Credit Cards: Visa, MC, AE. Beds: QDT. Meals: B&B.

"We were so delighted with our hosts and their lovely home! We had never tried B&B before and must admit we were a little nervous about the experience, but we had a marvelous time! I don't think we'll ever stay in a motel again!"

Richmond

Bensonhouse of Richmond at Monument Avenue

2036 Monument Ave
Richmond VA 23220
(804) 648-7560

This gracious recently restored historic home is a showcase of brightly colored walls, fireplaces, and detailed windows. The innkeepers have renovated five

Richmond homes and love collecting antiques, art, and new friends.

**Rates: $66-$84. Season: All year.
3 Rooms. 1 Private Baths. 2 Shared Baths. Guest phone available. Children 12 & up. TV available. Credit Cards: Visa, MC, AE. Beds: QT. Meals: B&B.

"We had a fabulous trip! One of the highlights was the night we spent in Richmond. We loved the house and thoroughly enjoyed our stay. We have done quite a few B&B's and your service rates a 10! Many thanks!"

The Catlin-Abbott House

2304 East Broad St
Richmond VA 23223
(804) 780-3746

Circa 1845. On historic Church Hill, the house was built for William Catlin by one of the finest brick masons in the country. This richly appointed inn is one block to St. John's Church, the site of Patrick Henry's famous *Liberty or Death* speech.

Location: Historic district.
**Rates: $72.50.
Innkeeper(s): Dr. & Mrs. James Abbott.

Scottsville

Guesthouse of Chester

For reservations contact Guesthouses of Charlottesville, Virginia.
Scottsville VA 24590
(804) 979-7264

Circa 1847. This elegant Greek Revival estate stands on seven acres of shaded lawns, century-old English

boxwood, and a half-acre water-lily pond. The builder, Joseph C. Wright, was a retired landscape architect from Chester, England. General Sheridan and Colonel George Custer (Little Big Horn) visited the local Confederate Army Commander here. Recently transplanted from New York, the innkeepers breed and show borzois. The home is furnished with antiques and oriental rugs and features eight fireplaces.

Location: Twenty-five minutes south of Charlottesville.

Rates: $50-$60. Season: All year.
Innkeeper(s): Gordon & Richard.
5 Rooms. 1 Private Baths. 2 Shared Baths. Guest phone available.
Children 8 & up. Pets OK. TV available. Handicap access provided.
Smoking OK. Beds: QDT. Meals: Full gourmet breakfasts.

"*Hospitality, generosity and cordiality are unmatched. Staying with you was like staying with old friends.*"

"*We couldn't have stayed at a more beautiful place.*"

"*Overwhelmed at the charm of Chester.*"

Staunton

Frederick House
Frederick and New Streets
Staunton VA 24401
(703) 885-4220

Circa 1810. The three historic homes that comprise Frederick House played a significant role in the history of Staunton, the oldest city in the Shenandoah

Valley. The houses were added onto each other and appear as one. Original staircases and woodwork are highlighted throughout. The inn is convenient to fine restaurants, Mary Baldwin College, and Woodrow Wilson's birthplace.

Location: Downtown Historic Staunton.
**Rates: $30-$50. Season: All year.
Innkeeper(s): Joe and Evy Harman.
11 Rooms. 11 Private Baths. Conference Room. Guest phone in room. Children. TV in room. Smoking not permitted. Credit Cards: Visa, MC, AE, DC. Beds: KQT. Meals: B&B.

"*Thanks for making the room so squeaky clean and comfortable! I enjoyed staying here and being the recipient of Virginia hospitality.*"

"*It was a real pleasure to stay in a place with such a warm and home-like atmosphere. The original house has so many Jeffersonian characteristics, there must be a connection. It's almost identical to Pavilion Seven at the University of Virginia.*"

Vesuvius

Sugar Tree Inn
Hwy 56
Vesuvius VA 24483
(703) 377-2197

Circa 1870. On twenty acres of woodland, Sugar Tree provides mountain views from its large front porch. Furnished in a rustic style, the inn has a library, greenhouse dining room, a living room, a tavern and seven guest rooms.

Location: One mile west of Blue Ridge Parkway.
Rates: $80.
Innkeeper(s): Smoky & Geneva Schroeder.

Williamsburg

Bensonhouse of Williamsburg
Contact Bensonhouse of Richmond to make reservations.
Williamsburg VA 23185
(804) 648-7560

Circa 1760-1983. A copy of the eighteenth-century Sheldon's Tavern in Litchfield, Connecticut, this home is located one mile from Colonial Williamsburg

and the College of William and Mary, in a quiet, wooded area. A palladian-style window, antique heart pine wide-plank floors from Philadelphia, and oak paneling from an old Indiana church are special features. For reservations, contact Bensonhouse, 2036 Monument Avenue, Richmond, VA 23220.

Location: One block to Colonial Williamsburg.
**Rates: $68-$72.

1 Rooms. 1 Private Baths. Guest phone available. Children. TV available. Credit Cards: Visa, MC, AE. Beds: QC and sofa bed for children. Meals: Full breakfast.

"You certainly chose wisely when you matched us with our hosts! You have a great thing going with the brochure, maps and wonderful houses. We went to several B&B's in other parts of the country and none were better!"

Riverfront House Bed & Breakfast
See: Mathews, VA.

Washington

Anohomish

Countryman Bed & Breakfast
11 Cedar
Anohomish WA 98290
(206) 568-9622
  Circa 1896.

Location: Thirty miles north of Seattle.
**Rates: $45-$55.
Innkeeper(s): Larry & Sandy Countryman.

Bainbridge Island

Bombay House
8490 Beck Rd NE
Bainbridge Island WA 98110
(206) 842-3926
  Circa 1907. The old Victorian Captain's House is set high atop Blakely Hill, amidst beautiful unstructured gardens exploding with color. It boasts a quaint widow's walk and an old fashioned gazebo overlooking picturesque sailboats and ferries cruising through Rich Passage.

**Rates: $50-$78. Season: All year.
Innkeeper(s): Bunny Cameron & Roger Kanchuk.
5 Rooms. 3 Private Baths. 1 Shared Baths. Conference Room. Guest phone available. Children. TV available. Handicap access provided. Smoking OK. Credit Cards: AE. Beds: KT. Meals: Continental plus breakfast.
  "Your breakfast was marvelous! No lunch today!"
  "Only a relaxing thirty-minute ferry ride from downtown Seattle. Truly a world away."

Bellingham

North Garden Inn
1014 North Garden
Bellingham WA 98225
(206) 671-7828
  Circa 1897. This Victorian home in the National Register has many rooms with views of Bellingham Bay and surrounding islands. A grand staircase leads down to two grand pianos in performance condition.

Location: Overlooking Bellingham Bay.
Rates: $40.
Innkeeper(s): Frank & Barbara Defreytas.

Bingen

The Grand Old House
Hwy 14 PO Box 667
Bingen WA 98605
(509) 493-2838
  Circa 1860. The Grand Old House was built by the first white settlers in the area to replace the original homestead that had been burned to the ground by the Yakima Indians. A full gourmet breakfast is served.

Location: Columbia River Gorge.
**Rates: $25-$65.
Innkeeper(s): Cyndy & Greg de Bruler.

Eastsound

Outlook Inn
Box 210 Main St
Eastsound WA 98245
(206) 376-2200

Circa 1888. In the heart of Orcas Island, the inn has recently been refurbished with turn-of-the-century an-

tiques. Rooms feature four-poster canopy beds, brass beds, and marble topped tables.

Location: Orcas Island.
**Rates: $39 & up.
Innkeeper(s): Bev Ely.

Turtleback Farm Inn
Rt 1 PO Box 650, Crow Valley Rd, Orcas Island
Eastsound WA 98245
(206) 376-4914

Circa 1890. This folk national design farmhouse was considered one of the finest homes on Orcas Island in

the early 1900s. Altered, abused and finally abandoned in the '50s, the building was restored and expanded from the ground up in 1985 with particular attention to authenticity and detail.

Location: Six miles from ferry landing, 2.4 miles from West Sound.
**Rates: $50-$90. Season: All year.
Innkeeper(s): William C. & Susan C. Fletcher.
7 Rooms. 7 Private Baths. Guest phone available. Children By prior arrangement. TV available. Handicap access provided. Credit Cards: Visa, MC. Beds: KQT. Meals: B&B.

"A five star B&B on our rating scale, tastefully decorated. The breakfast, served in a cheerful dining room, surpasses all other B&B's in our opinion."

Greenbank

Guest House Bed & Breakfast
835 E Christenson Rd
Greenbank WA 98253
(206) 678-3115

Circa 1920. This is a cozy Whidbey Island home with art-deco touches on twenty-five acres of forest and meadows. Deer wander by the wildlife pond, storybook cottages, and a luxurious log lodge for two. Guests come back for the croaking frog serenades, the marine and mountain views, and the lush greenery.

Location: Whidbey Island, 1 mile north of St. Michelle Visitor's Center.
**Rates: $65-$130. Season: All year.
Innkeeper(s): Don & Mary Jane Creger.
5 Rooms. 5 Private Baths. Hot Tub. Swimming Pool. Guest phone available. TV available. Credit Cards: Visa, MC, AE, DC. Beds: KQDT. Meals: Continental and full breakfast, depending on accommodation chosen.

Kirkland

Shumway Mansion
11410 100 Ave NE
Kirkland WA 98033
(206) 823-2303

Circa 1909. This resplendent twenty-two room, 10,000 sq. ft. mansion is situated on more than two acres overlooking Juanita Bay. With a large ballroom, and veranda with Lake Washington views, few could guess that only a short time ago the building was hoisted on hydraulic lifts and pulled three miles across town to its present site, three blocks from the beach.

Location: East side of Lake Washington, 25 minutes to downtown Seattle.
**Rates: $47.50-$62.50. Season: All year.
Innkeeper(s): Richard & Salli Harris.
7 Rooms. 7 Private Baths. Conference Room. Guest phone available. Children 12 & up. TV available. Credit Cards: Visa, MC. Beds: QT. Meals: B&B.

Langlay

Saratoga Inn
4850 South Coles Rd
Langlay WA 98260
(206) 221-7526

Circa 1892. This Cape Cod shingle house features gables and hardwood floors and is furnished with

Queen Anne and Chippendale furniture. Guest can enjoy the living room with fireplace, decks, gardens, and a tree house. The inn sits on twenty-five acres and overlooks the Saratoga Passage and mountains.

Location: Whidbey Island, 1 hour north of Seattle.
**Rates: $65-$85. Season: All year.
Innkeeper(s): Debbie and Ted Jones.
5 Rooms. 5 Private Baths. Credit Cards: Visa. Meals: Continental Plus.

Orcas

Orcas Hotel
Near the Ferry Landing.
Orcas WA 98280
(206) 376-4300

Circa 1900. In the National Register, the three-story Victorian inn has been a landmark to travelers and boaters since the early 1900s. It was restored in 1985. An open porch stretches around three sides and is filled with white wicker furniture. From this vantage point guests enjoy views of terraced lawns and flower beds of peonies, daffodils, iris and roses. A white picket fence and a vista of sea and islands complete the picture.

Location: Overlooking the Ferry Landing.
**Rates: $48-$75. Season: All year.
Innkeeper(s): John & Barbara Jamieson.
12 Rooms. 3 Private Baths. 6 Shared Baths. Conference Room. Guest phone available. Children. TV available. Handicap access

provided. Smoking OK. Credit Cards: Visa, MC, AE. Beds: QTC. Meals: B&B and gourmet restaurant.

"Our stay in your delightful Orcas Hotel was a highlight of our visit to the Coast. Two nights of sound sleep were bliss under your roof. Lovely menus, delicious cuisine, excellent service, and fire in the fireplace. A glory touch! Serenity! Romanticism!"

Port Angeles

Tudor Inn
1108 South Oak
Port Angeles WA 98362
(206) 452-3138

Circa 1910. This English Tudor inn has been tastefully restored to display its original wood work and fir

stairway featuring antique brass stair rods. Guests can enjoy stone fireplaces in the living room and study. A large terraced garden with 100-foot oak trees graces the property.

Location: 11 blocks south of the Harbor.
**Rates: $40-$70.
Innkeeper(s): Jane & Jerry Glass.

5 Rooms. 1 Private Baths. 2 Shared Baths. Guest phone available. Children 10 and up. TV available. Credit Cards: Visa, MC. Beds: KQTD. Meals: B&B.

"Thanks for the warm, gracious, and delightful hospitality." Shelly (Fabera) and Mike Farrell (M*A*S*H).

"Thanks for making this weekend such a special time. We will return."

"Most interesting and international."

Port Townsend

Heritage House Inn
305 Pierce St
Port Townsend WA 98368
(206) 385-6800

Circa 1880. This stately Italianate was built by famed wooden boat builder, John Fuge. In the National Register, it was once owned by Francis Pettygrove

who helped found and name Portland, Oregon. When visiting the inn, ask to see the unusual fold-down bath tub on wheels. Because of the mild climate and low rainfall (less than half that of Seattle), Port Townsend's many Victorian homes have successfully withstood the ravages of time, and contain the best examples of Victorian architecture north of San Francisco.

Location: Corner of Washington & Pierce.
Rates: $40-$76. Season: All year.
Innkeeper(s): Pat & Jim Broughton, Bob & Carolyn Ellis.
6 Rooms. 4 Private Baths. 2 Shared Baths. Guest phone available. Children 8 & up. TV available. Handicap access provided. Credit Cards: Visa, MC. Beds: QD. Meals: Continental plus breakfast.

Lizzie's
731 Pierce St
Port Townsend WA 98368
(206) 385-4168

Circa 1887. Named for Lizzie Grant, a sea captain's wife, this Italianate Victorian is elegant, imaginative, and full of light. In addition to the gracious interiors, the inn commands an outstanding view of Port Townsend Bay, Puget Sound, and the Olympic and Cascade mountain ranges. Lizzie's is known for its elaborate and delicious breakfasts. Guests are encouraged to help themselves to seconds!

Location: Two hours NW of seattle on Olympic Peninsula off Hwy 101.
Rates: $42-$79.
Innkeeper(s): Bill & Patti Wickline.

"As they say in show biz, you're a hard act to follow."
"Sumptuous breakfasts, delightful hosts - a truly memorable time."
"The hospitality here is a warm and comfortable as the beds."
"A real place of taste and class amid the rough and tumble wilderness."

Starrett House Inn
744 Clay St
Port Townsend WA 98368
(206) 385-3205

Circa 1889. In his twenties George Starrett came from Maine to Port Townsend and became the major residential builder during its boom. In 1889 he reported he had built one house a week since he came to town -- more than 350 houses. The Starrett House was a $6,000 gift to his wife, the former Ann Van Bokkelen, daughter of a Port Townsend pioneer. It was a truly remarkable house and considered to be of national significance. Starrett had artist George Chapman paint his interpretations of the four seasons on the ceiling of the octagonal tower. Chapman's paintings of young women dressed differently for each season are framed by an elaborate, free-hung spiral staircase. Winter's costume was the most delicate and shocked the locals who considered it "lewd." Guests now can enjoy the remarkable structure.

Rates: $42-$73. Season: All year.
8 Rooms. 1 Private Baths. 4 Shared Baths. Conference Room. Guest phone available. Children 13 & up. Credit Cards: Visa, MC. Beds: QD. Meals: Continental breakfast.

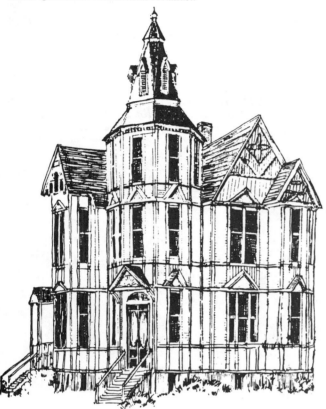

"A wonderful historic Victorian home...beautifully furnished...magnificent spiral staircase."

"Elegant yet comfortable. Thanks so much for everything, we will be back again."

Seattle

Bombay House
See: Bainbridge, WA.

Chambered Nautilus B&B Inn
5005 22nd NE
Seattle WA 98105
(206) 522-2536

Circa 1915. This blue Georgian Colonial was built by an English family. Three large dormers and Palladian doors balance the front of the house. Coved ceilings, fireplaces, and Persian rugs create an elegant

counterpoint to country furnishings. Many of the large guest rooms have French doors and balconies.

Location: Near University & Washington.
**Rates: $55-$75. Season: All year.
Innkeeper(s): Deborah Sweet & Kate McDill.
6 Rooms. 3 Shared Baths. Conference Room. Guest phone available. Children 12 & up. Credit Cards: All. Beds: Q. Meals: B&B.

"Wonderful nurturing place - the calm and warmth are felt everywhere."

"Food for the mind, body and spirit - more than I expected - thank you."

"Everything was great - the place, room, flowers and the sumptuous breakfasts!"

Chelsea Station Bed & Breakfast Inn
4915 Linden Ave N
Seattle WA 98103
(206) 547-6077

Circa 1920. The inn is a Federal Colonial home, located in a tranquil country setting in the midst of the city. A secluded hot tub is tucked away privately in one of the carriage houses. Seattle's Woodland Park Zoo and the Rose Gardens are only a few steps away. away. The inn has some twenty-nine varieties of its own special roses, including a Mint Julep.

Location: Three miles from Downtown, at the Zoo.
**Rates: $49-$73. Season: All year.
Innkeeper(s): Dick and Mary Lou Jones.
7 Rooms. 5 Private Baths. 2 Shared Baths. Hot Tub. Conference Room. Guest phone available. Children 10 & up. TV available. Credit Cards: All. Beds: KC. Meals: Full breakfast.

College Inn Guest House
4000 University Way NE
Seattle WA 98105
(206) 633-4441
  Circa 1908.

Location: Near the University of Washington.
**Rates: $35-$45.
Innkeeper(s): Jim & Judy Oliver.

Lizzie's
See: Port Townsend, WA.

Saratoga Inn
See: Langlay, WA.

Shumway Mansion
See: Kirkland, WA.

The Williams House
1505 Fourth Ave North
Seattle WA 98109
(206) 285-0810
  Circa 1905. Built by a midwestern cart builder, the inn features much original woodwork and gas light fixtures including an original ornate gas fireplace. It is situated atop Queen Anne Hill with many rooms having commanding views of mountains, lakes, Puget Sound, and the downtown Seattle skyline.

**Rates: $45-$70. Season: All year.
Innkeeper(s): Susan and Doug Williams.
5 Rooms. 1 Private Baths. 3 Shared Baths. Conference Room. Guest phone available. Children. TV available. Credit Cards: Visa, MC, AE, DC. Beds: KQD. Meals: Continental-plus breakfast.

Washington, D. C.

Washington

Adams Inn
1744 Lanier Pl NW
Washington DC 20009
(202) 745-3600

Circa 1913. This restored turn-of-the-century townhouse has fireplaces, a library, parlor, and fifteen guest rooms all furnished home-style. Former residents of this neighborhood were Tallulah Bankhead, Woodrow Wilson, and Al Jolson. The area is home to diplomats, radio and television personalities, professors, attorneys, and government workers. A notable firehouse across the street holds the record for the fastest response of a horse-drawn fire apparatus! The Adams-Morgan area is the city's most diverse and interesting neighborhood.

Location: Adams-Morgan area within walking distance to major convention hotels. Two miles north of the White House.
**Rates: $35-$70. Season: All year.
Innkeeper(s): Sybille Cooke.
15 Rooms. 6 Private Baths. 11 Shared Baths. Conference Room. Guest phone available. Children. TV available. Credit Cards: All. Beds: DT. Meals: Continental-plus breakfast.

"We enjoyed your friendly hospitality and the home-like atmosphere. Your suggestions on selecting from the many restaurants in your neighborhood and helping plan our visit were appreciated."

"I will come back again." (Librarian researching at the Smithsonian.)

Kalorama Guest House
1854 Mintwood Place NW
Washington DC 20009
(202) 667-6369

Circa 1900. The Kalorama is a group of charming turn-of-the-century Victorian townhouses located in a quiet downtown residential neighborhood. Decorated with Victorian and Edwardian antiques and period artwork the inn features original wainscoting, fireplace mantles, and claw-footed tubs. Its thirty-one rooms are located in six houses and are appointed with brass beds, plush comforters, oriental rugs, and sunny bay windows. Each house is hosted year round to provide a warm and friendly experience. Sherry is served by the fireplace each afternoon. Ethnic restaurants and the subway are a short walk. Just down Kalorama Road are the Chinese Embassy, the French Embassy, and the stately Massachusetts Avenue diplomatic residences. Another short walk brings guests to several major convention hotels.

Location: Downtown residential neighborhood, 10 minutes to the Mall and the White house. A short walk to the Washington Hilton, the Sheraton Washington, the Shoreham and the Highland House.
**Rates: $35-$65. Season: All year.
Innkeeper(s): Rick Fenstemaker, Janet Brown & Kay Williams.
31 Rooms. 12 Private Baths. 19 Shared Baths. Conference Room. Guest phone available. Children. TV available. Smoking OK. Credit Cards: Visa, MC, AE. Beds: QDT. Meals: Continental-plus breakfast.

The Norris House Inn
See: Leesburg, VA.

West Virginia

Caldwell

The Greenbrier River Inn
US 60
Caldwell WV 24925
(304) 647-5652

Circa 1824. Built by Henry B. Hunter as a stagecoach stop, the Greenbrier has been completely

restored. During the Civil War, the building was almost burned by a Union commander. Inside the house, a woman, too sick to be moved, had to be checked by the Union doctor. He agreed she was ill, and the house was left unscathed, except for some shelling from cannons during a crossfire between the Confederate and Union forces after the battle of Lewisburg. Robert E. Lee is said to have been here and a party was hosted for President Van Buren. The inn is tucked behind a giant elm tree and provides a southern mansion experience for guests. It has a small boat launch and provides fishing and tennis.

Location: Between Lewisburg and White Sulphur Springs.
Rates: $55. Season: All year.
Innkeeper(s): Joan & Jim Jeter.

7 Rooms. 7 Private Baths. Guest phone available. Children. Pets OK. TV available. Smoking OK. Credit Cards: Visa, MC. Beds: KTC. Meals: B&B.

Gerrardstown

Prospect Hill
PO Box 135
Gerrardstown WV 25420
(304) 229-3346

Circa 1789. An excellent example of a well-to-do gentlemen's home in the eighteenth century, this Georgian mansion was the home of William Wilson, a

member of Thomas Jefferson's cabinet. During the Civil War it is said that Mrs. Wilson stood on the first landing and Union soldiers shot around her, trying to discover where the slaves had been hidden. A metal detector indicates bullets in the shape of a large inverted 'U' in the wall. A hand painted mural of colonial scenes winds up the staircase wall to the third floor. There are 225 acres with graceful woodlands, ponds stocked with bass, orchard groves, and berry patches. In the National Register, the estate once had 2,000 acres and seventy-five resident slaves.

Location: Nine miles from Martinsburg.
Rates: $65-$85. Season: All year.
Innkeeper(s): Hazel D. Hudock.

3 Rooms. 3 Private Baths. Guest phone available. Children. TV available. Handicap access provided. Smoking OK. Credit Cards: Visa, MC. Beds: QD. Meals: Full country breakfast.

"Prospect Hill is beautiful and is on my recommended list to friends."

Lewisburg

The General Lewis
301 E Washington St
Lewisburg WV 24901
(304) 645-2600

Circa 1834. Patrick Henry and Thomas Jefferson registered at the inn's walnut desk. Once located in a local hot springs resort this area was popular with Virginia aristocrats. Lewisburg is in the National

Register and has many gracious historic homes and churches. An old stage coach that traveled between the springs on the James River and Kanawha Turnpike rests under an arbor. Memory Hall displays household items and tools once used by the local pioneers.

Rates: $40-$65. Season: All year.
Innkeeper(s): Rodney Fisher.
27 Rooms. 27 Private Baths. Swimming Pool. Children. Pets OK. Handicap access provided. Smoking OK. Credit Cards: Visa, MC, AE. Beds: DTC. Meals: EP.

"The staff is wonderful at making us feel at home, and we can be as much a part of the inn as we want."

"Anyone who enjoys old country inns should find a stop at this place to be a delightful and memorable experience." Nancy Clark, *Wonderful West Virginia.*

Middleway

Gilbert House Bed & Breakfast
Rt 1 PO Box 160
Middleway WV 25430
(304) 725-0637

Circa 1760. A magnificent greystone of early Georgian design, the Gilbert House boasts the state's oldest flagstone sidewalk. The inn is elegantly appointed with fine antique oriental rugs, tasteful art, and antique furnishings. During restoration, interesting graffiti found on the upstairs bedroom walls included a drawing of president James Polk and a child's growth chart from the 1800s. Listed in the National Register of Historic Places, Middleway is a place passed over by time. (The B&O Railroad was voted down, and an economic decline followed.) The village contains one of the country's most well-preserved collections of 18th century log homes.

Location: Near Harpers Ferry, Charles Town and Shepherdstown.
**Rates: $75-$125. Season: All year.
Innkeeper(s): Jean & Bernie Heiler.
3 Rooms. 3 Private Baths. Conference Room. Guest phone available. TV available. Credit Cards: Visa, MC. Beds: QT. Meals: B&B.

"Our stay at the Gilbert House could not have been more perfect. Your house is so elegant and yet so cozy. More importantly, you are wonderful innkeepers who make people feel at home. We will tell all our friends!"

"Our weekend was delightful, and we thank you both for your hospitality. The breakfasts were perfectly sumptuous, and we were both proud of the history we garnered from the two of you. We loved our guided walking tour!"

"Being at your inn was a wonderful experience and just goes to show that taking a spur of the moment trip can be a great adventure."

"Whenever we do our 'Honeymoon Show-and-Tell' we are reminded of the wonderful time we had and all you did to make it spectacular. Of course, everyone is jealous!"

Moorefield

Hickory Hill Farm
Rt 1 PO Box 355
Moorefield WV 26836
(304) 538-2511

Circa 1809. Two hundred years of farming and family living have taken place on Hickory Hill, a working farm on an enchanting bluff overlooking the river. A kiln was built on the farm and then a sawmill for the cutting and dressing of lumber. The two-story brick Federal house took years to complete and is considered to be one of the finest architectural gems in the South Branch Valley. Woodwork throughout the inn is hand carved, and the mantels and door frames are decorated with a repeated pattern of sunbursts combined with borders of fluting. A large, open porch runs across the back of the house, inviting

guests to enjoy the view. It contains a fascinating written history of the people who have lived here. One note, dated 1819, states, "I am all alone in my glory." Other notes of equal interest are still etched in the planks of the porch.

Location: On the South Branch of the Potomac River, 9 miles north of Moorefield.
Rates: $44-$65. Season: All year.
Innkeeper(s): Louis Shomette.
2 Rooms. 2 Private Baths. Guest phone available. Children. TV available. Smoking OK. Beds: DC.

"I have passed this place for years, and it is just as beautiful inside as out."

White Sulphur Springs

The General Lewis
See: Lewisburg, WV.

Wisconsin

Baraboo

The Barrister's House
226 9th Ave, PO Box 166
Baraboo WI 53913
(608) 356-3344

Circa 1932. Built by a prominent Baraboo attorney, this stately home was designed by architect Frank

Riley (builder of the governor's mansion) to replicate the warmth and grace of colonial New England homes. The fireplaces, crystal chandeliers, library and veranda are favorites with guests.

Rates: $45-$55. Season: Open daily June to August, weekends only Se
Innkeeper(s): Glen & Mary Schulz.
4 Rooms. 4 Private Baths. Guest phone available. Children by prior arrangement. Beds: Q. Meals: Continental-plus breakfast.

"Your home is simply wonderful and we've enjoyed every moment here. We hate to leave. Lovely rooms, gracious hosts, delicious food! A special place to remember."

Bayfield

Old Rittenhouse Inn
301 Rittenhouse Ave, PO Box 584-1
Bayfield WI 54814
(715) 779-5111

Circa 1890. In Bayfield's historic district, this rambling Queen Anne Victorian mansion was built by Civil War General Allen C. Fuller, using cedar shingles and the local brownstone for which Bayfield was famous. Antique furnishings abound throughout the inn, which has twelve working fireplaces. Under-

neath massive gables a wraparound veranda is filled with geraniums and petunias in wicker boxes. The porch provides an abundance of white wicker furnishings from which to enjoy the spectacular view of Lake Superior.

Location: On Bayfield's main street, 5 blocks from Lake Superior shore.
Rates: $59-$99. Season: All seasons. Weekends November to April.
Innkeeper(s): Jerry & Mary Phillips.
9 Rooms. 9 Private Baths. Conference Room. Children. Handicap access provided. Credit Cards: Visa, MC, AE. Beds: KQC. Meals: B&B and gourmet restaurant.

"The whole decor, the room, the staff, and the food were superb! Your personalities and talents give a great warmth to the inn."

"...among the most amazing morning meals that ever graced a table." Gourmet Magazine.

Cedarburg

Stagecoach Inn Bed & Breakfast
W61 N520 Washington Ave
Cedarburg WI 53012
(414) 375-0208

Circa 1853. Restored by historian Brook Brown, this stone inn in the Greek Revival style was originally used as a stagecoach stop between Milwaukee and Greenbay. It includes both an old bar and a tavern, and although no longer offering good stabling or a large stockyard for stagecoach horses, the inn still restores the spirits of weary travelers.

Location: Downtown historic district.
**Rates: $35-$75. Season: All year.
Innkeeper(s): Brook & Liz Brown.
9 Rooms. 9 Private Baths. Conference Room. Guest phone available. TV available. Credit Cards: Visa, MC, AE, Discover. Beds: D. Meals: Continental-plus breakfast.

The Washington House Inn
W62 N573 Washington Ave
Cedarburg WI 53012
(414) 375-3550

Circa 1886. Completely renovated, this original "Cream City" brick building is decorated in a light-hearted country-Victorian style featuring antiques as well as whirlpool baths. Some of the rooms have brick

and rough stone walls with wood-plank floors. An original guest registry, over a hundred years old, was a gift to the inn from a Cedarburg resident.

Location: In the heart of the Cedarburg historic district.
**Rates: $49-$99. Season: All year.
Innkeeper(s): Judith Drefahl.
20 Rooms. 20 Private Baths. Jacuzzi Tubs. Conference Room. Guest phone in room. Children. TV in room. Handicap access provided. Smoking OK. Credit Cards: All. Beds: KQDTC. Meals: B&B.

"Your inn is excellent...just what people hope an inn could be like."

Ellison Bay

The Griffin Inn
11976 Mink River Rd
Ellison Bay WI 54210
(414) 854-4306

Circa 1910. The Griffin Inn, one of Door County's historic buildings, is a New England-style country inn

set on nearly five acres. Large verandas, a gracious lobby, old-fashioned gazebo, and library are among the amenities enjoyed by guests. Choose between cottages or guest rooms on the second floor. You'll always find one of Laurie's handmade quilts to snuggle under. Outside there are five acres of lawns graced with maple trees, providing the syrup your hostess serves with her crunchy French toast at breakfast.

Location: Door County Penninsula, 2 blocks east of Hwy 42.
**Rates: $52. Season: All year.
Innkeeper(s): Laurie & Jim Roberts.
10 Rooms. 3 Shared Baths. Conference Room. Guest phone available. Children 6 & up. Beds: DT. Meals: Full breakfast.

"Wonderful New England style inn...Jim and Laurie may be new to innkeeping, but not to the art of hospitality."

Hazel Green

Wisconsin House Stagecoach Inn
2105 Main
Hazel Green WI 53811
(608) 854-2233

Circa 1846. Built of native oak with clapboard siding and "six-over-six" windows with shutters, the inn has withstood the ravages of time, including an 1876 tornado that completely devastated the village. The

builder Jefferson Crawford and his descendants lived here for over one hundred years. Ulysses S. Grant spent a good deal of time here as a guest helping the Crawford widow to settle her husband's estate.

Location: SW Wisconsin, center of the village.
Rates: $35-$55. Season: All year.
Innkeeper(s): John & Betha Mueller.
5 Rooms. 2 Private Baths. 3 Shared Baths. Guest phone available. Children who are well behaved are welcome. TV available. Smoking OK. Beds: DT. Meals: Old-fashioned full breakfast.

"Words can't explain what a unique and fun weekend this has been. Our hearts feel very warm and full of love, that there are still real people like you in the world."

Milwaukee

Ogden House
2237 N Lake Dr
Milwaukee WI 53202
(414) 272-2740

Circa 1916. Listed in the National Register of Historic Places, the inn is located in the North Point-South Historic District. Ogden House was built in the Federal style with Georgian influences for Miss Ogden, who lived to be 101 years old. She was one of the founders of the Milwaukee County Historical Society. The house is set on a bluff overlooking Lake Michigan.

Location: One block from Lake Michigan, 1 mile north of downtown.
Rates: $55-$65. Season: All year.
Innkeeper(s): Mary Jane & John Moss.
2 Rooms. 2 Private Baths. Guest phone available. TV available. Smoking OK. Beds: Q. Meals: Hearty continental breakfast.

The Washington House Inn
See: Cedarburg, WI.

Sister Bay

Renaissance Inn
414 Maple Dr
Sister Bay WI 54234
(414) 854-5107

Circa 1903. Before its debut as a bed and breakfast this turn-of-the-century building was a bait and tackle shop, a boardinghouse, and a butcher shop. Renovations on the building, as well as the collection of all appointments which now grace the building, took many months. Renaissance art is featured in the inn, a property in the National Historic Register.

Location: Just off Hwy 42.
Rates: $50-$70. Call about winter weekend specials. Season: All year.
Innkeeper(s): John R. and Jo Dee Faller.
5 Rooms. 5 Private Baths. Guest phone available. Children 14 & up. TV available. Smoking OK. Credit Cards: Visa, MC, AE. Beds: D. Meals: Full breakfast and gourmet seafood restaurant.

Sturgeon Bay

White Lace Inn
16 N 5th Ave
Sturgeon Bay WI 54235
(414) 743-1105

Circa 1903. White Lace Inn is three Victorian houses. One house is an ornate, late Queen Anne, asymmetrical in design; a second house was built in 1885; a third was built during 1885-1904. The inn is adjacent to two districts listed in the National Register. Often the site for romantic wedding festivities, one suite has a two-sided fireplace, magnificent walnut Eastlake Bed, English country fabrics, and a two-person whirlpool tub.

Location: Door County, Lake Michigan on one side of Penninsula, Green Bay on the other.
Rates: $55-$120. Season: All year.
Innkeeper(s): Dennis & Bonnie Statz.

15 Rooms. 15 Private Baths. Guest phone available. Children 12 & up. TV available. Smoking and non-smoking rooms available. Credit Cards: Visa, MC, AE. Beds: Q. Meals: Continental plus.

"Each guest room is such an overwhelming visual feast, such a dazzling...fusion of colors, textures and beautiful objects...It is one of these rare gems that established a tradition the day it opened." Wisconsin Trails.

"Very relaxing and romantic. We usually do not return to the same inn twice, but will make our first exception for this inn."

"It gave us a memory we will never forget!"

Wausau

Rosenberry Inn
511 Franklin St
Wausau WI 54401
(715) 842-5733

Circa 1908. This stucco and brick inn was built in the midwestern Prairie School style, stressing horizontal lines, overhanging eaves, and massive porch supports. The stained glass windows feature a waterlily design and geometric motifs. Rosenberry is listed in the National Register.

Location: Downtown area.
Rates: $40-$45. Season: All year.
Innkeeper(s): Gerald & Patricia Artz & son, Doug.
8 Rooms. 8 Private Baths. Children. TV available. Smoking OK. Credit Cards: Visa, MC. Beds: DT. Meals: Continental breakfast.

Wyoming

Cody

The Lockhart Inn
109 West Yellowstone Ave
Cody WY 82414
(307) 587-6074

Circa 1890. An old pioneer home, the Lockhart Inn is named after author Caroline Lockhart who lived here at the turn-of-the-century. Cody is fifty miles from the entrance to Yellowstone National Park.

Rates: $50.
Innkeeper(s): Cindy & Mark Baldwin.
6 Rooms. 6 Private Baths. Children. Smoking OK. Credit Cards: Visa, MC. Meals: Full breakfast.

Evanston

Pine Gables Bed & Breakfast
1049 Center St
Evanston WY 82930
(307) 789-2069

Circa 1883. Pine Gables is a Victorian mansion in the historic district. An antique shop at the inn has been the source of many of the inn's fine furnishings.

Location: Eighty miles from Salt Lake City.
Rates: $30-$35.
Innkeeper(s): Jesse & Arthur Monroe.
6 Rooms. 2 Private Baths. Children. TV available. Credit Cards: Visa, MC, CB, DC. Meals: Continental breakfast.

Glenrock

Hotel Higgins
416 West Birch
Glenrock WY 82637
(307) 436-9212

Circa 1900. This old hotel has the original terrazzo tile floors and many authentic antiques. Deer Creek, a few minutes away, was the headquarters of the Pony Express.

Location: Eighteen miles from Casper, on the Oregon Trail.
Rates: $29-$46. Season: All year.
Innkeeper(s): Jack & Margaret Doll.
10 Rooms. 7 Private Baths. 3 Shared Baths. Children. Smoking OK. Credit Cards: Visa, MC, AE. Meals: Full breakfast.

Lander

Miner's Delight Inn
Atlantic City Rt, PO Box 205
Lander WY 82520
(307) 332-3513

Circa 1899. Constructed of hand-hewn logs this inn is listed in the National Register. There are three rooms inside and three cabins on the grounds.

Rates: $25-$40. Season: Thursday to Sunday, May 15 to October 15.
Innkeeper(s): Georgina & Paul Newman.
6 Rooms. 2 Private Baths. Children.

Rawlins

Ferris Mansion
607 W Maple St
Rawlins WY 82301
(307) 324-3961

Circa 1903. This brick Victorian is three stories tall and is listed in the National Register. There is a parlor and a library as well as a large old porch complete with an inviting swing.

Rates: $25.
Innkeeper(s): Janice Lubbers.
2 Rooms. 2 Private Baths. Meals: Continental Breakfast.

U. S. Territories

Puerto Rico

Virgin Islands

Condado, San Juan

El Canario Inn
1317 Ashford Ave
Condado, San Juan PR 00907
(809) 722-3861
  Circa 1938. Located in this tropical climate, the inn is close to white sandy beaches. It features twenty-five pleasant rooms.

Location: Heart of the Condado, near the beach.
**Rates: $38-$75.
Innkeeper(s): Keith & Judy Olson.

St. Croix

Pink Fancy
27 Prince St, Christiansted
St. Croix VI 00820
(809) 773-8460 (800) 524-2045
  Circa 1780. A Danish townhouse is the basis of this historic group of four buildings made of stone and white clapboard. Pink shutters and black wrought iron accentuate the private self-catering apartments situated around a swimming pool. The building was at one time a private club for the rich plantation owners on the island. It was opened as a hotel by a Ziegfield follies star, Jane Gotleib. Soon writers and artists began frequenting the inn and it has remained a popular retreat.

Location: Downtown.
**Rates: $60-$150. Season: All year.
Innkeeper(s): Sam Dillon.
13 Rooms. 13 Private Baths. Swimming Pool. Guest phone available. Children. Smoking OK. Beds: QT. Meals: Continental breakfast.
  "...the cleanest, airiest, most intimate and distinctive small hotel on the Island."

Non-member Inns and Guesthouses

he following pages contain the names and addresses of inns and guesthouses believed to be of historic significance. However, they did not register with the Association of American Historic Inns and Guesthouses prior to publication. There are many fine quality inns in this list; therefore we include them here for your information.

We suggest that if you are interested in making reservations with any of these that you drop them a postcard or give them a call. Please be sure to mention that you saw them in **The Official Guide to American Historic Bed & Breakfast Inns and Guesthouses**.

We also encourage you to use the **Inn Evaluation Form** included in the back of this book.

Although we have made every attempt to verify the information included in this list, there remains the possibility of error or of change. Therefore the list is presented without any warranty. Corrections and changes, if any, and if brought to our attention, will be made in subsequent editions.

Alabama

Rutherford Johnson House
PO Box 202
Franklin AL 36444
(205) 282-4423

Kraft Korner
90 Carlile Dr.
Mobile AL 36619
(205) 666-6819

Malaga Inn
359 Church St.
Mobile AL 36602
Circa: 1862
(205) 438-4701

Alaska

McCarthy B&B
Box 111241
Anchorage AK 99511

Favorite Bay Inn
PO Box 101
Angoon AK 99820
(907) 788-3123

Fort William Seward B&B
House-1, PO Box 5
Haines AK 99827
(907) 766-2856

Fifth & Franklin B&B
505-TN Franklin
Juneau AK 99801

Mullins House
526 Seward St.
Juneau AK 99802
(907) 586-2959

Scandia Haus
PO Box 689, 206 Nordic Dr.
Petersburg AK 99833
(907) 772-4281

Irene's Inn
PO Box 543
Skagway AK 99840
(907) 983-2520

Skagway Inn
PO 292
Skagway AK 99840
Circa: 1899
(907) 983-2294

Fairview Inn
PO Box 379
Talkeetna AK 99676
Circa: 1921
(907) 733-2423

Tanakee Inn
167 S. Franklin
Tenakee Springs AK 99801
(907) 586-1000

1260 Inn
Mi 1260, AK Hwy.
Tok AK 99780
(907) 778-2205

Arizona

Inn At Castle Rock
PO Box 1161, 112 Tombstone Canyon
Bisbee AZ 85603
(602) 432-7195

Adobe Inn-Carefree
PO Box 1081, Elbow Bend & Sidewinder
Carefree AZ 85377
(602) 488-4444

Garland's Oak Creek Lodge
PO 152, Hwy. 89a
Sedona AZ 86336
Circa: 1940
(602) 282-3343

Desert Needlework Ranch
1645 N. Harrison Rd.
Tucson AZ 85715

Circa: 1930
(602) 885-6264

Kay El Bar Ranch
PO Box 2480
Wickenburg AZ 85358
Circa: 1926
(602) 684-7593

Arkansas

Benton B&B House
45 Benton St.
Eureka Springs AR 72632

Bridgeford Cottage
263 Spring St.
Eureka Springs AR 72632

Cabin On The Boardwalk
Box 492, 185 Spring
Eureka Springs AR 72632

Crescent Cottage Inn
211 Spring St.
Eureka Springs AR 72632
(501) 253-6022

Crescent Hotel
Prospect St.
Eureka Springs AR 72632

Devon Cottage
26 Eureka St.
Eureka Springs AR 72632
Circa: 1905
(501) 253-9169

Elmwood House
110 Spring St. #62B
Eureka Springs AR 72632

Eloise's Doll House
5 Summit 62 B
Eureka Springs AR 72632

Lookout Cottage
12 Lookout Cir.
Eureka Springs AR 72632

Main Street Inn
217 N. Main St.
Eureka Springs AR 72632

Maplewood B&B
4 Armstrong St.
Eureka Springs AR 72632
(501) 253-8053

New Orleans Hotel
63 Spring St.
Eureka Springs AR 72632
Circa: 1892
(501) 253-8630

Paul's Place Rose Room
5 Ridgeway
Eureka Springs AR 72632

Redbud Manor
7 Kings Hwy.
Eureka Springs AR 72632

Sunnyside Cottage
5 Ridgeway
Eureka Springs AR 72632

Tatman-Garrett House
Box 171
Eureka Springs AR 72632

The Basin Park Hotel
Prospect St.
Eureka Springs AR 72632

The Inn On Depot
Grade
75 Hillside Ave.
Eureka Springs AR 72632

The Old Homestead
78-82 Armstrong St.
Eureka Springs AR 72632

The Palace Hotel
135 Spring St.
Eureka Springs AR 72632

The Piedmont House
165 Spring St.
Eureka Springs AR 72632

The School House Inn
15 Kansas St.
Eureka Springs AR 72632

Owen Street Guest Cottage
20 Owen St.
Eurekea Springs AR 72632

Eton House
1485 Eton
Fayetteville AR 72701
(501) 521-6344

Merry Go Round Cottage
412 North 8th
Fort Smith AR 72901
Circa: 1895
(800) 643-2131, (501) 783-3472

Oak Tree Inn
Vinegar Hill & 110 W.
Heber Springs AR 72543
(501) 362-8870

Edwardian Inn
317 S. Biscoe
Helena AR 72342
Circa: 1904
(401) 338-9155

Stillmeadow Farm
Reproduction
Rt 1, Box 434-d
Hot Springs AR 71913

Megan-Lorien House
426 Spring St.
Hot Springs National Park AR
71901

Old Country Jail
PO Box 157
Washington AR 71862
Circa: 1872
(501) 983-2178

California

Kenton Mine Lodge
Box 942
Alleghany CA 95910
(916) 287-3212

Mine House Inn
Box 245
Amador City CA 95601
(209) 267-5900

Apple Lane Inn
6265 Soquel Dr.
Aptos CA 95003
Circa: 1870
(408) 475-6868

Bayview Hotel
8041 Soquel Dr
Aptos CA 95003
(408) 688-1927

Rose Victorian Inn
789 Valley Rd.

Arroyo Grande CA 93420
Circa: 1885
(805) 481-5566

Glenmore Plaza Hotel
120 Sumner Ave.
Avalon CA 90704
(213) 510-0017

Island Inn
PO Box 467, 125 Metropole
Avalon CA 90704
Circa: 1906
(213) 510-1623

The Inn On Mt. Ada
Box 2560, 207 Wrigley Rd.
Avalon CA 90704

Union Hotel
401 First St.
Benicia CA 94510
Circa: 1882
(707) 746-0100

Gramma's Inn
2740 Telegraph
Berkeley CA 94705
(415) 549-2145

Old Blue Hotel
2520 Durant Ave
Berkeley CA 94704
(415) 549-9281

Deetjen's Big Sur Inn
Hwy. 1
Big Sur CA 93920
(408) 667-2377

Bolinas Villa
PO Box 40, 23 Brighton Ave.
Bolinas CA 94924
(415) 868-1650

Toll House Inn
Box 268, 15301 Hwy 25
Boonville CA 95415
Circa: 1912

Brannan Cottage Inn
109 Wapoo Ave.
Calistoga CA 94515
(707) 942-4200

Culver's, A Country Inn
1805 Foothill Blvd
Calistoga CA 94515
Circa: 1875

Foothill House
3037 Foothill Blvd
Calistoga CA 94515
Circa: 1890

Larkmead Country Inn
1103 Larkmead Ln
Calistoga CA 94515
Circa: 1900

Mount View Hotel
1457 Lincoln Ave.
Calistoga CA 94515
Circa: 1917

Trailside Inn
4201 Silverado Trail
Calistoga CA 94515
(707) 942-4106

Wine Wayinn
1009 Foothill Blvd
Calistoga CA 94515
Circa: 1915

Holiday House
Box 782, Camino Real At 7th
Ave
Carmel CA 93921
Circa: 1905

Lincoln Green Inn
Box 2747
Carmel CA 93921
(408) 624-1880

Martin House B&b
26270 Dolores St
Carmel CA 93921

Pine Inn
Ocean & Monte Verde St
Carmel CA 93921

Sea View Inn
Box 4318
Carmel CA 93921
Circa: 1910

The Stonehouse Inn
Box 2517
Carmel CA 93921
Circa: 1906

Ye Olde Shelford House
29955 River Rd.
Cloverdale CA 95425
(707) 894-5956

Bear River Mountain Farm
21725 Placer Hills Rd.
Colfax CA 95713
(916) 878-8314

Coloma Country Inn
PO Box 502, #2 High St.
Coloma CA 95613
(916) 622-6919

Sierra Nevada House
PO Box 268
Coloma CA 95613
(916) 622-5856, (916) 933-0547

Vineyard House
Cold Spring Rd, Po Box 176
Coloma CA 95613
Circa: 1878
(916) 622-2217

Fallon Hotel
PO Box 1870, Washington St.
Columbia CA 95310
Circa: 1856
(209) 532-1470

O'rourke Mansion
1765 Lurline Rd.
Colusa CA 95932
(916) 458-5625, 458-4166

Jeffrey Hotel
PO Box 4
Coulterville CA 95311
(209) 878-3400

The Partridge Inn
521 First St
Davis CA 95616
(916) 753-1211

Dinsmore Lodge
Hwy. 36
Dinsmore CA 95526
Circa: 1901
(707) 574-6466

Sierra Shangri-la
PO Box 285
Downieville CA 95936
Circa: 1939
(916) 289-3455

Elk Cove Inn
PO Box 367
Elk CA 95432
Circa: 1883

(707) 877-3321

Green Dolphin Inn
PO Box 132, 6145 S. Hwy.1
Elk CA 95432
(707) 877-3342

Scott Valley Inn
PO Box 261, 642 Main St.
Etna CA 96027
(916) 467-3229

Eagle House
139 Second St.
Eureka CA 95501
Circa: 1886
(707) 442-2334

Heuer's Victorian Inn
1302 E. St.
Eureka CA 95501
Circa: 1890
(707) 442-7334

Old Town B&B Inn
1521 Third St.
Eureka CA 95501
Circa: 1871
(707) 445-3951

Steven's House
917 Third St.
Eureka CA 95501
(707) 445-9080

Shaw House Inn
PO Box 250, 703 Main St.
Ferndale CA 95536
Circa: 1854
(707) 786-9958

Captain Capps
32980 Gibney Lane
Fort Bragg CA 95437
(707) 964-1415

Casa Del Noyo Inn
500 Casa Del Noyo Dr.
Fort Bragg CA 95437
Circa: 1868
(707) 964-9991

Colonial Inn
PO Box 565, 533 E. Fir
Fort Bragg CA 95437
Circa: 1912
(707) 964-9979

Green Apple Inn

530 Bohemian Hwy.
Freestone CA 95472
Circa: 1860
(707) 874-2526

Lord Bradley's Inn
43344 Mission Blvd., Mission
San Jose
Fremont CA 94539
(415) 490-0520

The Victorian
1003 S Orange Ave
Fresno CA 93702

Benbow Inn
445 Lake Benbow Dr.
Garberville CA 95440
Circa: 1928
(707) 923-2124

Campbell Ranch
1475 Canyon Rd.
Geyserville CA 95441
(707) 857-3476

Isis Oasis
20889 Geyserville Ave
Geyserville CA 95441
Circa: 1895

The Hope-Bosworth House
Box 42, 21238 Geyserville Ave
Geyserville CA 95441
Circa: 1904

The Hope-Merrill House
Box 42, 21253 Geyserville Ave
Geyserville CA 95441
Circa: 1870

Stone Tree Ranch
PO Box 173, 7910 Sonoma
Mtn. Rd.
Glen Ellen CA 95442
(707) 996-8173

Circle Bar B Ranch
1800 Refugio Rd.
Goleta CA 93117
Circa: 1940
(805) 968-1113

Annie Horan's
415 W. Main St.
Grass Valley CA 95945
(916) 272-2418

Golden Ore House B&B
448 S. Auburn
Grass Valley CA 95945
(916) 272-6870, 272-6872

**Holbrooke Hotel & Pur-
cell House**
212 W. Main
Grass Valley CA 95945
(916) 273-1353

Swan-Levine House
328 S. Church St.
Grass Valley CA 95945
Circa: 1870
(915) 272-1873

Hotel Charlotte
PO Box 884
Groveland CA 95321
(209) 962-6455

Gualala Hotel
PO Box 675
Gualala CA 95445
Circa: 1903
(707) 884-3441

St. Orres
PO Box 523
Gualala CA 95445
Circa: 1820
(707) 884-3303

Whale Watch Inn
35100 Hwy. 1
Gualala CA 95445
(707) 884-3667

Creekside Inn
16180 Neeley Rd.
Guerneville CA 95446
(707) 869-3623

Ridenhour Ranch
12850 River Rd.
Guerneville CA 95446
Circa: 1906
(707) 887-1033

Santa Nella House
12130 Hwy. 116
Guerneville CA 95466
Circa: 1870
(707) 869-9488

Mill Rose Inn
615 Mill St.
Half Moon Bay CA 94019

Circa: 1903
(415) 726-3425

Victorian Inn
322 N. Irwin St.
Hanford CA 93230
Circa: 1890
(209) 584-9286

Belle Du Jour Farm
16276 Healdsburg Ave
Healdsburg CA 95448
Circa: 1870
(707) 433-7892

Madrona Manor
PO Box 818 1001 Westside
Healdsburg CA 95448
Circa: 1881

Thatcher Hotel
13401 S. Hwy. 101
Hopland CA 95449
(707) 744-1061

Winnedumah Inn
PO Box 209, 211 N. Edwards
Independence CA 93526
Circa: 1926
(619) 878-2040

Blackthorne Inn
PO Box 712
Inverness CA 94937
(415) 663-8621

Ann Marie's
410 Stasal St.
Jackson CA 95642
Circa: 1892
(20() 223-1452

Broadway Hotel
225 Broadway
Jackson CA 95642
(209) 223-3503

Court Street Inn
215 Court St.
Jackson CA 95642
Circa: 1872
(209) 223-0416

Gate House Inn
1330 Jackson Gate Rd.
Jackson CA 95642
Circa: 1890
(209) 223-3500

Mon Petite Chateau
15091 Lyons Valley Rd.
Jamul CA 92035
(619) 463-8955

Stillwater Cove Ranch
Jenner CA 95450
(707) 847-3227

Pine Hills Lodge
2960 La Posada Way
Julian CA 92036
Circa: 1912
(619) 765-1100

Storybrook Inn
PO Box 365, Sky Forest
Lake Arrowhead CA 92385
(714) 336-1483

Glendeven
8221 N. Hwy. 1
Little River CA 95456
Circa: 1867
(707) 937-0083

Heritage House
Little River CA 95456
Circa: 1877
(707) 937-5885

Little River Inn
Little River CA 95456
Circa: 1853
(707) 937-5942

Union Hotel
PO Box 616, 362 Bell St.
Los Alamos CA 93440
Circa: 1900
(805) 344-2744

La Hacienda Inn
18840 Saratoga Rd.
Los Gatos CA 95030
(408) 354-9230

Los Gatos Hotel
31 E. Main St.
Los Gatos CA 95030
Circa: 1890
(408) 354-4440

Tamarack Lodge
Tamarack Lodge Rd.
Mammoth Lakes CA 93546
Circa: 1924
(619) 934-2442

**1201 Main Stree Guest
House**
PO Box 803
Mendocino CA 95460
Circa: 1861

Agate Cove Inn
PO Box 1150
Mendocino CA 95460
Circa: 1860
(707) 937-1551

Ames Lodge
PO Box 207
Mendocino CA 95460
(707) 937-0811

Blue Heron Inn
390 Kasten St
Mendocino CA 95460
(707) 937-4323

Headlands Inn
PO Box 132
Mendocino CA 95460
Circa: 1868
(707) 937-4431

Kelly's Attic
PO Box 858, 699 Ukiah St.
Mendocino CA 95460
Circa: 1860
(707) 937-5588, 937-5559

Main Street Guest House
PO Box 108, 1021 Main St.
Mendocino CA 95460
(707) 937-5150

**Mendocino Bay Trading
Co.**
PO Box 817, 750 Albion St.
Mendocino CA 95460
Circa: 1882
(707) 937-5266

Mendocino Hotel
PO Box 587, 45080 Main St.
Mendocino CA 95460
Circa: 1878
(707) 937-0511

Sea Gull Inn
PO Box 317
Mendocino CA 95460
Circa: 1880
(707) 937-5204

Sears House Inn
PO Box 844
Mendocino CA 95460
Circa: 1870
(707) 937-4076

Whitegate Inn
PO Box 150, 499 Howard St.
Mendocino CA 95460
Circa: 1880
(707) 937-4892

Nethercott Inn
PO Box 671
Middletown CA 95461
Circa: 1871
(707) 987-3362

Mountain Home Inn
810 Panoramic Hwy.
Mill Valley CA 94941
(415) 381-9000

Hotel Leger
PO Box 50
Mokelumne Hill CA 95245
Circa: 1851
(209) 286-1401

San Ysidro Ranch
900 San Ysidro Ln.
Montecito CA 93108

Merritt House
386 Pacific St.
Monterey CA 93940
Circa: 1830
(408) 646-9640

Old Monterey Inn
500 Martin St.
Monterey CA 93940
Circa: 1929
(408) 375-8284

The Jabberwock
598 Laine St.
Monterey CA 93940
Circa: 1911
(408) 372-4777

The Spindrift Inn
Box 3196, 652 Cannery Row
Monterey CA 93940

Pelican Inn
10 Pacific Way
Muir Beach CA 94965
(415) 383-6000

Black Surrey Inn
1815 Silverado Terrace
Murphys CA 94559
(707) 255-1197

Churchill Manor
485 Brown St.
Murphys CA 94559
(707) 253-7733

Dunbar House
PO Box 1375
Murphys CA 95247
Circa: 1880
(209) 728-2897

Arbor Guest House
1436 G Street
Napa CA 94559
(707) 252-8144

Beazley House
1910 First St.
Napa CA 94559
Circa: 1902
(707) 257-1649

Old World Inn
1301 Jefferson
Napa CA 94559
(707) 257-0112

Sybron House
7400 St. Helena Hwy.
Napa CA 94559
(707) 944-2785

Yesterhouse Inn
643 Third St.
Napa CA 94559
Circa: 1896
(707) 257-0550

National Hotel
211 Broad St.
Nevada City CA 95959
Circa: 1852
(916) 263-4551

Red Castle Inn
109 Prospect St.
Nevada City CA 95959
Circa: 1850
(916) 265-5135

The Linanes
Box 1297, 130 E Dana St
Nipomo CA 93444
(805) 929 5444

Ye Old South Fork Inn
57665 Rd. 225
North Fork CA 93643
(209) 877-7025

Rockridge B&B
5428 Thomas Ave
Oakland CA 94618
(415) 655-1223

Ojai Manor Hotel
210 E. Matilija
Ojai CA 93023
(805) 646-0961

Wheeler Hot Springs
PO 250, 16825 Maricopa
Ojai CA 93023

Bear Valley Inn
PO Box 33, 88 Bear Valley
Olema CA 94950
Circa: 1876
(415) 663-1777

Olema Inn
PO Box 10
Olema CA 94950
Circa: 1876
(415) 663-8441

Christy Hill
1650 Squaw Valley Rd Box
2449
Olympic Valley CA 95730
(916) 583-8551

Centrella Hotel
PO Box 884, 612 Central
Pacific Grove CA 93950
Circa: 1889
(408) 372-3372

Gosby House Inn
643 Lighthouse Ave.
Pacific Grove CA 93950
Circa: 1887
(408) 375-1287

Martine Inn
255 Ocean View Blvd.
Pacific Grove CA 93950
Circa: 1899
(408) 373-3388

Ingleside Inn
200 W. Ramon Rd.
Palm Springs CA 92262
Circa: 1920
(619) 325-0046

Donneymac Irish Inn
119 N. Meridith
Pasadena CA 91106
(818) 440-0066

Barbara Welch
524 Howard
Petaluma CA 94952

Philo Pottery Inn
PO Box 166, 8550 Rte. 128
Philo CA 95466
(707) 895-3069

Fleming-Jones Home-
stead
3170 Newton Rd.
Placerville CA 95667
Circa: 1883
(916) 626-5840

James Blair House
2985 Clay St.
Placerville CA 95667
Circa: 1901
(916) 626-6136

Rupley House
PO Box 1709
Placerville CA 95667
Circa: 1929
(916) 626-0630

East Brother Light Sta-
tion Inc.
117 Park Pt.
Point Richmond CA 94801
Circa: 1873
(415) 233-2385

Morey Mansion
190 Terracina Blvd.
Redlands CA 92373
(714) 793-7970

Hotel Burgess
1726 11th St.
Reedley CA 93654
Circa: 1911
(209) 638-6315

Nelle Lethers
4561 Orange Grove Ave
Riverside CA 92501
(714) 683-3246

Rancho Caymus Inn
PO Box 78
Rutherford CA 94573

(707) 963-1777

Amber House
1315 22nd St.
Sacramento CA 95816
Circa: 1905
(916) 444-8085

Aunt Abigail's
2120 G. St.
Sacramento CA 95816
Circa: 1910
(916) 441-5007

Bear Flag Inn
2814 I St.
Sacramento CA 95816
Circa: 1906
(916) 448-5417

Driver Mansion Inn
2019 21st St.
Sacramento CA 95818
(916) 455-5243

Morning Glory
700 22nd St.
Sacramento CA 95816
Circa: 1906
(916) 447-7829

Tres Petite Auberge
811 26th St.
Sacramento CA 95816
Circa: 1890
(916) 446-6566

Black Bart Inn
PO Box 576, 55 St. Charles
San Andreas CA 95249
Circa: 1893
(209) 754-3808

Robin's Nest
PO Box 1408, 247 W. St. Charles
San Andreas CA 95249
(209) 754-1076

Edgemont Inn
1955 Edgemont St.
San Diego CA 92102

Alamo Square Inn
719 Scott St.
San Francisco CA 94117
Circa: 1895
(415) 922-2055

Andrews Hotel
624 Post St.
San Francisco CA 94109
(800) 622-0557, (415) 563-6877

Archbishop's Mansion
1000 Fulton St
San Francisco CA 94117
(415) 563-7872

B&B Near The Park
1387 Sixth Ave
San Francisco CA 94122
(415) 753-3574

Edward II Inn
3155 Scott St.
San Francisco CA 94123
(415) 921-9776

Emperor Norton Inn
615 Post St.
San Francisco CA 94109
(415) 775-2567

Fay Mansion Inn
834 Grove St.
San Francisco CA 94117
Circa: 1874
(415) 921-1816

Grove Inn
890 Grove St.
San Francisco CA 94117
(415) 929-0780

Hotel Louise
845 Bush St.
San Francisco CA 94108
(415) 775-1755

Inn At Union Square
440 Post St.
San Francisco CA 94102
(415) 397-3510

Inn On Castro
321 Castro St.
San Francisco CA 94114
Circa: 1910
(415) 861-0321

Jackson Court
2198 Jackson St.
San Francisco CA 94115
(415) 929-7670

Masonic Manor
1468 Masonic Ave

San Francisco CA 94117
(415) 621-3365

Ole Rafael B&B
528 C St.
San Francisco CA 94901

Pension San Francisco
1668 Market St.
San Francisco CA 94102
(415) 864-1271

Riley's Bed & Breakfast
1234 Sixth Ave.
San Francisco CA 94122
(415) 731-0788

Sherman House
2160 Green St
San Francisco CA 94123
(415) 563-3600

Sprekels Mansion
737 Buena Vista West
San Francisco CA 94117
Circa: 1887
(416) 861-3008

Stanyon Park Hotel
750 Stanyon St.
San Francisco CA 94117
(415) 751-1000

Stewart-Grinsell House
2963 Laguna St.
San Francisco CA 94123
Circa: 1890
(415) 346-0424

The Red Victorian
1665 Haight St.
San Francisco CA 94117
(415) 864-1978

Union Street Inn
2229 Union St.
San Francisco CA 94123
(415) 345-0424

Victorian Inn On The Park
301 Lyon St.
San Francisco CA 94117
Circa: 1889
(415) 931-1830

Warner Embassy
1198 Fulton St.
San Francisco CA 94117

(415) 931-6301

White Swan Inn
845 Bush St.
San Francisco CA 94108
(415) 775-1755

Bed And Breakfast San Juan
PO Box 613
San Juan Bautista CA 95045
Circa: 1858
(408) 623-4101

Heritage Inn
978 Olive St.
San Luis Obispo CA 93401
Circa: 1890
(805) 544-7440

Bath Street Inn
1720 Bath St.
Santa Barbara CA 93101
Circa: 1875
(805) 682-9680

Blue Quail Inn
1908 Bath St.
Santa Barbara CA 93101
(805) 687-2300

Glenborough Inn
1327 Bath St.
Santa Barbara CA 93101
Circa: 1890
(805) 966-0589

Hitchcock House
431 Corona Del Mar
Santa Barbara CA 93103
Circa: 1920
(805) 962-3989

Tiffany Inn
1323 De La Vina
Santa Barbara CA 93101
(805) 963-2283

Villa Rosa
15 Chapala St.
Santa Barbara CA 93101
(805)966-0851

Darling House
314 W. Cliff Dr.
Santa Cruz CA 95060
Circa: 1910
(408) 458-1958

Glen Tavern Inn
134 N. Mill St.
Santa Paula CA 93060
(805) 525-6658

Laurelwood
232 N. 8th St.
Santa Paula CA 93060

The Lemon Tree Inn
299 W. Santa Paula St.
Santa Paula CA 93060

Inn At The Belvedere
727 Mendocino Ave.
Santa Rosa CA 95401
Circa: 1901
(707) 575-1857

Melitta Station Inn
5850 Melita Rd.
Santa Rosa CA 95405
(707) 538-7712

Pygmalion House
331 Orange St.
Santa Rosa CA 95407
Circa: 1880
(707) 526-3407

Alta Mira Hotel
125 Bulkley St.
Sausalito CA 94965
(415) 332-1350

Sausalito Hotel
16 El Portal
Sausalito CA 94965
(415) 332-4155

Campbell Hot Springs
Box 234 #1 Campbell Hot
Springs Rd
Sierraville CA 96126
(916) 994-8984

Sonoma Hotel
110 W Spain St Box 1326
Sonoma CA 95476
(707) 996-2996

Thistle Dew Inn
171 W Spain St Box 1326
Sonoma CA 95476
(707) 938-2909

Trojan Horse Inn
19455 Sonoma Hwy
Sonoma CA 95476

(707) 996-2430

Victorian Garden Inn
316 E Napa St
Sonoma CA 95476
(707) 996-5339

Gunn House
286 S. Washington St.
Sonora CA 95370
Circa: 1851
(209) 532-3421

Jameson's
22157 Feather River
Sonora CA 95370
(209) 532-1248

Llamahall Guest Ranch
18170 Wards Ferry Rd.
Sonora CA 95370
(209) 532-7264

Lulu Belle's
85 Gold St.
Sonora CA 95370
Circa: 1883
(209) 533-3455

Serenity
PO Box 3484
Sonora CA 95370
Circa: 1860
(209) 533-1441

Sonora Inn
160 S. Washington
Sonora CA 95370
(209) 532-7468

Willow Springs Country
Inn
20599 Kings Ct.
Soulsbyville CA 95372
Circa: 1880
(209) 533-2030

Christiana Inn
PO Box 18298
South Lake Tahoe CA 95706
(916) 544-7337

Ambrose Bierce House
1515 Main St.
St. Helena CA 94574
Circa: 1870
(707) 963-3003

Bell Creek Bed & Breakfast
3220 Silverado Trail
St. Helena CA 94574
Circa: 1900
(707) 963-2383

Chalet Bernensis
225 St. Helena Hwy.
St. Helena CA 94574
Circa: 1884
(707) 963-4423

Cornerstone Hotel
1308 Main St.
St. Helena CA 94574
(707) 963-1891

Deer Run Bed & Breakfast
3996 Spring Mtn. Rd.
St. Helena CA 94574
(707) 963-3794

Hotel Saint Helena
1309 Main St.
St. Helena CA 94574
(707) 963-4388

Ink House
1575 St. Helena Hwy.
St. Helena CA 94574
Circa: 1884
(707) 963-3890

Prager Winery B&B
1281 Lewelling Ln.
St. Helena CA 94574
(707) 963-3713

Shady Oaks Country Inn
399 Zinfandel
St. Helena CA 94574
(707) 963-1190

The Cinnamon Bear
1407 Kearney
St. Helena CA 94574
Circa: 1904
(707) 963-4653

Wine Country Cottage
400 Meadow Wood Ln.
St. Helena CA 94574
(707) 963-4633

Trubody Ranch B&B
5444 St. Helena Hwy.
St. Helena CA 94574

(707) 255-5907

Botto Country Inn
11 Sutter Hill Rd
Sutter Creek CA 95685
(209) 267-5519

Hanford House
PO Box 847
Sutter Creek CA 95685
(209) 267-0747

The Foxes
PO Box 159, 77 Main St.
Sutter Creek CA 95685
Circa: 1862
(209) 267-5882

Timberhill Ranch
35755 Hauser Bridge Rd.
Timbercove CA 95421
(707) 847-3477

Trinidad Bed & Breakfast
PO Box Au
Trinidad CA 95570
(707) 677-0840

Alta Hotel
PO Box 2118
Truckee CA 95734
Circa: 1902
(916) 587-6668

Mountain View Inn
PO Box 8579, Off Hwy. 267
Truckee CA 95737
(916) 587-2545

Oak Hill Ranche
Box 307
Tuolumne CA 95379
(209) 928-4717

Sanford House
306 S. Pine
Ukiah CA 95482
(707) 462-1653

Inn At Valley Ford
PO Box 439, 14395 Hwy. 1
Valley Ford CA 94972
Circa: 1860
(707) 876-3182

Baker Inn
1093 Poli St.
Ventura CA 93001

(805) 652-0143

Roseholm
51 Sulphur Mt. Rd.
Ventura CA 93001
(805) 649-4014

St. George Hotel
PO Box 9
Volcano CA 95689
(209) 296-4458

Hocker-Bartlett House
PO Box 1511, 807 Main St.
Weaverville CA 96093
Circa: 1860
(916) 623-4403

Cobweb Palace
PO Box 132
Westport CA 95488
Circa: 1883
(707) 964-5588

Wilbur Hot Springs
Williams CA 95987
(916) 473-2306

Magnolia Hotel
Drawer M, 6529 Yount St.
Yountville CA 94599
Circa: 1870

Napa Valley Railway Inn
Box 2568, 6503 Washington
Yountville CA 94599

The Webber Place
Box 2873
Yountville CA 94599
Circa: 1850

The Wicks
560 Cooper Ave
Yuba City CA 95991
(916) 674-7951

Colorado

Lazy H Ranch
Box 248
Allenspark CO 80510

Christmas Inn
232 W. Main St.
Aspen CO 81611
(303) 925-3822

Copper Horse House
328 W. Main
Aspen CO 81611
Circa: 1886

Hearthstone House
134 E. Hyman St.
Aspen CO 81611

Innsbruck Inn
233 W. Main St.
Aspen CO 81611

Little Red Ski Haus
118 E. Cooper
Aspen CO 81611
Circa: 1888

Molly Gibson Lodge
120 W. Hopkins
Aspen CO 81611

Snow Queen Lodge
124 E. Cooper
Aspen CO 81611

Tipple Inn
747 S. Galena St.
Aspen CO 81611

Ullr Lodge
520w. Main St.
Aspen CO 81611

Briar Rose B&B
2151 Arapahoe
Boulder CO 80302
Circa: 1897

Fireside Inn
212 Wellington PO Box 2252
Breckenridge CO 80424

Two Ten Casey
PO Box 154
Central City CO 80427

Nordic Inn
PO Box 939
Crested Butte CO 81224

The Oxford
1600 17th St
Denver CO 80202
Circa: 1891
800 228 5838

**Bed And Breakfast
Durango**
PO Box 544
Durango CO 81301
Circa: 1878
303 247 2223

Victorian Inn
2117 W. Second Ave.
Durango CO 81301
Circa: 1880

Aspen Lodge
Longs Peak Rte
Estes Park CO 80517
Circa: 1915
303 586 4241

Helmshire Inn
1204 S. College
Ft. Collins CO 80524

Columbine Lodge
Box 267
Green Mountain Falls CO
80819
Circa: 1895

Outlook Lodge
Box 5
Green Mountain Falls CO
80819
Circa: 1889

Blue Lake Ranch
16919 Hwy. 140
Hesperus CO 81326

Nippersink
106 Spencer Ave
Manitou Springs CO 80829
Circa: 1885

Goldminer Hotel
Eldora Star Rt
Nederland CO 80466
Circa: 1897

Baker's Manor
317 Second St.
Ouray CO 81427
Circa: 1881

House Of Yesteryear
Box 440
Ouray CO 81427

St. Elmo Hotel
426 Main St.

Ouray CO 81427
Circa: 1897

Weisbaden Spa & Lodge
Box 349
Ouray CO 81427
Circa: 1895

Jackson Hotel
220 S. Main St.
Poncha Springs CO 81242
Circa: 1878

Historic Redstone Inn
82 Redstone Blvd.
Redstone CO 81623

Poor Farm Country Inn
8495 CO. Rd. 160
Salida CO 81201

Alma House
PO Box 780
Silverton CO 81433
Circa: 1898

Teller House Hotel
1250 Greene St
Silverton CO 81433
303 387 5423

Bear Pole Ranch
Star Rt. 1 Box Bb
Steamboat Springs CO 80487

Sky Valley Lodge
Box 2153
Steamboat Springs CO 80477

The House On The Hill
PO Box 770598
Steamboat Springs CO 80477

Dahl House
PO Box 695
Telluride CO 81435
Circa: 1890

Johnstone Inn
PO Box 546
Telluride CO 81435

New Sheridan Hotel
231 W. Colorado Ave.
Telluride CO 81435
Circa: 1895

Connecticut

Chimney Crest Manor
5 Founders Dr.
Bristol CT 06010

Inn At Chester
318 W Main St
Chester CT 06412
Circa: 1776
203 526 4961

Harbor View On Holly Place
63 Pratt Rd.
Clinton CT 06413

Harbor House Inn
50 River Rd
Cos Cob CT 06807
Circa: 1860
203 661 5845

Bishop's Gate
Goodspeed Landing
East Haddam CT 06423
Circa: 1818

Stonecroft Inn
17 Main St.
East Haddam CT 06423

Pricilla Sobol
138 Clark Hill
East Hampton CT 06424

Griswold Inn
Essex CT 06426
Circa: 1775

Palmer Inn
25 Church St. Noank
Groton CT 06340
Circa: 1907

Copper Beach Inn
Main Street
Ivoryton CT 06442

Ivoryton Inn
Main St
Ivoryton CT 06442
203 767 0422

Constitution Oak Farm
Beardsley Rd
Kent CT 06757
Circa: 1830

203 354 6495

Kenneth Waldorph
Box 307
Kent CT 06757

The Candlelight
Kent CT 06757
203 927 3407

B&B At Laharan Farm
350 Rte. 81
Killingworth CT 06417
Circa: 1800

Wake Robin Inn
Rte 41
Lakeville CT 06039
203 435 2515

Tucker Hill Inn
96 Tucker Hill Rd.
Middlebury CT 06762
(203) 758-8334

Fowler House
PO Box 432
Moodus CT 06469
Circa: 1890

Comolli's Guest House
36 Bruggeman Pl.
Mystic CT 06355

Inn At Mystic
Jct Rt 1 & 27
Mystic CT 06355
Circa: 1904
203 536 9604

Whalers Inne
PO Box 488t
Mystic CT 06355
Circa: 1900
203 536 1506

Maples Inn
179 Oenoke Ridge
New Canaan CT 06840
Circa: 1908

Roger Sherman Inn
195 Oenoke Ridge
New Canaan CT 06840
Circa: 1740
(203) 955-4541

Queen Anne
265 Williams St.

New London CT 06320

Homestead Inn
5 Elm St.
New Milford CT 06776
Circa: 1830

Birches Inn
West Shore Rd
New Preston CT 06777
Circa: 1920
203 868 0229

Boulders Inn
Rt 45
New Preston CT 06777
Circa: 1895
203 868 7918

Hopkins Inn
Hopkins Rd.
New Preston CT 06777

Hawley Manor Inn
19 Main St
Newton CT 06470
Circa: 1780
203 426 4456

Blackberry River Inn
Route 44
Norfolk CT 06058
Circa: 1763

Mountain View Inn
Rt. 272
Norfolk CT 06058
Circa: 1875

Weaver's House
Rte. 44
Norfolk CT 06058
(203) 542-5108

Harbor House Inn
165 Shore Rd
Old Greenwich CT 06850
203 637 0145

Bee And Thistle Inn
100 Lyme St.
Old Lyme CT 06371
Circa: 1756

Red Brook Inn
PO Box 237
Old Mystic CT 06372

Castle Inn-Cornfield Pt.
Hartland Dr.
Old Saybrook CT 06475
Circa: 1900

Feishaw Tavern
Five Mile River Road
Putnam CT 06260
Circa: 1742

Stonehenge
Route 7
Ridgefield CT 06877

The Elms Inn
500 Main St.
Ridgefield CT 06877
Circa: 1760

West Lane Inn
22 West Ln.
Ridgefield CT 06877
Circa: 1890

Old Riverton Inn
PO Box 6 Rt. 20
Riverton CT 06065
Circa: 1796

Ragamont Inn
Main St
Salisbury CT 06068
Circa: 1702
203 435 2372

Undermountain Inn
Rt 41
Salisbury CT 06068
203 435 0242

White Hart Inn
Villiage Green
Salisbury CT 06068
Circa: 1800

Yesterday's Yankee
Rte. 44 East
Salisbury CT 06068
(203) 435-9539

Altnaveigh Inn
957 Storrs Rd
Storrs CT 06268
Circa: 1734
203 429 4490

Farmhouse On The Hill
418 Gurleyville Rd.
Storrs CT 06268

Mayflower Inn
Rt 47
Washington CT 06793
Circa: 1894
203 868 0515

Captain Stannard House
138 S. Main St.
Westbrook CT 06498

Cotswold Inn
76 Myrtle Ave.
Westport CT 06880

Longshore Inn
280 Compo Rd South
Westport CT 06883
203 226 3316

Curtis House
Main St.
Woodbury CT 06798
Circa: 1700

Delaware

166 Ocean View
PO Box 275, 166 Ocean View
Pkwy
Bethany Beach DE 19930
Circa: 1909
(302) 539 3707

Homestead Guests
721 Garfield Pkwy.
Bethany Beach DE 19930
Circa: 1909

Sea-Vista Villas
Box 62
Bethany Beach DE 19930

The Addy Sea
P. Box 275
Bethany Beach DE 19930
Circa: 1900

The Sandbox
Box 62
Bethany Beach DE 19930
(302) 539 3354

Corner Cupboard Inn
50 Park Ave.
Rehoboth Beach DE 19971
Circa: 1932

Lord Baltimore Lodge
16 Baltimore Ave
Rehoboth Beach DE 19971
Circa: 1875
(302) 227 2855

Peasant Inn Lodge
31 Olive Ave.
Rehoboth Beach DE 19971
Circa: 1928

Sea Lodge
15 Hickman St
Rehoboth Beach DE 19971

The Abbey
31 Maryland Ave
Rehoboth Beach DE 19971
Circa: 1900
(302) 227 7023

Gladstone In
119 Commerce St
Smyrna DE 19977
(302) 653 8294

Florida

Cabbage Key Inn
PO Box 489
Bokeelia FL 33922
813 283 2278

Banyan House
624 Fontana Ln.
Bradenton FL 33529

Historic Island Hotel
Box 460
Cedar Key FL 32625

Hotel Place St. Michel
162 Alcazar Ave.
Coral Gables FL 33134
Circa: 1926

Rod & Gun Club
PO Box G
Everglades City FL 33929
Circa: 1883

Bailey House
PO Box 805
Fernandina Beach FL 32034
Circa: 1895

Greyfield Inn
Box 878 cumberland Isl.

Fernandina Beach FL 32034
Circa: 1904

Seaside Inn
1998 South Fletcher Ave.
Fernandina Beach FL 32034

Seminole Country Inn
15885 warfield
Indianatown FL 33456
Circa: 1925

Crown Hotel
109 N. Seminole Ave.
Inverness FL 32650
Circa: 1880

The Manor Inn
1630 Copeland St.
Jacksonville FL 32204

Colours Key West
410 Fleming St.
Key West FL 33040

Eaton Lodge
511 Eaton St.
Key West FL 33040
Circa: 1880

Eden House
1015 Fleming
Key West FL 33040
Circa: 1924

Heron House
512 Simonton St.
Key West FL 33040

Island City House
411 William St
Key West FL 33040
Circa: 1880
305 294 5702

Beaumont House
206 S Beaumont Ave
Kissimee FL 32741
Circa: 1900
305 846 7916

Kenwood Inn
38 Marine St.
St. Augustine FL 32084
Circa: 1865

Victorian House B&B
11 Cadiz St.
St. Augustine FL 32084

Wescott House
146 Avendia Menendez
St. Augustine FL 32084
Circa: 1880

Wakulla Springs Lodge
1 Spring Dr
Wakulla Springs FL 32305
Circa: 1930

Georgia

The Serpentine Inn
1416 S Milledge Ave
Athens GA 30605
(404) 353-8548

Beverly Hills Inn
65 Sheridan Dr. Ne
Atlanta GA 30305
Circa: 1929

Shellmont B&B Lodge
821 Piedmont Ne
Atlanta GA 30308

Telfair Inns
326 Greene St
Augusta GA 30901
Circa: 1860
800 282 2405

Laprade's
Rt 1, Hwy. 197
Clarkesville GA 30523
Circa: 1916

De Loffre House
812 Broadway
Columbus GA 31901
Circa: 1863

Forest Hills Mt. Resort
Rte. 3
Dahlonega GA 30533

Smith House
202 S. Chestatee St.
Dahlonega GA 30533

Dunlap House
635 Green St
Gainesville GA 30501

Hartwell Inn
504 W. Howell St.
Hartwell GA 30643

Derdenhof Inn
PO Box 405
Helen GA 30545

Lake Rabun Hotel
Rt 1 PO Box 101
Lakemont GA 30552
Circa: 1922
(404) 782-4946

1842 Inn
353 College St
Macon GA 31201

Hutnick House
273 Orange St
Macon GA 31201

La Petite Maison
1165 Dures Lane
Macon GA 31201
(912) 742-4674

Arden Hall
1052 Arden Dr. SW
Marietta GA 30060

York House
Box 126
Mountain City GA 30562
Circa: 1896

Stovall House
Rt. 1 Box 152
Sautee GA 30571
Circa: 1837

17 Hdred 90 Inn
307 E. President
Savannah GA 31401
Circa: 1790

Ballastone Inn
14 E. Oglethorpe
Savannah GA 31401
Circa: 1835

Barrister House
25 W Perry St
Savannah GA 31401

Charlton Court
403 E. Charlton St.
Savannah GA 31401
Circa: 1860

Comer House
2 East Taylor St.
Savannah GA 31401

Eliza Thompson House
5 W. Jones St.
Savannah GA 31401
Circa: 1847

Foley House Inn
14 W. Hull St.
Savannah GA 31401
Circa: 1896

Forsyth Inn
102 West Hall St.
Savannah GA 31401

Greystone Inn
214 E. Jones St.
Savannah GA 31401

Liberty Inn 1834
128 W. Liberty St.
Savannah GA 31401
Circa: 1834

Magnolia Place Inn
503 Whitaker St.
Savannah GA 31401

Mary Lee's House
PO Box 607
Savannah GA 31402
Circa: 1854

Mulberry Inn
601 E. Bay St.
Savannah GA 31402

Oglethorpe Inn
PO Box 9803
Savannah GA 31412
(912) 232-2700

Pulaski Square Inn
203 W. Charlton
Savannah GA 31401

Stoddard-Cooper House
19 W. Perry St.
Savannah GA 31401
Circa: 1854

Riverview Hotel
105 Osborne St.
St. Mary's GA 31558
Circa: 1916

Little St. Simons Island
PO Box 1078 G
St. Simons Island GA 31522
Circa: 1917

Statesboro Inn B&B
301 South
Statesboro GA 30458
(912) 489-8628

Susina Plantation Inn
Rte. 3 Box 1010
Thomasville GA 31792
Circa: 1841

The Golden Fox
Rt 2 Box 691
Thomson GA 30824
Circa: 1870
(404) 595-5395

Hawaii

Deep Creek Inn
Bonner's Ferry HI 83805

Idaho

Ellsworth Inn
715 3rd Ave S.
Hailey ID 83333

Whitaker House
410 Railroad Ave.#10
Sandpoint ID 83466

Idaho Rocky Mtn. Ranch
HC64 Box 9934
Stanley ID 8327
Circa: 1935

Redfish Lake Lodge
PO Box 9
Stanley ID 83278
Circa: 1935
(208) 774-3536

Illinois

Colonial Inn
Rt 3 Grand Detour
Dixon IL 61021
Circa: 1890
(815) 652-4422

Aldrich Guest House
900 Third Street
Galena IL 61036

Bedford House
Rt.20 West
Galena IL 61036
Circa: 1850

Belle Aire Mansion
11410 Rt 20 West
Galena IL 61036
Circa: 1834
(815) 777-0893

Colonial Guest House
1004 Park Ave.
Galena IL 61036
Circa: 1826

Comfort Guest House
1000 Third St.
Galena IL 61036

Creekside Guest House
3825 West Miner Rd.
Galena IL 61036

Felt Manor
125 S Prospect St
Galena IL 61036
Circa: 1840
(815) 777-9093

Fricke Guest House
119 South Bench St.
Galena IL 61036

Gallery Guest Suite
204 1/2 S Main St
Galena IL 61036
(815) 777-1222

Lafayette Guest House
911 Third St
Galena IL 61036
Circa: 1850
(815) 777-1160

Log Cabin Guest House
11661 W. Chetlain Ln.
Galena IL 61036

Mother's Country Inn
349 Spring St.
Galena IL 61036

Pillsbury's Guest House
713 S Bench St
Galena IL 61036
Circa: 1836
(815) 777-1611

Illinois (continued)

Ryan Mansion Inn
Rt. 20 West
Galena IL 61036
Circa: 1876

Victorian Mansion Guest
House
301 S High St
Galena IL 61036
Circa: 1861
(815) 777-0675

Riverview Mansion Hotel
Columbus Ave, PO Box 56
Golconda IL 62938
Circa: 1894
(618) 638-3001

The Mansion Of Golcon-
da
Bed & Breakfast
Golconda IL 62938

Bennett-Curtis House
302 W. Taylor
Gratt Park IL 60940

Wittmond Hotel
C/O Calhoun Herald
Harden IL 62017
(818) 883-2345

Old Illiopolis Hotel
608 Mary St
Illiopolis IL 62539
(217) 486-6451

Deer Path Inn
255 E Illinois Rd
Lake Forest IL 60045
(312) 234-2280

Hotel Nauvoo
Rt 96 Town Center PO 398
Nauvoo IL 62354
Circa: 1840
(217) 453-2211

Memory Lane Lodge
409 N. Canyon Park Rd.
Stockton IL 61085
(815)947-2726

Gray Goose Bed &
Breakfast
1206 S. Vine
Urbana IL 61801

Herrings Maple Lane
Farm
3114 Rush Creek Rd.
Stockton IL 61085

Indiana

Sherman House
Batesville IN 47006
Circa: 1852
(812) 934-2407

The Gray Goose
1835 Indian Boundary Rd.
Chesterton IN 46304

Barn House
10656 E. 63rd St.
Indianapolis IN 46236

Duneland Beach Inn
3311 Potawatomi
Michigan City IN 46360
Circa: 1920

Patchwork Quilt
11748 CR # 2
Middlebury IN 46540

New Harmony Inn
North St
New Harmony IN 47631
(812) 682-4491

Victorian House
RR1 Box 27
Roachdale IN 46172

Green Meadow
R2 State Rd. 5 Box 592
Shipshewana IN 46565

Iowa

Guest House Motor Inn
Motel
Amana IA 52203
(319) 622-3599

Hotel Brooklyn
154 Front St.
Brooklyn IA 52211
Circa: 1895

Little House Vacations
Elkader IA 52043

(319) 783-7774

Hotel Manning
100 Van Buren St
Keosauqua IA 52565
Circa: 1854
(319) 293-3232

Mason House Inn
RR 2 - Bentonsport
Keosauqua IA 52565
(319) 592-3133

Fitzgerald's Inn
106 3rd St
Lansing IA 52151
(319) 538-4872

Decker Hotel
128 N. Main
Maquoketa IA 52060

Historic Harlan House
122 N Jefferson St PO 110
Mt Pleasant IA 52641
Circa: 1857
(319) 385-3126

Strawtown Inn
Llll Washington St
Pella IA 50219
(515) 628-2681

Old World Inn
Spillville IA 52168
(319) 562-3739

Kansas

Rosalea's Hotel
121 W Main St
Harper KS 67058
Circa: 1880

Kimble Cliff
Rt 1, Box 139
Manhattan KS 66502

Anchor Hill Lodge
Rt 1
Rogersville KS 65742

B&B On Our Farm
Rt.1 Box 132
Wakefield KS 67487

Kentucky

Bruntwood 1802, Mrs.
Bare
714 N. 3 St.
Bardstown KY 40004

Boone Tavern Hotel
Main Street
Berea KY 40403
(606) 986-9358/9359

Doe Run Inn
Rte.2
Brandenburg KY 40108
Circa: 1820

Beaumont Inn
638 Beaumont Dr
Harrodsburg KY 40330
Circa: 1835
(606) 734-3381

Rokeby Hall
318 South Mill St
Lexington KY 40508
(606) 252-2368

Louisiana

A La Bonne Veillee
Rt 3 #2, Box 2270
Abbeville LA 70510

Mount Hope Plantation
8151 Highland Rd
Baton Rouge LA 70808
Circa: 1817
(504) 766-8600

Brame-Bennet House
227 S Baton Rouge St
Clinton LA 70722
Circa: 1839
(504) 683-5241

Avondale Plantation
Box 8187
Clinton LA 70722

Tezcuco Plantation
Rt. 1 Box 157
Convent LA 70723
Circa: 1855

Inn At Asphodel
Rt. 2 Box 89

Jackson LA 70748
Circa: 1830

Ti Frere's House
1905 Verot School Rd.
Lafayette LA 70508

Madewood Plantation
Route 2 Box 478
Napoleonville LA 70390

Mintmere Plantation
1400 E. Main
New Iberia LA 70560
Circa: 1857

A Creole House
1013 St Ann St
New Orleans LA 70116
Circa: 1820
504 524 8076

A Hotel, the Frenchman
417 Frenchman St.
New Orleans LA 70116

Andrew Jackson Hotel
919 Royal St
New Orleans LA 70166
Circa: 1880
504 561 5881

Burgundy Inn
911 Burgundy St
New Orleans LA 70116
Circa: 1780
504 524 0141, 800 535 7785

Club LA Pension
501 Canal St
New Orleans LA 70130
Circa: 1821

Dauzat House
337 Burgandy St.
New Orleans LA 70130

French Quarter Maisons
1130 Chartres St.
New Orleans LA 70116

Hansel And Gretel
House
916 Burgundy St
New Orleans LA 70116
Circa: 1880
504 524 0141

Hedgewood
2427 St. Charles Ave.
New Orleans LA 70130
Circa: 1840

Hotel Villa Convento
616 Ursulines St.
New Orleans LA 70116
Circa: 1820

Lafitte Guest House
1003 Bourbon St.
New Orleans LA 70116
Circa: 1849

Lamothe House
621 Esplanade Ave.
New Orleans LA 70116
Circa: 1840

Longpre's Gardens
1726 Prytania St.
New Orleans LA 70130

Maison Chartres
508 Chartres St
New Orleans LA 70130
Circa: 1835
504 529 2172

Marquette Hostel
2253 Carondelet St.
New Orleans LA 70130

Noble Arms Inn
1006 Royal St.
New Orleans LA 70116
Circa: 1820

Old World Inn
1330 Prytania
New Orleans LA 70130

Park View
7004 St. Charles St.
New Orleans LA 70118
Circa: 1884

Prince Conti Hotel
830 Conti St
New Orleans LA 70112
504 529 4172

St Peter House
1005 St Peter St
New Orleans LA 70116
Circa: 1850
504 524 9232

St. Charles Guest House
1748 Prytania St.
New Orleans LA 70130

Terrell House
1441 Magazine St.
New Orleans LA 70130

Pointe Coupee B&B
605 E. Main St.
New Roads LA 70760

Bondy House &
Claiborne House
Box 386, 304 Court St.
New Roads LA 70760

Estorge House
427 N. Market St.
Opelousas LA 70570
Circa: 1827

Cottage Plantation
Rt 5 PO Box 425
St. Francisville LA 70775
Circa: 1795
504 635 3674

Myrtles Plantation
PO Box 387
St. Francisville LA 70775
Circa: 1796

Maison De Fontenot
Rt 5, Box 1740
Sulphur LA 70663

Oak Alley Plantation
Rt. 2 Box 10 Hwy. 18
Vacherie LA 70090
Circa: 1880

Old Lyons House
1335 Horridge St.
Vinton LA 70668

Wakefield Plantaion
PO Box 41
Wakefield LA 70784
Circa: 1834

Glencoe Plantation
PO Box 178
Wilson LA 70789
Circa: 1903

Maine

The Olde Berry Inn
Kennebunk Road
Alfred ME 04002
(207) 324-0603

Crosby's Bed & Breakfast
51 Green St.
Augusta ME 04330

Cloverleaf Cottage B&B
RFD 1 Box 326
Bailey Island ME 04003

Driftwood Inn
Bailey Island ME 04003

Bayview Inn & Hotel
111 Eden St.
Bar Harbor ME 04609

Central House
60 Cottage St.
Bar Harbor ME 04609

Clefstone Manor
92 Eden St.
Bar Harbor ME 04609
Circa: 1880

Dow Cottage Inn
227 Main St.
Bar Harbor ME 04609
Circa: 1830

Holbrook Inn
74 Mount Desert
Bar Harbor ME 04609
Circa: 1880

Ledgelawn Inn
66 Mount Desert
Bar Harbor ME 04609
Circa: 1904

Shady Maples
Rd #1 Box 360
Bar Harbor ME 04609

Stratford House Inn
45 Mount Desert St.
Bar Harbor ME 04609

The Atlantean Inn
11 Atlantic Ave
Bar Harbor ME 04609

The Inn On High
15 High St.
Bar Harbor ME 04609

The Maples
16 Roberts Ave
Bar Harbor ME 04609

Thornhedge
47 Mt. Desert St.
Bar Harbor ME 04609
Circa: 1900

Town Guest House
12 Atlantic Ave.
Bar Harbor ME 04609
Circa: 1894

Pointy Head Inn
Rte. 102 A
Bass Harbor ME 04653

Grane's Fairhaven Inn
N. Bath Rd.
Bath ME 04530
Circa: 1790

Glad II
60 Pearl St
Bath ME 04530

Levitt Family B&B
50 Pearl St
Bath ME 04530

Dragonwick Inn B&B
Rt 3 Belmont Ave.
Belfast ME 04915

Horatio Johnson House
36 Church St.
Belfast ME 04915
(207) 338-5153

Penobscot Meadows
Rt. 1
Belfast ME 04915

Bakers B&B
Box 2090 RFD 2
Bethel ME 04217

Chapman Inn
PO Box 206
Bethel ME 04217

The Pointed Fir
PO Box 745

Bethel ME 04217
(207) 824-2251

Altenhofen House
Peters Point
Blue Hill ME 04614
Circa: 1810

Arcady Down East
South St.
Blue Hill ME 04614

Blue Hill Farm Country Inn
Route 15
Blue Hill ME 04614
Circa: 1832

Green Shutters Inn
PO Box. 543
Boothbay Harbor ME 04538

Hilltop House
44 Mckown Hill
Boothbay Harbor ME 04538
Circa: 1830

Howard House
Route 27
Boothbay Harbor ME 04538

Seafarer Guest House
38 Union St
Boothbay Harbor ME 04538

Thistle Inn
PO Box 176
Boothbay Harbor ME 04538
Circa: 1850

Topside
Mckown Hill
Boothbay Harbor ME 04538

Welch House
36 Mckown St.
Boothbay Harbor ME 04538
Circa: 1840

Westgate Guest House
18 West St.
Boothbay Harbor ME 04538
Circa: 1903

The Maples
PO Box 75, RR 1
Bowdoinham ME 04008
(207) 666-3012

Mountainside B&B
PO Box 290
Bridgton ME 04009

Noble House
PO Box 86
Bridgton ME 04009

North Woods B&B
55 North High St
Bridgton ME 04009

The 1859 Guest House
60 S. High St.
Bridgton ME 04009
Circa: 1859
(207)647-2508

Middlefield Farm
PO Box 4
Bristol ME 04539

Breezemere Farm
Box 290
Brooksville ME 04617
Circa: 1850

The Glen Mountain House
PO Box 176
Bryant Pond ME 04219

Jed Prouty Tavern
Box 550
Bucksport ME 04416

Aubergine
6 Belmont Ave.
Camden ME 04843
Circa: 1890

Chestnut House
69 Chestnut St
Camden ME 04843

Edgecomb-Coles House
64 High St.
Camden ME 04843

Goodspeeds Guest House
60 Mountain St.
Camden ME 04843

Hawthorne
9 High St.
Camden ME 04843

High Tide Inn
Camden ME 04843
Circa: 1940

Hosmer House
4 Pleasant St.
Camden ME 04843

J. Sloan Inn
49 Mountain St.
Camden ME 04843

Lord Camden Inn
24 Main St.
Camden ME 04843

Norumbega Inn
61 High St.
Camden ME 04843

Owl And The Turtle
8 Bay View
Camden ME 04843

Park Street Inn
90 Mechanic Street
Camden ME 04843

The Swan House
49 Mountain Street
Camden ME 04843

Whitehall Inn
52 High St.
Camden ME 04843

Crescent Beach Inn
Rt. 77
Cape Elizabeth ME 04107

Cape Neddick House
Rt. 1 PO Box 70
Cape Neddick ME 03902

Sea Chimes B&B
Shore Rd.
Cape Neddick ME 03902

Wooden Goose Inn
PO Box 195 Rt. 1
Cape Neddick ME 03902

Castine Inn
PO Box 41
Castine ME 04421
Circa: 1898

Pentagoet Inn
PO Box 4
Castine ME 04421
Circa: 1894

Westways On Kezar
Lake
Rte. 5
Center Lovell ME 04016

Chebeague Inn
Chebeague Island ME 04017
(207)967-3118

Ricker House
Box 256
Cherryfield ME 04622

Cornish Country Inn
Box 206
Cornish ME 04020

The Brannon Bunker
PO Box 045, Hcr 64
Damariscotta ME 04543
(207) 563-5941

Pilgrim's Inn
Main St.
Deer Isle ME 04627
Circa: 1793

Lincoln House Inn
Routes 1 & 86
Dennysville ME 04628
Circa: 1787

Ben-Loch Inn
PO Box 1020, RFD 1
Dixmont ME 04932
(207) 257-4768

The Foxcroft
25 West Main St
Dover-Foxcroft ME 04426

Waterford Inne
Box 49
East Waterford ME 04233

Victoria's B&B
58 Pine St
Ellsworth ME 04605

Inn At Cold Stream Pond
PO Box 76
Enfield ME 04433

Grey Havens Inn
Box 82
Five Islands ME 04546

Harraseeket Inn
162 Main St.
Freeport ME 04032

Old Red Farm
RR2 Box 242 Desert Rd
Freeport ME 04032
(207) 865-4550

The Oxford House Inn
105 Main St
Fryeburg ME 04037

Country Squire B&B
Box 178 Mighty St RR1
Gorham ME 04038

Greenville Inn
PO Box 1194
Greenville ME 04441
Circa: 1895

Trebor Inn
PO Box 299
Guilford ME 04443

Crocker House
Hancock ME 04640
Circa: 1884

Dark Harbor House Inn
Box 185
Islesboro ME 04848

Gablewood
Main Road
Islesboro ME 04848

Captain Littlefield Inn
26 Fletcher St.
Kennebunk ME 04043

Kennebunk Inn 1799
45 Main St.
Kennebunk ME 04043
Circa: 1799

1802 House
Box 774 locke St.
Kennebunkport ME 04046
Circa: 1802

Breakwater
PO Box 1160

Kennebunkport ME 04046

Captain Fairfield House
PO Box 202
Kennebunkport ME 04046

Captain Jefferds Inn
Box 691
Kennebunkport ME 04046
Circa: 1804

Chetwynd House
PO Box 130
Kennebunkport ME 04046
Circa: 1840

Dock Square Inn
PO Box 1123
Kennebunkport ME 04046

English Meadows
Rt. 35
Kennebunkport ME 04046

English Robin
R1 Box 194
Kennebunkport ME 04046

Flakeyard Farm
RFD 2
Kennebunkport ME 04046

North Street Guest
House
Box 1229
Kennebunkport ME 04046

Ocean View
72 Beach Ave.
Kennebunkport ME 04046

Rivermeadow B&B
Box 1293
Kennebunkport ME 04043

Seaside Inn
Gooch's Beach
Kennebunkport ME 04046

The Green Heron Inn
Ocean Ave.
Kennebunkport ME 04046
Circa: 1908

Tides Inn By The Sea
Goose Rock Beach
Kennebunkport ME 04046
Circa: 1900

White Barn Inn
Beach St.
Kennebunkport ME 04046
Circa: 1800

Whitten Hill House
Box 248
Kennebunkport ME 04046

Country Cupboard B&B
RFD 1 Box 1270
Kingfield ME 04947

County Cupboard
Rt. 27 N Main St.
Kingfield ME 04947

Herbert Inn
PO Box 67
Kingfield ME 04947

Three Stanley Avenue
PO Box 169
Kingfield ME 04947

Witner's Inn
Box 44
Kingfield ME 04947
Circa: 1800

Melfair Farm B&B
365 Wilson Rd.
Kittery ME 03904

Harbor's Watch
Box 42 RFD 1
Kittery Point ME 03905

Longville
PO Box 75
Lincolnville ME 04849

Yougtown Inn
Rt. 52
Lincolnville ME 04849

North House 1792
Box 165
Lincolnville Beach ME 04849

Old Tavern Inn
PO Box 445
Litchfield ME 04350

Eggemoggin Inn
Little Deer Isle ME 04650
Circa: 1906

Home Port Inn
45 Main St.
Lubec ME 04652

The Moorings
Manset ME 04679
Circa: 1780

Mill Pond House
Mrs. Korpinen
Martinsville ME 04860

Island Inn
Shore Rd.
Monhegan Island ME 04852
Circa: 1850

Feather Bed Inn
Box 65
Mount Vernon ME 04352
Circa: 1856

Charmwoods
Naples ME 04055

The Augustus Bove
House
RR 1 Box 501
Naples ME 04055

Bradley Inn
361 Pemaquid Pt.
New Harbor ME 04554
Circa: 1890

Mill Pond Inn
RFD 1 Box 245
Newcastle ME 04553

The Captain's House
PO Box 516
Newcastle ME 04553

The Markert House
PO Box 224, Glidden St.
Newcastle ME 04553
(207) 563-1309

Norridgewock Colonial
Inn
RFD 1 Box 1190
Norridgewock ME 04957

Channelridge Farm
358 Cross Pt. Rd.
North Edgecomb ME 04556

Pulpit Harbor Inn
Crabtree Point Rd.
North Haven ME 04853

Grey Rock Inn
Northeast Harbor ME 04662

Harbourside Inn
Northeast Harbor ME 04662
Circa: 1888

Admiral's Loft
97 Main St.
Ogunquit ME 03907
Circa: 1830

Blue Shutters
6 Beachmere Pl.
Ogunquit ME 03907

Blue Water Inn
Beach St.
Ogunquit ME 03907

Channing Hall
3 Pine Hill Rd.
Ogunquit ME 03907

Clipper Ship Guest
House
46 N. Main St.
Ogunquit ME 03907

Gazebo
PO Box 668 Rt. 1
Ogunquit ME 03907

Hartwell House
116 Shore Rd.
Ogunquit ME 03907

Inn At 77 Shore Road
77 Shore Rd.
Ogunquit ME 03907
Circa: 1840

Lemon Tree Inn
Box 564
Ogunquit ME 03907

Ogunquit House
PO Box 1883
Ogunquit ME 03907

Seafair Inn
24 Shore Rd. Box 1221
Ogunquit ME 03907
Circa: 1890

Yardarm Village Inn
PO Box 773
Ogunquit ME 03907

Little River Inn
Rt. 130
Pemaquid ME 04588

Copper Light
PO Box 67
Port Clyde ME 04855
(207) 372-8510

Ocean House
Box 66
Port Clyde ME 04855

Carleton Gardens
43 Carleton St.
Portland ME 04102
(207) 772-3458

Inn At Carleton
46 Carleton St.
Portland ME 04102

The Poet's Inne
180 State St Rte 77
Portland ME 04102

Oceanside Meadows Inn
Box 85
Prospect Harbor ME 04669

Davis Lodge
Rt 4
Rangeley ME 04970

Farmhouse Inn
PO Box 173
Rangeley ME 04970

Benjamin Riggs House
PO Box 440
Robinhood ME 04530
(207) 371-2256

Old Granite Inn
546 Main St.
Rockland ME 04841

Sign Of The Unicorn
191 Beauchamp Av.
Rockport ME 04856

Allen's Inn
279 Main St.
Sanford ME 04073

Carriage House Inn
Rte. 1 E. Main St.
Searsport ME 04974
Circa: 1849

Homeport Inn
Box 148
Searsport ME 04974

Buck's Harbor Inn
Rt. 176 PO Box 268
South Brooksville ME 04617

Thomas Inn & Playhouse
PO Box 128
South Casco ME 04077
Circa: 1850

Albonegon Inn
Capitol Island
Southport ME 04538

Claremont
Southwest Harbor ME 04679
Circa: 1884

Harbor Lights Home
Rte. 102
Southwest Harbor ME 04679
Circa: 1880

Penury Hall
Main St Box 68
Southwest Harbor ME 04679

The Island House
Box 1006
Southwest Harbor ME 04679

Rosehip
Box 346
Stonington ME 04681

Widow's Walk
Box 150
Stratton ME 04982
Circa: 1897

Goose Cove Lodge
Deer Isle.
Sunset ME 04683

Surry Inn
Surry ME 04684

Time & Tide
Box 90 RFD 1
Surry ME 04684

East Wind Inn & Meeting House
PO Box 149
Tenants Harbor ME 04680
Circa: 1860

Crab Apple Acres
Rte. 201
The Forks ME 04985
Circa: 1835

Gracie's Bed & Breakfast
52 Main St.
Thomaston ME 04861

The Belvedere
163 Main St.
Thomaston ME 04861

The Walker Wilson House
2 Melcher Place
Topsham ME 04086

Shepard Hill B&B
PO Box 338
Union ME 04862

Fox Island Inn
Carver St.
Vinalhaven ME 04863

James & Lobby Hopkins
Main St.
Waldoboro ME 04572

The Roaring Lion
Box 756
Waldoboro ME 04572

The Bittersweet Inn
Box 013
Walpole ME 04573

Windward Farm
Young's Hill Rd.
Washington ME 04574

Artemus Ward House
Waterford ME 04088
Circa: 1805

Kedarburn Inn
Rte. 35 Box A-1
Waterford ME 04088

Lake House
Rtes 35 & 37

Waterford ME 04088

Kawanhee Inn
Lake Webb
Weld ME 04285

Weld Inn
Box 8
Weld ME 04285
Circa: 1893

Bayview Inn B&B
RR1-2131
Wells ME 04090

Grey Gull Inn
321 Webhannet Dr.
Wells ME 04090
Circa: 1893

The Haven
Church St.
Wells Beach ME 04090
(207) 646-4194

King's Inn
PO Box 92
West Bethel ME 04286

Harbor Hill Inn
Box 280
Winter Harbor ME 04693

Squire Tarbox
Rd 2 Box 2160
Wiscasset ME 04578
Circa: 1765

The Stacked Arms
RR 2 PO Box 146
Wiscasset ME 04578
(207) 882-5436

A Summer Place
D 1 Box 196
York ME 03909

Dickside Guest Qtrs.
PO Box 205
York ME 03909
Circa: 1880

Scotland Bridge Inn
PO Box 521
York ME 03909

The Wild Rose Of York
78 Long Sands Rd
York ME 03909

Lilac Inn
Box 1325 3 Ridge Rd.
York Beach ME 03910

The Benetts
3 Broadway
York Beach ME 03910

The Inn At Harmon Park
York St
York Harbor ME 03911

Maryland

Gibson's Lodging
110-114 Prince George
Annapolis MD 21401

Maryland Inn
16 Church Circle
Annapolis MD 21401
(301) 263-2641

Reynolds Tavern
4 Church Circle
Annapolis MD 21401
(301) 263-2641

Robert Johnson House
23 State Circle
Annapolis MD 21401
(301) 263-2641

State House Inn
15 State Circle
Annapolis MD 21401
(301) 263-2641

Eagles Mere B&B
102 E. Montgomery
Baltimore MD 21230

Society Hill Hotel
58 W. Biddle St.
Baltimore MD 21201
Circa: 1890

Winslow Home
8217 Caraway St.
Bethesda MD 20818

Ye Lantern Inn
PO Box 310
Betterton MD 21610
(301) 348-5809

Inn At Buckeystown
3521 Buckeystown Pike

Buckeystown MD 21717
Circa: 1890

Sarke Plantation
Rt. 3 Box 139
Cambridge MD 21613

Greak Own Manor
Rt. 2 Box 766
Chestertown MD 21620

Sophie Kerr House
Rt. 3 Box 7-b
Denton MD 21629

Spring Bank Farm Inn
7945 Worman's Mill
Frederick MD 21701
Circa: 1881

Tran Crossing
121 E. Patrick St.
Frederick MD 21701

Foutaindale Inn
4253 Old National Pike
Middletown MD 21769

1876 House
110 N. Morris St.
Oxford MD 21654

Washington Hotel & Inn
Somerset Ave.
Princess Anne MD 21853
Circa: 1744

Inn At Antietam
PO Box 119
Sharpsburg MD 21782

Capt. & Ms. J's Guest House
Calvert & A St.
Solomons MD 20688

Locust Inn
Box 254
Solomons MD 20688
Circa: 1860

Kemp House Inn
412 S. Talbot St.
St. Michaels MD 21663

The Inn At Perry Cabin
St. Michaels MD 21663
Circa: 1810

Glenburn
3515 Runnymede Rd.
Taneytown MD 21787

Governor's Ordinary
Church & Water Box 156
Vienna MD 21869

Nanticoke Manor House
Church St. & Water Box 248
Vienna MD 21869
Circa: 1700

Judge Thomas House
195 Willis St
Westminster MD 21157
(301) 876 6686

Rosebud Inn
4 N. Main St.
Woodsboro MD 21798
Circa: 1920

Massachusetts

The Amity House
194 Amity St.
Amherst MA 01002
(413) 549-6446

Gold Leaf Inn
Box 477
Ashfield MA 01330
(413) 628-3392

Captain Samuel Eddy
House
609 Oxford St
Auburn MA 01501
(617) 832-5282

B&B On Beautiful Cape
Cod
110 Salt Rock Rd
Barnstable MA 02630
(617) 362-6556

Captain Isaiah's House
33 Pleasant St.
Bass River MA 02664

Old Cape Inn
108 Old Main St.
Bass River MA 02664
Circa: 1815

The Anchorage
122 South Shore Dr.
Bass River MA 02664
(617) 398-8265

Stonehedge
119 Sawyer hill Rd
Berlin MA 01503
Circa: 1735
617 838 2574

The White House
P.o. Box 447
Block Island MA 02807
(401) 466-2653

Bed & Breakfast
133 Paul Gore St.
Boston MA 02118
(617) 522-5366

Boston Terrace
Townhouse
60 Chandler St.
Boston MA 02116
Circa: 1870

Victorian B&B
35 Greenwich Park
Boston MA 02118
(617) 247-1599

Bramble Inn
Rt. 6a 2019 Main St
Brewster MA 02631
Circa: 1861

Inn Of The Golden Ox
1360 Main St
Brewster MA 02631
Circa: 1836
617 896 3111

Old Manse Inn
1861 Main St.
Brewster MA 02631

Beacon Plaza
1459 Beacon St
Brookline MA 02146
(617) 232-6550

Beacon Street Guest
House
1047 Beacon St.
Brookline MA 02146

A Cambridge House
P.o. Box 211

Cambridge MA 02140
(617) 491-6300

Harvard Square B&B
Of Cambridge
Box 211
Cambridge MA 02140
(617) 491-6300

The Copper Beach Inn
497 Main St.
Centerville MA 02632
(617) 771-5488

The Old Hundred House
1211 Craigville Beach Rd
Centerville MA 02632
(617) 775-6166

Forest Way Farm
Rt 8a (heath)
Charlemont MA 01339
(413) 337-8321

Bow Roof House
59 Queen Anne Rd
Chatham MA 02633
(617) 945-1346

Cyrus Kent House
63 Cross St.
Chatham MA 02633

Queen Anne Inn
70 Queen Anne Rd
Chatham MA 02633
Circa: 1840
617 945 0394

Town House Inn &
Lodge
11 Library Ln.
Chatham MA 02633
Circa: 1881

The Pleasant Pheasant
296 Heath St.,
Chestnut Hill MA 02167
(617) 566-4178

Grandmother's House
Rt 1 Box 37 Rte 112n
Colrain MA 01340
(413) 624-3771

Colonial Inn
48 Monument Square
Concord MA 01742
Circa: 1716

617 369 9200

Allen's B&B
60 Nickerson Ln Box 222
Cotuit MA 02635
(617) 428-5702

Windfields Farm
Rt 1 Box 170 Bush Rd
Cummington MA 01026
(413) 684-3786

Dalton House
955 Main St.
Dalton MA 01226
(413) 684-3854

Salem Village B&B
34 Centre St
Danvers MA 01923
(617) 774-7851

Deerfield Inn
The Street
Deerfield MA 01342
Circa: 1884

Winsor House Inn
PO Box 287 Shs 390
Washington St.
Duxbury MA 02331

Nauset House Inn
143 Beach Rd PO 774
East Orleans MA 02643
Circa: 1810
617 255 2195

Whalewalk Inn
169 Bridge Rd.
Eastham MA 02642
Circa: 1830

Ashley Inn
129 Main St.
Edgartown MA 02539

Chadwick House
67 Winter St
Edgartown MA 02539
(617) 627-4435

Daggat House
PO 1333 59 N. Water St.
Edgartown MA 02539

Edgartown Heritage
Hotel
227 Upper Main St

Edgartown MA 02539
(617) 627-5161

Governor Bradford Inn
128 Main St
Edgartown MA 02539
(617) 627-9510

Kelly House
PO Box 1637
Edgartown MA 02539
Circa: 1742
617 627 4394

Point Way Inn
PO Box 128
Edgartown MA 02539
Circa: 1832
617 627 8633

Elm Arch Inn
Elm Arch Way
Falmouth MA 02540

Grafton Inn
261 Grand Ave. S.
Falmouth MA 02540

The Inn At One Main St
One Main St
Falmouth MA 02540
(617) 540-7469

The Moorings Lodge
207 Grand Ave
Falmouth MA 02540
(617) 540-2370

Blue Shutters Inn
1 Nautilus Rd
Gloucester MA 01930
Circa: 1900
617 281 2706

Gray Manor
14 Atlantic Rd
Gloucester MA 01930
Circa: 1925
617 283 5409

Williams Guest House
136 Bass Ave.
Gloucester MA 01930

Thornewood
Rt. 7 & Rt. 183
Great Barrington MA 01230

Turning Point Inn
RD2 Box 140 3 Lake Buel Rd.
Great Barrington MA 01230

Windflower Inn
Egremont Star Rt, PO 25 Rt 23
Great Barrington MA 01230
Circa: 1860
413 528 2720

Victorian Inn At Harwich
Box 340 102 Parallel St
Harwich Center MA 02645
(617) 432-8335

Country Inn
86 Sisson Rd
Harwichport MA 02646
617 432 2769

Dunscroft Inn
24 Pilgrim Rd, Cape Cod
Harwich Port MA 02646

Harbor Breeze
326 Lower County Rd
Harwich Port MA 02646
(617) 432-0337

The Inn On Bank St.
88 Bank Street
Harwich Port MA 02646
(617) 432-3206

Yankee Pedler Inn
1866 Northampton St.
Holyoke MA 01040

The Laurels
18 Ash Street
Hopkinton MA 01748
(617) 435-5410

Park Square Village
156 Main ST.
Hyannis MA 02601

Sea Breeze By The Beach
397 Sea St. Cape Cod
Hyannis MA 02601

The Acorn House
240 Sea Street
Hyannis MA 02601
(617) 771-4071

1777 Greylock House
58 Greylock St.
Lee MA 01238

Haus Andreas
Rr 1 Box 605 B
Lee MA 01238
Circa: 1928

Morgan House
33 Main St
Lee MA 01238
413 243 0181

The Donahoes
Fairview St Box 231
Lee MA 01238
(413) 243-1496

Birchwood Inn
7 Hubbard St Box 131
Lenox MA 01240
(413) 637-2600

Cliffwood Inn
25 Cliffwood Street
Lenox MA 01240
Circa: 1890
(617) 637-3330

Cornell House
197 Pittsfield Rd.
Lenox MA 01240
Circa: 1890

Garden Gables Inn
141 Main St
Lenox MA 01240
Circa: 1890
413 637 0193

The Quincy Lodge
19 Stockbridge Rd
Lenox MA 01240
(413) 637-9750

Village Inn
16 Church St
Lenox MA 01240
(413) 637 0020

Walker House
74 Walker St.
Lenox MA 01240
Circa: 1804

Wheatleigh
PO Box 824
Lenox MA 01240

413 637 0610

Old Corner Inn
2 Harbor St
Manchester MA 01944
Circa: 1865
617 526 4996

Tidecrest
Spray Ave
Marblehead MA 01945
Circa: 1830
(617) 631-4515

Bay Breeze
PO 307
Monument Beach MA 02553

1739 House
43 Centre St
Nantucket MA 02554
(617) 228-0120

76 Main Street
76 Main St. Box E
Nantucket MA 02554
Circa: 1883

Anchor Inn
66 Centre St
Nantucket MA 02554
(617) 228-0072

B&B
One Cottage Court
Nantucket MA 02554
Circa: 1830
(617) 228-2486

Carlisle House
26 N. Water St.
Nantucket MA 02554

Carriage House
4 Ray's Ct
Nantucket MA 02554
Circa: 1865
617 228 0326

Century House
10 Cliff Rd. Box 603
Nantucket MA 02554

Cliff House
34 Cliff Rd
Nantucket MA 02554
(617) 228-2154

Corner House
49 Centre St.
Nantucket MA 02554

Eighteen Gardner Street
18 Gardner St.
Nantucket MA 02554
Circa: 1835

Fair Winds
4 Ash St
Nantucket MA 02554
Circa: 1885
(617) 228-4899

Four Ash Street
4 Ash Street
Nantucket MA 02554
Circa: 1795

Four Seasons Guest
House
2 Chestnut St
Nantucket MA 02554
Circa: 1850
617 228 0326

Halliday's Nantucket
House
2 East York St Box 165
Nantucket MA 02554
Circa: 1820
(617) 228-9450

Hawthorne House
2 Chestnut St
Nantucket MA 02554
Circa: 1849
(617) 228-1468

Hussey House
15 N Water St
Nantucket MA 02554
Circa: 1795
(617) 228-0747

India House
37 India St
Nantucket MA 02554
Circa: 1803
617 228 9043

Ivy Lodge
2 Chester St
Nantucket MA 02554
Circa: 1790
(617) 228-0305

Jared Coffin House
29 Broad St.
Nantucket MA 02554

Martin's Guest House
61 Centre St PO 743
Nantucket MA 02554
Circa: 1803
617 228 0678

Paul West House
5 Liberty St
Nantucket MA 02554
Circa: 1748
(617) 228-2495

Periwinkle Guest House
9 N. Water St.
Nantucket MA 02554
Circa: 1846

Phillips House
54 Fair St
Nantucket MA 02554
Circa: 1786
(617) 228-9217

Quaker House
5 Chestnut St.
Nantucket MA 02554

Roberts House
11 India St
Nantucket MA 02554
Circa: 1846
617 228 9009

Ruben Joy Homestead
107 Main St
Nantucket MA 02554
Circa: 1720
(617) 228-1703

Ships Inn
13 Fair St.
Nantucket MA 02554
Circa: 1812

Stumble Inne
109 Orange St
Nantucket MA 02554
Circa: 1704
(617) 228-4482

Ten Hussey
Ten Hussey St
Nantucket MA 02554
Circa: 1786
(617) 228-9552

The House At Ten Gay
Street
10 Gay St
Nantucket MA 02554
Circa: 1830
(617) 228-4425

The Hungry Whale
8 Derrymore Rd
Nantucket MA 02554
Circa: 1900
(617) 228-0793

West Moor Inn
Off Cliff Road
Nantucket MA 02554

Langhaar House
Sr 70 Box 123a
New Marlborough MA 01230

Old Inn On The Green
Star Rt. 70
New Marlborough MA 01230

Benjamin Choate House
25 Tyng St.
Newburyport MA 01950
Circa: 1794

Essex Street Inn
7 Essex St
Newburyport MA 01950
617 465 3145

Garrison Inn
On Brown Square
Newburyport MA 01950
Circa: 1809
617 465 0910

Morrill Place Inn
209 High St.
Newburyport MA 01950

Windsor House
38 Federal St.
Newburyport MA 01950

The Penny House
Rt 6 Box 238
North Falmouth MA 02651
(617) 255-6632

Centennial House
94 Main St
Northfield MA 01360
(413) 498-5921

Northfield Country
House
School St. Rr .1 Pob 79a
Northfield MA 01360
Circa: 1901

The Knoll
230 North Main
Northhampton MA 01060
(413) 584-8164

Attleboro House
11 Lake Ave Box 1564
Oak Bluffs MA 02557
(617) 693-4346

South Wind
Circuit & Pequot Ave
Oak Bluffs MA 02557
(617) 693-5031

East Bay Lodge
East Bay Rd PO Box N
Osterville MA 02655
Circa: 1800
617 428 6961

Greer B&B
193 Wendell Ave
Pittsfield MA 01201
(413) 443-3669

Another Place Inn
240 Sandwich St
Plymouth MA 02360
(617) 746-0126

Colonial House Inn
207 Sandwich St.
Plymouth MA 02360
Circa: 1855

Country Inn At Princeton
30 Mountain Rd.
Princeton MA 01540
Circa: 1890

Hill House
PO Box 276, 105 Merriam Rd.
Princeton MA 01541
(617) 464-2061

1807 House
54 Commercial St
Provincetown MA 02657

Asheton House
3 Cook St
Provincetown MA 02657

Circa: 1806
617 487 9966

Bradford Gardens Inn
178 Bradford St.
Provincetown MA 02657
Circa: 1820

Captain Lysander Inn
96 Commercial St
Provincetown MA 02657
Circa: 1850
617 487 2253

Elephant Walk Inn
156 Bradford St.
Provincetown MA 02657

Hargood House
493 Commercial St
Provincetown MA 02657
Circa: 1820
617 487 1324

Ocean's Inn
386 Commercial St
Provincetown MA 02657
617 437 0358

Rose And Crown
158 Commercial St.
Provincetown MA 02657
Circa 1780

White Wind Inn
174 Commercial St
Provincetown MA 02657
Circa: 1840
617 487 1526

Windamar House
568 Commercial St
Provincetown MA 02657
Circa: 1840
617 487 0599

Gilbert's B&B
30 Spring St.
Rehoboth MA 02769
(617) 252-6416

Perryville Inn
157 Perryville Rd.
Rehoboth MA 02769

Cogswell Guest House
Rt 41
Richmond MA 01254
413 698 2750

Pierson Place
Rt 41
Richmond MA 01254
617 698 2750

Westgate
Rt 295
Richmond MA 01254
(413) 698-2657

Addison Choate Inn
49 Broadway
Rockport MA 01966
Circa: 1851

Cable House
Norwood Ave
Rockport MA 01966
Circa: 1882
617 546 6383

Eden Pines Inn
Eden Rd
Rockport MA 01966
617 546 2505

Gibney Guest House
74 Main St
Rockport MA 01966
Circa: 1886

Rocky Shore Inn
Eden Rd.
Rockport MA 01966

Seacrest Manor
131 Marmion Way
Rockport MA 01966
617 546 2211

Seaward Inn
62 Marmion Way
Rockport MA 01966
Circa: 1912
617 546 3471

Tuck Inn
17 High St
Rockport MA 01966
Circa: 1785
617 546 6252

Yankee Clipper Inn
Pob 2399 99 Granite St.
Rockport MA 01966
Circa: 1840

Amelia Payson Guest House
16 Winter St
Salem MA 01970
(617) 744-8304

Stephen Daniels House
1 Daniels St.
Salem MA 01970
Circa: 1667

Suzannah Flint House
98 Essex St
Salem MA 01970
617 744 5281

Quince Tree
164 Main St.
Sandwich MA 02563

Centuryhurst Guest House
Box 486 Main St
Sheffield MA 01257
(413) 229-8131

Ivanhoe Country House
Rt 41 Undermountain Rd
Sheffield MA 01257
413 229 2143

Stagecoach Hill Inn
Rt 41
Sheffield MA 01257
413 229 8585

Staveleigh House
Pob 608
Shefield MA 01257

Parson Hubbard House
Old Village Rd
Shelburne Falls MA 01370
(413) 625-9730

1780 Egremont Inn
Old Sheffield Rd.
South Egremont MA 01258
Circa: 1780

Weathervane Inn
PO 388
South Egremont MA 01258
413 528 9580

Federal House Inn
Rt 102 Main St
South Lee MA 01260
413 243 1824

Historic Merrell Tavern Inn
Rte. 102 Main St.
South Lee MA 01260

River Street Guest House
9 River St
South Yarmouth MA 02664
(617) 398-8946

Sterling Inn
Rt. 12 Pob 609
Sterline MA 01564

Inn At Stockbridge
Rt 7 PO Box 2033
Stockbridge MA 01262
413 298 3337

Chamberlain House
PO Box 187
Sturbridge MA 01566
617 347 3313

Colonel Ebenezer Craft's
Pob 187
Sturbridge MA 01566
Circa: 1786

Sudbury B&B
3 Drum Ln
Sudbury MA 01776
(617) 443-2860

Wood Farm
40 Worcester Rd.
Townsend MA 01469

Capron House
2 Capron St
Uxbridge MA 01569
(617) 278-2214

Bayberry
Rfd 1 Box 546 old Courthouse Rd.
Vineyard Haven MA 02568

Captain Dexter House
100 Main St. box 2457
Vineyard Haven MA 02568
Circa: 1843

Geyer's Heritage House
16 Greenwood Ave Box 2475
Vineyard Haven MA 02568
(617) 693-5977

Lothrop Merry House
Owen Park Box 1939
Vineyard Haven MA 02568

Tuckerman House
45 William St Box 194
Vineyard Haven MA 02568
(617) 693-0417

Wildwood Inn
121 Church St.
Ware MA 01082

Holden Inn
Commercial St, PO 816
Wellfleet MA 02667
Circa: 1840
617 349 3450

Inn At Duck Creeke
Pob 364
Wellfleet MA 02667

The Old Rose Cottage
24 Worcester St
West Boylston MA 01583
(617) 835-4034

Brookfield House Inn
Route 9
West Brookfield MA 01585
Circa: 1863

Beach Side Lodge, The Edwards
140 Lower County Rd.
West Dennis MA 02670

The Beach House
61 Uncle Stephen's Rd.
West Dennis, Cape Cod MA 02670

Elms
Pob 895
West Falmouth MA 02574

Sjoholm Bed And Breakfast Inn
17 Chase Rd Box 430
West Falmouth MA 02574
617 540 5706

Barnaby Inn
PO Box 151
West Harwich MA 02671
617 432 6789

Lion Head Inn
186 Belmont Rd PO 444
West Harwich MA 02671
Circa: 1804
617 432 7766

Sunny Pines
77 Main Street
West Harwich MA 02671
(617) 432-9628

Westbridge Inn
Main St PO Box 378
West Stockbride MA 01266
413 232 7120

Old Parsonage B&B
Box 137 State Rd
West Tisbury MA 02575
(617) 693-4289

Manor House
57 Maine Ave.
West Yarmouth MA 02673
Circa: 1920

Heywood House
207 W Main St
Westborough MA 01581
(617) 366-2161

Outlook Farm
Rt 66
Westhampton MA 01027
(413) 527-0633

The Victorian
583 Linwood Ave
Whitinsville MA 01588
617 234 2500

Twin Maples B&B
106 South St
Williamsburg MA 01096
(413) 268-7925

Marlborough
320 Woods Hole
Woods Hole MA 02543

Worthington Inn At Four Corners Farm
Rt 143
Worthington MA 01098
(413) 238-4441

Old Yarmouth Inn
223 Main ST
Yarmouth Port MA 02675

Circa: 1698
617 362 3191

One Centre Street Inn
1 Centre St. Yarmouth Port
Yarmouth Port MA 02675

Village Inn
92 Main, Rt 6a, PO 1
Yarmouth Port MA 02675
Circa: 1795
617 362 3182

Michigan

D's Bed & Breakfast
110 Park
Albion MI 49224
(517) 629-2976

Torch Lake B&B
Box 165
Alden MI 49612
(616) 331-6424

Terrace Inn
216 Fairview Ave.
Bay View MI 49770

Windermere Inn
747 Crystal Dr
Beulah MI 49617
(616) 882-7264

Bridge Street Inn
113 Michigan Ave
Charlevoix MI 49720
(616) 547-6606

Channelview Inn
217 Park Ave
Charlevoix MI 49720
(616) 547-6180

Redwing
3176 Shady Oak Dr
Columbiaville MI 48421
(313) 793-4301

Miller School Inn
2959 Roosevelt Rd
Conklin MI 49403
(616) 677-1026

Oakbrook Inn
7256 E Court St
Davison MI 48423
(313) 653-1744

The House On The Hill
Lake St Box 206
Ellsworth MI 49729
(616) 588-6304

Avon House
518 Avon St.
Flint MI 48503

Winter Inn
100 N Lafayette
Greenville MI 48838
(616) 754-7108

Hansen's Guest House
102 W Adams
Homer MI 49245
(517) 568-3001

Chaffin Farms B&B
3239 W St Charles Rd
Ithaca MI 48847
(617) 463-4081

Stuart Avenue B&B
405 Stuart Ave.
Kalamazoo MI 49007

Pebble House
15197
Lakeside MI 49116

The Stagecoach Stop
0-4819 Leonard Rd W Box 18
Lamont MI 49430
(616) 677-3940

Governor's Inn
7277 Simons St
Lexington MI 48450
Circa: 1859
(313) 359-5770

Vicki Van's B&B
5076 S Lakeshore Rd
Lexington MI 48450
(313) 369-5533

Bogan Lake Inn
Box 482
Mackinac Island MI 49757
(906) 847-3439

Haan Cottage B&B
Box 1268
Mackinac Island MI 49757

Iroquois Hotel-On-the-
Beach
Mackinac Island MI 49757
906 847 3321

Metivier Inn
Box 285
Mackinac Island MI 49757
(906) 847-6234

Thuya B&B Cottage
Box 459
Mackinac Island MI 49757
(906) 847-3400

E E Douville House
111 Fine St
Manistee MI 49660
(616) 723-8654

Leelanau Country Inn
149 E Harbor Hwy
Maple City MI 49664
(616) 228-5060

National House Inn
102 S Parkview
Marshal MI 49068
Circa: 1835

Helmer House Inn
Rt. 3 Country Rd. 417
Mcmillan MI 49853

Blue Lake Lodge
9765 Blue Lake Lodge Ln Box
1
Mecosta MI 48823
(616) 972-8391

The Mendon Country
Inn
440 W Main St
Mendon MI 49072
(616) 496-8132

Morning Glory Inn
8709 Old Channel Trail
Montague MI 49437
(616) 894-8237

Little Bohemia
115 S Whittaker
New Buffalo MI 49117
(616) 469-1440

Old Mill Pond Inn
202 W Third St
Northport MI 49670

(616) 386-7341

Plum Lane Inn
Box 74
Northport MI 49670
(616) 386-5774

Wood How Lodge
Rt.1 Box 44
Northport MI 49670

Stonegate Inn
10831 Cleveland
Nunica MI 49448
(616) 837-9267

Merkel Manor
623 N Park St
Owosso MI 48867
(517) 725-5600

Mulberry House
1251 N Shiawassee St
Owosso MI 48867
(517) 723-4890

R & R Farm-ranch
308 E Hibbard Rd
Owosso MI 48867
(517) 723-2553

The J B Cain's
4650 Waugh Rd
Owosso MI 48867
(517) 723-4708

Bear & The Bay
421 Charlevoix Ave
Petoskey MI 49770
(616) 347-6077

Gull's Way
118 Boulder Lane
Petoskey MI 49770
(616) 347-9891

Stafford's Bay View Inn
Box 3
Petoskey MI 49770
Circa: 1886

Garfield Inn
8544 Lake St
Port Austin MI 48467
(517) 738-5254

Victorian Inn
1229 Seventh St.
Port Huron MI 48060

Raymond House Inn
M-25 111 S. Ridge St.
Port Sanilac MI 48469

Weber House
527 James
Portland MI 48875
(517) 647-4671

Osceola Inn
110 E Upton
Reed City MI 49677
Circa: 1892
(616) 832-5537

Montague Inn
1581 S Washington Ave
Saginaw MI 48601
(517) 752-3939

Colonial House Inn
90 N. State St.
Saint Ignace MI 49781

Jann's Guest House
132 Mason St
Saugatuck MI 49453
(616) 857-8851

Kemah Guest House
633 Pleasant St.
Saugatuck MI 49453

Wickwood
510 Butler St.
Saugatuck MI 49453

Last Resort
86 North Shore Dr.
South Haven MI 49090

The Ross
229 Michigan Ave
South Haven MI 49090
(616) 637-2256

Victoria Resort
241 Oak
South Haven MI 49090

Clifford Lake Hotel
561 Clifford Lake Dr.
Stanton MI 48888

Pink Palace Farms
6095 Baldwin Rd
Swartz Creek MI 48473
(313) 655-4076

Neahtawanta Inn
1308 Neahtawanta Rd
Traverse City MI 49684
(616) 223-7315

Cedar Creek
12666 W Bayshore Dr
Traverse City MI 49684
(616) 947-5643

Victorian Villa Gues-
thouse
601 N. Broadway
Union City MI 49094
Circa: 1876

Gordon Beach Inn
16240 Lakeshore Rd.
Union Pier MI 49129

Minnesota

Grand View Lodge
Rt. 6 Box 22
Brainerd MN 56401

The Mansion
3600 London Rd.
Duluth MN 55804

Kuchenbecker Farm
Rrf 1 PObox 107
Elmare MN 56027

Cascade Lodge
PO Box 693
Grand Marais MN 55604
Circa: 1930
218 387 1112

East Bay Hotel
Grand Marais MN 55604
Circa: 1909
218 387 2800

Gunflint Lodge
Pob 100 Gt-bb
Grand Marais MN 55604

Young's Island
Gunflint Tr. 67-1
Grand Marais MN 55604

Thorwood
4th & Pine
Hastings MN 55033

The Rahilly House
304 S. Oak St.
Lake City MN 55041

Pine Edge Inn
308 First St. Se
Little Falls MN 56345
Circa: 1823

Evelo's Bed & Breakfast
2301 Bryant Ave. S.
Minneapolis MN 55405
Circa: 1897

Schumacher's New
Prague
212 W Main St
New Prague MN 65071
Circa: 1898
612 758 2133

Archer House
212 Division St.
Northfield MN 55057

Lowell House B&B
531 Wood St.
Old Frontenac MN 55026
Circa: 1856

Sheep Shedde Inn
Hwy 212 & 71 W
Olivia MN 56277
Circa: 1938

The Calumet
PO Box 111
Pipestone MN 56164
Circa: 1883
507 825-5658

Canterbury Inn B&B
723 2nd St. Sw
Rochester MN 55902

Palmer House Hotel
500 Sinclair Lewis Ave.
Sauk Centre MN 56378
Circa: 1901

Country Bed & Breakfast
32030 Ranch Tr.
Shafer MN 55074

Lowell Inn
102 N. Second St.
Stillwater MN 55082
Circa: 1930

Historic Taylor Falls Jail
102 Government Rd.
Taylors Falls MN 55084

Anderson House
333 Main St, PO Box 262
Wabasha MN 55981
Circa: 1856
(612) 565-4524

The Hotel
129 W. Third St.
Winona MN 55987
Circa: 1892
(507) 452-5460

Mississippi

Edgewood
412 Storm A Ve.
Brookhaven MS 39601
Circa: 1890
(601) 833-2001

Mount Holly
Box 140
Chatam MS 38731

Liberty Hall
Rt 4, Armstrong Rd.
Columbus MS 39701

Rosewood Manor
719 7 St.
Columbus MS 39701

Temple Heights
515 9 St. N.
Columbus MS 39701

Fairview
734 Fairview St.
Jackson MS 39202

Dixie
211 S Wall St.
Natchez MS 39120
Circa: 1795
(601) 442-2525

Dunleith
84 Homochitto
Natchez MS 39120

Guest House Of Natchez
210 N. Pearl St.
Natchez MS 39120
Circa: 1840

(601)445-6000

Hope Farm
147 Homochitto St.
Natchez MS 39120

Linden
1 Linden Place
Natchez MS 39120
Circa: 1800

Ravennaside
601 S. Union St.
Natchez MS 39120
Circa: 1870

Silver Street Inn
1 Silver St.
Natchez MS 39120
Circa: 1840

Texada
212 S. Wall St.
Natchez MS 39120
Circa: 1792
(601) 445-4283

The Burn
712 N. Union St.
Natchez MS 39120
Circa: 1832

Oliver-britt House
512 Van Buren Av.
Oxford MS 38655

Balfour House
1002 Crawford St.
Vicksburg MS 39180

Duff Green Mansion
1114 First East St.
Vicksburg MS 39180

Gray Oaks
4142 Rifle Range Rd.
Vicksburg MS 39180

Manor House
2011 Cherry St.
Vicksburg MS 39180
Circa: 1906
(601) 638-0683

Old Feld Home
2108 Cherry St.
Vicksburg MS 39180

Missouri

Borgman's B&B
Arrow Rock MO 65320

Gallatin B&B Inn
200 E. Grand
Gallatin MO 64640

Fifth Street B&B
213 S. Fifth St.
Hannibal MO 63401

Victorian Guest House
#3 Stillwell
Hannibal MO 63401

Der Klingerbau Inn
108 E. 2d. St.
Herman MO 65041
Circa: 1878

Marshwood
PO 10352
Kansas City MO 64111

Mcnally House B&B
1105 S. 15
St. Joseph MO 64503

La Fayette House
1825 Lafayette Ave.
St. Louis MO 63204

Schwegmann House
438 West Front
Washington MO 63090

Montana

Lazy K Bar Ranch
Box 550
Big Sky MT 59011

Lehrkind Mansion
719 N. Wallace
Bozeman MT 59715

Silver Forest Inn
15325 Bridger Canyon Rd.
Bozeman MT 59715

Copper King Mansion
219 West Granite
Butte MT 59701
(406) 782-7580

Izaak Walton Inn
PO Box 653
Essex MT 59916
Circa: 1939
Ask (406) Operator For Essex
Phone No. 1

The Corner House
345 4 Ave. E.
Kalispell MT 59901

Nevada City Hotel
Nevada City MT 59755

Pitcher Guest House
2 So. Platt Pob 1148
Red Lodge MT 59068

Foxwood Inn
Box 404
White Sulphur Springs MT
59645

Nebraska

Bel-Horst Inn
Belgrade NE 68623
Circa: 1907

Fort Robinson Inn
Box 392
Crawford NE 69339
Circa: 1909

Offutt House
140 N 39th St.
Omaha NE 68131
(402) 553-0951

Nevada

Elliot-Chartz House
412 N. Nevada St.
Carson City NV 89701

Orchard House
Box 77
Genoa NV 89411

Gold Hill Hotel
Box 304
Gold Hill NV 89440

Old Pioneer Garden
Star Rt. Unionvile #79
Imlay NV 89418

Wingfield House
219 Court St.
Reno NV 89501

Hardwicke House
Box 96
Silver City NV 89429

Edith Palmer's Country Inn
Box 756 south B Street
Virginia City NV 89440

Stauffer House
82 Lay St.
Winnemucca NV 89445

Robric Ranch
Box 2
Yerington NV 89447

New Hampshire

Oak Birch Inn
Rt 28a (23)
Alton Bay NH 03810

Breezy Point Inn
Rfd-1 Box 302
Antrim NH 03440

Maplehurst Inn
Route 202
Antrim NH 03440

Steele Homestead Inn
Rr1 Box 78 Rt. 9
Antrim NH 03440
Circa: 1810

Uplands Inn
Miltimore Rd.
Antrim NH 03440
Circa: 1840

Cheney House
PO Box 683
Ashland NH 03217
Circa: 1895

Country Options-c. Willey House
PO 443
Ashland NH 03217

David's Inn
Bennington Sq.

Bennington NH 03442
Circa: 1788

Shepherd's Inn
PO 70
Bethlehem NH 03574
Circa: 1892

The Highlands Inn
PO 118 C
Bethlehem NH 03574

Victorian
16 Summer St
Bristol NH 03222
(603) 744-6157

Village Guest House
PO Box 222
Campton NH 03223
Circa: 1825
(603) 726-4449

Inn On Canaan Street
The Kremzners
Canaan NH 03741
(603) 523-7310

Dearborn Place
Box 997
Center Harbor NH 03226
(603) 253-6711

Hitching Post Inn
Old Rte. 16
Center Ossipee NH 03814
Circa: 1850
(603) 539-4482

Corner House Inn
Main St. PO 204
Center Sandwich NH 03227

Indian Shutters Inn
Rte. 12
Charlestown NH 03603
Circa: 1791
(603) 826-4445

Hitching Post B&B
Dover Rd. R.d. #2
Chichester NH 03263
Circa: 1786

Staffords-in-the-field
Chocorua NH 03817

The Farmhouse
PO 14 page Hill Rd.

Chocorua NH 03817

Wyman Farm
Rt 8 Box 437
Concord NH 03301
(603) 783-4467

Inn At Danbury
Rte. 104
Danbury NH 03230

Country House
2 Stagecoach Rd.
Durham NH 03824

Six Chimneys
Star Rt Box 114
East Hebron NH 03232
Circa: 1791

Delford Inn
Centre St.
East Sullivan NH 03445

Inn At Crystal Lake
Rt 163
Eaton Center NH 03832

Palmer House Inn
Rte 153
Eaton Center NH 03832
Circa: 1884

Rockhouse Mountain Farm
Eaton Center NH 03832
(603) 447-2880

Limner Haus
Box 126
Elkins NH 03233
Circa: 1786

Moose Mountain Lodge
Moose Mountain
Etna NH 03750

The "G" Clef
Ashbrook Rd.
Exeter NH 03833
(603) 772-8850

Amos Parker House
119 West
Fitzwilliam NH 03447

Barntique
Sugar Hill Rd

Fitzwilliam NH 03447

Fern Hill
PO Box 13
Fitzwilliam NH 03447
Circa: 1790
(603) 585-6672

Fitzwilliam Inn
Fitzwilliam NH 03447
Circa: 1796

Inn At Crotched Mountain
Mountain Rd.
Francestown NH 03043
(603) 588-6840

The Francestown B&B
Box 236
Francestown Village NH 03043

Franconia Inn
Easton Rd
Franconia NH 03580
(603) 823-5542

Hilltop Inn
Rte 117
Franconia NH 03580

Lovett's Inn
Rt 18 Profile Rd.
Franconia NH 03580
Circa: 1785
(603) 823-7761

Pinestead Farm Lodge
Rte. 116 Rfd 1
Franconia NH 03580
Circa: 1899

Sugar Hill Inn
Rte. 117
Franconia NH 03580
Circa: 1748

Webster Lake Inn
Webster Ave.
Franklin NH 03235
(603) 934-4050

Freedom House
PO Box 338, 1 Maple Street
Freedom NH 03836
(603) 539-4815

Cartway House Inn
Old Lake Shore Rd.

Gilford NH 03246
Circa: 1771
(603) 528-1172

Kings Grant Inn
RFD 5 PO Box 385
Gilford NH 03246
(603) 293-4431

The Historic Tavern Inn
Box 365
Gilmonton NH 03237
(603) 267-7349

Bernerhof Inn
Box 381 Rte. 302
Glen NH 03838
Circa: 1890

The Gables
139 Main St.
Gorham NH 03581
(603) 466-2875

The Gorham House Inn
55 Main St.
Gorham NH 03581
(603) 466-2271

Cutter's Loft
Rt 31
Goshen NH 03752
(603) 863-5306

Grafton Inn
Rt 4 Box 445
Grafton NH 03240

Blue Heron Inn
124 Landing Rd
Hampton NH 03842
(603) 926-9666

Boar's Head
12 Dumas
Hampton Beach NH 03842
(603) 926-3911

Century House
552 Ocean Blvd.
Hampton Beach NH 03842
Circa: 1803

The Grayhurst
11 F St.
Hampton Beach NH 03842
Circa: 1890

John Hancock Inn
Main St.
Hancock NH 03449
Circa: 1789
(603) 525-3318

Trumbull House
Box C29
Hanover NH 03755
(603) 643-1400

Haverhill Inn
Darmouth Col. Hwy.
Haverhill NH 03765
Circa: 1810

Colby Hill Inn
Box 778
Henniker NH 03242
Circa: 1800

Hanscom House B&B
Henniker NH 03242

Meeting House Inn
RFD #2 Flanders Rd.
Henniker NH 03242

Stonebridge Inn
Rt. 9 Box 82
Hillsborough NH 03244
Circa: 1830

Stonewall Farm
Rd2 Box 200
Hillsborough NH 03244
Circa: 1785

New England Inn
Rte. 16a
Intervale NH 03845
Circa: 1815
(603) 356-5541

The Forest A Country Inn
PO Box 37
Intervale NH 03845

Blake House
Pinkham Notch Rd., PO Box 246
Jackson NH 03846
(603) 383-9057

Christmas Farm Inn
Rt. 16 B PO 176
Jackson NH 03846
Circa: 1780

Inn At Thorn Hill
PO Box Ac
Jackson NH 03846
Circa: 1895
(603) 383-4242

Whitney's Village Inn
Rte. 16b, PO Box W
Jackson NH 03846
Circa: 1842
(603) 383-6886, (800) 272-2550

Wildcat Inn
Main St., PO Box T
Jackson NH 03846
(603) 383-4245

Nestlenook Inn
PO Q
Jackson Village NH 03846

Lilac Hill Farm
5 Ingalls Road
Jaffrey NH 03452
(603) 532-7278

Woodbound Inn
Woodbound Rd.
Jaffrey NH 03452
Circa: 1892
(603) 532-8341

Monadnock Inn
Main St. Box 103
Jaffrey Center NH 03454
Circa: 1840

Carriage Barn Guesthouse
358 Main St
Keene NH 03431

Hickory Stick Farm
RFD 2
Laconia NH 03246

Mackissock House
1047 Union Av.
Laconia NH 03246

Parade Rest Inn
Parade Rd
Laconia NH 03269
(603) 524-3152

Perry Point House
Lower Bay Rd
Laconia NH 03269
(603) 524-0087

Charpentier B&B
Box 562
Lincoln NH 03251
(603) 745-8517

1895 House
74 Pleasant St.
Littleton NH 03561
Circa: 1895

Edencroft Manor
Rte. 135
Littleton NH 03561
Circa: 1890
(603) 444-6776

Lyme Inn
Route 10
Lyme NH 03768
Circa: 1809

Marjorie's House
Rt 10
Lyme NH 03768

Thatcher Hill Inn
Thatcher Hill Rd
Marlborough NH 03455

Tolman Pond
PO RFD
Marlborough NH 03455

Ram In The Thicket
Off Rte. 101, Maple St.
Milford NH 03055

Victoria Place
88 Nashua St Rte 101-a
Milford NH 03055

Thirteen Colonies Farm
Rt 16
Milton NH 03887
(603) 652-4458

Olde Orchard Inn
Box 256
Moultonboro NH 03254
(603) 476-5004

Maple Hill Farm
Rr1 Box 1620
New London NH 03257
Circa: 1824

New London Inn
Box 8 Main St
New London NH 03257

Circa: 1792
(603) 526-2791

Pleasant Lake Inn
PO Box 1030, N Pleasant St
New London NH 03257
Circa: 1790
(603) 526-6271

Haley House Farm
Rt 1 N River
Newmarket NH 03857
(603) 679-8713

Cranmore Inn
PO Box 885
North Conway NH 03860
(603) 356-5502

Nereledge Inn & White
Horse Pub
River Rd Off Main St
North Conway NH 03860

Old Red Inn & Cottages
Rt. 16 Box 467
North Conway NH 03860
Circa: 1819

Stonehurst Manor
Rt 16
North Conway NH 03860

Wildflowers Guest House
Box 597
North Conway NH 03860

Cascade Lodge
222 Main St.
North Woodstock NH 03262
(603) 745-2722

Ledgeland
Box 278
North Woodstock NH 03260
(603) 745-3951

Woodstock Inn
Rte. 3, Box 118, Main St.
North Woodstock NH 03262
(603) 745-3951

Lake Shore Farm
Jeness Pond Rd.
Northwood NH 03261
Circa: 1848
(603) 942-5521

Meadow Farm B&B
Jeness Pond Road
Northwood NH 03261
Circa: 1770
(603) 942-8619

Acorn Lodge
PO Box 144, Duncan Lake
Ossipee NH 03864
(603) 539-2151

White Goose Inn
PO Box 17
Oxford NH 03777
(603) 353-4812

Salzburg Inn
Gov. Steele Estate
Peterborough NH 03458

Willows Inn
PO Box 527
Peterborough NH 03458
Circa: 1830

Northway House
RFD 1, U.s. Rte. 3 North
Plymouth NH 03264
(603) 536-2838

The Glynn House
1-93 On Rt 3
Plymouth NH 03264

Inn At Christian Shore
335 Maplewood, PO Box 1474
Portsmouth NH 03801
Circa: 1800
(603) 431-6770

Inn At Strawberry Banke
314 Court St.
Portsmouth NH 03801
(603) 436-7242

Martin Hill Inn
404 Islington St.
Portsmouth NH 03801
Circa: 1810
(603) 436-2287

Sheafe Street Inn
3 Sheafe St.
Portsmouth NH 03801
Circa: 1815
(603) 436-9104

Grassy Pond House
Rindge NH 03461

Tokfarm Inn
PO Box 229, Wood Ave.
Rindge NH 03461
Circa: 1880
(603) 899-6646

Rock Ledge Manor B&B
1413 Ocean
Rye NH 03870
Circa: 1880
(603) 431-1413

Wakefield Inn
Rt 1 Box 1014
Sanbornville NH 03872

Philbrook Farm Inn
North Rd.
Shelburne NH 03581
Circa: 1861
(603) 466-3831

Snowvillage Inn
Box 83, Foss Mt. Rd.
Snowville NH 03849
(603) 447-2818

Stoddard Inn
Rte. 123
Stoddard NH 03464
Circa: 1830
(603) 446-7873

Province Inn
PO Box 309, Bow Lake
Strafford NH 03884
(603) 664-2457

Ledgeland
Sugar Hill NH 03585
(603) 823-5341

The Homestead
Sugar Hill NH 03585
Circa: 1802
(603) 823-5564

Dexter's Inn
Stagecoach Rd., PO Box 5
Sunapee NH 03782
(603) 763-5571

Haus Edelweiss
Box 609
Sunapee NH 03782
(603) 763-2100

Inn At Sunapee
PO Box 336

Sunapee NH 03782
(603) 763-4444

Loma Lodge
RFD 1, PO Box 592, Rte. 103b
Sunapee NH 03782
(603) 763-4849

Old Governor's House
Lower Main & Myrtle
Sunapee NH 03782
(603) 763-9918

Seven Hearths Inn
Old Route 11
Sunapee NH 03782
(603) 763-5657

Times Ten Inn
Rte. 103B, PO Box 572
Sunapee NH 03782
Circa: 1820
(603) 763-5120

Village House At Sutton Mills
Box 151
Sutton Mills NH 03221
(603) 927-4765

Birchwood Inn
Rte. 45
Temple NH 03084
(603) 878-3285

Country Place
RFD 2, PO Box 342, Rte. 132n
Tilton NH 03276
(603) 286-8551

The Black Swan Inn
308 W Main St
Tilton NH 03276
(603) 286-4524

Tilton Manor
28 Chestnut St
Tilton NH 03276
(603) 268-3457

Charlie Napoli's Headmasters Inn
Troy NH 03465

Thimbleberry B&B
Parker Rd
Twin Mountain NH 03595
(603) 846-2211

The 1801 House
Box 35
Walpole NH 03608
Circa: 1801

Silver Squirrel Inn
PO Box 363, Show's Brook Rd.
Waterville Valley NH 03223
(603) 236-8325

Hobson House
Town Common
Wentworth NH 03282
(603) 764-9460

Wentworth Inn & Art Gallery
Ellsworth Hill Rd, Off Rte. 25
Wentworth NH 03282
(603) 764-9923

Maria Atwood Inn
RFD 2, Rte 3a
West Franklin NH 03235
(603) 934-3666

Crap Apple Inn
RFD 2, Box 200b, Rte.25
West Plymouth NH 03264
Circa: 1835

Kimball Hill Inn
Kimball Hill Rd., PO Box 03264
Whitefield NH 03598
(603) 837-2284

The 1875 Mountain Inn
The Dieterichs
Whitefield NH 03598
Circa: 1875
(603) 837-2220

Ram In The Thicket
Maple St.
Wilton NH 03086
(603) 654-6440

Lakeview Inn
Rt 109 N Main St
Wolfeboro NH 03894

New Jersey

Sands Of Avon
42 Sylvania Ave.
Avon-by-the-sea NJ 07717
Circa: 1890

(201) 776-8386

Bay Head Sands
2 Twilight Rd.
Bay Head NJ 08742
Circa: 1920
(201) 899-7016

Conover's Bay Head Inn
646 Main Ave.
Bay Head NJ 08742
Circa: 1912
(201) 892-4664

St. Rita Hotel
127 Engleside
Beach Haven NJ 08008
(609) 492-9192

Victorian Rose
719 Columbia Ave
Cape Island, Cape May NJ 08204
(609) 884 2497

Abigail Adams B&B
12 Jackson St.
Cape May NJ 08204
Circa: 1888
(609) 884-1371

Bell Shields House
501 Hughes St.
Cape May NJ 08204
(609) 884-8512

Brass Bed Inn
719 Columbia Ave.
Cape May NJ 08204
(609) 884-8075

Captain Mey's Inn
202 Ocean St.
Cape May NJ 08204
(609) 884-7793

Hanson House
111 Ocean St.
Cape May NJ 08204

Humphrey Hughes House
29 Ocean St.
Cape May NJ 08204
Circa: 1903
(609) 884-4428

Mooring
801 Stockton Ave.

Cape May NJ 08204
(609) 884-5425

Poor Richard's Inn
17 Jackson St.
Cape May NJ 08204
(609) 884-3536

Queen Victoria
102 Ocean St.
Cape May NJ 08204
(609) 884-8702

Windward House
24 Jackson St.
Cape May NJ 08204
(609) 884-3368

Publick House Inn
111 Main St
Chester NJ 07930
(201) 879-6878

The Belocchios
33 Hillside Ave.
Cresskill NJ 07626

Hunterdon House
12 Bridge St.
Frenchtown NJ 08825
(201) 996-3632

National Hotel
31 Race St.
Frenchtown NJ 08825
Circa: 1851
(201) 996-4871

Studio of John F. Peto
102 Cedar Ave.
Island Heights NJ 08732
Circa: 1889
(201) 270-6058

Coryell House
44 Coryell St.
Lambertville NJ 08530
(609) 397-2750

York Street House
42 York St.
Lambertville NJ 08530

Chesnut Hill
PO Box N, 63 Church St.
Milford NJ 08848
Circa: 1860
(201) 995-9761

Marboro Inn
334 Grove St.
Montclair NJ 07042
(201) 783-5300

Pine Tree Inn
10 Main Ave.
Ocean Grove NJ 07756
(201) 775-3264

Major Gandy's
180 Shore Rd.
Ocean View NJ 08230

Ashling Cottage
106 Sussex Ave.
Spring Lake NJ 07762
(201) 449-3553

Chateau
500 Warren Ave.
Spring Lake NJ 07762
(201) 974-2000

Johnson House
25 Tuttle Ave.
Spring Lake NJ 07762
(201) 449-1860

Kenilworth
1505 Ocean Ave.
Spring Lake NJ 07762
Circa: 1882
(201) 449-5327

Stone Post Inn
115 Washington Ave
Spring Lake NJ 07762
(201) 449-1212

Victoria House
214 Monmouth Ave.
Spring Lake NJ 07762
(201) 974-1882

Colligan's Stockton Inn
Rte. 29
Stockton NJ 08559
(609) 397-1250

Woolverton Inn
Rd 3, PO Box 233
Stockton NJ 08559
Circa: 1793
(609) 397-0802

New Mexico

Hacienda Rancho De
Chimayo
Box 11 State Road 520
Chimayo NM 87522
(505) 351-2222

La Posada De Chimayo
PO Box 463
Chimayo NM 87522
(505) 351-4605

The Lodge
PO Box 497
Cloudcroft NM 88317
(505) 682-2566

Galisteo Inn
Box 4
Galisteo NM 87540
(505) 982-1506

Llewellyn House
618 S. Alameda
Las Cruces NM 88005
(505) 526-3327

Chinguague Compound
PO Box 1118g
San Juan Pueblo NM 87566
(505) 852-2194

El Paradero
220 W. Manhattan
Santa Fe NM 87501
Circa: 1912
(505) 988-1177

Pueblo Bonito
138 W. Manhattan
Santa Fe NM 87501
(505) 984-1670

The Rim House
PO Box 1537
Santa Fe NM 87501

Las Palomas Conf.
Center
PO Box 6689
Taos NM 87571
(505) 758-9456

New York

Springside Inn
Box 520
Auburn NY 13021
(315)252-7247

Mulligan Farm
5403 Barber Road
Avon NY 14414
Circa: 1852

The Great South Bay Inn
160 South County Rd.
Bellport, Long Island NY 11713
(516) 286-8588

The Red House Country
Inn
Picnic Area Road
Burdett NY 14818

Glen Durham
Rt 2, Box 816
Cairo NY 12413

Gasho Inn
Rt 32
Central Valley NY 10917

Thousand Islands Inn
335 Riverside Dr.
Clayton NY 13624
Circa: 1897
(315) 686-3030

Green's Victorian B&B
Rt 44 & 55
Clintondale NY 12515
Circa: 1860

One Market Street
1 Market St.
Cold Spring NY 10516
Circa: 1810

The Old Post Inn
43 Main St.
Cold Spring NY 10516

Cooper Inn
PO Box 311
Cooperstown NY 13326
(607) 547-2567

The J. P. Sillhouse
63 Chestnut St
Cooperstown NY 13326

Maidstone Arms
207 Main St.
East Hampton NY 11937
(516) 324-5006

Inn At Lake Joseph
PO Box 81
Forestburgh NY 12777
(914) 791-9506

Frankfort Hill B&B
399 Brockway Rd.
Frankfort NY 13340

The Golden Eagle Inn
Garrison's Landing NY 10524
Circa: 1848

The Cobblestones
Rt 2
Geneva NY 14456
Circa: 1848

Randy Wade
Box 5
Greenport NY 11944

Gill House Inn
Henderson Harbor NY 13651
Circa: 1860

Captain Schoonmaker's
House
PO Box 37, Rte. 2
High Falls NY 12440
Circa: 1760
(914) 687-7946

House On The Hill
Box 86
High Falls NY 12440
Circa: 1825

L'Hostellerie Bressane
Corner Rtes. 22 & 23
Hillsdale NY 12529
Circa: 1780

The Stagecoach Inn
Old Military Rd.
Lake Placid NY 12946
Circa: 1830

The Federal House Bed
& Breakfast
175 Ludlowville Rd
Lansing NY 14882

Napoli Stagecoach Inn
Little Valley NY 14755
Circa: 1830

Lanza's Country Inn
PO Box 446, Rd 2
Livingston Manor NY 12758
(914) 439-5070

Tinell's Hathaway House
Rt 41, Box 621 Solon
McGraw NY 13101

Maple Shade B&B
Rt 1 Box 105
Milford NY 13807

Mt. Tremper Inn
Rt 212 & Wittenberg Rd.
Mt. Tremper NY 12457
Circa: 1850

New Lebanon Guest House
Rt 20
New Lebanon NY 12125
Circa: 1853

Ujjala's B&B
2 Forest Glen
New Paltz NY 12561
Circa: 1910
(914) 255-6360

White House Farm
211 Phillies Bridge Rd
New Paltz NY 12561

Bayside Guest House
Box 34
Olcott NY 14126

Dannfield
50 Canada Rd
Painted Post NY 14870
Circa: 1828

Fox Run Vineyards Bed & Breakfast
670 Rte 14 Rd 1
Penn Yan NY 14527

The Tibbitts House
100 Columbia Turnpike
Rensselaer NY 12144
Circa: 1860

The Libby House
Box 343
Riverhead NY 11901

The Rose Mansion & Gardens
625 Mt Hope Ave
Rochester NY 14620

The Schmids
Rt 1, Box 1114
Schuylerville NY 12871

Locustwood Country Inn
3568 Rte. 89
Seneca Falls NY 13148
Circa: 1820

Two Brooks Bed & Breakfast
Rt 42
Shandaken NY 12480

The Bowditch House
166 North Ferry Rd.
Shelter Island NY 11965

Maxwell Creek Inn
7563 Lake Rd
Sodus NY 14551
Circa: 1840

Country Inn
200 Hill St.
Southampton NY 11968
Circa: 1880

Village Latch
101 Hill St
Southampton NY 11968
(503) 283-2160

Millhof Inn
Rt 43
Stephentown NY 12168
Circa: 1930

Baker's B&B
Rt 2 Box 80
Stone Ridge NY 12484
Circa: 1780

North Carolina

Ray House
83 Hillside St.
Asheville NC 28801

Circa: 1891
(704) 252-0106

Balsam Lodge
PO Box 279, Valley Dr.
Balsam NC 28707
Circa: 1906
(704) 456-6528

Old Mill Inn
PO Box 252, Hwy 64/74
Bat Cave NC 28710
(701) 625-4256

Stonehearth Inn
Rt 74 PO Box 9
Bat Cave NC 28710
Circa: 1940
(704) 625-9990

Belford House B&B
129 Craven St
Beaufort NC 28516
(919) 728-6031

Captain's Quarters
315 Ann St
Beaufort NC 28516
(919) 728-7711

The Cedars At Beaufort
305 Front St.
Beaufort NC 28516

The Shotgun House
406 Ann St., Box 833
Beaufort NC 28516

Red Rocker Inn
3888 40 Way S.
Black Mountain NC 28711
Circa: 1894

Maple Lodge
PO Box 66, Sunset Drive
Blowing Rock NC 28605
(704) 295-3331

Sunshine Inn
Box 528
Blowing Rock NC 28605

The Inn At Brevard
410 E. Main St.
Brevard NC 28712
Circa: 1890
(704) 884-2105

Womble Inn
301 W. Main St.
Brevard NC 28712
(704) 884-4770

Folkestone Lodge
Rt 1 Box 310
Bryson City NC 28713
Circa: 1926
(704) 488-2730

Nu-Wray Inn
PO Box 156
Burnsville NC 28714
Circa: 1830
(704) 682-2329

Hampton Manor
3327 Carmel Rd.
Charlotte NC 28211

Morehead Inn
1122 E. Morehead St.
Charlotte NC 28204

Overcarsh House
326 W Eighth St.
Charlotte NC 28202
(704) 334-8477

Gingerbread Inn
PO Box 187, Hwy. 74
Chimney Rock NC 28720
(704) 625-4038

Tanglewood Manor
PO Box 1040
Clemmons NC 27012
Circa: 1859
(919) 766-0591

Jarrett House
PO Box 219
Dillsboro NC 28725
Circa: 1884
(704) 586-9964

Mulberry Hill
R7 D4
Edenton NC 27923
(919) 482-4175

Trestle House Inn
Rt 4 PO Box 370
Edenton NC 27932

(919) 482-2282

Woodfield Inn
PO Box 98
Flat Rock NC 28731
Circa: 1852
(704) 693-6016

Franklin Terrace
67 Harrison Ave
Franklin NC 28734
Circa: 1880
(704) 524-7907

Poor Richards Summit Inn
PO Box 511
Franklin NC 28734
Circa: 1898
(704) 524-2006

Glendale Springs Inn
Glendale Springs NC 28629
(919) 982-2102

Mountain High
Big Ridge Rd
Glenville NC 28736
(704) 743-3094

Leftwich House
215 E. Harden St.
Graham NC 27253
(919) 226-5978

Echo Mountain Inn
2849 Laurel Park Hwy.
Hendersonville NC 28739
Circa: 1896

Havenshire Inn
Rte. 4 Box 455
Hendersonville NC 28739
(704) 692-4097

Waverly
783 N. Main St.
Hendersonville NC 28739
Circa: 1890
(704) 69309193

Highlands Inn
PO Box 1030
Highlands NC 28741
Circa: 1880
(704) 526-9380

Old Edwards Inn
4th & Main St

Highlands NC 28741
Circa: 1870
(704) 526-5036

Ye Olde Cherokee Inn
Rt 1 PO Box 315
Kill Devil Hills NC 27948
(919) 441-6127

Brookside Lodge
7 Lakeshore Dr.
Lake Junaluska NC 28745
(704) 456-8897

Providence Lodge
PO Box 212, 1 Atkins Loop
Lake Junaluska NC 28745
(704) 456-6486

Sunset Inn
PO Box 925, 21 N. Lakeshore Dr.
Lake Junaluska NC 28745
(704) 456-3620

Lodge On Lake Lure
Rte. 1 PO Box 529a
Lake Lure NC 28746
(704) 625-2789

Greystone Inn
Greystone Lane
Lake Toxaway NC 28747
(800) 824-5766, (704) 966-4700

Baird House
121 S. Main St
Mars Hill NC 28754
(704) 689-5722

Pine Ridge Inn
2893 W. Pine St.
Mt. Airy NC 27030
(919) 789-5034

Colony Beach Inn
PO Box 87
Nags Head NC 27959
(919) 441-3666

Boyette House
PO Box 39
Ocracoke NC 27960
(919) 928-4261

Island Inn
Box 9
Ocracoke NC 27960
Circa: 1901

The Beach House
Box 443
Ocracoke NC 27960

Pines Country Inn
Hart Rd.
Pisgah Forest NC 28768
Circa: 1883
(704) 877-3131

Orchard Inn
PO Box 725
Saluda NC 28773
Circa: 1900
(704) 749-5471

Green River Plantation
The Guy Odoms
Shelby NC 28150

Dosher Plantation House B&B
Rt 5 Box 100
Southport NC 28461
(917) 457-5554

Melrose Inn
211 Melrose
Tryon NC 28782
Circa: 1880

Pine Crest Inn
PO Box 1030, 200 Pine Crest Ln.
Tryon NC 28982
(704) 859-9135

The Squire's Vintage Inn
Rt 2 Box 130r
Warsaw NC 28398
(919) 473-5466

Haywood Street Inn
409 Haywood St.
Waynesville NC 28786

Piedmont Inn
630 Eagle's Nest Rd.
Waynesville NC 28786

Worth House
412 S. Third St.
Wilmington NC 28401
(919) 762-8562

Colonel Ludlow House
Summit & W. 5th
Winston-salem NC 27101
Circa: 1887

(919) 777-1887

Ohio

Portage House
601 Copley Rd.
Akron OH 44320
Circa: 1917
(216) 535-9236

Frederick Fitting House
72 Fitting Ave.
Bellville OH 44813
(419) 886-4283

Tudor House
P.o. Box
Cleveland OH 44118
(216) 321-3213

Pleasant Journey Inn
4247 Roswell Rd. S.W.
Dellroy OH 44620
(216) 735-2987

Granville Inn
314 E. Broadway
Granville OH 43023
Circa: 1812

Inn At Honey Run
6920 Country Rd. 203
Millersburg OH 44654
(216) 674-0011

Old Island House Inn
Box K, 102 Madison St.
Port Clinton OH 43452
Circa: 1886

Cider Mill
PO Box 441
Zoar OH 44697
Circa: 1863
(216) 874-3133

Oregon

Iris Inn
59 Manzanita St
Ashland OR 97520
Circa: 1905

McCall House
153 Oak St.
Ashland OR 97520
Circa: 1883
(503) 482-9296

Morical House
688 N Main St
Ashland OR 97520
Circa: 1880

Oak Street Station
239 Oak St
Ashland OR 97520
(503) 482-1726

Scenic View B&B
467 Scenic Dr.
Ashland OR 97520
Circa: 1910
(503) 482-2315

Winchester Inn
35 S 2nd St
Ashland OR 97520
Circa: 1886

Ashland's Main St. Inn
142 W. Main St.
Ashland OR 97520
(503) 488-0969

Sea Dreamer Inn
15167 Mcvay Lane
Brookings OR 97415
(503) 469-6629

The Hudson House
37700 Highway 101 S
Cloverdale OR 97112
(503) 472-4814

Campus Cottage
1136 E 19 Ave
Eugene OR 97403
Circa: 1922

Jefferson House
752 Jefferson
Eugene OR 97402
(503) 484-5504

Timesways Inn
1006 Taylor St
Eugene OR 97402
Circa: 1891

Frenchglen Hotel
Frenchglen OR 97736
Circa: 1914
(503) 493-2565

Guest House At Gardiner By The Sea
401 Front St

Gardiner OR 97441
(503) 271-4005

Lawnridge House
1304 Nw Lawnridge
Grants Pass OR 97526
(503) 479-5186

Clear Creek Farm B&B
Rte Box 138
Halfway OR 97834
(503) 742-2238

Columbia Gorge Hotel
4000 W. Cliff Dr.
Hood River OR 97031
Circa: 1921
(503) 386-5566

Davidson House
887 Monmouth St
Independence OR 97351
(503) 838-3280

Farmhouse Bed & Breakfast
755 E. California St.
Jacksonville OR 97530

Judge Touvelle House
455 N. Oregon St.
Jacksonville OR 97530

Wallowa Lake Lodge
Joseph OR 97846
Circa: 1926

A Gran-Mother's House
12524 Sw Bonnes Ferry Road
Lake Oswego OR 97034
(503) 244-4361

Madras
343 C Street At Hwy 26
Madras OR 97741
(503) 475-2345

Mattey House
10221 Ne Mattey Lane
Mcminnville OR 97128
(5030 434-5058

Madelaine's
735 8th Box 913
Port Orford OR 97465
(503) 332-4373

Old Portland Estate
1870 Se Exeter Drive

Portland OR 97202
(503) 236-6533

Peninsula Guest House
2911 N. Russet
Portland OR 97217
(503) 289-9141

Harbison House
1845 Commercial Se
Salem OR 97302
(503) 581-8118

The Boarding House
208 N. Holladay Dr
Seaside OR 97138
(503) 738-9055

The Gilbert House
341 Beach Dr
Seaside OR 97138
(503) 738-9770

Bigelow B&B
606 Washington
The Dalles OR 97058
(503) 298-8239

Pennsylvania

Coachaus
107-111 N. 8th St.
Allentown PA 18102

Horseshoe Farm
Rt 1, Box 228
Annville PA 17003

East Shore House B&B
Box 12
Beach Lake PA 18405

Jean Bonnet Tavern
Rt 2, Box 188
Bedford PA 15522

Grandmaws
Rt 3, Box 239
Benton PA 17814

Ogline's B&B
1001 E. Main St.
Berlin PA 15530

Sunday's Mill Farm
Rt 2, Box 419
Bernville PA 19506

The Greystone
Blue Ridge Summit PA 17214

Brookview Manor B&B Inn
Rt 1, Box 365
Canadensis PA 18325

Overlook Inn
Dutch Hill Rd.
Canadensis PA 18325

Pine Knob
Rte. 447
Canadensis PA 18325
(717) 595-2532

Pump House Inn
Sky Top Road
Canadensis PA 18325

Cedar Run Inn
Rte. 414
Cedar Run PA 17727
(717) 353-6241

Noah's Ark
Rte. 1, PO Box 425
Central City PA 15926

Hill House
Creek Rd.
Chadds Ford PA 19317

Winding Glen Farm
PO Box 160
Christiana PA 17509
Circa: 1770
(215) 593-5535

Tara
Box 475, 3665 Valley View
Clark PA 16113

La Anna Guest House
Rd2, PO Box 1051
Cresco PA 18326
(717) 676-4225

Mountain House
Mountain Rd.
Delaware Water Gap PA 18327

Duck Hill Farm
Rt 1
Downington PA 19335

Doylestown Inn
18 W. State St.
Doylestown PA 18901
(215) 345-6610

The Inn At Fordhook
Farm
105 New Britain Rd.
Doylestown, Bucks County PA
18901

Eagles Mere Inn
Po Box 356
Eagles Mere PA 17731

Shady Lane Lodge
Allegheny Av.
Eagles Mere PA 17731

Evermay-on-the-
Delaware
River Rd.
Erwinna PA 18920
(215) 294-9100

Golden Pheasant Inn
River Rd.
Erwinna PA 18920
Circa: 1857

Duling Kurtz House
146 S. Whitford Rd.
Exton PA 19341

Historic Fairfield Inn
Box 96
Fairfield PA 17320

Glasbern
PO Box 250, R.d. 1
Fogelsville PA 18051-9743
(215) 285-4723

Quaker Manor House
1165 Pinetown Rd.
Fort Washington PA 19034

Hobby House B&B
174 Srader Grove Rd.
Freeport PA 16229

Swinn's Lodging
31 E. Lincoln Ave.
Gettysburg PA 17325

Gettystown Inn
89 Steinwehr Ave.
Gettysburg PA 17325

The Old Appleford Inn
218 Carlisle St.
Gettysburg PA 17325

Log Cabin B&B
Box 393 Rt. 11
Hallstead PA 18822

The Corner Inn
Box 777
Hallstead PA 18822

Academy Street B&B
528 Academy St.
Hawley PA 18428

Settlers Inn
4 Main Av.
Hawley PA 18428

Aunt Susie's Country
Vacations
Rt 1, Box 225
Hesston PA 16647

Shady Elms Farm B&B
Rt 1, Box 188
Hickory PA 15340

Brun Run Estate
132 Logan Blvd.
Hollidaysburg PA 16648

Hotel Wayne
1202 Main St.
Honesdale PA 18431
(717) 253-3290

Das Tannen-lied
Rte. 1
Jamestown PA 16134
Circa: 1872

Ye Olde Library B&B
310 S. Main St.
Jersey Shore PA 17740

Harry Packer Mansion
Packer Hill
Jim Thorpe PA 18229

Bucksville House
Rt 2, Box 146
Kintnersville PA 18930

Groff Tourist Farm
Home
R.d.1 Box 36

Kinzer PA 17353

Bethania Farm
PO Box 228
Kinzers PA 17535
(717) 442-4939

The Koller's
Rt 2, Box 400a
Kunkletown PA 18058

Peddler's Village Lodg-
ing
Rte. 263
Lahaska PA 18931
(215) 794-7438

Buena Kotte B&B
2020 Marietta Ave.
Lancaster PA 17603

Gertrude Garber
1768 Highland Ave.
Langhorne PA 19047

Ligonier Country Inn
Po Box 46 Rt. 30 E.
Laughlintown PA 15655

Loom Room
Box 1420
Leesport PA 19533

Turtle Hill Rd. B&B
Rt 1, 111 Turtle Hill Rd.
Leola PA 17540

Pineapple Inn
439 Market St.
Lewisburg PA 17837

Grant House B&B
244 West Church St.
Ligonier PA 15658

General Sutter Inn
14 E. Main St.
Lititz PA 17543
Circa: 1764

General Sutter Inn
14 E. Main St.
Lititz PA 17643
(717) 626-2115

Black Bass Hotel
River Rd.
Lumberville PA 18933

The Great Valley House
110 Swedesford Rd. Rd 3
Malvern PA 19355
(215) 644-6759

Three Center Square Inn
Po Box 428
Maytown PA 17550

Restless Oak B&B
Box 241
Mcelhatten PA 17748

Stranahan House B&B
117 E. Market St.
Mercer PA 16137

Black Walnut Inn
509 Fire Tower Rd.
Milford PA 18337

Cliff Park Inn
Cliff Park Rd.
Milford PA 18337
(717) 296-6491

Walnut Hill B&B
Rt 1, Box 113
Millersville PA 17551

Cameron Estate Inn
R.d.1 Box 305
Mount Joy PA 17552

Rocky Acre Farm
Rd 3
Mount Joy PA 17552
(717) 653-4449

The Bodine House B&B
307 S. Main St.
Muncy PA 17756

Tulpehocken Manor Inn
650 W. Lincoln Ave.
Myerstown PA 17067

Waltman's B&B
Rt 1, Box 87
New Albany PA 18833

Centre Bridge Inn
Rts. 32 & 263
New Hope PA 18938

Hotel Du Village
N. River Rd.
New Hope PA 18938

(215) 862-9911

Inn At Phillips Mill
North River Rd.
New Hope PA 18938

Logan Inn
10 W. Ferry St.
New Hope PA 18938

Pineapple Hill
1324 River Road
New Hope PA 18938
Circa: 1800

Whitehall Inn
R.d.2 Box 250
New Hope PA 18938

White Cloud Sylvan Retreat
Rd 1 Box 215
Newfoundland PA 18445

Windward Inn
51 Freeport Rd.
North East PA 16428

Maple Lane Farm
505 Paradise Ln.
Paradise PA 17562

Neffdale Farm
604 Strasburg Rd.
Paradise PA 17562
(717) 687-7837

Rayba Acres Farm
183 Black Horse Rd
Paradise PA 17562
(717) 687-6729

Pleasant Grove Farm
Rt 1, Box 132
Peach Bottom PA 17563

The Benfield Mill #302
624 E. Walnut St.
Perkasie PA 18944

Society Hill Hotel
301 Chestnut
Philadelphia PA 19106

Inn Of Innisfree
Box 108
Point Pleasant PA 18950

Tattersall Inn
Po Box 569
Point Pleasant PA 18950

Coventry Forge Inn
Rd 2
Pottstown PA 19464

Fairway Farm Bed & Breakfast
Vaughn Rd.
Pottstown PA 19464

Sign Of Sorrel Horse
Rd 3
Quakertown PA 18951

Bogert House
140 Main St.
Ridgway PA 15853

Riegelsville Hotel
10-12 Delaware Rd.
Riegelsville PA 18077

Century Inn
Route 40
Scenery Hill PA 15360

Pine Wood Acre
Rt 1, Box 278
Scottdale PA 15683-9567

The Blue Lion Inn
350 S. Market St.
Selinsgrove PA 17870

Haag's Hotel
Main St.
Shartlesville PA 19554

Smoketown Village Tourist Home
2495 Old Ph Pike
Smoketown PA 17576

Charles Bauerlein
Box 369
Spring House PA 19477

Inn At Starlight Lake
Starlight PA 18461
Circa: 1909
(717) 798-2519

Siloan
Village Rd. Box 82
Strasburg PA 17579

Strasburg Village Inn
1 W. Main St.
Strasburg PA 17579

Jefferson Inn
Rt 2, Box 36
Thompson PA 18465

Victorian Guest House
118 York Av.
Towanda PA 18848

Bridgeton House
Po Box 167
Upper Black Eddy PA 18972

Tara
1 Bridgeton Hill
Upper Black Eddy PA 18972

Upper Black Eddy Inn
Rt. 32-river Rd.
Upper Black Eddy PA 18972

Willows
40 Kinzua Rd.
Warren PA 16365

Woodhill Farms Inn
130 Glenwood Dr.
Washington Crossing PA 18977

Altheim B&B
Box 2081, 104 Walnut St.
Waterford PA 16441

Point House Lodge
Church St.
Waterville PA 17776

Jesse Robinson Manor
141 Main St.
Wellsboro PA 16901

Crooked Winsor
409 S. Church St.
West Chester PA 19382

The Coreys
2522 Wexford Run Rd.
Wexford PA 15090

Reighard House
1323 E. Third St.
Williamsport PA 17701

Green Gables B&B
2532 Willow St. Pike

Willow Street PA 17584

Woodward Inn
Box 177
Woodward PA 16882

Wycombe Inn
Po Box 204
Wycombe PA 18980

Fairhaven
Rd 12 Box 445
York PA 17406

Inn At Mundis Mill
Rt 1, Box 15, Mundis Race Rd.
York PA 17402

Rhode Island

1661 Inn
PO Box 1
Block Island RI 02807
Circa: 1661
(401) 466-2421, 466-2063

Blue Dory Inn
Dodge Street
Block Island RI 02807
(401) 466-2254

Hotel Manisses
PO Box 1
Block Island RI 02807
Circa: 1872
(401) 466-2836

Inn At Old Harbor
PO Box 718
Block Island RI 02807
(401) 466-2212

Seacrest Inn
207 High St.
Block Island RI 02807
(401) 466-2882

General Stanton Inn
PO Box 222, Rte. 1a
Charlestown RI 02813
(401) 364-8888

Bay Voyage Inn
Jamestown RI 02835
(401) 423-0540

Calico Cat Guest House
14 Union St.

Jamestown RI 02835
(401) 423-2641

Stone Towers
152 Tuckerman Ave.
Middletown RI 02840
(401) 846-3227

Four Gables
12 S. Pier Rd.
Narragansett RI 02882
Circa: 1898
(401) 789-6948

Ilverthorpe Cottage
41 Robinson St.
Narragansett RI 02882
Circa: 1896
(401) 789-2392

Louis Sherry Cottage
59 Gibson Ave.
Narragansett RI 02882
(401) 783-8626

Richards' Guest House
104 Robinson St.
Narragansett RI 02882
(401) 789-7746

Sea Gull Guest House
50 Narragansett Ave.
Narragansett RI 02882
(401) 783-4636

Starr Cottage
68 Caswell St.
Narragansett RI 02882
Circa: 1883
(401) 783-2411

Summer House Inn
87 Narragansett Ave.
Narragansett RI 02882
(401) 783-0123

Admiral Benbow Inn
93 Pelham St.
Newport RI 02840
Circa: 1855
(401) 846-4256, 846-1615

Captain Samuel Guest
House
3 Willow St., Historic Point
Newport RI 02840
(401) 846-5486

Cliffside Inn
2 Seaview Ave.
Newport RI 02840
(401) 847-1811

Covell Guest House
43 Farewell St.
Newport RI 02840
Circa: 1810
(401) 847-8872

Dennis Guest House
59 Washington St.
Newport RI 02840

Easton's Inn On The
Beach
30 Wave Ave.
Newport RI 02840
(401) 846-0310

Ellery Park House
44 Farewell St.
Newport RI 02840
(401) 847-6320

Guest House Internation-
al
28 Weaver Ave.
Newport RI 02840
(401) 847-1501

Harborside Inn
Christie's Landing
Newport RI 02840
(401) 846-6600

Inn At Castle Hill
Ocean Dr.
Newport RI 02840
(401) 849-3800

Inntowne
6 Mary St.
Newport RI 02840
(401) 846-9200

Merritt House Guest
57 2nd St.
Newport RI 02840
(401) 847-4289

Moulton-Weaver House
4 Training Station Rd.
Newport RI 02840
Circa: 1805
(401)847-0133

Oceancliff
Ocean Dr.
Newport RI 02840
(401) 847-7777

Sunnyside Mansion
25 Old Beach Rd.
Newport RI 02840
Circa: 1886
(401) 849-3114

The Brinley Victorian
Inn
23 Brinley St.
Newport RI 02840

The Inn At Castle Hill
Ocean Dr.
Newport RI 02840

Wayside
Bellevue Ave.
Newport RI 02840
Circa: 1876

Yankee Peddler Inn
113 Touro St.
Newport RI 02840
Circa: 1830
(401) 846-1323

Yellow Cottage
82 Gibbs Ave.
Newport RI 02840
Circa: 1900
(401) 847-6568, 849-4212

Twin Spruce Tourist
Home
515 Turnpike Ave.
Portsmouth RI 02871
(401) 682-0673

Stone Bridge Inn
1 Lawton Ave.
Tiverton RI 02878
Circa: 1682
(401) 624-6601

Larchwood Inn
176 Main St.
Wakefield RI 02879
Circa: 1831
(401) 783-1709, 783-5454

Longvue Guest House
311 Shore Rdl, Rte. 1a
Westerly RI 02891
(401) 322-0465

Shelter Harbor Inn
Rte. 1
Westerly RI 02891
(401) 322-8883

South Carolina

Belmont Inn
106 E. Pickens St.
Abbeville SC 29620
(803) 459-9625

Holley Inn
235 Richland Ave
Aiken SC 29801
(803) 648-4265

Pine Knoll Inn
305 Lancaster St
Aiken SC 29801
(803) 649-5939

The Brodie Residence
422 York St
Aiken SC 29801
(803) 648-1445

Wilcox Inn
Colleton Ave At Whiskey Rd
Aiken SC 29801
(803) 649-1377

Evergreen Inn
1109 S Main
Anderson SC 29841
(803) 225-1109

Rhett House Inn
1009 Craven St.
Beaufort SC 29902
(803) 525-1166

Twelve Oaks Inn
PO Box 4126, Rte. 2 Box 293
Beaufort SC 29902
(803) 525-1371

The Cedars
Box 117 1325 Williston Rd
Beech Island SC 29841
(803) 827-0248

Aberdeen
1409 Broad St
Camden SC 29020
(803) 432-2524

Fair Oaks
1308 Fair St.
Camden SC 29020
(803) 432-1499

The Inn
1308 19 Broad St
Camden SC 29020
Circa: 1800
(803) 425-1806

1837 Bed & Breakfast
126 Wentworth St.
Charleston SC 29401
(803) 723-7166

Barksdale House Inn
27 George St
Charleston SC 29401
(803) 577-4800

Battery Carriage House
20 S. Battery St.
Charleston SC 29401
Circa: 1845
(803) 723-9881

Bed & Breakfast
36 Meeting St
Charleston SC 29401
(803) 722-1034

Church Street Inn
177 Church St
Charleston SC 29401
Circa: 1890
(800) 845-7638

Coach House
39 E Battery Pl
Charleston SC 29401
Circa: 1810
(803) 722-8145

Elliot House Inn
78 Queen St.
Charleston SC 29401
Circa: 1865
(803) 723-1855

Hayne House
30 King St.
Charleston SC 29401
(803) 577-2633

Holland's Guest House
15 New St.
Charleston SC 29401
(803) 723-0090

Indigo Inn, Eighteenth
Century Recreation
1 Maiden Lane
Charleston SC 29401
Circa: 1979
(803) 577-5900

Jasmine House
64 Hasell St.
Charleston SC 29401
Circa: 1843
(803) 577-5900

Kings Courtyard Inn
198 King St.
Charleston SC 29401
(803) 723-7000

Meeting Street Inn
173 Meeting St.
Charleston SC 29401
Circa: 1870
(800) 845-7638, (803) 723-9881

Palmer Home
5 East Battery
Charleston SC 29401
(803) 723-1574

Sweet Grass Inn
23 Vendue Range
Charleston SC 29401
Circa: 1800
(803) 723-9980

Sword Gate Inn
111 Tradd St.
Charleston SC 29401
Circa: 1800
(803) 723-8518

Two Meeting Street Inn
2 Meeting St
Charleston SC 29401
Circa: 1890
(803) 723-7322

Vendue Inn/Sweet Grass
19 Vendue Range
Charleston SC 29401
Circa: 1824
(803) 577-7970

Spears Bed & Breakfast
501 Kershaw St
Cheraw SC 29520
(803) 537-7733

Coosaw Plantation
Dale SC 29401
(803) 846-8225

Adams House
212 Augusta Rd.
Edgefield SC 29824

The Village Inn
Court House Square
Edgefield SC 29824
(803) 637-3789

The John Lawton House
159 Third St E
Estill SC 29918
(803) 625-3240

Shaw House
8 Cypress Ct.
Georgetown SC 29440
(801) 546-9663

The Inn On The Square
104 Court St
Greenwood SC 29646
(803) 223-4488

Guilds Inn
101 Pitt St
Mt Pleasant SC 29464
(803) 881-0510

Webster Manor
115 E James St
Mullins SC 29574
(803) 464-9632

Serendipity, An Inn
407 71st. Ave. N
Myrtle Beach SC 29577
(803) 449-5268

Russell Street Inn
491 Russell St
Orangeburg SC 29115
(803) 531-2030

Liberty Hall Inn
Pendleton SC 29670
(803) 646-7500

The Palmettos
2014 Middle St., PO Box 706
Sullivan's Island SC 29482
(803) 883-3389

Forest Hill Manor
Rt 2 Box 725

Union SC 29379
(803) 427-4525

Tennessee

Lookout Mountain
Guest House
4415 Guild Trail
Chattanooga TN 37409
Circa: 1927
(615) 821-8307

Leconte Lodge
PO Box 350
Gatlinburg TN 37738
Circa: 1930
(615) 436-4473

Three Chimneys
1302 White Ave.
Knoxville TN 37916
Circa: 1896
(615) 521-4970

Lynchburg B&B
PO Box 34, Mec. St.
Lynchburg TN 37532
(615) 759-7158

Walnut House
Rt 2
Monterey TN 38574

Clardy's Guest House
435 E. Main St.
Murfreesboro TN 37130
Circa: 1898
(615) 893-6030

Leawood-Williams Estate
PO Box 24
Shiloh TN 38376
(901) 689-5106

Texas

Gast Haus Lodge
944 High St
Comfort TX 78013
(512) 995-2304

Reiffert-Mugge Inn
304 West Prairie St
Cuero TX 77954
(512) 275-2626

Lickskillet Inn
PO Box 85, Fayette St.
Fayetteville TX 78940
Circa: 1850
(409) 378-2846

Indian Lodge
PO Box 786
Fort Davis TX 79734
Circa: 1933
(915) 426-3254

Baron's Creek Inn
110 East Creek St
Fredericksburg TX 78624
(512) 997-9398

Dickens Loft
2021 The Strand
Galveston TX 77550
(409) 762-1653

J.F. Smith House Inn
2217 Broadway
Galveston TX 77550

Tremont House
2300 Ship's Mechanic Row
Galveston TX 77550
(409) 763-0300

Victorian Inn
511 17th St
Galveston TX 77550
(409) 762-3235

Louise Witkowski
800 Third St.
Graham TX 76046

Nutt House
Town Square
Granbury TX 76048
Circa: 1893
(817) 573-5612

Excelsior House
211 W. Austin
Jefferson TX 75657
Circa: 1850
(214) 665-2513

Hale House
702 South Lee
Jefferson TX 75657

New Jefferson Inn
124 Austin St.
Jefferson TX 75657

(214) 665-2631

Pride House
409 Broadway
Jefferson TX 75657
Circa: 1888
(214) 665-2675

The Magnolias
209 Broadway
Jefferson TX 75657
Circa: 1867
(214) 665-2754

William Clark House
201 W. Henderson
Jefferson TX 75657
Circa: 1855
(214) 665-8880

Wise Manor
312 Houston St.
Jefferson TX 75657
Circa: 1874
(214) 665-2386

The Roper House
Rt 2 Box 31
Marble Falls TX 78654
(512) 693-5561

Three Oaks
609 N. Washington Ave.
Marshall TX 75670
(214) 938-6123

La Posada
100 N Main
McAllen TX 78501
(800) 292-5659

Gruene Mansion Inn
New Braunfels TX 78130
(512) 629-2641

Prince Solms Inn
295 East San Antonio
New Braunfels TX 78130
(512) 625-9169

La Borde House
601 E. Main St.
Rio Grande City TX 78582
Circa: 1897
(512) 487-5101

Inn At Salado
North Main At Pace Park
Salado TX 76571

(817) 947-8200

Menger Hotel
204 Alamo Plaza
San Antonio TX 78205
(512) 223-4361

Aquarena Springs Inn
1 Aquarena Dr.
San Marcos TX 78666
Circa: 1929
(512) 396-8901

Crystal River Inn
326 West Hopkins
San Marcos TX 78666
(512) 396-3739

Weimar Country Inn
Jackson Square
Weimar TX 78962
(409) 725-8888

Utah

Center Street B&B
169 East Center St
Logan UT 84321
(801) 752-3443

The Birch Trees B&B
315 Boulevard
Logan UT 84321
(801) 753-1331

The Homestead
700 N. Homestead Dr.
Midway UT 84049
Circa: 1886
(801) 654-1103, 377-9149

Mansion House B&B
298 South State St
Mt Pleasant UT 84647
(801) 462-3031

505 Woodside
Box 2446
Park City UT 84060
(801) 649-4841

Chez Fontaine
45 North 300 East
Provo UT 84601
(801) 375-8484

The Pullman
415 South University Ave

Provo UT 84601
(801) 374 8141

Burr House
195 West Main St
Salina UT 84654
(801) 529-7320

Saltair B&B
164 South 9th East
Salt Lake City UT 84102
(801) 533-8184

Green Gate Village Historic B&B Inn
62-78 West Tabernacle
St George UT 84770
(801) 628-6999

Seven Wives Inn
217 North 100 West
St George UT 84770
(801) 628-3737

Vermont

Sycamore Inn
PO Box 2485, Rt 7
Arlington VT 05250
Circa: 1786
(802) 362-2284

The Silver Lake House
PO Box 13, North Rd.
Barnard VT 05081
(802) 234-9957

Old Homestead Inn
PO Box 35
Barnet VT 05821
(802) 633-4100

Bennington Hus
208 Washington Avenue
Bennington VT 05201
(802) 447-7972

Captain's House
Bennington VT 05701

Poplar Manor
Rte. 2
Bethel VT 05032
Circa: 1810
(802) 234-5426

Stone Mill Farm
PO Box 203

Brandon VT 05735
Circa: 1773
(802) 247-6137

Mill Brook B&B
PO Box 301, Rte. 44
Brownesville VT 05037
(802) 484-7283

Inn At Mt. Ascutney
Brook Rd.
Brownsville VT 05037
Circa: 1802
(802) 484-7725

Chester House
Box 218
Chester VT 05143
(802) 875-2871

Mountain Top Inn
Chittenden VT 05737
Circa: 1880
(800) 445-2100

Gary Meadow Dairy Farm
PO Box 11, RR 1
Craftsbury VT 05826
Circa: 1884
(802) 586-2536

Inn On The Common
Main St.
Craftsbury VT 05826
(802) 586-9619

Dorset Inn
Dorset VT 05251
Circa: 1796
(802) 867-5500, 867-9392

Burke Green
PO Box 81, RR1
East Burke VT 05832
Circa: 1840
(802) 467-3472

Varnum's
143 Weed Rd.
Essex Junction VT 05452
Circa: 1792
(802) 899-4577

The Vermont Marble Inn
12 West Park Drive
Fair Haven VT 05743
(802) 265-8383

Foggy Hollow Farm
Rt 104
Fairfax VT 05454
Circa: 1857

Fair Meadow Dairy Farm
PO Box 430, Rte. 235
Franklin VT 05457
Circa: 1853
(802) 285-2132

The Hayes House
Grafton VT 05146

Kincraft Inn
PO Box 96, Rte. 100
Hancock VT 05748
(802) 767-3734

Sherburne Valley Inn
Rte. 4
Killington VT 05751
Circa: 1900
(802) 422-9888

River Meadow Farm
PO Box 822
Manchester Center VT 05255
Circa: 1829
(802) 362-3700

Whetstone Inn
Marlboro VT 05344

Middlebury Inn
Courthouse Square
Middlebury VT 05753
Circa: 1827
(800) 842-4666

Camel's Hump View Farm
Rt 100b
Moretown VT 05660
Circa: 1831
(802) 496-3614

The Hortonville Inn
Rd #1 Box 14
Mt Holly VT 05758
(802) 259-2587

North Hero House
North Hero VT 05474
Circa: 1890
(802) 372-8237

Lake House Inn At Lake Fairlee
PO Box 65, Rte. 244
Post Mills VT 05058
Circa: 1871
(802) 333-4025

Lake St. Catherine Inn
PO Box 129
Poultney VT 05764
Circa: 1920
(802) 287-9347

Putney Inn
Depot Rd.
Putney VT 05346
Circa: 1830
(802) 387-6617

Peaceful Acres
PO Box 114
Ripton VT 05466
(802) 388-2076

The Evergreen
Sandgate VT 05250
Circa: 1935
(802) 375-2272

Shoreham Inn
Rte. 74 West
Shoreham VT 05770
Circa: 1799
(802) 897-5081

Green Mountain Tea Room
PO Box 400, Rte. 7
South Wallingford VT 05773
(802) 446-2611

Bittersweet Inn
Rte 100 South
Stowe VT 05672
(802) 253-7787

Foxfire Inn
RD 2, Rte.100
Stowe VT 05672
(802) 253-4887

Gables Inn
Mountain Rd.
Stowe VT 05672
(802) 253-7730

Emersons' Guest House
82 Main St.
Vergennes VT 05491

(802) 877-3293

Captain Henry Chase House
Rt 4, Box 788
West Brattleboro VT 05301

Doveberry Inn
Rte. 100
West Dover VT 05356
(802) 464-5652

Lincoln Covered Bridge Inn
Rte. 4
West Woodstock VT 05091
(802) 457-3312

Darcroft's Schoolhouse
Rte. 100
Wilmington VT 05363
Circa: 1837
(802) 464-2631

Cambria House
43 Pleasant St.
Woodstock VT 05091
Circa: 1880
(802) 457-3077

The Jackson House At Woodstock
Rt 4 West
Woodstock VT 05091

Virginia

Martha Washington Inn
150 W. Main St.
Abingdon VA 24210
Circa: 1830
(703) 628-3161

Little River Inn
PO Box 116
Aldie VA 22001
Circa: 1819
(703) 327-6742

Alexandria Lodgings
PO Box 416
Alexandria VA 22313
(703) 836-5575

The Old Mansion
Bowling Green VA 22427

English Inn
316 14th St. Nw
Charlottesville VA 22903
Circa: 1920
(804) 295-7707

Sims Mitchell House
Box 846, 242 Whittle St SW
Chatham VA 24531

Channel Bass Inn
100 Church St.
Chincoteague VA 23336
Circa: 1871
(804) 336-6148

Year Of The Horse Inn
600 S. Main St.
Chincoteague VA 22336

Fredericksburg Inn
1707 Princess Anne St.
Fredericksburg VA 22401
Circa: 1928
(703) 371-8300

Kenmore Inn
1200 Princess Anne St.
Fredericksburg VA 22401
(703) 371-7622

Shenandoah Springs
Country Inn
Haywood VA 22722

King Carter Inn
PO Box 425
Irvington VA 22480
Circa: 1890
(804) 438-6053

Laurel Brigade Inn
20 W. Market St.
Leesburg VA 22075
Circa: 1759
(703) 777-1010

Alexander-Withrow
House
3 W. Washington
Lexington VA 24450
Circa: 1789
(703) 463-2044

Maple Hall
11 N. Main St.
Lexington VA 24450

McCampbell Inn
11 N. Main St.
Lexington VA 24450
Circa: 1809
(703) 463-2044

Ravenswood Inn
PO Box 250
Mathews VA 23109
(804) 725-7272

Luck House
PO Box 919, 205 E.
Washington St.
Middleburg VA 22117
(703) 687-5387

Red Fox Inn & Tavern
PO Box 385, 2 E. Washington
St.
Middleburg VA 22117
Circa: 1728
(703) 687-6301

Wayside Inn Since 1797
7783 Main St.
Middletown VA 22645
Circa: 1797
(703) 869-1797

Crossroads Inn
PO Box 36
North Garden VA 22959
Circa: 1818
(804) 293-6382

Colonial Manor Inn
PO Box 94, Market St.
Onacock VA 23417
Circa: 1890
(804) 787-3521

Hidden Inn
249 Caroline St.
Orange VA 22950
(703) 672-3625

Duncan Lee House
PO Box 15131
Richmond VA 22314
(804) 321-6277

Conyers House
Slate Mills Rd.
Sperryville VA 22740
Circa: 1770
(703) 987-8025

Hotel Strasburg
201 Holliday St.

Strasburg VA 22657
(703) 465-9191

Prospect Hill
PO Box 55, RD 1 Rt 613
Trevillians VA 23170
Circa: 1732
(703) 967-0844

1763 Inn
PO Box 19, Rt 1
Upperville VA 22176
(703) 592-3848

Inn At Gristmill Square
PO Box 229
Warm Springs VA 24484
(703) 839-2231

Meadow Lane Lodge
PO Box 110, Star Rte. A
Warm Springs VA 24484
(703) 839-5959

L'Augerge Provencale
PO Box 203, Rt1, On Rte 340
White Post VA 22663
(703) 837-1375

Cedars
616 Jamestown Rd.
Williamsburg VA 23185
(804) 229-3591

Washington

Channel House
2902 Oakes Ave.
Anacortes WA 98221
Circa: 1902
(206) 293-9382

Nantucket Inn
3402 Commercial Ave.
Anacortes WA 98221
Circa: 1925
(206) 293-6007

Alexander's Country Inn
Highway 706
Ashford WA 98304
(206) 569-2300

National Park Inn
Mt. Ranier Guest Services, Star
Rte.
Ashford WA 98304
Circa: 1920

(206) 569-2563

Em's Bed & Breakfast
PO Box 206, 304 Wapato
Chelan WA 98816
(509) 682-4149

Captain Whidbey
Coupeville WA 98239
Circa: 1907
(206) 678-4097

Victorian House
PO Box 761, 602 N. Main
Coupeville WA 98239
(206) 678-5305

Kangaroo House
5 North Beach Rd., Orcas Island
Eastsound WA 98245
(206) 376-2175

Pillars By The Sea
1367 E. Bayview
Freeland WA 98249
(205) 221-7736

San Juan Inn
PO Box 776
Friday Harbor WA 98250
Circa: 1873
(206) 378-2070

Tucker House B&B
260 B St
Friday Harbor WA 98250
(206) 378-2783

Olde Glencove Hotel
9418 Glencove Rd.
Gig Harbor WA 98335
(206) 884-2835

Bush House
PO Box 863, 5th & Index Aves.
Gold Bar WA 98251
Circa: 1898
(206) 363-1244

Katy's Inn
PO Box 304, 503 S. 3rd.
La Conner WA 98257
(206) 466-3366

La Conner Country Inn
PO Box 573, 2nd & Morris
La Conner WA 98257
(206) 466-3101

Caroline's Country Cottage
PO Box 459, 215 6th St.
Langley WA 98260
(206) 221-8709

Sally's B&B Manor
PO Box 459
Langley WA 98260
Circa: 1929
(206) 221-8709

The Orchard
619 3rd St.
Langley WA 98260
Circa: 1905
(206) 221-7880

Whidbey House
PO Box 156, 106 First St.
Langley WA 98260
Circa: 1934
(206) 221-7115

Edel Haus Bed & Breakfast
320 Ninth St.
Leavenworth WA 98826
Circa: 1930
(509) 548-4412

Haus Rohrback
12882 Ranger Rd.
Leavenworth WA 98826
(206) 548-7024

Betty's Place
PO Box 86
Lopez WA 98261
Circa: 1923
(206) 468-2470

Apple Tree Inn
43317 S N. Bend Wy.
North Bend WA 98045
(206) 888-3672

Puget View Guesthouse
7924 61st NE
Olympia WA 98506
(206) 459-1676

Arcadia Country Inn
1891 S. Jacob Miller Rd.
Port Townsend WA 98368
(206) 385-5245

Bishop Victorian Suites
714 Washington St.

Port Townsend WA 98368
Circa: 1892
(206) 385-6122

Hastings House
313 Walker St.
Port Townsend WA 98368
(206) 385-3553

Irish Acres
PO Box 466, 780 Arcadia W.
Port Townsend WA 98368
(206) 385-4485

James House
1238 Washington
Port Townsend WA 98368
Circa: 1889
(206) 385-1238

Lincoln Inn
538 Lincoln
Port Townsend WA 98368
(206) 385-6677

Manresa Castle
PO Box 564, 7th & Sheridan
Port Townsend WA 98368
Circa: 1892
(206) 385-5750

Palace Hotel
1004 Water St.
Port Townsend WA 98368
Circa: 1889
(206) 385-0773

Quimper Inn
1306 Franklin St.
Port Townsend WA 98368
Circa: 1880
(206) 385-1086

Manor Farm Inn
26069 Big Valley Rd.
Poulsbo WA 98370

Hotel De Haro
PO Box 1
Roche Harbor WA 98250
Circa: 1886
(206) 378-2155

Roche Harbor Resort
Roche Harbor WA 98250
(206) 378-2155

Bed & Breakfast Inn
PO Box 9902

Seattle WA 98109
(206) 285-5945

Burton House
PO Box 9902
Seattle WA 98109
(206) 285-5945

Galer Place
318 W. Galer St.
Seattle WA 98119
(206) 282-5339

Shelburne Inn
PO Box 250, Pacific Hwy. 103 & J
Seaview WA 98644
Circa: 1896
(206) 642-2442

Keenan House
2610 N. Warner
Tacoma WA 98407
Circa: 1890
(206) 752-0702

Tokeland Hotel
PO Box 117
Tokeland WA 98590
Circa: 1854
(206) 267-7700

River Bend Inn
PO Box 943, Rte. 2
Usk WA 99180
(509) 445-1476

Inn Of The White Salmon
PO Box 1446, 172 SE Jewett
White Salmon WA 98672
(509) 493-2335

Orchard Hill Inn
PO Box 130, Rt 2
White Salmon WA 98672
(509) 493-3024

Washington DC

Connecticut-Woodley
2647 Woodley Rd NW
Washington DC 20008
Circa: 1890
(202) 667-0218

Tabard Inn
1739 N St NW
Washington DC 20036

(202) 785-1277

The Manse
1307 Rhode Island Ave NW
Washington DC 20005
(202) 232-9150

West Virginia

The Country Inn
Berkeley Springs WV 25411
(304) 258-2210

The Manor
415 Fairfax St
Berkeley Springs WV 25411
(304) 258-1552

Hillbrook Inn
Rt 2, Box 152
Charlestown WV 25414

Marian's Guest House
731 Harrison Ave.
Elkins WV 26241
Circa: 1917
(304) 636-9883

Tichnell's Tourist Home
1367 Locust Ave.
Fairmont WV 26554
Circa: 1939
(304) 366-3811

Three Rivers Inn
PO Box 231
Gauley Bridge WV 25085
Circa: 1929
(304) 632-2121

Glen Ferris Inn
Glen Ferris WV 25090
Circa: 1853
(304) 632-1111

Fillmore Street B&B
Box 34
Harpers Ferry WV 25425

Spangler Manor
55 High St, Rt 3 Box 1402
Harpers Ferry WV 25425

Beekeeper Inn
Helvetia WV 26224
(304) 924-6435

The Current
Box 135
Hillsboro WV 25945

Heritage Station
11th St & Veterns Mem Blvd
Huntington WV 25701
(304) 523-6373

West Fork Inn
Rt 2 Box 212
Jane Lew WV 26378
(304) 745-4893

Valley View Farm
PO Box 467
Mathias WV 26812
(304) 897-5229

McMechen House Inn
109 N. Main St.
Moorefield WV 26836
(304) 538-2417

Kilmarnock Farms
PO Box 91, Rte. 1
Orlando WV 26412
(304) 452-8319

Riverside Inn
Rt 3
Pence Springs WV 24962
(304) 445 7469

Bavarian Inn & Lodge
Rt 1 Box 30
Shepherdstown WV 25443
(304) 876-2551

The Little Inn
PO Box 219, Princess At German St.
Shepherdstown WV 25443
(304) 876-2208

Thomas Shepherd Inn
Box 1162, German & Duke St
Shepherdstown WV 25443
(304) 876-3715

Morgan Orchard
Rt 2 Box 114
Sinks Grove WV 24976
(304) 772-3638

Wells Inn
316 Charles St.
Sistersville WV 26175
Circa: 1893

(304) 652-3111

The Chilton House
2 Sixth Ave
St Albans WV 25177
(304) 722-2918

Old Wilderness Inn
1 Old Wilderness Rd
Summerville WV 26651
(304) 872-3481

Countryside
PO Box 57
Summit Point WV 25446
Circa: 1930
(304) 725-2614

Dovers Inn
1001 Washington Pike
Wellburg WV 26070
(304) 737 0188

The Greenbrier
White Sulphur Springs WV
24986
(304) 536-1110

Wisconsin

Lane House
1111 S. Main
Alma WI 54610
Circa: 1863
(608) 685-4923

House Of Seven Gables
PO Box 204, 215 6th St.
Baraboo WI 53913
(608) 356-8387

Chez Joliet
PO Box 768, Bayfield
Bayfield WI 54814
Circa: 1890
(715) 779-5480

Cooper Hill House
33 S Sixth St Box 5
Bayfield WI 54814
(715) 779-5060

Greunke's Inn
17 Rittenhouse
Bayfield WI 54184
Circa: 1863
(715) 779-5480

The Mansion
7 Rice Ave.
Bayfield WI 54184
Circa: 1810
(715) 779-5408

Proud Mary
PO Box 193
Fish Creek WI 54212
Circa: 1870
(414) 868-3442

Whistling Swan Inn
Main St Box 193
Fish Creek WI 54212
(414) 868-3442

White Gull Inn
PO Box 175
Fish Creek WI 54212
Circa: 1896
(414) 868-3517

Monches Mill House
W301 N9430 Hwy E
Hartland WI 53029
(414) 966-7546

Sessler's Guest House
210 S. Jackson St.
Jamesville WI 53545

Seven Pines Lodge
Lewis WI 54851
Circa: 1903
(715) 653-2323

Captain Am's
105 East Boundary Road
Mequon WI 53092

Wilson House Inn
110 Dodge St Hwy 151
Mineral Point WI 53565
(608) 987-3600

The Evansen House
Rt 1, Box 18
New Lisbon WI 53950

Jamieson House
407 N. Franklin
Poynette WI 53955
Circa: 1883
(608) 635-4100

Page's Old Oak Inn
Hwy. 131 South
Soldiers Grove WI 54655

Circa: 1901
(608) 624-5217, 735-4683

Hardyns House
250 North Winstead
Spring Green WI 53588
(608) 588-7007

Lake House
PO Box 217, RR 2
Strum WI 54770
(715) 693-3519

Viroqua Heritage Inn
220 East Jefferson St.
Viroqua WI 54665
(608) 637-3306

Wolf River Lodge
White Lake WI 54491
Circa: 1920
(715) 882-2182

House On River Road
922 River Rd.
Wisconsin Dells WI 53965
(608) 253-5573, (608) 254-4428

Wyoming

Shoshone Lodge Resort
PO Box 790BB
Cody WY 82414
(307) 587-4044

Valley Ranch
100 Valley Ranch Rd.
Cody WY 82414
(307) 587-4661

Captain Bob Morris
PO Box 261 Teton Village
Jackson Hole WY 83025
(307) 733-4413

Jenny Lake Lodge
PO Box 240
Moran WY 83013
(307) 733-4677

Wolf Hotel
PO Box 1298, 101 E. Bridge
Saratoga WY 82331
(307) 326-5525

Boyer YL Ranch
PO Box 24
Savery WY 82332

(307) 383-7840

Heck Of A Hill Home-
stead
PO Box 105
Wilson WY 83014
(307) 733-8023

Snow Job
PO Box 371
Wilson WY 83014
(307) 739-9695

Puerto Rico

Parador Hacienda
Juanita
PO Box 838
Maricao PR 00706
(809) 838-2550

Caribe Playa Resort
B. 2730 Guardamaya
Patillas PR 00723

La Casa Del Frances
PO Box 458, Esperanza
Vieques PR 00765
(809) 741-3751

Reservation Services

Alabama

Bed and Breakfast, Birmingham, Inc., PO Box 31328, Birmingham, AL 35222, (205) 591-6406.

Bed and Breakfast Mobile, P.O. Box 66261 Mobile, AL 36606, (205) 473-2939.

Bed and Breakfast Montgomery, P.O. Box 31328, Birmingham, AL 35222, (205) 285-5421.

Alaska

Alaska Bed and Breakfast, 526 Seward St, Juneau, AK 99801, (907) 586-2959.

Alaska Guest Homes, 1941 Glacier Hwy, Juneau, AK 99801, (907) 586-1840.

Anchorage B'B, PO Box 10135, South Station, Anchorage, AK 99511. (907) 345-2222.

Fairbanks B&B, PO Box 74573, Fairbanks AK 99707, (907) 452-4967.

Ketchikan B'B, Box 7814, Ketchikan, Ak 99901. (907) 225-6044, 247-8444.

Stay With a Friend, 3605 Arctic Blvd, #173, Anchorage, AK 99503. (907) 274-6445.

Arizona

Barbara's B&B, PO Box 13603, Tucson, AZ 85732-3603. (602) 886-5847.

Bed and Breakfast in Arizona, (8433 N Black Canyon, Suite 160, Phoenix, AZ 85021, (602) 995-2831.

Bed & Breakfast-Scottsdale, PO Box 624, Scottsdale, AZ 85252. (602) 998-7044.

Mi Casa, Su Casa Bed & Breakfast, 1456 N. Scottsdale Rd., Suite 110, Tempe, AZ 85281 (602) 990-0682.

Arkansas

Bed & Breakfast in the Arkansas Ozarks, RT 1, PO Box 38, Calico Rock, AR 72519. (501) 297-8764.

Bed & Breakfast Reservations, 11 Singleton, Eureka Springs, AR 72632. (501) 253-9111.

B&B of Eureka Springs, PO Box 27, Eureka Springs, AR 72632. (501) 253-6767.

California

America Family Inn B&B, Box 349, San Francisco, CA 94101. (415) 931-3083. San Francisco, Monterey, Wine Country.

American Historic Homes B&B, P.O. Box 336, Dana Point, CA 92629, (714) 496-6953. National reservations.

B&B International, 151 Ardmore Rd, Kensington CA 94707. (415) 525-4569.

B&B of Los Angeles, 32127 Harborview Lane, Westlake Village CA 91361. (818) 889-7325, 889-8870. Southern California.

B&B of Southern California, Box 218, Fullerton CA 92632. (714) 738-8361. Southern California.

B&B Approved Hosts, 10890 Galvin, Ventura CA 93004. (805) 647-0651. Los Angeles.

California Houseguests International, 6051 Lindley Ave #6, Tarzana CA 91356. (818) 344-7878. Southern California.

California Coast B&B, 25624 Monte Nido Dr, Calabasas, CA 91302. (213) 999-3130.

Carolyn's B&B Homes, Box 84776, San Diego CA 92138. (619) 422-7009. San Diego.

Christian B&B of America, Box 388, San Juan Capistrano, CA 92693. (714) 496-7050. United States, Britain.

Co-Host, America's B&B, 11715, S Circle Dr, Whittier CA 90601. (213) 699-8427. California.

Dig's West, 8191 Crowley Circle, Buena Park CA 90621. (714) 739-1669. California.

Educators' Vacation Alternatives, 317 Piedmont Rd, Santa Barbara, CA 93105. (805) 687-2947. Membership organization for teachers.

Eye Openers B&B, Box 694, Altadena CA 91001. (818) 684-4428 or 797-2055. Los Angeles County.

B&B Homestay, Box 326, Cambria CA 93428. (805) 927-4613. Cambria.

Hospitality Plus, Box 388, San Juan Capistrano CA 92693. (714) 496-7050. California coastal cities and Yosemite.

Napa B&B Reservations, 1834 First St., Napa CA 94559. (707) 224-4667.

New Age Travel, 839 Second St, Suite 3, Encinitas CA 92024. (619) 436-9977.

Traveler's Bed & Breakfast, PO Box 1368, Chino, CA 91710. (714) 627-7971.

University B&B, 1387 Sixth Ave, San Francisco, CA 94122. (415) 661-8940.

Wine Country B&B, Box 3211, Santa Rosa CA 95403. (707) 578-1661. Santa Rosa area.

Colorado

Bed & Breakfast of Boulder, Inc, PO Box 6061, Boulder, CO 80302. (303) 442-6664.

Bed & Breakfast Colorado, PO Box 20596, Denver, CO 80220. (303) 442-6664.

B&B Rocky Mountains, Box 804, Colorado Springs CO 89901. (303) 630-3433. Colorado, Montana, New Mexico, Wyoming, Utah.

Vail B&B, Box 491, Vail CO 81658. (303) 949-1212.

Connecticut

Bed & Breakfast, Ltd in New Haven, PO Box 216, New Haven, CT 06518. (203) 469-3260.

Covered Bridge B&B, West Cornwall CT 06796. (203) 542-5944. Northwest corner of Connecticut and the Berkshires.

Nautilus B&B, 133 Phoenix Dr., Groton CT 06340. (203) 448-1538. All Connecticut.

Nutmeg B&B, 222 Girard Ave., Hartford CT 06105. (203) 236-6698. Connecticut.

Seacoast Landings, 21 Fuller St., New London CT 06329. (203) 442-1940. SE Connecticut.

Delaware

Bed & Breakfast of Delaware, 1804 Breen Lane, Wilmington, DE 19810. (302) 479-9500.

Florida

A&A B&B of Florida, Box 1316, Winterpark, FL 3278:. (305) 628-3233. Florida.

B&B Company, Box 262, S. Miami, FL 33243. (305) 661-3270. Southern Florida.

B&B of the Florida Keys, Box 1373, Marathon FL 33050. (305) 743-4118. Florida.

B&B of the Palm Beaches, 5 Man-O-War Drive, Marathon, FL 33050. (305) 743-4118.

B&B Suncoast Accommodations, 8690 Gulf Blvd., St Petersburg Beach FL 33706. (813) 360-1753. West Coast of Florida.

Open House B&B Registry, PO Box 43025, Palm Beach, FL 33480. (305) 842-5190.

Georgia

Atlanta Home Hospitality, 2472 Lauderdale Dr NE, Atlanta GA 30345. (404) 493-1930. Atlanta.

B&B Atlanta, 1801 Piedmont Ave, N.E., #208, Atlanta GA 30324. (404) 875-0525. Atlanta.

Quail Country Bed & Breakfast, Ltd, 1104 Old Monticello Rd, Thomasville, GA 31792. (912) 226-6882.

Savannah Historic Inns & Guesthouses, 1900 Lincoln St, Savannah, GA 31401. (912) 226-7218.

Hideaway B'B, PO Box 300, Blue Ridge GA 30513. (404) 632-2411.

Hawaii

B&B Hawaii, Box 449, Kapaa HI 96746. (808) 822-7771. Hawaii.

Pacific-Hawaii B&B, 19 Kai Nani Place, Kailua, Oahu, HI 96734. (808) 262-6026. Hawaii. B&B Honolulu, 3242 Kaohinani Dr, Honolulu, HI 96817. (808) 595-7533.

Go Native - Hawaii, PO Box 13115, Lansing MI 48901. (517) 349-9598.

Idaho

B&B of Idaho, PO Box 7323, Boise, ID 83707. (208) 336-5174.

Illinois

B&B Chicago, Inc, 3500 N Lake Shore Dr, Suite 17-D, Chicago, IL 60657. (312) 472-2294.

B&B of Chicago, Box 14088, Chicago IL 60614. (312) 951-0085.

Bed and Board America Inc, 7308 W. Madison St, Forest Park IL 50130. (312) 771-8100. Chicago and suburbs.

Kansas

Kansas City B&B, Box 14781, Lenexa, KS 66215. (913) 888-3636. Kansas City and suburbs.

Kentucky

Kentucky Homes B&B, 1431 St. James Court, Louisville, KY 40208. (502) 635-7341, 452-6629. Kentucky.

Bluegrass B&B, Route 1, Box 263, Versailles, KY 40383. (606) 873-3208. Central Kentucky.

Louisiana

B&B Inc., 1236 Decatur St, New Orleans LA 70116. (504) 525-4640. New Orleans.

New Orleans B&B, Box 8128, New Orleans LA 70182. (504) 822-5046. Louisiana.

Southern Comfort B&B Reservation Service, 2856 Hundred Oaks, Baton Rouge LA 70808. (504) 346-1928.

Bed, Bath & Breakfast, Box 52466, New Orleans LA 70152. (504) 897-3867 or 891-4862. New Orleans.

Louisiana Hospitality Services, Box 80717, Baton Rouge LA 70898. (504) 769-0366. Louisiana, Mississippi, Alabama & Arkansas.

Maine

B&B Down East, Box 547, Eastbrook, ME 04634, (207) 565-3517. Maine.

B&B of Maine, 32 Colonial Village, Falmouth, ME 04105, (207) 781-4528. Maine.

Chamber of Commerce, 142 Free St, Portland ME 04101.

The Maine Publicity Bureau, 97 Winthrop St, Hallowell, ME 04347.

Maryland

Armanda's B&B, 1428 Park Ave, Baltimore, MD 21217-4230. (301) 225-0001.

Sweet Dreams & Toast, Inc, PO Box 4835-0035, Washington DC 20008. (202) 483-9191.

The Traveller in Maryland, 33 West St, Annapolis, MD 21401. (301) 269-6232; 261-2233.

Massachusetts

Around Plymouth Bay, PO Box 6211, Plymouth, MA 02360. (617) 747-5075.

B&B Agency of Boston, 47 Commercial Wharf, Boston, MA 02110. (617) 720-3540.

B&B Associates Bay Colony LTD, Box 166 Babson Park, Boston, MA 02157. (617) 449-5302. Massachusetts, Maine, New Hampshire, Vermont, Connecticut.

B&B Brookline/Boston, Box 732, Brookline MA 02146. (617) 277-2292. Boston, Cape Cod and Northeast.

B&B Cambridge & Greater Boston, 73 Kirkland St, Cambridge MA 02138 (617) 576-1492 Boston, Cape Cod, Cambridge.

B&B Cape Cod, Box 341, West Hyannisport, MA 02672. (617) 775-2772. Cape Cod.

B&B Folks, 73 Providence Rd, Westford, MA 01886. (617) 692-3232.

B&B of Minuteman Country, B Linmoor Terrace, Lexington MA 02173. (617) 861-7063.

Be Our Guest B&B, Box 1333, Plymouth MA 02360, (617) 837-9867 Plymouth and area.

Berkshire Bed & Breakfast, Main St, Williamsburg, MA 01096-0211. (413) 268-7244.

Christian Hospitality, 636 Union St, Duxbury, MA 02332. (617) 834-8528. New England.

Folkstone B&B, PO Box 932, Boylston, MA 01505. (617) 869-2687.

Greater Boston Hospitality, Box 1142, Brookline MA 02146. (617) 277-5430. Boston and suburbs.

Host Homes of Boston, Box 117, Newton MA 02168. (617) 244-1308. Boston and suburbs.

House Guests, Cape Cod, Box 8-A, Dennis, MA 02638. (617) 398-0787.

Mayflower B&B, Box 172, Belmont MA 02178. (617) 484-0068. Boston metropolitan area.

New England B&B, 1045 Centre St, Newton Centre, MA 02159. (617) 244-2112; 498-9819.

Orleans B&B Associates, Box 1312, Orleans MA 02653. (617) 255-3824. Cape Cod.

Pineapple Hospitality Inc., 384 Rodney French Blvd., New Bedford MA 02744. (617) 990-1696. New England.

Michigan

Betsy Ross B&B, 3057 Betsy Ross DR, Bloomfield Hills MI 48013. (313) 646-5357 or 647-1158. Detroit and suburbs.

Frankenmuth Area B&B, 337 Trinklein St, Frankenmuth, MI 48734. (517) 652-8897.

Minnesota

B&B Registry, Box 80174, St Paul MN 55108. (612) 646-4238. National.

Mississippi

Lincoln, Ltd, Bed & Breakfast, PO Box 3479, Meridian, MS 39303. (601) 482-5483.

Natchez Pilgrimage Tours, Box 347, Natchez MS 39120. (601) 446-6631. (800) 647-6742.

Missouri

B&B St. Louis, 16 Green Acres, ST. Louis MO 63137. (314) 533-9299.

Lexington B&B, 115 N. 18th st., Lexington MO 64067. (816) 259-4163.

Missouri B&B River Country, #1 Grandview Heights, St. Louis MO 63131. (314) 965-4328.

Ozark Mountain Country B&B, Box 295, Branson MO 65616. (417) 334-4720 or 5077. Missouri & Arkansas Ozarks.

Truman Country B&B, 424 N. Pleasant, Independence MO 64050. (816) 254-6657. Missouri.

Montana

Western B&B Hosts, Box 322, Kalispell MT 59901. (406) 257-4476.

Nebraska

B&B of Nebraska, 1464 28th Ave., Columbus NE 68601. (402) 564-7591. Nebraska.

Swede Hospitality B&B, 1617 Ave A, Gothenburg, NE 69138. (308) 537-2680.

New Hampshire

New Hampshire Bed & Breakfast, RFD 3, Box 53, Laconia, NH 03246. (603) 279-8348.

New Jersey

Bed and Breakfast of New Jersey, Suite 132, 103 Godwin Ave, Midland Park, NJ 07432. (201) 444-7409.

Town & Country Bed & Breakfast, PO Box 301, Lambertville, NJ 08530. (609) 397-8399.

Bed & Breakfast of Northwest NJ, 11 Sunset Trail, Denville, NJ 07834. (201) 625-5129.

New Mexico

Bed and Breakfast Santa Fe, Inc, 218 E Buena Vista, Santa Fe, NM 87501. (505) 982-3332.

New York

Alternate Lodgings, Inc, PO Box 1782, East Hampton, NY 11937 (516) 324-9449.

The American Country Collection of B&B Homes, 984 Gloucester Place, Schenectady, NY 12309. (518) 370-4948.

A Reasonable Alternative, 117 Sprint St, Port Jefferson, NY 11777. (516) 928-4034.

B&B of Greater Syracuse, 143 Didama St, Syracuse, NY 13224. (315) 446-4199.

Bed & Breakfast of Long Island, PO Box 392, Old Westbury, NY 11568. (516) 334-6231.

Bed & Breakfast Rochester, Box 444, Fairport, NY 14450. (716) 223-8510, 223-8877.

Bed & Breakfast, USA, Ltd, PO Box 606, Croton-on-Hudson, NY 10520. (914) 271-6228.

Cherry Valley Ventures, 6119 Cherry Valley Turnpike, Lafayette, NY 13084. (315) 677-9723.

City Lights Bed & Breakfast, Ltd, 344 West 84th St, New York, NY 10024. (212) 877-3235.

Guest Quarters International Club, 207 E 85th St, Suite 166, New York, NY 10028. (212) 249-1014.

Hampton Bed & Breakfast, PO Box 378, East Moriches, NY 11940. (516) 878-8197.

Leatherstocking B&B, 389 Brockway Rd, Frankfort, NY 13340. (315) 733-0040.

New World Bed & Breakfast, Ltd, 150 Fifth Ave, Suite 771, New York, NY 10011. (212) 675-5600.

North Country Bed & Breakfast, PO Box 286, Lake Placid, NY 12946. (518) 523-3739.

Rainbow Hospitality Bed & Breakfast, 9348 Hennepin Ave, Niagara Falls, NY 14304. (716) 283-4794; 754-8877.

Traveler's Retreat, RD 3, Melvin Lane, Baldwinsville, NY 13027. (315) 638-8664.

Urban Ventures, PO Box 426, New York, NY 10024. (212) 594-5650.

North Carolina

Bed & Breakfast of Asheville, 217-B Merrimon Ave, Asheville, NC 28801. (704) 255-8367.

B&B in the Albemarle, PO Box 248, Everetts, NC 27825. (919) 792-4584.

Charlotte Bed & Breakfast, 1700-2 Delane Ave, Charlotte, NC 28211. (704) 366-0979.

Ohio

Buckeye Bed & Breakfast, PO Box 130, Powell, OH 43065. (614) 548-4555.

Columbus Bed & Breakfast Group, 769 S Third St, Columbus, OH 43206. (614) 443-3680.

Ohio Valley B&B, 6876 Taylor Mill Rd, Independence, KY 41051. (606) 356-7865.

Private Lodgings, PO Box 18590, Cleveland, OH 44118-0590. (216) 321-3213.

Oregon

Bed & Breakfast Oregon, 5733 SW Dickinson, Portland, OR 97219. (503) 245-0642.

Northwest Bed and Breakfast, 7707 SW Locust, Tigard, OR 97223. (503) 243-7616.

Pennsylvania

Bed & Breakfast Center City, 1804 Pine St, Philadelphia, PA 19103. (215) 735-1137.

Bed & Breakfast of Chester County, PO Box 825, Kennett Square, PA 19348. (215) 444-1367.

Bed & Breakfast of Lancaster County, PO Box 19, Mountville, PA. (717) 285-5956.

Bed & Breakfast of Philadelphia, PO Box 630, Chester Springs, PA 19425. (215) 827-9650.

B&B of Valley Forge, Valley Forge, PA 19481-0562. (215) 783-7838.

Bed & Breakfast of Southeast Pennsylvania, Box 278, RD1, Barto, PA 19504. (215) 845-3526.

The B&B Traveler, PO Box 21, Devon, PA 19333. (215) 687-3565.

Hershey B&B, PO Box 208, Hershey, PA 17033-0208. (717) 533-2928.

Pittsburgh Bed & Breakfast, 2190 Ben Franklin Dr, Pittsburgh, PA 15237. (412) 367-8080.

Rest & Repast, PO Box 126, Pine Grove Mills, PA 16868. (814) 238-1484.

Rhode Island

Bed & Breakfast of Rhode Island, Inc, PO Box 3291, Newport, RI 02840. (401) 849-1298.

Castle Keep Bed & Breakfast, 44 Everett St, Newport, RI 02804. (401) 846-0362.

Guest House Association of Newport, 23 Brinley St, Newport, RI 02840. (401) 849-7645.

South Carolina

Charleston Society Bed & Breakfast, 84 Murray Blvd, Charleston, SC 29401. (803) 723-4948.

Bay Street Accommodations, 601 Bay St, Beaufort, SC 29902. (803) 524-7720.

Historic Charleston Bed & Breakfast, 43 Legare St, Charleston, SC 29401. (803) 722-6606.

South Dakota

South Dakota Bed & Breakfast, PO Box 80137, Sioux Falls, SD 57116. (605) 528-6571.

Tennessee

Bed & Breakfast in Memphis, PO Box 41621, Memphis, TN 38104. (901) 726-5920.

Hospitality at Home, Rt 1, Box 318, Lenior City, TN 37771. (615) 693-3500.

Host Homes of Tennessee, PO Box 110227, Nashville, TN 37222-0227. (615) 331-5244.

Nashville Bed & Breakfast, PO Box 150651, Nashville, TN 37215. (615) 298-5674; 269-6555.

River Rendezvous, PO Box 240001, Memphis, TN 38124. (901) 767-5296.

Texas

Bed & Breakfast Hosts of San Antonio, 166 Rockhill, San Antonio, TX 78209. (512) 824-8036.

Bed & Breakfast Society, 330 W Main St, Fredericksburg, TX 78624. (512) 997-7150.

Bed & Breakfast Society of Houston, 921 Heights Blvd, Houston, TX 77008. (713) 868-4654.

Bed & Breakfast Texas Style, 4224 W Red Bird Lane, Dallas, TX 75237. (214) 298-5433; 298-8586.

Gasthaus Bed & Breakfast Lodging Services, 330 W Main St, Fredericksburg, TX 78624. (512) 997-4712.

Sand Dollar Hospitality B&B, 3605 Mendenhall, Corpus Christi, TX 78415. (512) 853-1222.

Vermont

American Bed & Breakfast in New England, Box 983, St Albans, VT 05478. (802) 524-4731.

Vermont Bed & Breakfast, Box 139 Browns Trace, Jericho, VT 05465. (802) 827-3827.

Virginia

Bed & Breakfast of Tidewater, PO Box 3343, Norfolk, VA 23514. (804) 627-1983; 627-9409.

Bensonhouse of Richmond and Williamsburg, 2036 Monument Ave, Richmond, VA 23220. (804) 648-7560.

Blue Ridge Bed & Breakfast, Rocks & Rills, Rt2, Box 249,l Berryville, VA 22611. (703) 955-1246.

Guesthouses - B&B, Inc, PO Box 5737, Charlottesville, VA 22905. (804) 979-7264; 979-8327.

Princely B&B, Ltd, 819 Prince ST, Alexandria, VA 22314. (703) 683-2159.

Rockbridge Reservations, PO Box 76, Brownsburg, VA 24415. (703) 348-5698.

Shenandoah Valley Bed & Breakfast, PO Box 305, Broadway, VA 22815. (703) 896-9702; 896-2579.

Sojourners Bed & Breakfast, 3609 Tanglewood Lane, Lynchburg VA 24503. (804) 384-1655.

The Travel Tree, PO Box 838, Williamsburg, VA 23187. (804) 253-1571.

Washington

BABS Bed & Breakfast Service, PO Box 5025, Bellingham, WA 98227. (206) 733-8642.

INNterlodging Co-op, PO Box 7044, Tacoma, WA 98407. (206) 756-0343.

Pacific Bed & Breakfast, 701 NW 60th St, Seattle, WA 98107. (206) 784-0539.

Travellers' Bed & Breakfast, PO Box 492, Mercer Island, WA 98040. (206) 232-2345.

Washington, D. C.

B&B League Ltd, 2855 29th St NW, Washington DC 20008. (202) 363-7767. Washington DC and United States.

B&B LTD of Washington DC, Box 12011, Washington DC 20005. (202) 328-3510. Downtown historic areas of DC.

Sweet Dreams & Toast, Box 4835-0035, Washington DC 20008. (202) 483-9191. DC.

Wisconsin

Bed & Breakfast Guest-Homes, Route 2, Algoma, WI 54201. (414) 743-9742.

Bed & Breakfast of Milwaukee, 3017 N Downer Ave, Milwaukee, WI 53211. (414) 271-2337.

Wyoming

Bed & Breakfast Rocky Mountains-Wyoming, PO Box 804, Colorado Springs, CO 80901. (307) 630-3433.

State Tourism Information

- Alaska Division of Tourism, Pouch E-445, Juneau AK 99811

- Bureau of Publicity and Information, 532 South Perry St, Montgomery AL 36104

- Dept. Parks & Tourism ,1 Capitol Mall, Little Rock AR 72201

- Arizona Office of Tourism, 1480 E Bethany Home Rd, Phoenix AZ 85014

- Office of Tourism, 1121 L St., First Floor, Sacramento CA 95814

- Colorado Dept. of Tourism, 1625 S. Broadway, #1700, Denver CO 80202

- Vacations, Dept. of Economic Development, 210 Washington St., Hartford CT 06106

- State Travel Service, P.O.Box 1401, 99 Kings Hwy, Dover DE 19903

- Division of Tourism, Visitor Inquiry Section, 126 Van Buren St., Tallahassee FL 32301

- Tour Georgia, P.O. Box 1776, Atlanta GA 30301

- Visitors Bureau, Waikiki Business Plaza, 2270 Kalakaua Ave., #801, Honolulu HI 96815

- Development Commission, Tourism Division, 600 E. Court Ave., Suite A, Des Moines IA 50309

- Tourism, Statehouse, Room 108, Boise ID 83720

- Tourist Information Center, 310 S. Michigan Ave., #108, Chicago IL 60604

- Tourism Development Division, 1 North Capitol Ave., #700, Indianapolis IN 46204

- Department of Economic Development, Travel and Tourism Division, 503 Kansas Ave, 6th Floor, Topeka KS 66603

- Kentucky Department of Travel Development, Capitol Plaza Tower, Frankfort KY 40601

- Office of Tourism, Inquiry Dept., P.O. Box 44291, Baton Rouge LA 70804

- Division of Tourism, Dept. of Commerce & Development, 100 Cambridge St., 13th Floor, Boston MA 02202

- Office of Tourist Development, 45 Calvert St, Annapolis MD 21401

- Publicity Bureau, 97 Winthrop St., Hallowell ME 04347

- Travel Bureau, Dept. of Commerce, P.O. Box 30226, Lansing MI 48909

- Office of Tourism, 240 Bremer Building, 419 N. Robert St, St. Paul MN 55101

- Division of Tourism, Truman Building, P.O. Box 1055, Jefferson City MO 65102

- Division of Tourism, Dept. of Economic Development, P.O. Box 22825, Jackson MS 39205

- Promotion Division, Department of Commerce, 1424 Ninth Ave., Helena MT 59620

- Travel & Tourism Division, Dept. of Commerce, Raleigh NC 27611

- Tourism Promotion, Liberty Memorial Building, State Capitol Grounds, Bismarck ND 58505

- Division of Travel & Tourism, Dept. of Economic Development, P.O. Box 94666, 301 Centennial Mall South, Lincoln NE 68509

- Office of Vacation Travel, P.O. Box 856, Concord NH 03301

- Division of Travel and Tourism, CN-826, Trenton NJ 08625

- Travel Division, Economic Development & Tourism Dept., Bataan Memorial Building, Room 751, Santa Fe NM 87503

- Commission on Tourism, Capitol Complex, 600 E. Williams St., Carson City NV 89710

- State Department of Commerce, Division of Tourism, 1 Commerce Plaza, Albany NY 12245

- Office of Travel and Tourism, P.O. Box 1001, Columbus OH 43216
- Tourism and Recreation Dept., Literature Distribution Dept., 215 N.E. 28th, Oklahoma City OK 73105
- Economic Development Dept., Tourism Division, 595 Cottage St., N.E., Salem OR 97310
- Bureau of Travel Development, Dept. of Commerce, 416 Forum Building, Harrisburg PA 17120
- Dept. of Economic Development, 7 Jackson Walkway, Providence RI 02903
- Dept. of Parks, Recreation, and Tourism, P.O. Box 71, Columbia SC 29202
- Tourism, Box 1000, Pierre SD 57501
- Dept. of Tourist Development, P.O. Box 23170, Nashville TN 37202
- Dept. of Highways & Public Transportation, Travel & Information Division, P.O. Box 5064, Austin TX 78763

- Travel Council, Council Hall, Capitol Hill, Salt Lake City UT 84114
- Division of Tourism, 202 North 9th St. #500, Richmond VA 23219
- Travel Division, 134 State St., Montpelier VT 05602
- State Dept. of Commerce & Economic Development, Tourism Development Division, General Administration Building, Olympia WA 98504
- Washington Convention and Visitors Association, 1575 Eye St., N.W. #250, Washington DC 20005
- Division of Tourism, P.O. Box 7606, Madison WI 53707
- Travel West Virginia, Capitol Complex, Charleston WV 25305
- Travel Commissions, Frank Norris Jr. Travel Center, Cheyenne WY 82002

Reservation Form

Guest Information

Names of people in party _____

_____

My Destination: _____

Purpose:_____

I expect to arrive (date): _____ at (time) _____.

I will depart (date): _____

I will stay _____ nights.

Number of people in my party: _____

Adults: _____

Children: _____ Ages: _____

Pets: _____

INN Information

Name of Inn:_____

Address:_____

City: _____ State: _____ Zip: _____

Phone: _____

Directions: _____

_____

Private bath: _____

Shared Bath: _____

Smoking: _____

Number of rooms needed: _____

Deposit due by: _____

Method of payment used: _____

Total Daily Rate of room(s): _____ $ _____

Total: (#Days X #Total Daily Rate) _____ $ _____

Tax:_____ $ _____

Total due: _____ $ _____

Date deposit mailed: _____ Amount of Deposit: _____ $ _____

Total due upon arrival:_____ $ _____

Please feel free to use this worksheet for all your accommodation needs. This worksheet can serve as a valuable check list and will help keep all your accommodation information together.

Association of American Historic Inns and Guesthouses

PO Box 336   Dana Point CA 92693   (714) 496-7050

Inn Evaluation Form

The B&B, Inn, or Guesthouse we visited: _____

	A	B	C	D	F
Location for our needs					
Cleanliness					
Bathroom facilities					
Beds					
Attitude & Friendliness of host					
Food & Presentation					
Worth the price					

A = Outstanding
B = Good
C = Average
D = Needs to be improved
F = Disaster

Any comments on the above: _____

_____

I especially appreciated: _____

_____

Suggestions for improvement: _____

_____

Name (optional): _____

Date of stay: _____

Please complete this form for each stay and mail to the address above.

Thank you.

American Historic Inns Book Club

Innkeeping Tapes

How to Start and Operate a Bed and Breakfast Inn

A set of six tapes from seminars given by Tim and Deborah Sakach.

Hundreds of prospective innkeepers have taken these classes and rated them highly. Do you have the right mix of entrepreneurial spirit, creativity, energy, and people skills to start and operate a quality bed and breakfast inn? This course will help you find out. Packed with valuable information and helpful tips.

Former students said:

"I certainly got my money's worth. I'm leaving with a renewed vitality."

"Excellent information on financing an inn and on cash flow management. I learned a great deal." Dave R., Innkeeper.

"Much preparation. Thoughtfully and sensitively shared."

Includes a wealth of information on topics such as:
- What location should you choose? (Location test provided.)
- Should you buy an existing inn, restore a historic property, or build your own?
- How much should you pay for an inn?
- How should it be financed?
- What are the regulations governing inns, and how can you meet them?
- How to estimate income and expenses.
- What is it like to be an innkeeper?
- How to manage an inn.
- How to obtain free advertising.
- How to develop a media kit.

$69.95

Innkeeping, How to Keep it Fun.

Cassette tape by Kathleen Salisbury, owner of Salisbury House in Los Angeles.

$9.95

How to Market Your Inn -- The Key to Success.

Cassette tape by Lynn Montgomery, innkeeper of Gold Mountain Manor and Emmy winning screen writer.

$9.95

Professional Inn Management.

Cassette tape by Jerry Seigel, innkeeper, Casa Laguna, and former hotel consultant for 20 years.

$9.95

Save! Order all nine tapes for $89.95.

Cookbooks

The American Bed & Breakfast Cookbook
By The Bed Post Writers Group

Recipes of regional specialties and old family favorites, all chosen by bed & breakfast hosts.

189 pages, $12.95

Best Recipes from New England Inns
By Sandra J. Taylor

More than 100 country inns share their traditional favorites and specialties of the house.

320 pages, $15.95

Best Recipes from New York State Inns
Edited by Georgia Orcult

A compilation of 250 recipes from sixty New York inns. These well-tested recipes are bound to be favorites.

320 pages, $16.95

The Country Innkeepers' Cookbook

By Wilf & Lois Copping

Favorite recipes of two Vermont innkeepers compiled by Yankee publishing.

224 pages, $10.95

The Dairy Hollow House Cookbook

By Crescent Dragonwagon

Over 400 Ozark recipes from The Dairy Hollow House in Arkansas. Poetry and stories about friendship, the seasons, and life are included throughout. A cookbook for both the body and soul.

400 pages, $19.95

The Pleasures of Afternoon Tea

By Angela Hynes

Do you know the difference between "Afternoon Tea", "High Tea" and "Power Tea"? This book by English author Angela Hynes explains it all and is a true education in the preparing and presenting of the famous "Afternoon Tea". 150 recipes.

160 pages, color illus., $16.95

Inn Restoration Resources

All About Old Buildings -- The Whole Preservation Catalog

Edited by Diane Maddex

A valuable source book for anyone who wants to save an old home or a whole home town.

436 pages, 900 illus., $24.95

The Brown Book: A Directory of Preservation Information

Edited by Diane Maddex, with Ellen R. Marsh

A "who's who" of preservation information and know how. It list organizations and sources supporting preservation.

160 pages, $17.95

Fabrics for Historic Buildings

By Jane C. Nylander

How can an appropriate fabric be selected to reupholster a family heirloom chair, make new draperies for a 100-year-old house, or restore the furnishings of an entire house to their original appearance? Tells how to research, order, and install the correct fabrics. A catalog of 550 fabric reproductions available today, organized by period, type, and manufacturer. It also tells how to recreate period effects.

160 pages, 95 illus., $12.95

Floor Coverings for Historic Buildings

By Helene Von Rosenstiel & Gail Caskey Winkler

How to research, order, and install appropriate reproductions of historic floor coverings. Includes all types of floor coverings -- Wilton, Brussels, tapestry, ingrain, and rag carpeting as well as linoleum, floorcloths, and hooked rugs. Covers 1750 through 1950s.

144 pages, 100 illus., Avail. Nov. 1987, $12.95

Wallpapers for Historic Buildings

By Richard C. Nylander

This invaluable book tells how to select the right wallpaper for an old house or historic home and provides a unique catalog of more than 350 authentically reproduced designs that are available today, organized by period, type and manufacturer. Includes details on how to research, select and install appropriate modern reproductions.

128 pages, 110 illus., $12.95

The Old House Journal Catalog

By The Old House Journal Corporation

Lists over 1,000 companies that sell items needed by the brave who restore old houses. Everything imaginable, over 10,000 items.

231 pages, $13.95

Respectful Rehabilitation: Answers to Your Questions About Old Buildings

By The National Park Service

Answers 150 of the most-asked questions about rehabilitating old houses and other historic buildings.

200 pages, 100 illus., $12.95

What Style Is It? A Guide to American Architecture

By John Poppeliers, S. Allen Chambers, Jr., and Nancy B. Schwartz

Historic American Buildings Survey. Of value to all who wish to identify and enjoy the architectural assets of a building.

112 pages, 150 illus., $7.95

Guidebooks

The Official Guide to American Historic Bed & Breakfast Inns and Guesthouses

By Tim and Deborah Sakach with the innkeepers and members of the Association of American Historic Inns and Guesthouses

Includes more than 2,000 historic inns and guesthouses throughout the United States. Considered by reviewers to be the "guide that outshines them all."

Contains history, anecdotes, and descriptions of more than 600 inns from the 17th, 18th, 19th, and early 20th centuries.

Recommended by USA Today, Library Journal, Publisher's Weekly, and many other publications.

288 pages, 300 illus., $14.95

American Historic Inns

P.O. Box 336-B
Dana Point CA 92629
(714) 496 6953

Order Form

Please print clearly. This will be used as the shipping label.

Name: _____

Address: _____

City: _____ State: _____ Zip: _____

Please send me the following books and tapes:

Qty	Description	Price Each	Total
_____	The Official Guide to American Historic Bed & Breakfast Inns and Guesthouses	$14.95	_____
_____	How to Start and Operate a Bed & Breakfast Inn (6 tapes)	$69.95	_____
_____	Innkeeping, How to Keep it Fun (1 tape)	$9.95	_____
_____	How to Market Your Inn -- The Key to Success (1 tape)	$9.95	_____
_____	Professional Inn Management (1 tape)	$9.95	_____
_____	*** All 9 tapes	$89.95	_____
_____	The American Bed & Breakfast Cookbook	$12.95	_____
_____	Best Recipes from New England Inns	$15.95	_____
_____	Best Recipes from New York State Inns	$16.95	_____
_____	The Country Innkeepers' Cookbook	$10.95	_____
_____	The Dairy Hollow House Cookbook	$19.95	_____
_____	The Pleasures of Afternoon Tea	$16.95	_____
_____	All About Old Buildings -- The Whole Preservation Catalog	$24.95	_____
_____	The Brown Book: A Directory of Preservation Information	$17.95	_____
_____	Fabrics for Historic Buildings	$12.95	_____
_____	Floor Coverings for Historic Buildings	$12.95	_____
_____	Wallpapers for Historic Buildings	$12.95	_____
_____	The Old House Journal Catalog	$13.95	_____
_____	Respectful Rehabilitation	$12.95	_____
_____	What Style Is it? A Guide to American Architecture	$7.95	_____

	Total		
_____	Shipping first book	$1.50	_____
_____	Shipping additional books	each $.50	_____
_____	California Residents 6% sales tax		_____
_____	Can't wait 3 to 4 weeks for book rate; Please expedite shipping	$4.00	_____
	Total Enclosed		_____